# WHEN HITLER TOOK AUSTRIA

# WHEN HITLER TOOK AUSTRIA

## A Memoir of Heroic Faith by the Chancellor's Son

Kurt von Schuschnigg

*With Janet von Schuschnigg*

IGNATIUS PRESS   SAN FRANCISCO

German edition: *Der lange Weg nach Hause: Der Sohn des Bundeskanzlers erinnert sich*
© 2008 by Amalthea Signum Verlag, Vienna, Austria

Photo Insert:
Photos 41 and 43, Austrian National Library, Picture Archives, Vienna
Photo 50, Associated Press
All others courtesy of the von Schuschnigg family

Cover photos:
Upper, "Chancellor Kurt von Schuschnigg with Son Kurti",
courtesy of von Schuschnigg family
Lower, "Hitler Triumphant in Mercedes during Austrian Anschluss",
Bildarchiv Preussischer Kulturbesitz, Berlin/Art Resource, New York

Cover design by John Herreid

*For my Fräulein Alice*

I wanted to enjoy the happiness of living and working in the place which some day would inevitably bring about the fulfillment of my most ardent and heartfelt wish: the union of my beloved homeland [Austria] with the common fatherland, the German Reich. Even today many would be unable to comprehend the greatness of such a longing. . . . Only he who has felt in his own skin what it means to be a German, deprived of the right to belong to his cherished fatherland, can measure the deep longing which burns at all times in the hearts of children separated from their mother country. It torments those whom it fills and denies them contentment and happiness until the gates of their father's house open, and in the common Reich, common blood gains peace and tranquility.

German Austria must return to the great German mother country. . . . Never will the German nation possess the moral right to engage in colonial politics until, at least, it embraces its own sons within a single state. Only when the Reich borders include the very last German, but can no longer guarantee his daily bread, will the moral right to acquire foreign soil arise from the distress of our own people. Their sword will become our plow, and from the tears of war the daily bread of future generations will grow.

Adolf Hitler, *Mein Kampf*

# CONTENTS

Foreword, *by Christoph Cardinal Schönborn*     1
*Preface*     3
*Introduction*     5

The First Reckoning     9
Reality     13
Shockwaves     28
Kriegsministerium     36
Devastation     45
Relocation     60
Kalksburg     74
Separation     88
Munich     108
Sachsenhausen     118
Summer Vacation     127
House of German Armaments     144
The German Navy     158
Recuperation     180
Out of Germany     201
Tirol     218
South of the Border     235
Resistance     248
The Ascent     265
The Long Way Home     288

*Epilogue*     305
*Acknowledgments*     307
*Bibliography*     309
*Index*     311

# FOREWORD

The memoir of Kurt von Schuschnigg, the son of the Austrian chancellor from 1934 to 1938, is a deeply personal, gripping, and impressive story. Recorded by his wife, Janet, his recollections can help those who were born after the events described here not only to understand the dramatic developments that occurred in Central Europe during the period between the two world wars, but also to absorb some of the atmosphere of the time.

Even today, in his own homeland, the image of Chancellor Schuschnigg is frequently distorted by "party hatred and favoritism", an intense partisan spirit. It is certainly true that the country whose government he led over the course of four years was not a democracy. But wasn't every level of society and every group complicit, to one degree or another, in shaping political outcomes? On a number of anniversaries of the events of the years from 1934 to 1938, the Austrian Catholic Church has confessed its own complicity—not because it has wished to conform to the fashion of the day, but because it has been moved by an inner conviction. But at the same time, one has to remember the fact that in Austria the years 1934 to 1938 were also a period of respite, when the country was a refuge for many people for whom the Nazi dictator—the very embodiment of evil in neighboring Germany—had left no chance of survival. This Austria, as numerous contemporary witnesses have testified, provided a breathing space in particular for Jewish citizens as well as for culture and science. Many things may have turned out wrong, but there is no denying that Kurt von Schuschnigg, along with many of those who struggled with him on behalf of an independent Austria, acted out of an explicit commitment to Christian ideals.

In Janet von Schuschnigg's preface there is a sentence that moves me deeply. Referring to her husband, she says: "His story of survival is a testimony to the faith, hope, and perseverance of the many people who, at great risk to themselves, resisted the evil of tyranny by doing good for others." The chancellor during the years from 1934 to 1938, along with members of his family, had to pay a high price for his resistance to the evil of tyranny. And it is clear from his son's recollections, that Schuschnigg was perfectly aware of the enthusiasm that a segment of the Austrian public had for the Nazi program—an enthusiasm that tragically evolved into the participation of many Austrians in the criminality of the Nazi regime.

This book is marked by a real love for the true Austria. One of the greatest benefits that I hope will result from its translation into English is that now the debate taking place in Austria over that era will be brought out into the wider world, and that what transpired at the time in Austria will be placed in a broader international context. I am profoundly grateful to Janet von Schuschnigg for this contribution to an American understanding of Austria's history during this period.

> † Christoph Cardinal Schönborn
> Archbishop of Vienna, Austria
> August 22, 2011

# PREFACE

Before I met my husband, Kurt von Schuschnigg, I did not speak a word of German. As an American I was familiar with the Family von Trapp from the Hollywood film *The Sound of Music*, but I had never heard the name von Schuschnigg.

By the time I met Kurt, he had already lived in America for some time, and the memories of his childhood and youth in Austria during the rise of Hitler were infrequent thoughts. Man's memory has amazing qualities. With discipline the mind can be razor sharp, precise; at other times, when confronted with traumatic experience, memory can become selective.

Recognizing the limits of my understanding of European history as related to Austria in particular, I was spurred on to broaden that knowledge. In doing so, I discovered a seemingly unlimited supply of information, most of which was either polemic or a distortion of the truth. My particular attention was dedicated to books about the Austrian battle to remain independent, the subsequent annexation of Austria by the Third Reich, and the following years until the war's end. The result of this new knowledge was the desire to relate the experiences of a boy whose coming of age was intertwined with these dramatic events.

This is the story of the von Schuschnigg family as told from the unique perspective of my husband. His account illuminates the long, pain-filled journey of this family, as seen through the eyes of one who was family member, witness to history, son of the Austrian chancellor, and victim.

Many years ago I asked him if he didn't hate people for what they inflicted on him and his family. His answer still amazes me today: "I don't blame them. One had to live during those times and to have been a part of those times to understand. One did what seemed necessary to survive. One lived in constant fear, especially during the war years. One was happy to wake up every morning and still be alive!"

3

His story of survival is a testimony to the faith, hope, and perseverance of the many people who, at great risk to themselves, resisted the evil of tyranny by doing good for others.

Janet von Schuschnigg
Kitzbühel, Austria
March 26, 2011

# INTRODUCTION

March 12, 1938: Madly waving people lined the highways and streets of Austria. Jubilant crowds filled squares and plazas. Excitement abounded as the army of the Third Reich marched into Austria escorted by the aircraft of the German Luftwaffe. Flags of the Third Reich were unfurled as the sound of jackboots echoed throughout the land. Many men raised their arms in salute—the greeting required by Hitler—as women threw flowers and blew kisses.

The German Eighth Army crossed into Austria between Bregenz and Schärding. By early morning military units rumbled into Salzburg; by midday they were in Innsbruck. Mile-long columns of artillery and Panzer tanks, which had been patiently awaiting orders since the end of February, had disembarked from the autobahn near Traunstein, Germany, while from Bad Aibling's new airfield, German planes had roared into the air and by nine fifteen A.M. had landed in Vienna. More than one hundred thousand German troops now occupied Austria.

A week earlier, the Reich commissioner for economic affairs, Wilhelm Keppler, had arrived with a new list of demands from Berlin. The Austrian Chancellor, Kurt von Schuschnigg, knew he was out of diplomatic options and time. In a final attempt to draw attention to the plight of Austria, he called for a plebiscite on Anschluss, the incorporation of the Austrian Republic into the Third Reich.

Recent polls had showed that between 65 and 70 percent of Austrians wanted to retain their independence, and the plebiscite was set for March 13. Efforts to keep the chancellor's plebiscite a secret prior to the formal announcement on March 9 had been in vain. A secretary, who was a German spy of long standing in the office of Austria's Fatherland Front Party, had informed Berlin.

On March 10 the Third Reich prepared to invade Austria, and Hitler's ultimatum was delivered to the chancellor on March 11. It was simple: cancel the plebiscite or German troops will march into

Austria. The führer could not afford the humiliation of a public rejection by the Austrian people and was determined to have their country as part of the Reich.

Phone calls and cables flew from Vienna to its ambassadors abroad. London, now implacably "neutral" in the matter, formally refused to react in any significant manner. These two German states should resolve their own differences.

In Paris the Chautemps cabinet had resigned the previous day, leaving the country without a government and producing a simple explanation for not intervening. France would not—could not—stand against Germany.

Italy's response was brief: "Under the circumstances the Italian government is unable to give advice."

After four years of unremitting struggle the Austrian chancellor had lost. Austria was left without any prospect or even hope of assistance. The week before the impending plebiscite he had tried to rally his countrymen with the patriotic cry: "Red, white, red until death!" Now with a two- or three-day supply of ammunition and a vastly outnumbered army, to resist German aggression would have been suicidal.

Just after two P.M. on March 11, Austria received yet another demand from Berlin. The chancellor and his cabinet were to resign, and the Austrian Nazi Arthur Seyss-Inquart, the newly appointed minister of the interior, would become the new chancellor; otherwise the German Wehrmacht would move that very evening.

Six hours later Kurt von Schuschnigg broadcast Hitler's ultimatum to the nation. Berlin had fabricated stories of Austrian civil disorder, of a government that was no longer in control, and of streams of blood running in the streets. "These", said the chancellor, "are lies from A to Z. President Miklas asks me to tell the people of Austria that we have yielded to force." He ended this address with the words, "God protect Austria!"

After taking leave of his cabinet and President Miklas, Schuschnigg with his aide-de-camp, Lt. Col. Georg Bartl, set out for the chancellor's residence. Bartl related a plan to fly Schuschnigg to Hungary, to which the chancellor replied, "I've stolen no silver spoons." Schuschnigg would remain in Austria and meet his fate. At eight A.M. on March 12, the German Eighth Army, under Gen. Fedor von Bock, crossed into Austria as it had planned to do. The authority of the German National Socialist Party had been established.

The former chancellor, Engelbert Dollfuss, had paid for his resistance to Anschluss with his assassination by the outlawed Austrian Nazi Party. Chancellor von Schuschnigg continued this resistance in the face of Hitler's untiring rhetoric advocating Germany's right to *Lebensraum*—increased land and raw materials. Those who believed in and profited from National Socialism now had their day.

With the Anschluss finally achieved, no voices remained to challenge Hitler's vision. The once independent Austrian Republic, now incorporated into Greater Germany and renamed Ostmark, would face an uncertain future.

Crowds on that March 12 included the unconvinced and the skeptical, as well as the curious. People gathered as if drawn by a magnet; but their presence did not endorse the new political environment, nor did it contradict the findings of recent government polls. Austrian Nazis were a minority in Austria, so what was the explanation?

The answer lies in the events of 1918 and before. Most of the vital ingredients that had combined to create the wealth of the former Austro-Hungarian Empire no longer existed within Austria's borders after World War I. Left behind was a modest bit of land, little more than a smudge on the European map, and this land had begun to feel isolated and orphaned. National pride, the sense of belonging to something great, was gone completely. The humiliation of defeat in war paled in comparison to the daily struggle people faced to feed their families. The devastation of war produced food shortages, which in turn triggered strikes and demonstrations. Inflation was rampant, and people carried bags of money to buy food.

Soon the Austrian middle class ceased to exist. Unemployment was everywhere, and prospects for young Austrians were bleak. The dismal situation bred discontent and its corollaries: extremist and violent political movements.

It would take time, years for some people, before Austrians understood what the welcome given to the army of the Third Reich actually meant. Moreover, in time it would be difficult to find anyone who admitted to have taken part in that welcome. The Anschluss had been carefully planned over a long period of time, and it served first as a testing ground, then as a springboard, for lebensraum; its consequences would be incalculable.

The arrival of the Third Reich signaled a wave of political arrests and a realignment of people and the military. Tens of thousands of political opponents were imprisoned, while 55 percent of Austria's generals, 40 percent of the colonels, and 17 percent of the other military officers were reassigned. Innumerable demotions included those of decorated veterans of the First World War who were declared "unworthy to serve". Also marked by the Reich was Chancellor von Schuschnigg.

The country, however, busied itself with thoughts of what good would flow to it from the Third Reich.

# The First Reckoning

By 1926, eight years after the end of the First World War and seven since the signing of the treaties of Versailles and Saint-Germain, the world was moving toward stability and prosperity.

On one side of the Atlantic the United States, led by their modest, conservative president, Calvin Coolidge, had a robust economy and thrived with just 1.8 percent unemployment. Americans undertook daring challenges such as the flight to the North Pole by Admiral Richard Byrd. Although a young nation, America had become a beacon to the rest of the world.

In England, King George V continued his reign, and Stanley Baldwin, prime minister and leader of the Conservative Party, was in firm control of the government. Unemployment, however, was high. The country awoke one day in May to find itself in a state of emergency caused by a local coal strike that had widened into a general strike.

Meanwhile France, economically weakened by inflation and an unstable franc, had rejected the left-wing government of the Cartel des Gauches. The French elected Raymond Poincaré and his conservatives hoping to revive the economy.

Italy had witnessed the political rise of a former journalist who had earned a reputation as a radical and a firebrand. With a heavy hand he had consolidated his power and by 1926 led the only political party whose existence was permitted. The party was that of the Fascists, and its founder, Benito Mussolini, was popularly known as Il Duce.

The struggle to succeed Lenin in the Soviet Union was well under way. Leon Trotsky's star was on the wane and Joseph Stalin's on the rise. Those countries lying between Russia and Austria were working busily and optimistically toward a better future.

In Austria anger had subsided since the expulsion of the Habsburgs, the dissolution of Austria-Hungary, and the period when returning imperial soldiers—too poor to buy civilian clothes—had been spat on and had the medals and insignia ripped off their uniforms. The political situation was not stable, however, as different factions sought to fill the power vacuum left by the monarchy.

In November 1926, Otto Bauer, the head of the Austrian Socialist Party threatened the country with the "dictatorship of the proletariat" in a speech given in Linz. Since the beginning of the 1920s, the Socialists had professed their hatred for both the Catholic Church and her clergy. In the view of the Socialists, the Church was suffocating free thinkers. That the Socialists loathed the very name Habsburg was also no surprise. The Habsburg dynasty, the Catholic Church, and the ruling Christian Social Party were all held to be obstructive to Socialist goals and Socialist ideals. This boded ill for the country—such was the state of the world when I joined it.

After a two-year engagement, my parents had married in 1924. By 1926 Father, then twenty-nine, had been practicing law for five years. Like many of his classmates, he had gone directly from his graduating class at Stella Matutina, the Jesuit college in Vorarlberg, to war in 1915. A year later he found himself in Italy, near Gorizia, where he remained through 1918, when he was taken prisoner along with his father, a general in the Austro-Hungarian Imperial Army. The two spent nearly a year as prisoners of war in Caserta.

When my father returned home, his first objective was to complete his education. Father possessed a keen mind, which the Jesuits had honed further. He earned his law degree from the University of Innsbruck a year early and at the top of his class. To open more career avenues he enrolled in a course at the Academy of Commerce. Papa often said that the sons of career military officers knew few luxuries other than a first-class education.

Father quickly established himself as a lawyer while Austria struggled to establish itself as a republic. With passion and concern he turned his focus toward Austria's post-war problems. Initially, in gatherings at the University of Innsbruck, he began to share his views on the future of Austria. These progressed to town hall meetings, where his impressed colleagues eventually persuaded him to declare his candidacy for the Austrian Parliament.

In 1927 he was elected senator and began to commute to Vienna. As with everything else he did, Father threw himself totally into this new phase of his life. After Mass on Sunday he took the train to Vienna. Returning Friday evening, he would spend Saturday traveling around his constituency, listening to the people and making speeches.

The qualities that had propelled Father into Parliament were noted by Monsignor Ignaz Seipel, the chancellor. In the then still very Catholic Austria, the priest was chairman of the Christian Social Party (1921–1930) and had once before served as the Austrian chancellor (1922–1924). He was appointed chancellor again in 1926 and would continue in this office until 1929.

Referred to as Doctor Seipel, the priest-chancellor took the young Kurt von Schuschnigg, with his strong faith and pure ideals, under his wing. Often in one another's company, Doctor Seipel became a mentor to Father.

My first vivid memory of childhood is associated with Saint Nicholas Day, a big holiday for children in some northern European countries. According to tradition, on December 6 children often receive candy or other special treats from the saint, but the devil Krampus leaves one of his switches in each family's home to remind children to be obedient and behave themselves. With one of these switches, I was introduced formally and painfully to the concept of justice. When I was five years old, about a week after Saint Nicholas and Krampus had visited, a huge, L-shaped, cherry-wood banquette arrived for my room. It had hinged seat cushions and would be used to store my toys. Admiring her acquisition, Mother exclaimed, "Wait until your father sees this!" Since Papa was available so seldom, it was left to me to endorse Mother's purchases.

I stowed my books and toys in the new banquette with great pride and in doing this discovered a forgotten set of miniature tools. The idea of making improvements to the banquette overwhelmed me. With my hammer in midair I heard Mother shriek, "Kurti! What on earth are you doing?"

I froze, and the hammer fell from my hand, creating a wholly unintended dent to my pattern. Mother's voice had a volume and octave I had never heard before. These were very bad signs followed by the words every child dreads: "Wait until your father sees what you've done!" Her firm, calm voice rendered those words more sinister.

I spent the rest of the afternoon in my room "thinking about what I had done"; and with my handiwork right in front of me, that wasn't difficult to do. Who knew that an expression of my individual taste would cause such a disturbance? Time passed. Dinner arrived on a tray. This wasn't a good sign nor was the limited conversation, which consisted of mere directives: "Sit up straight", "Use your napkin", and other such advice. I did as I was told.

Soon, I heard Father's voice in the other room, a sound that normally delighted me, but not now. My feelings divided between panic and dread when I heard Father's footsteps in the corridor followed by Mother's. The doorknob turned and the door swung open. I leapt up, shocked to see Father holding the Krampus switch! I knew the fiend had left it behind for just such an occasion.

Darting past my surprised parents, I shot down the hall and into the salon. As soon as I dove under the couch, I regretted my choice. I should have chosen my bed; there was more room underneath. Showing an agility that startled me, Father was on the floor and we were eye to eye. I tried to flatten myself against the wall, out of reach. It was a futile maneuver. Grasping my ankle, Father dragged me out as if I were a sack of potatoes. What followed is too painful to relate.

That loathsome piece of furniture was repaired—"at great expense". I would have liked to set fire to it. It remained in my room as a constant and painful warning.

# Reality

In 1932 we moved to Vienna. That January Father had been appointed minister of justice. Vienna was an incredible city for a six-year-old fresh from Innsbruck. My life had really begun: a new apartment, a new school, and new friends.

In May Engelbert Dollfuss became chancellor. Born in Lower Austria, he served as an officer in World War I, receiving eight decorations for bravery. Already with degrees in law and theology from his studies at the universities of Vienna and Berlin, he added a doctorate in economics, with the goal of solving the agrarian problems of his home state. After first serving as secretary of his state's Agriculture Association and then as president of its Chamber of Agriculture, he next headed the Austrian Railway System before being appointed minister of agriculture and forestry in 1931. Engelbert Dollfuss, devout Catholic and ardent patriot, was a diminutive man—a scant five feet tall—but what he lacked in height he more than compensated for with enormous personal charisma.

The new government's objectives were a balanced budget, lower unemployment, and a vigorous trade policy focused on Central Europe. A balanced budget was critically important because Austria's largest bank, the Creditanstalt, had failed in 1931, leaving Austria responsible for the bank's liabilities. Economic reconstruction was the crucial challenge facing Austria.

Chancellor Dollfuss secured a nine-million-pound (sterling) loan from the League of Nations, which stabilized the currency and, in so doing, guaranteed Austria's survival. Without this loan, taxes would have escalated out of control, and government subsidies to industries as well as aid to educational and cultural institutions would have been slashed. This, in turn, would have led to further unemployment and hardships for Austrians, who since the beginning of the First World War had suffered terribly.

The League of Nations' condition—not to enter into a customs union with Germany for twenty years—was widely criticized by

Austria's pan-German political groups. The leftist press also objected to the loan and directed distortions, irrelevant criticisms, and personal insults at Dollfuss. The more significant reaction, however, was from the indignant German press widely distributed in Austria: Frankfurt's *Zeitung*, Berlin's *Tageblatt*, and others. The critical reports caused the public, already concerned about an uncertain future, further worry.

Understanding the division in the country, Dollfuss had concluded his May 27 inaugural address by saying, "Conscious of the grave responsibility the present government bears in a time when everything depends on our economic recovery, our home affairs as well as our destiny with regard to foreign relations, I address this appeal: Recognize with us the gravity of the hour and cooperate with us. Otherwise, I fear the fate of our country has reached a crucial point."[1]

The Left, however, was not interested in cooperation with Dollfuss. Otto Bauer, a leader of the Social Democratic Party, was the student of Victor Adler, who was considered the father of the Austrian Socialist movement. In his criticisms of Dolfuss, Bauer made liberal use of Karl Marx's phrases—"the dictatorship of the proletariat" and "the overthrow of the bourgeoisie government by any means". To these he later added his own—"Austrofascism", which he applied to the government of Dolfuss formed after the Parliament dissolved itself the following year.

From the moment Dolfuss took office, Bauer and his party set out to bring down his government. After Dollfuss' inaugural address, Bauer stood up in Parliament and said, "We are ready to work that this land may be saved from the terrible economic fate still threatening it. But for this task of facilitating the formation of a government which could really assemble all the great and vital forces of the country, we regard as an essential condition a bitter, decisive and ruthless struggle against this government."[2] He ended by calling for a vote of no confidence, which did not pass but was a clear warning. The Socialists were intransigent and their resistance would continue.

---

[1] Engelbert Dollfuss to the National Council of Parliament, 27 May 1932, Parliament Archives, Vienna.

[2] Anton Hopfgartner, *Kurt Schuschnigg: Ein Mann gegen Hitler* (Vienna: Verlag Styria, 1989), 83.

The year 1932 also marked a rise in the disturbances throughout the country that had become routine. These organized disruptions of Austrian daily life coincided with the arrival in Vienna of Theo Habicht, leader of the Austrian National Socialist Workers Party (NSDAP), or Nazis. In addition, skirmishes between the right-wing Heimwehr and the left-wing Schutzbund were on the increase. These paramilitary groups arose in the turbulent years after World War I and were not under the control of the government. Popular since 1927, they had become increasingly important as a result of the restrictions imposed by the Treaty of Saint-Germain.[3] The Heimwehr had been formed largely by demobilized soldiers and proclaimed itself an ally of the government. The Schutzbund was an extension of the Austrian Socialist Party.

By the end of 1932, the Nazis had begun to concentrate their attention on the Jewish population. In December, holiday shoppers in Jewish stores were teargassed. The Nazi swastika began to appear on the sides of bridges, on benches and sidewalks, on milestone markers, and even on roads.

Family life, however, was wonderful; we were together again. Our apartment at Mariahilferstrasse 88 was not far from Papa's office on the Minoritenplatz. Mother adapted easily and was happy in Vienna. I barely had time to appreciate the move to Vienna, because my education began—in two different forms. I attended the Katholischer Schulverein, a public boys' school, and Elmayer's.

At school classes were in groups of twenty or so, and we were clearly expected to learn. As a shy newcomer, I hesitated to ask questions, in sharp contrast to the savvy local boys.

Knowing that she wouldn't laugh at me, I approached my mother one day and said, "One boy asked me if I was a Catholic, a Protestant, or a Jew."

"And what did you say?"

---

[3] The Treaty of Saint-Germain-en-Laye was signed Sept. 10, 1919, by the victors of WW I and the newly created Republic of Austria. The document dissolved the Austro-Hungarian Empire and recognized the independence of Hungary, Czechoslovakia, Poland, and the State of Slovenes, Croats, and Serbs (Yugoslavia). The new Austria ceded land to Czechoslovakia, Italy, Poland, Romania, and Yugoslavia and was made liable for war reparations. The Austro-Hungarian Navy was dismantled, and the Austrian Army was limited to 30,000 volunteers.

"I wasn't sure, so I just said, 'I am a Tiroler.' Was that wrong?"

Mother's answer was kinder and more elaborate than the brief comment made by my friend's mother: "Country bumpkin."

Elmayer's existed to prevent its students from turning into social buffoons. Instruction in dance and comportment was directed by Herr Rittmeister Wilhelm Elmayer. A dashing cavalry officer in the First World War, he had returned from the battlefront with a permanent limp. The gold-topped cane that he was forced to use only added to the aura of his imposing monocle. Herr Rittmeister was not a man to be taken lightly. "Uncle Willy" came from a decent background, but he thought it inadequate: decent was not quite aristocratic. His manner and bearing, however, were of good breeding—from the top of his immaculately combed brown hair to his mirror-polished, handmade shoes.

Elmayer classes were divided by age, and we six-year-olds were presented to a small group of ladies responsible for carrying out Uncle Willy's curriculum. He occasionally instructed, but only those whom he had personally selected. One was expected to excel under his tutelage. He combined strict military discipline with a sharp-shooter's eye; nothing escaped him. A misstep during a minuet— tripping over one's feet or, worse, one's partner's feet—and one was sent to stand in a corner, facing the wall. That particular form of "raising awareness" lasted only four or five minutes, and sooner or later everyone visited a corner. Uncle Willy was a kind man, and we all thought him wonderful. Our success as Elmayer students was the driving force in his life.

Sometimes students at the school were chosen to participate in theatrical benefit performances; to these Uncle Willy volunteered his own talent and time. We acted only as background. Uncle Willy considered these activities important for acquiring "presence". Sometimes we had to mill around in Biedermeier costumes; but, more often than not, we played the part of a snowflake, a bush, or something equally harmless.

We took these occasions extremely seriously. To do otherwise would be to betray Uncle Willy. Not one of us would allow as much as a leaf to fall from our costume. During one performance, the sapling beside me tried heroically to suppress a sneeze. He held his breath until his face turned purple and his eyes threatened to explode through his inch-thick glasses. Despite these herculean efforts, his sneeze imploded, jarring his body and knocking his spectacles onto the stage. I stared at him in horror. In one fluid motion the sapling rose, stepped forward, and lowered himself over his spectacles. But in doing so he stepped squarely on them and crushed them. His parents were not pleased, but Uncle Willy was delighted.

Adult conversations were dominated by one subject—the rapid growth of the NSDAP. Habicht was organizing the Nazi press as his first order of business. Originally a Communist, he was adept at methods to propagandize, influence, and terrorize a civil society; and as a result, the Nazis were gaining momentum.

By 1932 Habicht's presence was felt in the streets. Nazi demonstrators disrupted concerts and public meetings; even the cinema was not safe from them. Groups of Nazi-hired rabble-rousers blocked entrances and exits at the University of Vienna and massed in hallways, causing total confusion. The university had to be closed until the police restored order.

Habicht published the *Arbeitsbuch* (handbook) for the pro-Hitler movement in Austria. In it he declared, "Austria is the key point in the heart of Europe. Whoever possesses Austria controls Middle Europe." Habicht orchestrated the dissemination of Nazi propaganda throughout Austria. Planes regularly took off from Munich loaded with Nazi leaflets to be dropped over Austrian cities. German radio broadcast to those Austrians not reachable by other means. Contents never varied: discussions of culture and freedom, distortions and falsehoods about the Austrian government, and arguments in favor of union with Germany.

In April 1932, Joseph Goebbels, Hitler's future minister of propaganda and national enlightenment, arrived in Vienna during the election campaign to disseminate an idea that obsessed the Nazis: the true home of all Austrians was Germany. The vote on April 24 marked the first significant voter turnout for the Nazis in the states of Vienna, Lower Austria, and Salzburg. A year later, having carried 40 percent of all the votes, the Nazis were the strongest party in Innsbruck. By October 1933, Goebbels' propaganda expenses for Austria alone amounted to five million *Reichsmarks* (German currency, 1924–1948).

The Lindbergh kidnapping also occurred in March, and the report went far beyond the United States. All the European newspapers and magazines covered the story of the Lindbergh baby in detail, filling all parents with shock and horror. I was made to feel its consequences keenly.

In addition to my *Kinderfräulein* (governess), a plainclothes policeman followed our every step. He trailed ten feet behind, but that made little difference—he was as inconspicuous as a herd of cows. More mortifying was the fact that he sat every day in the hall outside my classroom. I pleaded for several weeks to be released from this surveillance and finally decided that I could no longer endure it. Father's status as a public figure, as well as the social and political turmoil of Vienna, was not lost on me. I just cared more about my immediate predicament.

I told my parents that I would rather take my chances with a kidnapper than suffer one day more of this torment. My classmates' mockery was constant. I stamped my foot to emphasize this point and was met with the words, "Don't you dare stamp your foot at your mother!" Having exhausted all my arguments, I fell silent. Some form of wordless communication seemed to take place between my parents and, finally, they yielded.

The next morning I awoke with an extraordinary sense of freedom and ease and, without a backward glance, set off for school. Hailing my friend Peter Mayer, I immediately shared my good news. He gave me a curious look, tilted his head, and rolled his eyes sideways, saying, "If that's so then he must have a twin."

"What!" I whipped around and saw the plainclothesman not thirty feet away reading a newspaper. Although his face was partially hidden, his checked suit, bowler hat, and brown, practical shoes were unmistakable. I had watched that combination follow me for weeks. I was speechless. Why hadn't he been told not to follow me?

I returned home, sulking. I confronted my mother and learned an ugly truth: for the welfare of their child, parents permitted themselves to lie. To soothe my feelings, several changes were put into practice.

"Shadow", as I called him, began to find ingenious ways to conceal himself. He made spectacular leaps behind trees (where available), ducked behind cars (if stationary), and resorted to that simplest of ploys, the U-turn. I got some satisfaction out of surprising him by whirling around suddenly and catching him off guard. He no longer sat in the school hallway but in the open coat closet. He was there. I knew he was there. He knew that I knew he was there. He must have wanted to strangle me for making his life difficult.

My two closest friends, Peter Mayer and Rudi Fugger, ignored this monstrous encumbrance. Peter was the sort of boy who was every mother's dream—hair always combed, socks pulled up; he seemed never to get dirty. Peter loved being an altar boy and could recite the Mass in Latin as proficiently as the priests. He was a stalwart friend whose company I would soon miss. Peter, his brother, and their parents would be forced to flee the country because, though fervent Catholics, there was a tincture of Jewish blood in the family.

Then there was Rudi: impetuous, fun loving, and reckless. Blonde, blue-eyed Rudi was thin and wiry. His electric eyes and easy grin always threatened trouble. Rudi was never a willing altar boy. The three of us were completely different, and we engaged in continuous bouts of one-upmanship.

Rudi: "I heard about a boy who fell asleep lying on the grass. A worm crawled in his mouth, down into his stomach, and ate out the whole thing!"

I: "Well, I heard that a caterpillar went in through a man's ear, died, and rotted out his brain."

Serious Peter, eyebrows knitted in concentration, watched our faces as we spoke then exploded, "You're both crazy! Your stomach would digest a worm, and a caterpillar is way too big to make it all the way through the ear to the brain. I don't believe it for a minute!"

Quietly intelligent, Peter was also down-to-earth. Our different qualities were complementary; perhaps that was why the three of us had such a steadying effect on one another.

The friendship between Rudi and me led to our mothers' becoming friends as well. Rudi's mother, Vera, was born Countess Czernin-Chudenitz, and she married Count Leopold Fugger-Babenhausen at an early age. In addition to Rudi, they had three other children: Nora, Rosemarie, and Sylvia. Rudi's parents lived apart: his mother in Vienna, his father in Germany. While this arrangement was unusual, it was better than breaking the unwritten eleventh commandment: "Thou shalt not divorce." In Catholic Austria and Bavaria one did not even whisper the word, and I never asked Rudi about his situation.

Mother and Vera were about the same age, and both were considered beauties. Mama had waving, short blonde hair, brilliant blue eyes, and a slightly full lower lip. Vera was somewhat taller and blonder with a generous mouth that seemed always poised for laughter. Like Mother she had beautiful pale skin. Vera's most distinguishing feature was her eyes—not their color but their shape: like large almonds slanting upward at the outside corners.

When Mother learned that Rudi's sisters often went to their father for the holidays, our family of three grew to five with the addition of Rudi and his mother. In the winter there was skiing, not in chic Kitzbühel but in low-key Saint Anton. The comfortable Hotel Post was right at the base of the Kandahar ski run. Rudi and I happily stayed under the watchful eye of my kinderfräulein at the hotel's modest annex, where we were not directly under the parental thumb.

In the summers, our destinations varied. In the Italian town of Sistiana I first learned the extent of Rudi's capacity for recklessness.

The aptly named Grand Hotel welcomed Mother, Father, and Aunt Vera. Rudi, my even-tempered kinderfräulein, and I occupied the modest but comfortable hotel annex next door. After a quick look at the interior and guests, we explored the grounds. Dropping down beside a pond—in fact, a hole filled with brown water—Rudi pronounced the place an old people's home as he began to toss pebbles into the water. Upon closer inspection we saw that it was full of tadpoles.

"Poor things," said Rudi, "stuck in that filth. They should have a better home."

His first thought was the water pitchers in the guests' rooms. I gasped at his suggestion, not so much over the deed as the prospect of getting caught. I shuddered at my thoughts of Father's reaction to tadpoles in water pitchers. Rudi, however, was convinced that should the worst happen, it would not go beyond the kinderfräulein. Risk, he claimed, was "part of the excitement"—as long as it did not involve his mother. Rudi had a healthy respect for her temper, and I'm sure that he frequently had been the cause of it.

After seeing the lay of the land, we drew up a plan. The guests were at breakfast when the rooms were cleaned, so that would be the decisive moment. As we had no intention of missing a meal, we presented ourselves early the next morning at the dining room, ate quickly, and were on our way out when the first guest appeared.

I shot up to our room and grabbed the jar of rescued tadpoles along with a small spoon with which to effect the transfer. Closing the door with my foot, I turned and ploughed straight into the stomach of the cleaning woman. I quickly put my hands behind my back wondering how long I could hold on to the tadpole jar. The thought of dropping it gave me strength. Somehow I squeezed past her to the top of the stairs, and as she took a step toward me, I bolted down the stairs to meet Rudi coming up. We darted into an empty room, and I quickly described the turn of events with the cleaning woman.

"Well, she didn't follow you. Come on!"

She was cleaning our bathroom as we quietly made our way to our base of operations, a curtained alcove in the hallway. Wasting no time, I poured a little water from the jar into the glass, and Rudi spooned in the tadpoles. A door slammed nearby. We flattened ourselves against the wall and held our breath. More opening and closing of doors followed with the sound of three or four voices, one of which belonged to the cleaning woman.

I peeked through the curtains and saw her. The only thing I had really noticed earlier was her ample stomach. Now I saw that middle age had fully descended; she was heavyset with a prominent moustache matching a coil of black hair resting on her neck. Her small, dark, darting eyes would miss nothing. Encased in a gray jumper, she disappeared and momentarily reappeared at her cart to fill an empty pitcher with water. This was our cue. As she carefully carried it back to the wooden bed stand, Rudi and I silently slid in behind her.

I tapped her on the arm. Rudi and I together knew, at best, seventeen words in Italian, none of which were verbs. I began with what I knew. "Signorina."

She turned toward me as Rudi, balancing the glass behind his back, slid behind her. I held up a coin and shrugged my shoulders as a question.

"Lire, li-re!" she said loudly so that, surely, I would understand. Rudi slipped the tadpoles into the pitcher as she counted with her fingers just how many lire the coin was worth.

"Grazie", I said, trying to keep a straight face.

We flew out of the room and collapsed behind the curtains in the hall. Weak from trying to suppress our laughter, we waited for our next opportunity. The sound of shuffling feet was followed by furniture being moved about and then the flapping of linen. Seconds later she came out for the pitcher and reentered the room with it. Rudi followed. I trailed Rudi, carrying the glass of tadpoles behind my back. We entered as she was replacing the water pitcher. Our reappearance excited her suspicions. She planted both hands on her hips and said, "Che cosa?"

Rudi indicated that he needed her help to tie his shoelaces, "Per favore."

Help? A six-year-old boy could not tie his own shoelaces? At least that is what we thought she must be saying. Her speech flowed and grew louder, and putting a severe strain on buttons that were already threatening rebellion, she bent and set to work on Rudi's shoelaces.

Behind Rudi was a full-length mirror, and plainly reflected in it was the pitcher on the table. She saw me slide the little creatures into their new home. Though well past her first youth, that cleaning woman moved like lightning. Our bottoms stinging, our necks firmly in the grip of her large hands, we were unceremoniously brought into the presence of the head cleaning woman. She, in turn, summoned our kinderfräulein, who displayed a side of herself hitherto unrevealed. It was a very unpleasant surprise. Still, she did not denounce us to the most dreaded of all authorities. From that day on, for the remainder of our vacation, we never lingered past mealtimes in the hotel dining room, and we carefully avoided our room during breakfast hours.

On the whole I was fortunate with my governesses, save one notable exception: a Frau Something-or-Other, a dour woman "of a certain age" who had been highly recommended by the nuns, from whom all those who touched our lives during my youth seemed to have come.

Frau Something wore only black throughout her blessedly short reign. There is nothing wrong with wearing clothes colored black, but Frau Something's natural disposition was such that her clothes served only as an unwelcome reminder of it. I knew right away that her mouth was not made to croon lullabies; she did not even have lips. Her hair was so tightly pulled against her scalp that it looked as if it had been painted on. Her prominent aquiline nose did nothing to alleviate the general severity of her face; it only just managed to separate her eyes. Should all this have failed to make an impression, there were the eyes themselves: small, black, beady, and hooded. When Frau Something sat with hands folded in her lap and eyes cast downward, it was difficult to tell whether she was awake or asleep.

Shortly after her arrival I came upon her in precisely this pose. On the table by her side lay a plate of cookies made by Liesl, queen of our kitchen. Thinking she was asleep, I approached the table. Aside from the ticking of the clock on the mantelpiece, there was no sound in the room. Noiselessly, I reached for one of Liesl's cookies. Swifter than a hunting falcon, out shot her hand and wrapped itself around my wrist. I stood there, as if frozen. Had I been an adult, I am quite certain that I would have had a heart attack. Her cold stare had the same effect on me as the snake charmer is said to have on the cobra. She did not utter a word. Then the clock struck the quarter hour and snapped me out of my trance. I wrested my hand free and shot out of that room at such speed that papers flew off the table in my wake. Even after I was safely out of her sight, I could feel those eyes boring into my back. I did not stop until I reached the kitchen.

It was Liesl's opinion that Frau Something was so thin that her body had no room for a heart. Well-padded Liesl was convinced that lean and mean were synonymous. I had no doubt that this was true in Frau Something's case. So forbidding was her entire demeanor that I suspected even Father was uncomfortable in her presence. I was certain that Mother was thoroughly intimidated by the woman. After suffering silently for several weeks, Mama, who had probably never dismissed anyone, finally had enough. It was then that Fräulein Alice Ottenreiter entered our lives.

Fräulein Alice was one of two daughters of good, hardworking parents and the first kinderfräulein whose name I remembered. Her father, a successful upholsterer, housed his family in a large, sunny apartment on Neubaugasse. Alice was well educated and had attended Sacre Coeur Gymnasium in Vienna; was a devout Catholic as was her whole family; spoke French and English in addition to her native German; and, had already been "in service" in Belgium and England.

In her midtwenties Fräulein Alice was about average height and had a trim, almost athletic figure. Her short light-brown hair was always maintained with a hint of style such that it complemented beautiful brown eyes that twinkled in a way that made a person feel he was sharing some secret joke with her.

Nothing in her pleasing appearance, her work experience, or the recommendations of the nuns would foretell the rarity of her strength and kindness; her heart was pure gold. She settled graciously into our routine. None of us could have envisioned then how completely we would come to be entwined in one another's lives. Fortunately, Fräulein Alice also had an excellent set of nerves, which were tested almost immediately after her arrival.

The lovely Augarten Palace, a property of the Austrian government, had been converted into private apartments for government officials. One of these had been allotted to Father, who since October 1932 had been minister of justice. In May 1933 he became minister of education. As such, in July he accompanied Chancellor Dollfuss to Rome to meet the papal nuncio, Cardinal Eugenio Pacelli. They were there to sign a concordat extending the cooperation between church and state regarding Catholic schools and religious education. The concordat stressed the attitude of the Catholic Church toward the social problems of the present times. Pope Pius XI's 1931 encyclical *Quadragesimo Anno* would be the foundation for Austria's form of government called *Ständestaat*, corporate state.[4]

---

[4] Ständestaat was a form of government with representation elected by professional and trade associations instead of by rival political parties, which at that time tended to divide along the class lines defined by Marx as capital and labor.

In an effort to remedy the social problems and civil unrest caused by the disparity of wealth created by modern industry, Pope Pius XI, as well as his predecessor Leo XIII, taught that civil institutions should be built upon associations that include both workers

With so many demands on his time, Father usually arrived home late in the evening and was never there long enough to enjoy the beauty of the structure or its surrounding grounds. Twice the size of the apartment on Mariahilferstrasse, it also had a variety of trees, well-tended gardens, and stables. Fräulein Alice and I were now surrounded by fresh air and had a safe environment in which to exercise. Confrontations between the Heimwehr and the Schutzbund had created zones that were out of bounds for us, including the Vienna City Park.

In Austrian politics, a realm not known for objectivity and forthrightness, Father had an unassailable reputation. With an unshakable faith and unwavering patriotism, he could not be swayed by bribery. Like so many countries, Austria had its share of those who sought to influence men in power by offering them gifts of every kind. It was well known that gifts offered to Father would either be returned immediately or refused on the spot. Other methods of influence would be employed, but the result would be the same. Presents would also arrive for "Little Kurti". Had it not been for a chance trip to Father's office, I would not have learned of them. That morning, Fräulein Alice and I had arrived just as Father's secretary was politely refusing delivery of a shiny, new, beribboned bicycle.

Chocolates seemed to arrive by the barrel. Donors of these were thanked on behalf of their ultimate recipients, the old and poor of Vienna, whose lives Mother worked tirelessly to improve through the Altwienerbund. This charity was very important to her, and the people it served were grateful for the chocolates. I, however, liked chocolates as much as cod-liver oil and would suffer through the unpleasantness of having a chocolate popped into my mouth by some well-wisher. Curiously, they never asked if I liked chocolates.

Father never wavered in his refusal to accept gifts. Once a crate of fruit arrived from his brother-in-law, who was a fruit exporter in the South Tirolean town of Bozen. This region had been Italian since the end of World War I, but Austria still subsidized those industries, such as fruit farms, owned and operated by Austrians.

and owners and not upon political parties that encourage enmity between them and can result in Communist-led revolutions.

Worried that such a gesture, even from a relative, could be misinterpreted, he had the crate sent back to my slightly indignant uncle. I resigned myself to the fact that no token of goodwill would ever come my way—nothing except the despised chocolates.

One afternoon Fräulein Alice and I were summoned to the stables. When we entered, one of the orderlies handed me a card with the inscription "For Kurti" and an unfamiliar signature. The orderly told me to close my eyes and then led me around the corner.

"Open your eyes!" he exclaimed.

With a theatrical wave of his arm, he presented a beautiful pony hitched to a sparkling new carriage. I looked at Fräulein Alice with my mouth ajar; she also was speechless. This gift was beyond my imagination, for I had never been spoiled with presents. We circled the apparition. Then I ran my hands over the pony. It was solid, real, and not an apparition. Though deliriously happy, I was astonished that Father had relented to such a degree. The pony pawed the ground and shook his head. We fed him carrots and racked our brains for a suitable name. When my mother returned, she was stunned and did not know from whom the pony and carriage came. She knew that nothing was delivered to the Augarten without Father's approval, so she shared our excitement.

The next morning, our dappled brown-and-white pony trotted out, pranced before us, and shook his forelock proudly. Fräulein Alice and I sat in the splendid, yellow coach with its chocolate-colored trim. The matching canvas top had been pulled down to reveal soft, fawn-colored leather seats. We attracted so many admiring looks that the orderly at the reins took a long detour and we arrived at school just as the bell rang. I ran as fast as I could and just missed being tardy. There was one late arrival—limping, panting Shadow.

After school, my friends were treated to a carriage ride. This delayed us, and we returned home past the usual hour. Father had just arrived when we made our late and conspicuous entrance. Having proceeded past the beautifully tended park of the Augarten, we came to a halt in front of him. Fräulein Alice and I both mistook his look of surprise for admiration; but the next instant, he wordlessly spun on his heel and stormed through the door, taking the stairs two at a time up to our apartment.

I looked at Fräulein Alice. There was no mistaking her unease. She took me to my room; and though she closed the door behind her, one would have had to have been deaf to miss what followed: "What the devil are you trying to do? Ruin me? What were you both thinking to accept such a gift? Wherever that pony and that carriage came from, send it back this minute!" Father's command was punctuated with the thunderous slamming of a door. Father had always been a door-slammer. Fortunately, all our apartments had solid doorframes. His outburst was Fräulein Alice's introduction to the temperamental nature of my family.

The shiny carriage with the dappled pony vanished and were never mentioned again. Only one person benefited from their disappearance—Shadow.

# Shockwaves

Adolf Hitler came to power in Germany on January 30, 1933.

On March 4, a bill important to the Social Democrats came before the Austrian Parliament. In Austria, the president of Parliament does not vote; however, the second and third presidents do vote. On this particular bill, the voting was tied.

On the advice of Otto Bauer, Karl Renner, a fellow Social Democrat and president of Parliament, resigned in order to break the tie. Now, the office of president would pass to Second President Rudolf Ramek, a member of Dollfuss' Christian Social Party. This transition would eliminate Ramek's vote, and the Social Democrats would gain two votes. To counter Renner's action Rudolf Ramek also resigned. Not wishing to be either party's pawn, the third president, Sepp Straffner of the Greater German Party, resigned too. Through these combined actions Parliament had dissolved itself.

Chancellor Dollfuss solved the constitutional crisis by reviving the Economic Empowering Law of 1917, which reestablished rule by decree. The law provided Dollfuss with a practical means by which Austria could protect itself from the forces that were working to destabilize the country. The greatest threat was Hitler's ambition to force the unification of Austria and Germany, which he had clearly put forth in *Mein Kampf*, but also undermining Austria was the spread of Communism. The stalemate in Parliament, caused by the intransigence of the Socialists was preventing the government from thwarting the growth of armed radical groups. The resignation of the three heads of Parliament was fortuitous for Chancellor Dollfuss, for it gave him the authority to confront the grave threats to Austrian independence. With his new powers, he outlawed the Socialist Party's militia, the Schutzbund, in March. Then on May 6, he banned the Communist Party, and on June 19 the NSDAP.

On May 27, Germany imposed a tariff of one thousand reichsmarks on every German traveling to Austria. The previous year, 1932, Germans had accounted for 60 percent of all tourists in four of the nine Austrian states: Tirol, Vorarlberg, Salzburg, and Carinthia. The tariff, which amounted to a blockade, was a catastrophe for them, but the intent of the new tax was to sabotage the Austrian economy.

Shortly after its Thousand-Mark Tariff, Germany unleashed in June a wave of Nazi bombings that threatened to cripple Austria. Throughout that summer innumerable caches of explosives were confiscated, yet the bombings rose to a rate of about 125 a month. The country was being steadily undermined by attacks on power plants, electric switching stations, railway stations, bridges, state buildings, and the offices of local and state police. There were simpler acts of sabotage as well, such as the cutting of telephone lines. Train service was frequently disrupted: a section of the line would be damaged, destroyed, or blocked with rocks.

Accompanying the terrorism were more assassination attempts on the chancellor, the vice-chancellor, and the minister of justice. Both foreign and domestic in origin, this terror warfare was meant to portray the Austrian government as incapable of protecting its citizens.

Because of the Treaty of Saint-Germain, the Austrian Army was inadequate to defend the country or patrol its borders. Another source of intimidation was the threat posed by the Austrian Legion, which operated along the German-Austrian border. When Dollfuss banned their party, these Austrian Nazis fled to Germany, where they were receiving military training. Reportedly, even the Nazi Habicht had viewed these storm troopers as a challenge to his authority and strongly objected to their presence.

In desperate need of neighbors of goodwill, Chancellor Dollfuss traveled to Italy and found a hoped-for warm reception. With little use for Hitler, Mussolini expressed his support for an independent Austria, which could serve as a useful buffer state between Germany and Italy. The thought of German troops on the Brenner Pass would not have been a pleasant one for the Italian dictator.

Dollfuss' aim was to reach a compromise in order to relieve German pressure on Austria before matters gyrated out of control. An optimist, he sent out unofficial feelers for a meeting with Hitler. Advised that the führer would receive an Austrian emissary in Munich on October 31, 1933, the chancellor sent Father. But upon his arrival, a party functionary informed Father that Hitler was not in Munich. Heinrich Himmler then took Father to see Rudolf Hess, who was surprised at the visit. Father left for Vienna after an hour of Nazi rhetoric.

By 1934 Nazi violence was the Austrian government's foremost concern—no one knew when or where it would erupt. Nazis were infiltrating the Heimwehr and adding recruits. Considering themselves a counterforce, left-leaning intellectuals were swelling the ranks of the Social Democrats and clandestinely enlarging and organizing the Shutzbund.

On February 12, Nazi terrorism reached a new high; upwards of forty bombs were detonated in a single day. Members of the government, as well as Austrian patriots, were sent letter bombs. One of these was slipped through the mail slot in the front door of our Innsbruck apartment. The letter bombs turned out to be the least of the bad news on that fateful day, for the government was faced with a bloody putsch by the Schutzbund.

When Emil Fey, vice-chancellor and minister of security, ordered a weapons search of the Social Democratic headquarters in Linz, gunfire erupted. Meanwhile in Vienna, power plants were sabotaged and phone lines cut, as snipers killed several policemen. The banned Schutzbund, the army of the Social Democrats, had risen from the underground.

Chancellor Dollfuss ordered troops into the troubled Karl Marx Hof, the Vienna municipal housing complex long since emptied of civilians and held by the Shutzbund. After three days of fierce fighting, the Shutzbund surrendered. The battle resulted in many casualties: the government forces counted 128 dead and 409 wounded. Schutzbund and civilian casualties amounted to 193 dead and 300 wounded.

Subsequently, the government discovered plans detailing the uprising and the usurpation of power. Official buildings were to be bombed out of existence and tribunals, already chosen, were to be set up.

In May, before the full heat of summer, the new US ambassador to Austria, George Messersmith, arrived in Vienna. His appointment would have been short had not a bomb hidden in the Hotel Bristol, where he was lodged, been discovered. It was powerful enough to have brought down the entire building.

One of my obligations as my father's son was to be present at parades and other official occasions wearing the uniform of Ostmärkische Sturmscharen, an organization that Father had founded. The term *Ostmark* referred to the eastern boundary of Charlemagne's empire that needed to be defended from non-Christian invaders. The Catholic paramilitary group was meant as a counterbalance to the Hitler Youth and to the Heimwehr. The recruits were members of Katholische Jugend, a Catholic youth group, as well as teachers and other professional adult men.

At the spring parade of 1934, thousands of spectators lined the Ringstrasse. All branches of the armed forces as well as the Sturmscharen and Heimwehr marched down the street. First Chancellor Dollfuss placed a wreath at the memorial to the Unknown Soldier on the Heldenplatz. Opposite the memorial was the reviewing stand comprised of members of the government, foreign dignitaries, and representatives of the Catholic Church. Escorted by Chancellor Dollfuss, I presented myself to the archbishop of Vienna, Cardinal Theodor Innitzer, and bent to kiss his ring. Simultaneously, my cap slid backward, and my flag almost slipped out of my hand. After that Mother firmly anchored my cap, and I no longer carried a flag.

That summer was exceptionally hot, causing those who could flee the city weather to do so. Mother took a group of her friends and mine out to the bathing spa at Klosterneuburg. Such an all-day outing was a special treat for us boys. We had finished lunch when Mother was called to the telephone. Assuming that it must be Father, I followed her out. As she listened her expression grew serious. After an inaudible exchange of words, Mother nodded and hung up. Taking my hand, we returned to the party in silence. She said that while her presence was urgently required in Vienna, the rest of us were to stay and enjoy ourselves. The driver would return for us at the end of the day. She kissed me goodbye, adding that I should be a good boy. I knew that I would be good—something wasn't right, and it was with a sense of uncertainty that I watched her leave.

Dollfuss had been shot. An attempt to take over the radio station had been foiled, but not before the Nazi conspirators broadcast false news that Dollfuss had resigned and was being replaced by Anton Rintelen. Once governor of Styria, he had been the Austrian ambassador to Italy since 1933. Later it was learned that he had attended numerous meetings between January and June 1934 with Rudolf Weydenhammer, a representative of Theo Habicht, the Nazi. The focus of their conversations had been the overthrow of the Austrian government.

Our swimming party concluded at the end of the day, and the driver returned us to the city. Alone in the car as we approached the Augarten, I saw policemen stationed along the road. More policemen and soldiers were in the park and ringed the building. Something was wrong. Armed and alert, these men made attempts to conceal their weapons from my sight. The driver went past our entrance to the far end of the building. I was told that I would spend the night with our neighbors, the Davids. I was surprised, for nothing like this had ever happened, and the Davids offered no explanation for the unusual arrangement.

I was given dinner at six P.M. and sent to bed. Despite the early hour, a full day of swimming and the excitement of whatever it was that was happening brought sleep on quickly. Later that night, I was awakened by loud, unfamiliar noises. I ran to the partially open window. In the distance I could see spots of light moving eerily through the darkness. There were shouts and the sharp sounds of small explosions. I knelt and rested my forearms on the windowsill.

Soon I realized the roaming beams were men with flashlights, and I knew I was listening to gunfire: the spitting noise had to be a machine gun, and the sporadic reports pistols and rifles. I could hear the shattering of glass, the thwacking of bullets striking and glancing off hard surfaces, and also the shouts of men, mixed with rapid volleys of gunfire.

Not knowing where my parents were, I said a quick prayer that they were safe. Suddenly, a bullet thudded loudly into a nearby tree—I nearly jumped out of my skin. Was it the Swastikas or the Reds? Maybe it was the banned Schutzbund soldiers. Whoever was responsible, I knew this was a serious situation. I could smell the acrid gun smoke of discharged ammunition. It filled the night air and floated into the bedroom. I thought of my tin soldiers and of the mock battles that I had conducted. There was no resemblance to this! From time to time, the sounds of battle subsided. Relaxing, I would rest on my heels, only to be jerked back to attention when another volley erupted.

At one point, sensing movement below my window, I squinted into the dark. I knelt there frozen, not daring to breathe. If I saw anything move, I would need to find someone, and quickly. It would have been easy for someone to climb up to my window and murder us all! It grew silent for a few moments. Then I heard a loud moan, followed by an ear-splitting explosion that rattled the room and caused my insides to jump. The battle had resumed.

For what seemed an eternity, I kept my vigil at the window until I was so tired that I decided to lie down on the floor. Then it came to me this might not be wise. If someone were to climb up and come through the window, I would have been what he stepped on! I returned to my bed and sat down. The battle seemed to be concentrated at the end of the building my family occupied. This time I fervently addressed my parents' guardian angels. Still no one had come to my room, and I was sorely tempted to find the Davids. Then I remembered that my mother had asked me to be "a good boy" and decided to stay where I was.

I leaned back against the headboard and waited. I was still in that position when the sky began to lighten and a servant came to fetch me. I was taken to my parents, who had been up the entire night in a different apartment in the Augarten. It was then I learned Chancellor Dollfuss had been killed by the Swastikas. They had tried the previous October but had only wounded him. This time they succeeded.

The Augarten Palace saw a flurry of repair activity that day. Mother was resting after being up all night. Father had left for the chancellery. Fräulein Alice had been able to make her way across Vienna and was arranging for our temporary quarters. I left the Davids' apartment feeling a degree of freedom. Outside I saw an army of police circling the grounds with weapons drawn.

I walked down to our entrance. The pockmarked facade, the litter outside, and the debris testified to the vicious fighting that had occurred last night. I could look at the damage and once more hear sounds of shattered glass, broken stone, and splintered wood. Workers were sifting through the wreckage and talking among themselves; I gathered that the government's men had fought a fierce gun battle with the Swastikas and that it had lasted until early in the morning. Noticing me, a worker shouted out words of caution.

Greatly enlightened by the conversations that I had overheard and not wanting Fräulein Alice to discover that I had gone missing, I returned to the other apartment.

They called themselves Swastikas, Brownshirts, or Nazis, and they were responsible for everything bad that was happening. Yesterday's events, however, raised a new question: If they could murder Dollfuss, who had the army and police to protect him, then who was safe? Underlining the question was our shattered apartment down there.

Workmen toiled round the clock. By the time Father was sworn in as chancellor, the renovation was complete. No outward trace remained of the would-be assassins' work. Bullet holes had been filled in, the rooms painted, and windows replaced. Shards of broken china and smashed crystal had been swept up. The smallest detail had been attended to with the greatest care. Massive arrangements of lilies lined the foyer, and roses and lilacs burst forth from cut-crystal vases in the main salon. This profusion of flowers had an added purpose—their mingled fragrances would eradicate the smell of gun smoke.

Nevertheless, as I walked with my parents from room to room, I knew life would never again be normal. The signs of physical havoc wrought that night had been erased, but memories associated with so many familiar objects that had been destroyed were still fresh in my mind.

These thoughts I kept to myself. Father was fine, but I sensed unease in Mother. Many of her things had been destroyed, but it wasn't the loss of china, crystal, or furniture that seemed to bother her. Small noises startled her, and she held my hand more often in public. She was clearly uncomfortable in crowds. Her eyes were always searching. She studied faces, as if trying to recognize someone or something.

We no longer rode around the city in the open landau, something I had always enjoyed. I could only hope for a speedy end to this phase of security. That night was never referred to again, nor was I told the details of Dollfuss' death. He had been shot by Nazis disguised as policemen. Wounded, Dollfuss lay on a couch for seven hours. His requests for a doctor and a priest were denied. Before dying he asked that Kurt von Schuschnigg succeed him.

After Dollfuss' assassination, the chancellor's residence was considered to be too accessible and insecure. We were packed up and moved into the fortress-like Ministry of War building, the Kriegsministerium.

While the household was being reestablished, Father dedicated himself to the task of ensuring the independence of the Austrian state. In the third week of August 1934, the new Austrian chancellor went to Italy to remind Mussolini that Austria relied on Italy's support.

Three weeks later, he stood before the representatives of the League of Nations in Geneva. The chancellor described the critical importance of an independent Austria. He asked League representatives to understand Austria's reaction to the putsch of February 12 and Dollfuss' assassination on July 25. Vengeance was not sought against "the enemies of yesterday"—Austria desired only to pursue its own destiny in peace. Those who sought to harm the Austrian economy would, he said, be punished as the law allowed. He recognized that the present Austrian form of government, a corporate state, might seem alien to democracies such as England and France, but their form of democracy was new to Austria and equally alien. Regardless of the kind of government in place, Austrian independence remained the vital issue. By the end of September, he had in hand a declaration from England, France, and Italy reaffirming their commitment to Austrian independence.

By no means was Austria alone in its desire for security. Hungarian Prime Minister Gyula Gömbös came to Austria at the beginning of November and stated his concern for Hungary's own security. After further discussions with Mussolini, the Austrian chancellor made a trip to Budapest. Creating a fire wall between Austria and Germany was the need of the hour.

# Kriegsministerium

Built around 1900 as the War Office of the Austro-Hungarian Empire, the Kriegsministerium occupied an entire city block. The entrance to our apartment was on the Stubenring,[1] at one end of the building. The Danube Canal flowed past the other end. We were connected to the rest of the building by the grand marble hallway that ran the length of the structure. It was eighteen feet high and wide enough to ride a bicycle or roller skate comfortably, without so much as grazing either of Father's orderlies—the stalwart Defregger and the sturdy Gsaller.

There was also room for my new four-legged friend, whom I named for the puppy's enthusiastic somersaulting around my bedroom floor. He became Purzel. Mother and Father had decided that I needed a companion in these enormous surroundings. Nothing could have made me happier. It was even better than having a baby brother or sister: I didn't have to wait for Purzel to become companionable. From the beginning, the black standard poodle had no idea he was a dog. He thought he was one of us in disguise. The puppy had come to us housebroken—one of Mother's prerequisites. I was a very lucky boy.

Enormous windows ran down the front of the Kriegsministerium and wrapped themselves around the sides of the building. On sunny days the building flooded with light, inviting exploration. I had traded the beautiful lawns and gardens of the Augarten for the marbled Kriegsministerium, but there was compensation: here I was considered safe and given the run of the place. I was free to wander its cavernous halls with Purzel for company.

On dark, wintry days, when those gargantuan spaces seemed to fill up with long shadows, I turned to my legions of toy soldiers—infantrymen and cavalrymen from every corner of Europe. There

---

[1] The Stubenring is a part of the larger Ringstrasse, a main street of Vienna rich in historical buildings.

were Hessian dragoons with their red coats, yellow shoulder knots, and white breeches; Austro-Hungarian officers with blue coats and crimson sashes; British grenadiers and fusiliers with bearskin caps. All of them had worthy opponents in Napoleon's army. Even the cast-iron Russians found employment.

When tired of staging battles, I turned to my stamps. I had built up my collection by my own efforts and had stamps from every corner of the world. The great jewel in my collection came to me as a gift—a complete set of first-issue Italian stamps from Benito Mussolini. Before handing me the present, Father explained why he had made this exception: it would have been an insult for Father to refuse a gift for his child from the Italian leader. The Italians were our only bulwark against Adolf Hitler's National Socialists, and Italy's goodwill was critical to the independence of Austria. I was many times over a lucky boy. Sometimes I wondered if it ever occurred to my parents that Purzel and these quiet hobbies of mine rendered being sent to my room ineffective as punishment.

Alone one day, Purzel having been taken to the veterinarian, I set out on an adventure. Beginning at the end of our hallway, I systematically opened one door, then the next, and so on. I intended to inspect each and gain a detailed knowledge of all the rooms. Reception rooms, large and small, were interspersed with a variety of offices, pantries, closets, and a great neo-rococo ballroom. After a glance at several ordinary offices, I burst through the next door and came face-to-face with a surprised and less than pleased minister of commerce, Fritz Stockinger.

His sudden reaction to my unexpected entry caused the small Persian kitten that had been resting on a nearby table to spring onto the minister's desk, which was covered with papers. Had the kitten aimed at the very large and full inkwell, it could not have done a better job knocking it over.

Minister Stockinger sat paralyzed, watching a river of blue ink soak everything in its path. Stifling a curse, he burst into action. With one hand, he whipped out his handkerchief to arrest the ever-spreading flow of ink across the desk; with his other hand, he snatched up the wastebasket and shot it under the rivulets of ink now streaming over the edge of the desk.

I stood there frozen—my mouth open. With nimbleness not unexpected—it was Stockinger who had overpowered Dollfuss' would-be assassin the first time the chancellor had been shot in October 1933—he swooped up the kitten in one fluid movement and took several purposeful steps toward the open window. His face was the color of a man whose collar was much too tight.

"Please, don't hurt it, sir", I implored.

He whirled toward me. "You want the thing? Take it and get out of here this instant!"

I called out a hasty thank you and fled with the kitten to our apartment. After calming it down, I began to wonder how my parents were going to react to news of this incident.

Fräulein Alice had been the first to have doubts about the kitten. It had stuck her with its claws, once and then again. "Like two pins", she said in English: thus the name Pinpin.

"There is Purzel to consider, Kurti! Dogs and cats are not natural friends", Mother explained at lunch. "It is just the way they are created. Keeping peace between them borders on the impossible."

"Please let me try", I begged. "Minister Stockinger turned the color of these plums, he was so angry, and he nearly threw Pinpin out the window!"

"Darling, Minister Stockinger would not have thrown the kitten out of the window. When not provoked he is a very nice man", she sighed. "Very well, but it's going to be your responsibility to see that Purzel and Pinpin are kept separated no matter how hard it is and no matter how much trouble. Is that clear?"

"Yes, Mother. Thank you so much!" After a hug that was enthusiastic enough nearly to unseat her, I went off to make my arrangements.

The living quarters first. Purzel had seniority; I could not simply throw him out of my room to make way for the upstart kitten. Pinpin would have to go to the kitchen and keep Liesl company. After all, Liesl liked animals.

"What? A cat in my kitchen? Not on your life! I like dogs. You tell a dog to go sit in a corner and it does. A cat goes and does whatever it pleases. No!"

After pleading and then begging, I finally wore her down. Pinpin was allowed to stay in the kitchen. This arrangement was not altogether successful. Every time Liesl opened the door, the kitten shot out. When I was within earshot, I had retrieval duty.

Pinpin had developed a passion for Mother's pale-yellow silk curtains. Clawing her way up them at top speed, she managed to create fresh patterns in the silk. It was my good fortune that Pinpin's claw marks escaped Mother's notice, but something had to be done.

The two orderlies, Gsaller and Defregger, had a curtain-free duty room. I relocated Pinpin, but this assignment did not last long. The next day, I entered with Pinpin's milk and accidentally knocked the duty book onto the floor. It landed with a resounding thud, scaring the kitten through the wedge of the partially open door.

"Pfui! Come back here!" I shouted. Aware this was a futile command, I hastily put down the milk, sloshing it all over myself. Then I heard Mother yell, "Somebody catch that cat!" To describe her voice as unhappy would have been an understatement. Had she caught the kitten, she would have thrown it out the window. When I reached the salon, I heard a dreaded sound: "Ziz–ziz-ziz." Pinpin had scampered up the curtains and was sitting atop the silk-covered cornice in front of Mother.

I had no choice other than to evict Purzel from my room and with a sinking feeling and sense of futility install the kitten in his place. While ostensibly with Liesl in the kitchen, Purzel had taken up sentry duty outside my door, forcing me to slide sideways in and out of my room. I considered using the ledge outside my window to enter the adjoining room; but I knew if Mother spotted me, it would have been the proverbial straw that broke the camel's back.

Two days later all hell broke loose. Mother and I were going to the *Altersheim* (home for the elderly). When she called, "Kurti, we leave in five minutes", my clothes were on the bed, where Fräulein Alice had put them a long while before. I was conducting the Battle of Aspern-Essling on the floor of my room. Nearly falling over my own feet, I leapt up and snatched my clothes. Wriggling and hopping, I was fully dressed in about twenty-five seconds. Mother would have to comb my hair in the car. I ran to the door, feeling vaguely that I had forgotten something, and yanked it open. There, waiting patiently was Purzel. Before I could shout no, Purzel was halfway to the slumbering Pinpin. The kitten leapt from the bed to the dresser; then, a living projectile, she shot through the door with Purzel in hot pursuit.

39

They went yowling through the hall, past both salons, through the front door, thoughtfully left open for Fräulein Alice, and out into the hallway. They streaked past Gsaller, and he took off in pursuit of my two fast-disappearing pets. Trailing far behind, I saw Gsaller slide into a right turn before he vanished. I tried to erase the picture that flashed into my mind—a triumphant Purzel with Pinpin dangling lifelessly from his mouth.

I caught up in time to watch Pinpin execute the leap of her life. Cornered by the fiercely growling Purzel, twenty times her size, Pinpin knew she was about to become a doggie appetizer. Spotting an open window, she sprang onto the table beneath it, and then onto the windowsill. A split second later, she flew out the window and landed below on the thick glass roof of the porte cochere. Unable to follow, Purzel went berserk. He leapt up and down, barking frantically at the vanished kitten.

Gsaller made an instant assessment of the situation and swung himself onto the frail table, which miraculously sustained his weight, then up and onto the ledge of the window frame. He swiveled around and called out over his shoulder, "She is just sitting out here." These were his last words before he jumped to the roof of the porte cochere. Before one could even mouth the word *idiot*, Gsaller crashed through the glass followed by Pinpin.

Against all probability there was neither car nor driver, nor anyone else, below. Completely unharmed, the kitten darted to the street and leapt upon the first thing she saw—a lady in a silk dress. The lady's escort extricated Pinpin but not before substantial damage had occurred to her clothes. A guard who ran out to help took charge of Pinpin while another guard went in search of smelling salts and an ambulance.

The injured Gsaller was taken to the hospital, and, much later than planned, I meekly accompanied Mother to the altersheim. My mother had a remarkable ability to remain calm in trying circumstances and did so on this occasion. The thought of Father's reaction occupied my attention for the rest of the day.

At breakfast the following morning, Liesl told me that his lips seemed to disappear when he read the headlines in the newspaper: "Wildcat of Schuschnigg Attacks Lady in Front of Kriegsministerium!" I did not look forward to the rest of the day and asked myself, "What is the worst thing that can happen now?" Not wishing to dare fate, I changed it to "What is the best thing that can happen?" Either question came to the same thing: forfeiting my allowance until I had paid for the lady's dress, Gsaller's hospital bills, and the porte cochere. It would take me the rest of my life.

Just before bedtime, I was summoned by Father. I marched in and stood, knees unsteady, waiting. He sat.

"Kurti, you understand that you neglected your responsibility?"

"Yes, sir."

"You understand how serious the consequences were?"

"Yes, Papa", the flood began. "I am really, really sorry. I am so sorry that Gsaller hurt himself. I am sorry that the lady's dress was ruined, and I am sorry that the glass roof was broken. I am extra, extra sorry that it was in the newspaper."

Raising an eyebrow at the mention of the newspaper, Father seemed to soften. "Come here, my son."

He reached out and lifted me onto his lap. This was a welcome turn of events. He explained that it had not been fair to keep Pinpin in the same household with a dog, especially one as energetic as Purzel, and that it was natural for a kitten to like to climb. We had to do the right thing for Pinpin. Father said he had found a wonderful new home for her. She was going to the zoo to live with other wild cats, and I could visit her whenever I wished. Relief flooded over me. Pinpin would be safe and happy after all, and Purzel could return to my room. I was also relieved to learn that Gsaller hadn't broken any bones. He would be back the next day with a twisted wrist and a few stitches. All this—*and* I was debt free.

One of the spectacular aspects of the Kriegsministerium was its splendid ballroom overlooking the Stubenring. Marbled walls studded with ornate mirrors soared up to a graceful, high ceiling from which hung heavy chandeliers. Gilt-edged chairs upholstered in red velvet lined the walls, and groupings of sofas and armchairs provided additional seating. The centerpiece of the ballroom was a magnificent grand piano.

My parents shared a passion for music. Mother ensured that once a week the room was graced by the presence of some of the great musical talent of the day. These were my parents' favorite evenings.

My activities in the ballroom were common by comparison. Mother would have children's parties for me and my friends. She would put considerable energy and imagination into the arrangements, and the results were always a success. The parties were full of cleverly contrived and ingenious games, and there was more than enough lemon and orange soda as well as Liesl's confections to make us thoroughly ill.

What we liked most were the afternoons with the *Märchentante*, professional narrators of fairy tales. The märchentante were accomplished actresses, somewhat past their prime. They would hold us spellbound for hours on end. Their material seemed unlimited: from Wilhelm Busch's illustrated stories, later to be called comic strips, to the fabulous tales by the Brothers Grimm. So vivid and compelling were the märchentante that we could smell the poisoned apple into which Snow White bit and shivered with cold as we crept behind Hansel and Gretel in the forest. We lived every minute of each adventure. Seeing the effect they had on us must have been its own reward for the märchentante.

Mother combed through the available pool of talent—off-duty army personnel—to find the perfect Saint Nicholas and Krampus for a *Fasching*[2] party. She was hoping for an inspiring performance; we wanted only to be scared to death.

When Saint Nicholas and Krampus were announced, a hush fell over the ballroom while scores of eyes looked in anticipation toward the entrance. In swept the sainted bishop resplendent in miter and gold vestments. He struck his jeweled staff on the floor in rhythm with his every step. This imposing figure with a long white beard strode to the middle of the room, halted, and stared thoughtfully into each face as if to learn which of the twitching, excited little souls would be rescued from the devil's grasp. Silently he turned back toward the door. Reminiscent of Moses facing the Red Sea, Saint Nicholas raised both arms toward the heavens. He paused for a second then brought them down violently—thundering his staff against the floor.

A blood-curdling shriek sounded in the corridor and in leapt the devil incarnate—Krampus! Every child in that room convulsed

---

[2] Fasching is the German word for carnival, the festive period leading up to the somber arrival of Ash Wednesday and Lent.

in fright. A fire-breathing, child-eating dragon would not have scared us more. In one hand the fiend clutched a handful of switches, in the other, the very chains of hell. Krampus whirled and jumped about, his dark, shiny horns glistening in the light as his great tail lashed about behind him. He was dressed in black from head to toe, and the high, rigid collar of his cape fanned out behind his head. Crimson-rimmed eyes sprang out at us from his ashen face as the red slash of his mouth emitted one horrifying cackle after another. The rattling of chains accompanied his every gesture. This terrifying presence froze us in our seats. We knew, of course, that he was not real—we knew that before he came in. But if evil had a face, then we were looking at it.

Krampus swaggered around the room, pausing from time to time to pinch one of us under the chin. To one child, "Heard you haven't been such a good boy at school, eh?" Then to the next, "Can't be trusted to obey your mother all the time, can you, little girl?"

Saint Nicholas finally banished him to a corner, where he crouched, growling and glowering at us. Then the saint distributed fruit, nuts, and presents. The cakes, ice creams, and cookies Liesl had taken pride in for the past two days would follow, as would plenty of games.

Saint Nicholas processed purposefully around the entire ballroom before turning to deliver his parting words. He solemnly implored the gathering to heed the importance of being good, concluding with these ominous words: "Remember, whatever you do, I will know."

Meanwhile, evil Krampus paced back and forth in his corner. When his turn came, he let out a wild, piercing howl and, rattling his chains, jumped in the air. He then slithered over to Saint Nicholas and hissed, "I too know what you do. I will watch you very carefully!" Gasps filled the room. With great flourishes of their capes, the two swept out to riotous applause.

We knew that Saint Nicholas and Krampus were only ordinary soldiers, but just then, for those brief moments, they were really the saint and the devil. Rushing to the windows, we hoped to see them disappear into the clouds or in a billow of fire. Craning our necks, we watched them leave screaming, "Saint Nicholas! Krampus! Up here! Up here!" Saint Nicholas extended both arms and then disappeared into the police van. Shaking his fistful of chains and brandishing his switches, Krampus turned and, with a final cackle, followed Saint Nicholas. His tail was disappearing and we were drifting back toward the ballroom when we heard a horrifying scream. We flew back to the windows and waited breathlessly, but neither Saint Nicholas nor Krampus reappeared. The police van shot away with wheels squealing and siren blaring—that qualified as an encore.

Mother and I went to the altersheim the next day. Our driver, Tichy, greeted us. He said that Sargeant Schmidt was much better and relayed his thanks to Mother for her solicitude.

"What does Tichy mean, Mother?" I asked, less out of curiosity than for the pleasure of having a conversation with my mother.

"He was thanking me for my concern over Sargeant Schmidt's health, Kurti."

"Why? He was fine yesterday." I knew that Sargeant Schmidt had played Krampus and helped Tichy from time to time.

"Well, after the performance, Sargeant Schmidt had an accident of sorts."

"What kind of accident?"

Mother hesitated and then said thoughtfully, "It seems that Sargeant Schmidt's tail was attached by a long nail to a thin piece of wood in the back of his tights. He wasn't supposed to sit down and, well, he forgot."

I sat silently for a moment, curiously looking at her. Finally, the implication dawned on me. I slapped my knees and rocked back on my seat howling with laughter. "I'll bet he never, ever makes that mistake again!"

Mother struggled to keep a straight face but she too dissolved into laughter. Almost choking, she said, "I'll bet he doesn't ever volunteer for Krampus again either!" She dabbed at her eyes with her handkerchief. "The poor man! The poor man!"

Then we drove off to cheer up the old people.

# Devastation

The situation in Austria was the result of a complicated set of circumstances, policies, and events dating back to the period before the First World War. The republic was slowly pulling itself out of the catastrophic financial condition in which it had found itself in 1918. The repayment of the League of Nations loans and the Thousand-Mark Tariff imposed by Germany created enormous difficulties. The plague of inflation had receded, however, and the economy was growing.

The year 1935 opened with great fanfare: the chancellor announced that the Vienna Opera Ball would be sponsored by the Republic of Austria. In addition to celebrating the priceless contribution of Austrian musicians and composers to the music-loving world, the government sought to boost tourism, which in turn would help the economy. Little else in the running of the country was as uncomplicated as the Opera Ball.

\* \* \*

July 13, 1935: Tires screeched, metal buckled, and bodies flew through the air choking with smoke and dust: surely I was having a nightmare, for everything was moving too quickly. As in a kaleidoscope, the pieces were all jumbled up. My face felt wet in the breeze, and I thought it was Purzel trying to wake me: "Down, boy; go away!"

"Kurti! Kurti!" Fräulein Alice's voice anxiously called me, and I opened my eyes.

The sun was beating down on me, so I squinted. My head was in Fräulein's Alice's lap, but where was the car? What were we doing on the grass, and what was she saying to me? Turning my head I saw Father—white-faced and somber.

"Papa! What's the matter? Are you sick?"

Father began wiping my face, and the handkerchief was red. The sky was spinning round. "Don't let him move, Fräulein Alice", I heard Father say. "Keep him still!" That is the only thing I wanted to do anyway. Then I saw Liesl. She was turning her head and gasping, so I looked in the same direction and saw two grim-faced secret service men carrying something; no, carrying a person: a pair of legs extended from a white linen skirt. They carried her to the stretcher, then to the ambulance. Pale as Father, her eyes were closed and she wasn't moving; she looked like a little, limp doll.

Fräulein Alice focused on the stretcher. She was crying, tears streaming down her face. I had never seen Fräulein Alice cry. I looked toward Liesl; she was crying too. They both looked at me, and then, full of dread, I knew.

I closed my eyes tightly and felt a spinning sensation. Arms picked me up and carried me to the other car. Fräulein Alice put one arm around me and held a handkerchief against one side of my face. Colonel Bartl and a secret service man helped Father into the car. He reached over and smoothed back my hair. The expression on his face was awful, and his eyes . . . his eyes were dead. He took my hand and held it in both of his, and I felt my eyes closing.

Later, much later, I awoke in the Brothers of Charity Hospital in Linz.

"You have been such a brave boy!" said Fräulein Alice, straightening my bedclothes for the two-hundredth time in two weeks. "Soon we will go to Saint Gilgen. Liesl said there is a whole lake of fish just waiting for you to catch them, and she'll cook them for dinner. You can eat your very own fish!"

Well, it was a happier thought than most of the ones I had since I was able to stay awake long enough to think. The gashes on my forehead and cheek were beginning to look a little better, and my face, although stiff, was only slightly sore.

The doctor who ran the hospital was standing at my bedside. After clamping his icy stethoscope one last time on my protesting flesh, he nodded and declared himself satisfied with my progress. "I am very relieved that no major muscles were severed. You know you are a very lucky boy. The glass partition that fell on you could have done much more damage. Your guardian angel must have been sitting on your shoulder, young man!" He was a kind man and wanted to cheer me up.

"Herr Doktor," I said, "I wish he would have been sitting on my mother's shoulder."

Of the six of us in the car that morning, Father and Fräulein Alice were the only passengers to escape relatively unharmed. Fräulein Alice suffered only a sore neck and torn clothes. Father had been thrown clear of the wreck. He was badly bruised but otherwise not hurt, that is, not physically hurt.

Father's wounds were internal—a deep emotional pain. He was devastated by the loss of the shimmering radiance that had been my mother. In public Father was stoic as he went about the business of Austria. The black armband he wore was his only public concession to private emotion. He brought an inconsolable grief to Saint Gilgen on weekends. Even then it was evidenced only by a rare sob as he sat alone in his darkened room. Father did not refer to the accident, but his sunken, dark-ringed eyes held the same unspoken, unanswerable question that I had: "Why Mother?"

Fräulein Alice said that the police were trying to piece together what had happened. The investigation had begun with the driver, Tichy. Along with the secret service man seated beside him in the car, Tichy was still in the hospital. Sargeant Tichy had a spotless military record and been carefully profiled before becoming our driver. He had led a blameless life, was moderate in his habits, and was the picture of health. In the two years that he had been with us, he had never missed a day of work

The afternoon before the accident, on his way home from the Kriegsministerium, Tichy stopped at the same *Gasthaus* (tavern) that he visited every day. According to the owner, Tichy had only his one customary glass of beer, but he did not leave the gasthaus until three o'clock the next morning. The only explanation for this seemed to be the glass of beer. The owner said that a stranger had bought it for him. Noticing Tichy later slumped over his table, the owner had tried to rouse him. Because of the owner's regard for Tichy, he let him.sleep until closing time. In the end, the staff drenched him with cold water. Tichy finally came to and managed to make his way home. He had just enough time to shower and change. He reported to the Kriegsministerium at five A.M. to assist in loading the cars bound for Saint Gilgen.

The police surmised that Tichy, proud of his position as the chancellor's driver, had probably talked about the Saint Gilgen trip one afternoon in the gasthaus. The chief of police was convinced that

Tichy, because of his regular habits, had been followed for some time. The Marxists and the Nazis were both hostile to the government and therefore also to Father. This was common knowledge.

In the police chief's mind, there was little doubt that Tichy's beer had been drugged. There was no other logical explanation for either the incident at the gasthaus or for an experienced driver crashing into a tree, at a normal speed, in the full light of day. After Dollfuss' assassination and the attack on the Augarten Palace, suspicion was quickly placed on the Nazis; proving it, however, was an entirely different matter.

Some speculated that the car had been sabotaged or a tire had been shot. There was only one skid mark leading to the crash site. The front tire that made the skid mark was destroyed during the crash and was useless as a clue; however, it was on the side of the car that would have turned the vehicle into the direction it went. The parts of the car's brake system that were destroyed in the crash made proving a brake failure or sabotage of the brakes all but impossible.

Fräulein Alice did all she could to help my body and my mind heal. She had taken a room at a nearby hotel and was at the hospital every day, all day. Father and Grandfather traveled back and forth to visit me, but neither spoke of Mother or the accident. Fräulein Alice took a radically different approach.

"Kurti," Fräulein Alice said, "it is important for you to know that your mother did not suffer. When the car collided with the tree, her head hit the edge of the open roof. The impact broke her neck instantly. The doctor said she experienced no pain—it was like instantly going to sleep, and when she awoke she was in heaven. I know it is difficult, but you must always try to think of it that way."

I hoped that was true, about the pain. The images in my dreams: the crushed hulk of metal that had been our black landau; the white linen skirt moving in the morning breeze; the two secret service men carrying my beautiful, dead mother—how long would these images last?

Father, Grandfather, and Fräulein Alice were at Mother's funeral in Vienna. My grandmother was ill and unable to attend. Father and Grandfather promised they would take me to her grave as soon as I was strong enough. Fräulein Alice continually tried to raise my spirits. It was a terribly depressing time.

Fräulein Alice described the funeral Mass in great detail. I studied the photographs she brought to the hospital. "Kurti, look at the mountain of flowers your mother has! You know how much she loved flowers!" A visit to her grave could not have left me more depressed than those black-and-white photographs. I could not think about Mother lying in the dark earth.

Grandfather came to collect Fräulein Alice and me at the hospital. The kind people at the hospital wished me well. The doctors patted me on my head, and the nurses murmured kindnesses. It was then that I had my first cheerful thought—I would not have to put up with chocolates, pudding, or anything else I didn't like. I would, at least temporarily, have my own way. The chief doctor's parting words were that one day my scars would make me look distinguished—I took little comfort in that.

Saint Gilgen was a different world. It wasn't my injuries that made life at the hospital difficult, but the constant sympathy. In Saint Gilgen I had Purzel—cheerful and uncomplicated. He was either happy or hungry. I had the rest of my family: Father, Fräulein Alice, Liesl, and even the secret service men about the property. They were now as familiar a presence as Liesl or Colonel Bartl.

Our villa on Wolfgangsee, a beautiful Alpine lake in the Salzkammergut region, had been Mother's discovery. The sturdy lakeside villa, built at the turn of the twentieth century, was painted a soft cream color and had cinnamon-tinted shutters and trim. From the road it deceptively appeared to be a small, one-story structure with an abbreviated upper floor under a low roof. This narrow road was the only access to the house, which pleased the government security detail. From the lakeside it was an entirely different structure: four stories—two with balconies. On one of these I would sit in the evenings, sometimes with Father but more often with Fräulein Alice, watching the sunset. An evening breeze would ripple through the trees surrounding the lake with a scent of its own. The waning sun tinted the clouds shades of orange, pink, and peach. A fading palette of colors yielded to a moon rising above the Schafberg and Zwölferhorn mountains. Beside the lake was peaceful and quiet: one heard only the ducks, the crickets, the water lapping against shore and dock, and the mountain streams flowing into the valleys.

When Father came to Saint Gilgen for the weekend, his state of mind was a matter of great concern to the two people closest to us. From my balcony one day, I overheard Liesl talking to Fräulein Alice.

"Alice, it's so sad! How long do you think things will go on this way with the chancellor? I just hope for the boy's sake that things change."

Fräulein Alice sighed. "You know, Liesl, he adored her; and on top of her death, Kurti's being injured was another blow. When the chancellor is out in public or with any of his staff, he is fine. Well, you know what I mean. Here, when he goes to his room in the evening, he just sits in the dark. It worries me."

It worried me too. I longed to see happiness in Father's eyes again. I would rather have him angry than like this. I was familiar with his anger. It came, exploded, and then disappeared, but this lifelessness was awful.

Once I came upon him sitting on the balcony just before dinner. It was one of the rare, wonderful occasions when he was alone. I walked over to his chair, but he did not notice me. He stared unfocused at the lake. I put my hands over his eyes and exclaimed, "Papa!" Reaching up, he removed my hands and smiled; but it was the sad smile that I had come to know well. It was as if all happiness had been gouged out of him.

The days passed in our household as if we were traveling in a car with one flat tire. The car hobbled along slowly, and none of the passengers was comfortable. Since my return from the hospital, I rested in the afternoon. Fräulein Alice would open the door to the balcony, open the windows, kiss me on the forehead, and then leave. The balcony door had large glass panes. Left open at an angle, it reflected the window boxes thick with red and white geraniums nestling in dense green leaves. The pleasure of lying there, surrounded by flowers and their mirror-born duplicates, was wasted on me. Mother had so loved flowers, and I bore this constant reminder of her like a punishment—only I didn't know what I had done to deserve it.

At last the pace of life on the weekends started to change. It began as a trickle of family and friends. Then, government officials were added to the stream. The atmosphere began gradually to lighten.

"Fräulein Alice, who has Father brought with him this weekend?"

"Well, Kurti, let's see—Doctor Pernter is here. He's the minister of education—one of your father's earlier positions. Remember? You like him. Colonel Bartl, of course, and also Doctor Buresch, the finance minister, are here. Two of your father's friends and their wives are coming, but just for dinner." The only assurance I had of my father's company was for Sunday Mass in the Saint Gilgen church. I rarely saw him in Vienna, so since our arrival I had hoped for more. A protest had already formed in my mind but one had to be careful with Fräulein Alice. Sometimes she used the You-are-too-old-for-that admonishment, which made complaining all the more difficult. Even so, on this day I just couldn't restrain myself and said sarcastically. "Oh, great! This weekend is really going to be fun!" I folded my arms across my chest, cocked my head, and waited for her reaction.

"Kurti, you know that your father can't possibly get all the things done he needs to get done without having to work here. You are being selfish." Then, placing her hands on her hips she leaned toward me and announced triumphantly, "What you don't know is your father told me to bring you down to the dock after lunch to go rowing."

"Really, Fräulein Alice?" I said, knocking over my chair in my enthusiasm.

"Yes, really!" she laughed.

"Fräulein Alice, I am going to row Father all the way across the lake. I'll get the worms and the fishing poles."

"No worms and no fishing poles, Kurti."

"All right, all right."

I rowed so powerfully that I surprised myself, and Father was proud; that was my reward. How wonderful to have him all to myself—I rattled on cheerfully about nothing. Father had serious matters on his mind and said these subjects required considerable thought. While it was important to become physically strong, it was more important to be strong mentally. He said that I was "doing a fine job on both".

"My son, we cannot always have things as we would wish them to be, even when we wish for good things."

I knew he meant Mother.

"We must always be grateful for the gifts God sends us for however long they last; and, although one door may close, another will eventually open." What he said next caused me to pause, my oars suspended in midair. "The day of the accident the police had stopped to question a man waiting at a point just ahead of us on the road. He turned out to be a Swastika armed with a bomb. Had it not been for the accident we might all be dead."

I slowly dipped the oars back in the water and continued to row in silence. To me these Swastikas from Germany were a thousand times worse than the Reds from Russia.

After a moment I asked, "But Papa, why can't we stop them?"

"If it were a simple affair we would, but this isn't the same sort of battle that you fight with your soldiers. It is more like a game of hide-and-seek. They commit their acts of terror and try to make people, especially workers, distrust the government."

"But why?"

"The shortest answer is that, above all else, they want Austria to become part of Germany, but the majority of Austrians want to stay Austrian. That is why we can't afford to relax our vigilance— not even for a minute."

This was the first time Father had talked to me as an adult. While diligently listening to him, I vowed never again to complain about the secret service men. I fervently hoped that Father's guardian angel would keep a constant vigil over him—there were only the two of us now.

As the summer wore on, Father and I developed routines. Contrary to the belief that when the heart dies the body dies too, life went on for us both. Fräulein Alice became everything she could be for me. With a mother's judgment, she was full of wisdom and love.

Fräulein Alice took me often to the church in town, and we always lit candles for Mother and Father. It was with Fräulein Alice that I dug for worms and rowed to the numerous coves on the lake. She fished with me and taught me how to make campfires that cooked our trout and corn at day's end. Sometimes we hiked to a nearby stream or sat on the end of the dock. Together we caught a good portion of the trout in the lake.

I found that Liesl did not take the same pleasure in our fishing successes. Taking the day's catch to the kitchen one afternoon, I stuck my head around the door and said, "Liesl, guess what?"

She must have had inkling, for she slowly placed her partially peeled apple on the counter and waited in silence.

"I have a surprise for dinner!" I said and triumphantly presented my bucket of entrees that were still flapping about.

She hesitated for a moment and then, incapable of containing herself, she exploded. "What? More trout?" Liesl's appreciation for the fish I brought had been declining since the first bucket. She had not reckoned on our being such successful fishermen. "I am going to start lighting candles in church for rain! I have beautiful medallions of venison from the butcher for tonight's dinner."

I explained as if to a child, "Liesl, you know that Father loves trout."

"Yes, but not every single day. And neither do I!" Her voice had increased in volume. Her hands positioned on her hips made her elbows stick straight out. I had seen Liesl in such moods, and I was beginning to smell defeat in the air.

"Please, Liesl. I just want Father to know that I caught these for him. It's like a little gift from me."

She mulled this over for a moment; my hopes rose an inch.

"All right, Kurti. I will tell you what. I am going to make a bargain with you. I will cook these for dinner, this time. But in the future, we are not having fish of any kind more than three times a week, and that includes Friday. You know we can't eat meat on Fridays anyway. Now that doesn't mean that you can't go fishing. Fish all you want, but from now on you will give the extra fish you catch to Stephan." Stephan had replaced Tichy as our driver. "We will tell your father that you caught them for him, but as the dinner menu was already planned, you gave them to Stephan."

This was not exactly what I wanted. "Well," I began very slowly but was cut off.

"This is not a discussion, Kurti. Your father needs his strength, and that means eating meat as well as fish. Now, off you go. Find Fräulein Alice and tell her I'd like to see her for a moment." And that was that.

Fräulein Alice announced one clear, sunny morning that we were going for tea to Bad Ischl. A half-hour drive only to drink a cup of tea seemed excessive, but we were going to the Café Zauner. In 1832, Johann Zauner brought his expert knowledge of Viennese baking to the spa town of Bad Ischl, and his legacy continued. Grateful spa guests delighted in its art nouveau interior, high ceilings, and subtle lighting from countless milk glass fixtures while listening to the occasional Mozart sonata or Liszt fugue played on the upstairs piano. The Zauner had a reputation for serving the lightest of pastries and the most delicate of confections. It could also boast the patronage of Emperor Franz Josef. Café Zauner had become an institution. Though not expressed, the outing was meant to increase my awareness of the civility of the afternoon tea ritual.

I was in a dilemma. The day before I found a small snake in the garden and had taken it to my room. The possibility of Liesl accidentally coming across it flashed through my mind. I could not leave the snake behind. Having no other choice, I would have to take the snake with me. We set out for the Café Zauner that summer afternoon with the smallest member of our party safely coiled up in my pocket.

Frau Zauner herself seated us. I took stock of our surroundings. The room was completely full, but no conversation was louder than mumbled Mass responses in church.

"Fräulein Alice, it's awfully quiet in here."

"Well, Kurti, it's a tearoom not a sports stadium. Now, let's look at the menu."

I chose my favorite, a *Himbeerkuchen* (raspberry tart) with a lake of whipped cream on the side. Fräulein Alice settled for an *Apfelkuchen* (apple tart).

My eyes wandered to the table in front of us—two ladies seated there seemingly against their will. The older lady, elegantly dressed, looked disinterestedly at her younger, plainly dressed table companion. Not the hint of a smile passed between them. The older lady would nod patronizingly from time to time. Her companion was obviously agitated and grew more and more so as she spoke. I felt sorry for her.

For what followed there is no reasonable explanation. I reached into my pocket and took out the snake under cover of the tablecloth. Without thinking of the consequences, I dropped it on the floor. Holding my breath, I willed it toward the two ladies, praying that a waiter, in the middle of the perfect tea presentation at an adjacent table, would not step on my little friend. In a flash the snake slithered under the correct table and disappeared beneath its huge covering.

Then it happened. With eyes like saucers, the younger lady looked quickly under the table. I had meant for the snake to notice the older lady. Instead it had started up the stocking-sheathed leg of her companion. An ear-splitting scream pierced the entire tearoom. A moment of stunned silence followed; then no less than five waiters and one chef rushed in. The young lady sprang to her feet, not only taking the tablecloth with her but also toppling the table itself and rendering its porcelain, tea, and confections airborne. Holding her skirt above her knees, she shrieked and swiped wildly at her leg with her napkin. The older lady stared incredulously. Whipped cream dripped from her face; a mangled piece of cake lay in her lap. One heartbeat later, another crystal-shattering scream filled the room: "Snake!" The effect was that of a bugler's call to the cavalry. The Café Zauner emptied onto sidewalk and street.

Most of my himbeerkuchen was still on my plate—I regretted my timing. Fräulein Alice grabbed my arm and pulled so firmly that I practically flew out of my seat. In seconds we had joined the others outside. An ever growing circle of curious pedestrians ringed the café. In Bad Ischl's normally quiet late afternoon, news traveled quickly that something had happened at the Café Zauner.

It was too late to consider the well-being of my snake. It was beyond rescue, for the master of the kitchen flew by, brandishing a knife that looked sharper than Father's razor and three times longer than my poor snake. A hush had fallen over the crowd, and I prayed for a miracle. The minutes ticked by. When passersby stopped to ask the predictable question, the unpredictable answer, "Snake!", was followed by a sharp intake of breath and, "Mein Gott!" None were willing to leave before the final resolution. The minutes ticked by—the crowd grew restive.

Finally the chef reappeared and declared the Zauner snake free. The crowd moved hesitatingly toward the entrance. I had taken but one step when Fräulein Alice's hand descended firmly on my shoulder. The drama had so absorbed me that I had forgotten her presence.

"Kurti, you wait here, exactly on this spot. Don't move! I have to fetch my purse, but I'll be right back!" A few minutes later she was pushing me down the street and murmuring something about quality slipping everywhere these days.

Frau Zauner's voice followed the departing patrons. "A serpent doesn't just slither down the street and decide to have a cup of tea!" I felt sorry for her. Who could have imagined such an extreme reaction to a harmless little snake?

I realized that I could never tell anyone about this. Not even tight-lipped Peter Mayer. It was just too dangerous. I was also shocked by Fräulein Alice's reaction. The thought that suspicion might fall on me, and the attendant consequences, did not bear contemplation.

Father summoned me that evening. I presented myself, washed and ready for bed. When he asked about our trip to Café Zauner, I said evasively that I had enjoyed my afternoon. Fräulein Alice stood nearby with a sphinx-like expression on her face. Father asked if I had known that we really had been a party of three that afternoon. I felt my heart contract. He continued, "Your Shadow was there." Shadow had been at the Café Zauner? How could I have missed him? Shadow had seen me drop my snake—Father knew everything.

Now came the payback for endless hours spent in the closet at school and all those acrobatic leaps behind trees, fences, and a variety of parked vehicles. Since the episode of the banquette and the Krampus switch, I had been spared corporal punishment. Recalling the stunned expression of the elderly lady with the cake in her lap and the ensuing pandemonium, I squeezed my eyes shut and braced myself for what was surely to follow. Unfortunately, I had already planted myself within easy reach of Father. Seconds passed; still nothing happened. I opened my eyes. Father was looking at me with a peculiar expression quickly replaced by a stern, parental look. The length of his verbal reprimand broke all previous records and covered every aspect of the incident. I left with Fräulein Alice, who mercifully made just one observation: "Your reckless prank could have caused serious injury!"

Could have? It had. My garden snake was dead.

Summer soon gave way to autumn, and the villa on the Wolf-gangsee was left behind. The texture of life in the Kriegsministerium was entirely changed. A few weeks after Mother's funeral, Grandmother Anna von Schuschnigg had died. Father and I had lost our mothers within weeks of one another. Grandfather, now a widower like Papa, came to live with us. For the sake of convenience,

Father's aide-de-camp Colonel Bartl, though he had a wife and a son, had been living with us since Father became chancellor. So by the autumn of 1935, we were practically an all-male club. Fräulein Alice and Liesl provided the only touch of femininity.

In September 1935, Germany introduced what came to be known as the Nuremberg Laws, which among other things deprived Jews of German citizenship. In October, Italy began its campaign in Abyssinia. The former was not widely known, but the latter created a hue and cry. Italy's military invasion of Ethiopia alienated France and England and in effect nullified the Stresa Pact, which had only been signed the previous April. The Stresa signatories had agreed upon mutually beneficial foreign policy objectives, including continued Austrian independence.

No longer sure which allies he could count on, the Austrian chancellor set to work again on Czechoslovakia, wedging in a trip to the country the week before Christmas. In his ongoing attempt at unity on the home front, he proclaimed a Christmas amnesty. Of the 1,521 Social Democrats arrested in the February 12, 1934, Schutzbund uprising, 1,505 were released. Dealing with the Austrian Nazis, jailed for the attempted coup of July 25, 1934, was a more delicate proposition. There were 911 of these National Socialists in prison; 440 were released. Their amnesty however had an additional advantage; it would be recognized as a gesture of goodwill toward Germany. However, it also raised a troubling question: How many of those 440 freed National Socialists would resume their prior activities?

Father, in addition to becoming a widower, had another adjustment to his personal life thrust upon him. It came in two forms: "Aunt Zoë" (Baroness Zoë von Schildenfeld)—tall, imposing, commanding, and very much unmarried; and "Aunt Vera" (Countess Fugger-Babenhausen)—Mother's friend and Rudi Fugger's mother. Aunt Vera and her husband had divorced and were awaiting an annulment by the Catholic Church. In Austria, annulment was even more rare than divorce. By declaring the recipients' previous marriage invalid, it allowed them to marry "again" in the Church. I may have been the only one in Austria unaware of the race between these two Viennese hostesses, let alone the nature of the prize.

One day, I overheard a conversation between Fräulein Alice and Liesl in the kitchen. Fräulein Alice was perched on a stool beside the counter at which Liesl was working. The mountain of dough occupying Liesl's attention was in the process of being transformed into something better. Totally eclipsed by a large standing cabinet, I entered the kitchen. When I heard them mention Father, Aunt Zoë, and Aunt Vera, my curiosity was piqued. I knew that if I were to make my presence known, the conversation would change, as often happened. So I kept my position behind the cabinet, eavesdropping without shame. Absorbed by her notes of the day's schedule, Fräulein Alice was silent. Liesl was doing all the talking.

"Never an occasion goes by, not a musical evening nor a dinner, that either one or the other isn't present. Last night," Liesl paused for a deep intake of breath, "words almost failed me when I saw they were both here!" Words had never failed Liesl. "Baroness Schildenfeld at one end and Countess Fugger at the other—that had to be a lot to handle!" Another pause, then in a quieter tone of voice: "The poor chancellor hasn't a chance. One of them is going to succeed in the end. Mark my words."

"Yes," Fräulein Alice said eventually, without looking up from her notebook, "such things really are to be expected." Here she paused and looked pointedly at Liesl. "But not necessarily noticed."

Undeterred, Liesl went doggedly on. "But Countess Fugger certainly has an edge with the boys being such good friends. I wonder why Baroness Schildenfeld doesn't do something with that gray hair. She looks older than my own mother!" I agreed with Liesl.

"If you ask me, little Rudi Fugger is a permanent excuse to visit here." Liesl's mind, diverted by the task at hand, was leaping about like a frog. "No doubt about it. It'll be Countess Fugger in the end. Mark my words. She's way out in front in this race."

Fräulein Alice, though provoked, had not yet begun to bristle; but I could tell that she was not far from it. I knew she was fond of Liesl, as we all were. However, clearly discernible in Fräulein Alice's tone of voice was an unwillingness to discuss the subject. I knew that tone. Crisply snapping her notebook shut, Fräulein Alice said only, "That is that!"

And Liesl understood: the subject was closed. Shrugging her shoulders, she concentrated on taming the mass in front of her. Silence settled on the room. I decided that the most prudent course of action was to leave as I had entered, quietly. It was irritating, for I knew that this was not the ideal way to add to my stock of vital knowledge. But it was also true that the only information I ever got came to me through a happenstance such as this one.

Unlike previous years, that Christmas and New Year's were only a blur. Still, Father and Grandfather, Fräulein Alice and Liesl—all of them did their best to keep themselves and me as busy as we could all bear to be. There was no time to dwell on anything but our schedules. I tore around during the day with my friends, and in the evening, I fairly fell into bed. I woke most mornings to find a salami sandwich in my hand or on my night table. I sometimes went without seeing Father for days, but the sandwich was proof that he had seen me. I looked upon it as Father's equivalent of the fish I had caught for him in Saint Gilgen.

Father contended ceaselessly with the thrust and parry of domestic and international politics. He had a reputation for being thoughtful and deliberate in his actions, and this eliminated the possibility of his being bullied or intimidated; it frustrated many an opponent as well.

In an effort to shore up the Danube River Basin, Father began the new year by traveling to Czechoslovakia. Like Austria, Czechoslovakia was menaced by German expansionism. Its president, Edvard Beneš, was also eager for allies. As a result, by the time Hitler, thumbing his nose at the Treaty of Locarno, marched into the Rhineland on March 7, 1936, Austria had signed a trade agreement with Czechoslovakia. The two countries were working on consolidating Austria with the Little Entente (the alliance of Czechoslovakia, Romania, and Yugoslavia), to build a more solid Central European defense against Germany. Another check against German expansion was the extension of the Rome Protocols, which Dollfuss had originally signed in March 1934. Extending the Protocols ensured that Hungary, Italy, and Austria were still committed to economic and political cooperation.

Next on the Austrian chancellor's list was rearmament to counter the threat of the rapidly growing German military. The intransigence of the League of Nations had already cost him a year. Further delay in action would border on recklessness. On April 1, a year and a month after Germany had done so, Austria announced the reintroduction of compulsory military service. All military units were to be placed under the umbrella of the Fatherland Front.

# Relocation

One day in early spring, Fräulein Alice met me at school. A surprise was waiting for me. That morning, after I had left for school, an army of workers had descended upon the Kriegsministerium, gathered up our household and moved it to Belvedere, the former gardener's house, not the palace. Our entrance was diagonal to the *Südbahnhof* (southern train station). As we drove past it, Fräulein Alice pointed ahead to a two-story stucco building that interrupted a long, high wall. We turned there and followed the drive to the front of a handsome single-story house.

Its simple, yellow stucco exterior left one unprepared for an impressive interior. I stepped into an oval marble foyer with black-and-white tile flooring. Columns that supported a high ceiling punctuated its yellow damask-covered walls. Sculpted winged figures atop a table stood guard in the middle. I raised my eyebrows at Fräulein Alice. "Wait until you see the rest!" she said and steered me into another room. "It is important that we start here. I want to show you something very unusual."

A piano rested on an oriental rug of extraordinary dimensions: it covered almost the entire parquet floor. Behind the piano was a series of french windows. Sunlight flooded in; it reflected off the chandelier and spilled over the empire chairs and marble-topped tables. "As well proportioned and attractive as this room is, what I want you to see is over there."

She went to the handsome old armoires standing against the wall and, with a flourish, opened one of the doors to reveal nothing. This was puzzling. She gave me a broad smile and then stepped inside. "Now, Kurti, you will close this door firmly, then count to ten. Do not look away. Don't even blink! When you reach ten, open the door again. All right?"

There should have been a keyhole on the door, but I did not see one. That too was very puzzling. "And there is no keyhole for you

60

to look through, you silly goose." Horrible, the way she often knew exactly what I was thinking.

"I wasn't even considering looking through any keyhole!"

"Now, don't forget! First count to ten out loud."

"Yes, Fräulein Alice."

I closed the door firmly, counted evenly to ten as instructed, and then reopened the door. The armoire was empty! I stood there wondering, then I stepped inside and groped in the air. I ran my hands up and down the back of the armoire. There was a tap on my shoulder—I jumped. There she stood, smiling. She took my hand and placed it on something that felt metallic: a lever I had missed that protruded from the back corner of the armoire. I pressed down on the lever. A panel sprang open; the secret exit led outside, into the garden.

Now I was infected by Fräulein Alice's gaiety as she pulled me toward the adjoining Biedermeier salon. Sofas and chairs, in striped green-and-white silk, were placed throughout the room. Interspersed among them were wooden credenzas and commodes in rich shades of brown.

Fräulein Alice said, "Your mother's things look wonderful in this room. Don't they? You can spend all the time you want in here." Tousling my hair, she added, "There is very little that is breakable and not already used to your attentions. Next we come to the dining room!"

With a flick of a switch an enormous chandelier, with hundreds of crystal prisms, burst to life. Directly below it was a round, highly polished table. But the lighted display cabinets at each end of the room looked out of place; they were filled with old china that looked in need of cleaning. Fräulein Alice said, "That fine old china is supposed to look like that." Again she exercised that ability to read my mind!

Father's study was next. The first thing I saw was the farmer that Egger-Lienz had immortalized, still sowing grain from his full linen pouch. It was like seeing a friend. The painting made me feel less an intruder in a strange house. I sat down behind Father's desk. Facing me were the silver-framed photographs of Mother and me and those of my grandparents. They were the first things Papa would see when he sat down. We were all here, all together. I glanced into the adjacent bedroom and bath and was reassured by the sight of Father's brushes, combs, and all the other toiletries; they promised his daily presence.

We arrived at my room. It was enormous. The bedroom that I had left only that morning had been luxuriously large, but this one looked twice its size. "Fräulein Alice, I can't believe it! There's my entire train set—tracks, tunnels, trees, and train yard—and it doesn't even fill that whole corner!" I said, running over to it. "I've got enough room to skate or ride my bike in here!"

She raised an eyebrow and, half smiling, said, "Let's get one thing straight. There will be no, I repeat, no skating and no bike riding in this room, young man."

I threw open the doors of the wardrobes, peered out of each of my new windows into the back gardens. This was going to work out very well. Grandfather's room and bath were on my other side. That afforded him easy access to my train sets, which he loved as much as I did. Colonel Bartl's quarters, beyond Grandfather's rooms, were at the very end of the house. More than satisfied with my room, I said, "Fräulein Alice, he must have been some gardener to have lived like this!"

She laughed and said, "It did not look like this in the gardener's time, Kurti. A lot of people worked very hard to make this a lovely new home for your father and you. The Kriegsministerium was never meant to be a residence; this is much more suitable."

"Still, I'll bet that gardener would cry if he could see his old house now", I said. I was happier than I had been since we had all set out for the Wolfgangsee that first time so long ago.

"Kurti, come! There is still more."

We took the more conventional way out of the music room. Outside was a riot of color; huge flowerbeds were all in full bloom. Geraniums were as large as small trees. Rosebushes—with blooms in reds, yellows, whites, and pinks—vied for space. Begonias bordered beds of lilies and irises. Framing the entire back garden was a thick, high boxwood hedge.

"Who lives back there?" I asked, pointing toward the center of the hedge.

She waved me on. "Come!" The hedge concealed a door. Passing through it, Fräulein Alice said, "You see. It's not who but what lives behind."

In front of us was one of the parks of Belvedere Palace. It was not a formally laid park, but a natural wooded area. An enormous elm dominated the foreground. Beyond were oak and linden trees. There were groups of rhododendron and rolling carpets of grass criss-crossed by footpaths. We passed a large, round pool full of water lilies and wandered on in the direction of Belvedere proper. Fräulein Alice's pleasure in everything we had seen was delightfully childlike; she was practically bubbling over with excitement. "Can you imagine that we share all of this only with the nuns from the convent next door!" she chirped.

"We've got *nuns* next door?"

"It is the motherhouse of the Daughters of Divine Love, and the entrance is all the way over on the corner of Jacquingasse", Fräulein Alice said. Reading the dubious expression on my face she continued, "What are you thinking? That they'll be dropping over to have tea with you every day?" With a hint of sarcasm she added, "I imagine the good nuns already had a pretty well-established routine before we arrived, Kurti. Furthermore, unless we go out into the park on their designated days, we shall see very little of them. You know, they may not be so thrilled about sharing the park with us. Did you think of that?"

I had not, but I didn't really mind having the nuns as neighbors. I had only wondered if having nuns as neighbors might possibly be confining.

Fräulein Alice continued, "There is also the Botanical Garden that we have access to on the days it is closed to the public. Between the nuns and all this space, we have a little corner of heaven. Don't you agree?"

I thought of Purzel and how much he would enjoy himself here. It would take an effort to drag him back indoors. There was no doubt about it; we were both lucky.

Our new surroundings and the passage of time had a positive effect on Father and me, except for a small misfortune: I developed a case of double pneumonia followed by scarlet fever. Austria had the services of noted thoracic specialist Professor Heinrich Neumann, who would return me to health. The eminent doctor would later flee Austria and seek asylum in America, where he would become one of President Franklin D. Roosevelt's physicians. Later he became the personal physician of King Ibn Saud of Saudi Arabia. At this juncture, however, it was I who commanded his attention.

There was an increase in the corridor activity at the Belvedere house: doctors and nurses, towels, compresses, basins of water, and cold and hot drinks streaming back and forth. A silver lining began to appear in this dark cloud: new toy soldiers, more track for my—and Grandfather's—electric trains, and the occasional train tunnel or papier-mâché landscape seemed to appear from nowhere. I felt that all this qualified as spoils of war; after three weeks in bed, I felt I had earned them.

Once I was back to normal, I was often summoned to the salon to meet Father's visitors, but only after I had passed muster with Fräulein Alice. One afternoon, the Austrian armaments dealer Fritz Mandl and his wife arrived for tea. I had never met a husband and wife who had different last names. That Herr Mandl's wife answered to Fräulein was another mystery. A fount of practical wisdom, Fräulein Alice informed me that Hedwig Kiesler, Herr Mandl's wife, was a film star, and film stars were always called Fräulein even when they were married. I did not really care what her name was. Had I been a dog I would have lain at her feet. She was the most beautiful woman I had ever seen, and I glued myself to her side.

At one point Fräulein Kiesler playfully tweaked my nose and pulled my ears as one might do when playing with a puppy. I responded with a friendly smack on her posterior. To my great surprise, my hand came into contact with what can only be called anatomically unnatural. Fräulein Alice's face blanched, and her mouth fell open. I had just stepped over the line. Fortunately, Father was absorbed in a conversation with Herr Mandl and had not noticed. Upon reflection, I don't suppose the gesture would have endeared me to Herr Mandl either. Fräulein Kiesler was a good sport. She let me off with a wag of her finger and a rumpling of my hair.

Fräulein Alice and I said good-bye. As soon as we were out of Father's line of sight, Fräulein obtained a solid grip on the back of my neck and marched me in silence all the way to my room. Closing the door firmly, she sat me down and said, "Kurti, what did you do that you should never have done?"

"I slapped Fräulein Kiesler on her po?"

"Yes, you did. You are never, ever to do that to a lady again! Do you understand?"

I completely understood. I was told—twice—how fortunate I was that Father and Herr Mandl had missed my gross indiscretion. That was the only reason I was still able to sit on *my* posterior!

I still did not know what had caused Fräulein Kiesler's posterior to be so stone-like, and Fräulein Alice enlightened me. "It is a woman's undergarment called a girdle. It makes a lady look smaller and slimmer."

Curious, I looked around Fräulein Alice for a back view. Her face seemed to color slightly and she said, "You needn't look any further; a girdle is the furthest thing from my mind, and that is enough on the subject." Regardless of her tiny bit of vanity, Miss Kiesler was far and away the most beautiful visitor we ever had.

Years later, I learned that Fräulein Kiesler's movie *Ecstasy* contained a scene in which she swam naked in a lake. After she married Herr Mandl, he attempted to buy every existing copy of that film. She left Herr Mandl and Austria for America, where the movie caused her career to soar. Louis B. Mayer renamed her Hedy Lamarr.

Those trips to the reception room gave me glimpses of some of the extraordinary personalities of the time. Fräulein Alice would make sure I had my fast-filling autograph book before she took me to meet Father's guests. Baron Hans von Hammerstein-Equord, who before becoming Austrian minister of justice in 1936 was a well-known poet and writer (whose works I would later read), entered his name. Arturo Toscanini, an ardent anti-Fascist who would incur Mussolini's wrath, flee Italy, and become conductor of the NBC Symphony Orchestra created for him in 1937, was a visitor the same year. Another Italian guest was Umberto di Savoia, the prince who would later become the last king of Italy. A later visitor was the pretty, blonde soprano Lotte Lehmann, whose talent placed her on the cover of *Time* magazine in 1935. She would flee Nazi Germany in 1938 for America.

More and more gifted Jewish and Catholic personalities streamed out of Germany into Austria, including conductor and composer Bruno Walter and soprano Elisabeth Schumann, who both subsequently emmigrated to the United States. In addition to the musicians, authors and writers such as Carl Zuckmayer, Joseph Roth, and Dietrich von Hildebrand also passed through the Belvedere house before fleeing to the United States. This exodus caused Father later to write: "German culture, homeless in its old home found a new country ... Weimar had been exiled from the Third Reich and had found its home in Vienna."[1]

Of all those who passed through the salons at the Kriegsministerium and Belevedere, the one who remained most vivid in not only my memory but also Father's and that of Vienna's chief of police was the Prince of Wales.

That day I was positioning my toy soldiers for an important battle when Fräulein Alice entered. Her face wore the expression of single-mindedness that I had come to know well. Father was expecting a guest. I would change into a freshly ironed sailor shirt and my new shoes. The shoes were the telling factor; no ordinary guest would have rated them.

"Let me see your hands" resulted in a vigorous application of the nail brush followed by the wielding of my hairbrush.

"Fräulein Alice, can Purzel come with me?"

"Absolutely not."

Fräulein Alice, kind and normally unflappable, had not a trace of humor in the tone of her voice. That, and the military precision with which I was being groomed, were clearly signs of nervousness.

"Will you please tell me who is so important that I have to put on my new shoes?"

She turned me around and putting her hands on my shoulders said, "Kurti, the Prince of Wales is here. He will be England's next king."

"Fräulein Alice, what does a king *do*?"

"We have no time to discuss occupations. Now, let me see your bow."

This was not the first time that I had ever bowed, but it was the first time that I had ever had to rehearse it for Fräulein Alice.

"All right, that's fine. You are to be at your most polite; you are *not* to bring up the subject of a king's duties."

---

[1] Kurt Schuschnigg, *Im Kampf gegen Hitler: Die Überwindung der Anschlussidee* (Vienna: Verlag Fritz Molden, 1988), 65.

I was escorted to the door of the Biedermeier salon and propelled gently forward. Fräulein Alice slipped away. I approached Father and his guest, greeted them, and bowed. Then the Prince of Wales hoisted me up and sat me on his knee.

"What a big boy you are! Tell me, what is your favorite sport?"

Compared with English rugby my fishing successes probably came up short; however, I redeemed myself with my passion for skiing. Next he asked about the sights to see in our "beautiful Vienna". I told him the Prater, Vienna's celebrated amusement park, was wonderful, but I had to warn him about the circus. It smelled terribly!

I watched as he and Father chatted. A family friend had once described Father as sternly handsome. The future king, on the other hand, seemed to have a nice face but it was soft in appearance. I wondered how he would look with a crown and an ermine cape.

"Thank you, Kurti", Father said and then nodded toward the door.

I took my autograph book, thanked the Prince of Wales for signing it, and bowed once again. When I reached the entrance to the salon, the disembodied hand of Fräulein Alice materialized and led me away. All that bother for barely five minutes. Evening came, and I changed into my pajamas. When Fräulein Alice shook out my trousers, to both our amazement a five-schilling coin dropped onto the carpet.

"What's that?" I said diving for the coin.

"What indeed?" I heard Fräulein Alice say.

I had never had more money than my allowance of fifty *Groschen* (cents), and that was never with me long. I had no access to money other than what was to be found in the kitchen: Liesl's household cash was kept on a plate in the larder.

"Kurti, that is a lot of money. Where did it come from?"

At first I thought it was a joke, one of Fräulein Alice's conjuring tricks, but the expression on her face said the coin was not a trick.

"Fräulein Alice, it isn't mine"—an unfortunate choice of words.

"It certainly isn't yours! Let us try again. Where did you get this?"

Speechless, I looked up from the coin at Fräulein Alice. I knew what was coming: Father. In the library Fräulein Alice described the circumstances in which a coin had been found, and Father asked me where I had gotten it. My answer, the only answer I had, was closely followed by a resounding slap on the cheek. I had never before been struck on the cheek. I had felt the Krampus switch. I had occasionally been swatted on the behind but never on the cheek. Beyond the humiliation of the slap was the realization: my father thought me a thief and a liar. His displeasure was a terrible sadness. I saw little enough of my father as it was—I cursed the coin.

Many years later, the mystery of the five-schilling coin was explained. It had indeed been a conjuring trick, a sleight of hand. The Duke of Windsor, previously the Prince of Wales and for a brief period King Edward VIII, told me that he had slipped the coin into my pocket as I sat upon his knee that afternoon. What was meant to have been a delightful surprise went wrong because the recipient was known never to possess more than his allowance of fifty groschen.

Had it been a painful episode only for me, the royal visit would have created no waves, but that was not the case. Though Vienna had been only an intermediate stop in a hunting trip to southern Austria, His Royal Highness insisted, security risk or not, on traveling around the city informally with complete freedom of movement. He wanted to follow his impulses. This approach created havoc for Vienna's chief of police, who visibly aged in those few days and was brought to the point of pulling out what was left of his hair. All of his previous planning was thrown to the wind and new precautions put in place. He could only pray that no harm came to the prince.

It was necessary to put all of the best restaurants on alert. Fortunately the prince's dinner destination was usually passed on by the valet of His Royal Highness; then a flurry of activity followed. Reservations at that restaurant were canceled, and those patrons were replaced by government employees and their wives. Each evening the prince and his guests joined an animated public that was both well-dressed and in a festive mood. The best of kitchen and wine cellar was always available and also, wondrously, the best table.

These miraculous evenings made possible by a government staff assigned to the logistics of the royal visit were costly—appropriate evening attire, overtime, restaurant bills, and the cancellation of reservations in the other restaurants the prince could have chosen added up. The most unexpected expense, however, was the cost of several of the city's street lights. Emerging from a restaurant one night, after punishing an especially fine bottle of cognac, the Prince of Wales decided to take a little exercise in the form of target practice—he was an exceptionally good shot.

The final tally for the royal visit almost caused Father to tear out his own hair. However, the possibility of harm coming to the Prince of Wales in Austria was terrifying. It was the assassination of the heir to the Austro-Hungarian throne in Sarajevo that had precipitated the First World War. Thus, every expense, every inconvenience, and every precaution was both necessary and prudent.

With his father, George V, ailing, the Prince of Wales soon would become the king of England. His reign of eleven months would be one of the shortest reigns in England's history. He chose to give up his throne in favor of the woman he loved—the American divorcee Wallace Simpson.

In May 1936 Father found himself having to cope with two new delicate problems. Italy, Austria's strongest and only truly committed ally, had reached the point of annexing Abyssinia. Father personally disapproved of Fascism and Mussolini's aggression, but he could not publically pronounce this.

Ambassador Messersmith had already pointed out to his government the previous fall that Austria's immediate future was governed by her dependence on Italy for protection and economic assistance. Austrians would have chosen to rely upon England and France, he noted; however, both those nations were content to allow Italy a free hand in Austria if that meant maintaining the status quo. "The Austrians", Messersmith wrote, "therefore have really been put into a position by England and France of this principal dependence on Italy." [2]

The other problem was the telegram sent by Austria's vicechancellor, Prince Ernst von Starhemberg, congratulating Mussolini on the capture of Addis Ababa. Father could not tolerate this misrepresentation of the official Austrian position by the vicechancellor. England and France, nominally guarantors of Austria's independence, were simply outraged. At odds with Starhemberg

---

[2] George Messersmith to the US State Department, 20 September 1935, Records of the Department of State Relating to Internal Affairs of Austria, 1930–1944, National Archives and Records Administration, College Point, MD.

and the Heimwehr since the time of Dollfuss, Father had long wanted to end the independent existence of Austria's various paramilitary organizations but was unable to do so without the help of England and France. Traditionally, Austria's rulers had counted on the army for support, but neither Dollfuss nor Schuschnigg could place too much confidence in the military. Loyalty wasn't the issue—the strength of the military was. The severe limitations on the size of the Austrian Army imposed by the Treaty of Saint-Germain had contributed to the growth of the Heimwehr.

The Heimwehr had a double grip on Austrian politics. First, the Christian Socialist Party had needed the Heimwehr coalition to maintain a majority in Parliament; and second, the Heimwehr's Prince Starhemberg, ideologically in alignment with Fascism, had skillfully obtained support from Mussolini. There was constant anxiety, however, about Nazi infiltration of the Heimwehr. The group had become a burden to the government, and its presence was now seen as subversive.

When compulsory military service was reestablished and passed into law on October 10, 1936, the Front Militia came into existence. All volunteer organizations, including the Heimwehr, were officially disbanded.

The end of May 1936 brought both good and bad news. Gen. Alfred Jansa, chief of staff of the Austrian Army, informed Austrian envoy Theodor Hornbostel of a report Jansa had received from a reliable source: Hitler had ordered that "for the moment acts of violence in Austria should cease and martyrs . . . not be created." [3] The same source, however, had also reported that the Austrian Legion intended for the occupation of Austria numbered about twenty-five thousand men who had received two years of military training and had been placed in civilian jobs along the Austrian-German border. They could be mobilized in twenty-four hours.

Austria looked to Italy for its continued support, but due in large part to its African policy, Italy's relationship with France and England had severely deteriorated. Italy was now turning toward Germany. Mussolini was anxious that relations between Austria and Germany prosper, and to this end he exerted pressure on Austria.

---

[3] Schuschnigg, *Im Kampf gegen Hitler*, 194.

A level of detente with Germany had become absolutely necessary. Austria needed relief from German-sponsored terrorism, the Thousand-Mark Tariff, and the discrimination against trade with Austria that had been in place for the last three years. Lastly, but most importantly, Austria sought, and had been seeking since 1933, a guarantee that Germany would not meddle in Austrian internal affairs and would recognize Austrian sovereignty. On July 11, Germany agreed to renounce all claims on Austria. In exchange, Germany demanded political amnesty for Nazis in Austrian prisons and the appointment of representatives of the German National Opposition in Austria to participate in the Austrian government.

This agreement left room for the chancellor to maneuver. He believed that if the external pressure dissipated, the internal elements were containable. After their release, the jailed Nazis were likely to pose a considerable problem. On this point, however, the Germans were unyielding. By the end of 1936, the number of Nazis released from Austrian prisons would number 18,648. Those jailed for serious public crimes remained incarcerated. The chancellor steadfastly refused to admit Nazis to his cabinet. Instead, he appointed Edmund Glaise-Horstenau as minister without portfolio and Guido Schmidt as state secretary for foreign affairs. Although they favored stronger ties with Germany, they did not support Hitler; they belonged to the Fatherland Front and were thought of as loyal to their country.

In the end, the July 11 agreement demonstrated that Austria was prepared to be a good neighbor and, for the sake of peace, was reasonable in negotiations and pliable within bounds. There was an additional benefit to Austria: by signing the agreement Austria would be seen to have followed Mussolini's advice. The German ambassador to Italy, Ulrich von Hassell, observed, "Mussolini had seized the opportunity to express lively satisfaction over the agreement because it would bring to an end the unhappy situation of Austria as a football of foreign interests and above all remove the last and only mortgage on German-Italian relations." [4]

Hitler's reaction to his ambassador to Austria, Franz von Papen, was altogether different. Papen would write later: "[Hitler] broke

---

[4] Ibid.

into a flood of abuse. I had misled him, he said, into making exaggerated concessions in return for purely platonic undertakings by the Austrian government. The whole thing was a trap ... He was in one of those hysterical rages which I had experienced before, though never on the telephone." [5]

In Austria the July 11 agreement was viewed as a window of opportunity. With it Chancellor von Schuschnigg embarked on the delicate task of playing one dictator against the other. History would show, however, that from the very beginning the agreement was not worth the paper on which it had been printed.

A week after the agreement, the Spanish Civil War broke out. Italy aligned militarily and financially with General Franco, hoping for Germany's assistance. Quite soon, Italian aid to Austria, far from increasing, was completely cut off. Militarily and economically Italy had reached its limits. Fortunately, Austria's financial situation had improved somewhat. The League of Nations' financial controller for Austria resigned on August 6, citing there was no longer a need for his position.

The summer of 1936 in Saint Gilgen would be much better than the previous summer. Fräulein Alice's former Belgian employer, Monsieur Vincent Cols, intrigued by her descriptions of the Saint Gilgen area, arrived with his two children. Michel, who was my age, the beautiful Suzy, who was three years older, and I took on the summer together.

Under Fräulein Alice's watchful eye, we fished, swam, and grilled dinners over open fires. Michel and Suzy's company was the highlight of my summer. Their departure left a crater in my day, but at age ten one recovers quickly.

I could hike, swim, look for mushrooms in the woods, or just lie on the wharf—fishing pole and worms temporarily forgotten—and watch the coveys of birds in flight. As they glided in formation through the air with ease and grace, their movements seemed effortless.

Wonderful as this was—clear days and warm sun—equally so was the advance of a summer storm. In the distant sky dark gray clouds would gather. Birds, twittering hysterically, seemed to signal warnings to one another. Deep rumblings issued forth from

[5] Ibid., 200.

the advancing clouds, and bolts of lightning tore across the sky; cascades of rain came with electrifying cracks of thunder—it was magnificent.

Every color God had created was reflected in the millions of flowers nourished by those summer rains. Their blossoms blanketed everything in Austria's lake district from the hills and mountains down to the valley floors. At the close of those wonderful days, twilight gave way to the night with its mantle of stars and clear moonlight, which I would admire while lying on the porch with Purzel.

Life was, for the moment, perfect. It was in this frame of mind that I entered the Jesuit boarding school Kollegium Kalksburg.

# Kalksburg

"What a lucky boy you are, Kurti. You have a wonderful school and new friends waiting for you."

Fräulein Alice's voice broke through my thoughts as we drove through the outskirts of Mödling and approached the Jesuit school. Stephan, our driver, turned the car into Kalksburg's wide entrance.

"Yes, indeed," added Grandfather, "but we are going to be lonely without him. Aren't we, Purzel?"

Purzel wagged his tail.

There were many boys at Kalksburg, and I would be just another boy like all the others. My closest friends, Peter Mayer and Rudi Fugger, were going to different schools, but some of my other classmates would be here. Fräulein Alice was right. I was a lucky boy. A new life was in front of me. I wondered what she was going to do with herself in my absence. I had an uncomplicated affection for her and Purzel. They had been my anchors.

The car had barely rolled to a stop when I jumped out and headed toward the school's main doors. I glanced back for a split-second to check on Grandfather and careened straight into a black cassock.

"Not so fast, my son! Your family will never be able to keep up with you at this pace."

I had run into the general prefect, Father Hugo Montjoie. Grandfather introduced our party. In deference to Stephan, who had my luggage in hand, we then followed the good father's directions to my student dormitory.

A huge, gray room was divided into cubicles. High wooden partitions separated each bed, leaving just enough space on either side for a small wardrobe and a chest of drawers. A heavy curtain hanging at the foot of the bed could be pulled closed. Pitiless tubular lighting did nothing to soften the Spartan atmosphere.

Fräulein Alice spoke cheerfully as she observed my new quarters. This definitely meant she was surprised by the austerity. I was not. Father had described his alma mater, Stella Matutina, also a

Jesuit school. He had said Kalksberg would be similar, and it was. Then he had asked me how I felt about being on my own. I had told Father I thought boarding school was going to be a great adventure.

My first meal was something of a shock. I took the seat assigned to me on the wooden bench. We thanked God for the meal. My neighbor passed me a dish. I stared at the contents: *Greisbrei* (cream of wheat). I thanked God for this? Inwardly I moaned, for I hated cream of wheat even more than I hated chocolates. This was not an auspicious beginning. I turned automatically to pass on the bowl, but before I had released my hold on it, a command rang out from the head of the table: "Stop!" The table froze—forks and glasses hung in midair. "Kurt, you will eat your food", Father Zerlauth said in a way that left no room for interpretation. This was another bad omen; he knew my name.

"But, Father, it makes me sick."

"There are starving children in this world. You will eat the greisbrei."

I had heard this appeal to one's conscience from Fräulein Alice, but I did not have the nerve here to say, "They can have mine." I ate the pale mush and whatever else was presented to us as edible just like everyone else. That was lesson number one.

The questionable distinction of being addressed by name soon befell me again. Some weeks later, Father Montjoie stood up and tapped his glass. Silence ensued and all heads turned toward him. "Today this crate of oranges arrived from Bozen", he said. As the crate was being brought to the head table by two sturdy lay workers, he continued, "I will read the card out loud: 'To my grandson Kurti, from Grandfather'. Let us all thank Kurt von Schuschnigg for sharing these wonderful oranges with us."

"Danke, Kurt!" echoed through the dining room, immediately followed by the clatter of dishes and buzz of conversation as the business of eating resumed. I was happy my grandfather had remembered me, and I waited for the oranges to come around. When the crate reached our table: *empty*. Not even a leaf was left behind. This was lesson number two.

Holy Mass at six A.M. was part of the Kalksburg routine, even though I was sure God did not insist upon hearing from us that

75

early. Altar boy duty was mandatory, and all the boys were on a rotation. Regularly one had to be fully awake and in the sacristy ten minutes earlier to put on a cassock and surplice. After a breakfast of bread, butter, and tea, the day's activities had one objective: strengthening our minds and bodies. Eventually all the new students adapted to this routine, and I did so quite readily.

Relatives were permitted to visit once a month—part of the Jesuit plan to develop independence. In my case, visits were divided between Grandfather and Fräulein Alice. During her visit in November, Fräulein Alice told me we were going to Obladis, a ski area near Landeck. I had not seen Father since September, and I had visions of us skiing together, sharing meals: things that one might expect a father and his young son to do together. Given the current state of affairs in Austria, it was soon apparent that such expectations were unrealistic.

In October 1936, Germany and Italy signed an agreement formalizing a Rome-Berlin Axis, which left Austria without a guarantor. A month later, Germany signed the Anti-Comintern Pact with Japan.

A bright spot had been the formation of Father's new cabinet. Ambassador Messersmith wrote to Cordell Hull, the US secretary of state:

> There is not a single member of the Cabinet now who does not enjoy a good reputation, who does not have a good public and private record, whose hands are not known to be entirely clean, and who does not have either general confidence or that of a particular group of the population. Every single member of the Cabinet ... has particular qualifications for the post which he holds.... I am informed that the changes being reported upon have been received with general satisfaction in the country.[1]

Austria's international situation was not encouraging, but the domestic situation seemed under control. The chancellor had given a speech in Klagenfurt, a Nazi stronghold, and concluded by calling upon members of the Fatherland Front to fight defeatism, which would undermine the struggle against Communism and National

---

[1] George Messersmith to Cordell Hull, 1936, National Archives.

Socialism. Messersmith reported that Schuschnigg had reacted to German pressure and Austrian provocations

> in the most energetic fashion ... [He] served plain warning on all subversive elements in the state, Communist, Nazi or disgruntled Heimwehr, that activities against the Government would not be tolerated. In short, the Chancellor is still determined to follow the 'middle road', and in that resolve the Legation believes that he has the majority of the Austrian people behind him, and, what is perhaps momentarily even more important, the cooperation of the Army and the Police.[2]

After the reorganization of the chancellor's cabinet in early November, the Rome Protocol meetings with Italy and Hungary were conducted in Vienna. An obstacle between the Austrians and their objective of closer ties with the Little Entente was that Hungary still had claims on parts of Czechoslovakia. If Hungary brought up the issue, the chancellor would have to oppose both Hungary and Italy. He made every effort to prevent the subject from being raised, and in the end that was the only success of the meeting; shock waves from the news of the Rome-Berlin Axis were still ricocheting throughout the Little Entente and the Balkans.

Early in 1937, Austria signed an economic treaty with Germany, concluding six months of negotiations between the two countries. The result of seemingly endless negotiations, the agreement was in the end fairly empty of content. The successful aspect of the treaty was that Austria had avoided German economic dominance, for everyone who dealt with the Reich was paid in credits that could be redeemed only within the Reich.

Also in 1937 the Austrian chancellor had refused to allow the Austrian representative of the Nazis, Capt. Joseph Leopold, to form the Nationalistic Party that he wanted. Instead, the chancellor permitted the creation of a seven-man National Opposition Committee that would negotiate with the Austrian government. A diplomat in the American legation who was close to the chancellor explained to Ambassador Messersmith that Schuschnigg

---

[2] Ibid.

was using these negotiations with the Nazis to "disturb Signor Mussolini's complacency" before the chancellor's upcoming visit to Italy. Messersmith passed this information to Secretary Hull and wrote, "[Schuschnigg's] waiting policy in the face of subversive elements ... proved once again his adroitness in handling Austrian politics and his knowledge of the Austrian psychology." [3]

Hoping at least to maintain the status quo, the chancellor undertook a trip to Venice in April 1937 to ascertain where Mussolini stood and to allay the Italian dictator's anxieties about the rumored restoration of the Habsburg monarchy. The rumor was based on the fact that a portion of the Habsburg land confiscated after World War I had been returned to the Habsburgs in 1935. Further, the royal family had been granted permission to return to Austria as private citizens, after having lived in exile since November 1918. The Reich fabricated the story that the Habsburgs were returning to the throne as a wedge between Austria and Italy, and Berlin regularly denounced Austria for it. It also served to whip into a frenzy the countries of the Little Entente, which were formerly part of the Austro-Hungarian Empire. Germany's position was that a Habsburg monarchy in Austria would be sufficient reason to occupy Austria.

The Venice trip did have one positive outcome. Italy had recently signed new economic agreements with Yugoslavia. In light of these agreements, Mussolini had become doubtful that Italy could continue to import Austrian lumber. The chancellor managed to defer the discussion, citing the need for an expert economic advisor. The Austrian he dispatched to Italy returned with a one-year extension of Austria's timber arrangement. A serious economic setback was avoided.

As reported to the US State Department by American foreign service officer James B. Young, the Austrian chancellor would continue his policy of "maintaining Austrian independence, offending Germany as little as possible and of securing all support still available from Italy, particularly in the economic field". His policy was also aimed at "strengthening as much as possible relations with Prague, Vienna, and Budapest and to hope for sympathy and support

---

[3] George Messersmith to Cordell Hull, 1937, National Archives.

from England and France in the ratio as one re-arms and the other settles its internal problems."[4]

Since March, the Austrian government had been promoting a new domestic loan plan that would allow the government to cash in short-term treasury loans, but its main purpose was the creation of some fifty thousand jobs. Though the economy was growing stronger, government-sponsored work projects were still necessary to reduce unemployment. The government wanted every Austrian to have a job; those without were more susceptible to Nazi propaganda.

As reported by Messersmith to the US State Department:

> The Austrian Nazis were determined to sabotage the subscription effort from the beginning. They alleged falsely that the loan would be used to buy arms from Italy, that its real purpose was to finance the return of Otto von Habsburg, that banks were being forced to subscribe using the people's savings, and so on. In his speech in Graz on March 4, 1937, the Chancellor met the situation head-on, lashing out against those who were seeking to impair the success of the internal loan and, as a result, the work of economic reconstruction.[5]

In the end, the government secured the loan. In April, Young reported that "during February and March 1937 Schuschnigg had succeeded in out maneuvering his political opposition: the Nazi organization was in disorder and quarreling ... Nazi activity did not cease but ... many were beginning to believe that this activity was born of desperation."[6]

Meanwhile, King Leopold III was insisting that Belgium's claim of neutrality be respected.[7] This was a serious new complication. It meant that France could no longer use Belgian airfields and French troops would not be allowed to pass through Belgian territory to

---

[4] James B. Young to US State Department, 1937, National Archives.

[5] George Messersmith to US State Department, 1937, National Archives.

[6] James B. Young to US State Department, 1937, National Archives.

[7] After World War I, Belgium entered into the Locarno Treaty with France and Germany. The three countries agreed not to attack each other and promised to help defend any signatory country against aggression by another. When Germany reoccupied the Rhineland in 1936, King Leopold III declared that the treaty had been nullified and that his country must remain outside any resumption of conflict between Germany and France.

aid Czechoslovakia or Poland in the event of a German invasion. Thus both Czechoslovakia and Poland were left exposed and vulnerable.

If the goal of a stronger Central European bloc was to be achieved, amity between Hungary and Czechoslovakia was paramount. In May the Austrian president, the secretary of state, and the chancellor made a state visit to promote the initiative they had previously put forth in March. Hungary now had to choose its path. A week later, in the never-ending effort to sway the British, Secretary Schmidt again traveled to London.

By June 1937, I had readied myself mentally for the summer. I knew that when Father was in Vienna he had little spare time. His life was his work. When he was at home, without ministers or office retinue, he wrote speeches and maintained correspondence. Though I had hopes for seeing Father in Saint Gilgen, his sights were focused on the Austrian labor body. Seeking their understanding and support, Father addressed the Social Workers' Union. He explained the necessity of continuing the corporate-state form of government with representation by professional and trade associations, rather than by rival political parties, and emphasized the need for discipline in volatile times. His goal, he said, was to return to more normal representation in government after the threats to the country had abated.

When vacation arrived, Fräulein Alice and I were on our way to Saint Gilgen, but without Father. Ambassador Papen was increasing pressure on Austria to approve an Austro-German commission that would address Austria's alleged violations of the July 11 agreement. Messersmith reported to Secretary Hull: "Chancellor Schuschnigg refused to bend to German pressure and the meeting had to be postponed. When it finally met it was along the lines approved by Vienna."

As the domestic situation was in good order, the Austrian government tackled the Nazi issue more aggressively. A crackdown on all disturbances, however mild, followed. It was small wonder that as the summer wore on, we saw little of Father.

Summer warmth and sunshine gradually gave way to autumn; the days grew shorter, the air crisper. As if putting on a pair of comfortable old shoes, I returned to the routine at the Jesuit school.

The illusion of Italian support for Austria had disappeared. At the end of September, during Father's Prague meeting with Czechoslovakian Prime Minister Milan Hodza, Mussolini made a state visit to Germany. Hitler staged an impressive reception for him with parades, pomp, and ceremony. Mussolini promenaded through two rows of busts of Caesars and then into a Berlin decorated with Roman columns complete with Fascist symbols. Il Duce was impressed and Hitler knew it. Hitler was so confident of his power that in November he revealed to the German foreign minister, minister for war, and chiefs of staff the plan for the subjugation of Austria and Czechoslovakia in what is known as the Hossbach Memorandum. The next day Italy joined the Anti-Comintern Pact, formally allying herself with Germany and Japan. In December, Italy formally withdrew from the League of Nations.

The Christmas holidays arrived and with them, as always, Fräulein Alice. Eyeing my packed suitcase, she said cheerfully, "Let's take a look at what you've packed."

In my second year of independence at Kalksburg now, I took exception to her comment as implying I didn't know how to pack.

Noticing my annoyance she continued, "Of course you can pack for yourself, but I don't think you know we're going to Saint Anton!"

"Skiing?"

"Yes indeed, skiing!" she laughed. I dumped the contents of my suitcase on the floor and started packing with a different purpose.

The journey from Vienna to Saint Anton took about ten hours by train, but Father preferred this to motoring. The government coach in which he and his aides and ministers rode was attached to the overnight train, allowing them a full workday.

"Fräulein Alice, do we get to go with Father this time?" I asked at dinner.

"Of course. That is the whole idea of traveling by train, you silly goose."

She knew exactly what I meant: Would I have time with Father?

"Liesl went to great lengths to prepare all of your favorite dishes", Fräulein Alice said. "She is going to be hurt if you don't eat."

Seeing that her strategy to get my mind off Father wasn't working, she added, "We are going to be on the same train, Kurti, but not together. You know that your father is traveling with Colonel Bartl and some of the ministers who are complaining about not having enough time for Christmas. Every minute they can work on the train is a minute longer they'll have free in Saint Anton. It is important for all of them, but especially for your father. I don't think he gets more than four hours of sleep a night."

My dinner was on the brink of congealing, and I was famished. Cutting into the *Wiener Schnitzel* (Viennese veal cutlet), I reminded myself that I had expected Father to be busy. I focused on the better news that my friend Rudi would be in Saint Anton. Christmas was not going to be dull. The door opened and Liesl entered with a platter of frothy, golden *Salzburger Nockerln* (Salzburg-style soufflé). We don't get that at Kalksburg, I thought happily.

A frigid blast hit us as we stepped off the train into a wintry scene from a fairy tale. Mountains and trees, as far as the eye could see, were laden with snow. Boughs of holly festooned the small station and garnished the waiting sleighs. Ropes of tiny bells adorned the harnesses and jingled festively every time the horse stamped his hoof or shook his mane. Saint Anton was preparing for Christmas.

Garlands of fir, tied with thick red bows, hung on the front doors of the legendary Hotel Post. After the minute it took me to unpack in my room in the Post's annex, I dashed off in search of Rudi. I literally bumped into him coming around a corner.

Rudi's first words were, "Somebody did a great job with the reservations. I'm in the room next to yours!" Nothing remotely resembling a greeting. It was typical.

"I know, and Fräulein Alice is on the other side."

"What! I'm not the one who needs a nanny."

"Rudi, you know we wouldn't be allowed to stay in the annex by ourselves. What did you expect?"

We were both stopped short by the arrival of Fräulein Alice. She must have heard us, but all she said was, "There you are, Rudi. Good! Let's get you settled in your room." As we turned in the direction of our rooms, Rudi gave me a noncommittal glance and shrugged his shoulders. I merely smiled; yes, we would see.

Fräulein Alice had arranged for us to take lessons with two young skiers who were beginning to make names for themselves. With their growing accomplishments on the slopes, Hannes Schneider and Rudi Matt were attracting more attention to the sport. The graceful but difficult telemark skiing of Colonel Bartl's generation was now considered old-fashioned. Telemark had yielded to the new vogue for skiing fast.

There was another recent development: skijoring. Fräulein Alice herself had brought up the subject and made it perfectly clear that (a) it was dangerous and (b) we were not to participate. Rudi objected immediately.

"Even the brainless can hold a rope. The car does the work of pulling the skis."

"No!"

Without any pause whatsoever, Rudi launched an attack on another front. Could we not at least find our own way home after lessons? Fräulein Alice graciously agreed to this seemingly innocent request.

The following afternoon, as we were hoisting our skis onto our shoulders, a new American car stopped beside us. It was a shiny Ford station wagon with wood paneling. We were admiring it when out stepped Ronald Balcom and his wife, the Standard Oil heiress, Millicent Rogers. As the former wife of Count Ludwig von Salm, she was fluent in German. She had also become a friend of Austria and one of Father's supporters.

"Uncle Ronni!" Rudi shouted, waving his free arm.

Uncle Ronni waved back, and Aunt Millicent called out to us, "Hello Rudi! Hello Kurti! What are you two doing wandering around when you could be skiing?"

We hurried to Uncle Ronni's fantastically beautiful car and his even more fantastically beautiful wife. Without missing a beat, Rudi prevaricated, "Well, it's funny that you should ask. We've been waiting for someone who was supposed to take us skijoring, but it looks like we've been let down."

I did my best to keep my mouth from falling open.

"Is that right?" asked Uncle Ronni.

This was a comment rather than a question. They both looked at me. Late on the uptake, I nodded vigorously.

"We're on our way over to Saint Christoph's for tea. Would you boys like to hitch yourselves to the back of our car and join us?"

"Would we ever!"

Uncle Ronni's wife broke in here. "Ronni, darling," she observed, "do you think that's wise? It is a rather dangerous sport."

Uncle Ronni glanced from his wife to us, then back at her. "But, my angel, Rudi says they've done this before. Right boys?"

"Oh, many times, Uncle Ronni!" effortlessly rolled off Rudi's tongue.

Not as verbally nimble, I merely continued to nod.

"Good!" Uncle Ronni said, clapping us both on our backs. "There, you see, darling? They're practically professionals, and they just want to have a little fun. How can we say no?"

Impervious to her good sense, he turned to us. "Put on your skis, and I'll tie the ropes to the back bumper."

It was amazing that Uncle Ronni had ropes. I simply could not imagine Aunt Millicent skijoring, nor could I picture her allowing Uncle Ronni to do so. But Rudi and I needed no more urging; we hurriedly put on our skis. I did have a vaguely disturbing feeling about it though. What if Fräulein Alice found out?

As we picked up our ropes I said to Rudi, "That was a whopping big lie!"

Unimpressed, Rudi arched his eyebrows at me and said, "And just who is the beneficiary of that?"

"You boys all set?" called Uncle Ronni from his window.

"All set, Uncle Ronni!" we chorused.

Before one could think twice we were off. Aunt Millicent had turned herself around in her seat and watched with an expression of concern. I ignored it because I needed every bit of concentration that I could muster just to keep my balance. Uncle Ronni could not have driven at much more than a slow crawl, but to us it felt as if we were taking those curves at fifty miles an hour. I had just begun to feel faint stirrings of confidence when, completely without warning, Rudi deliberately slammed sideways into me. Then, laughing maniacally, he swung back to his side. Had I been able to risk freeing one hand, I certainly would have punched him. By the grace of God, I did just manage to stay upright. As I was contemplating retaliation, Aunt Millicent called out, "Stop that!", while vigorously shaking her head back and forth and wagging her finger at us. And so we did.

By the time the Ford station wagon pulled up in front of the hotel in Saint Christoph, the ropes were frozen solid in my hands. It might have been the cold, but it could easily have been the grip of fear. I was pleased to see that Rudi was in exactly the same state. Still, we had been on the ride of our lives!

"There! You see, Millicent? Professional skijorers!" Uncle Ronni jumped out of the car and cuffed each of us on the shoulder. "Well done! Did you enjoy it?"

Through frozen lips we articulated our assent as well as we could, but our enthusiasm was unmistakable.

"Come on, boys," he laughed, untying the ropes and helping us out of our skis, "put everything in the car, then come inside and we'll have tea."

He took Aunt Millicent's arm and led her into the hotel. As we followed them, I had one thought firmly in mind: I was motoring back.

Rudi was sitting on the backseat beside me when we pulled up to the Post Hotel. Hoping to slip in unnoticed, I asked Uncle Ronni to let us out at the hotel's main entrance, instead of at the annex. It was all for naught. There, clearly visible, was the waiting form of Fräulein Alice. Our lesson was to have ended some two hours ago. I did not want to guess how long she had been waiting out there. Rudi and I looked at each other for a long moment then climbed out of the car. Fräulein Alice introduced herself to Aunt Millicent and Uncle Ronni.

"We had an excellent afternoon, didn't we, boys?" said Uncle Ronni.

"Oh yes!" we sang out, as we scrambled to unload our skis.

I knew I needed a miracle, the sort where Fräulein Alice did not find out about the skijoring.

Aunt Millicent said, "How careless of us not to have had the boys call you. I'm so sorry."

Hoping to prevent discussion between Fräulein Alice and the Balcoms, I blurted out, "Fräulein Alice, Uncle Ronni and Aunt Millicent took us to Saint Christoph for tea. Rudi and I had three different kinds of *Kuchen* (cake), but it doesn't matter because we could still eat a cow, we're so hungry."

Clatter, clatter—down went skis and poles, a desperate diversionary tactic. Fräulein Alice was bending to help me pick them up when Uncle Ronni chose, most unfortunately, to boast of our prowess.

"Bet you didn't know what experts these boys are at skijoring!"

Before I could blink, Rudi—the coward—sang out his thanks and auf wiedersehen-ed his way into the Annex, tossing his skis and poles against the wall as he went inside. I hadn't the courage to look at Fräulein Alice. To her enormous credit, she graciously thanked the couple, saying not a word about my being forbidden to go skijoring.

"Give me the skis, Kurt."

It was bad when she called me Kurt. I obeyed, all the while avoiding her eye, but Fräulein Alice was not so easily evaded.

"Stand still and look at me."

This was more than bad; it was very bad.

"You know what you did today was seriously wrong, don't you?"

"Fräulein Alice, all we did was . . ."

I was brusquely cut off. "This is not a discussion concerning Rudi. I am concerned that you do what you are supposed to do. Equally important, that you don't do what you're not supposed to do. Now you come with me."

I meekly followed her straight to Rudi's door. He must have had his ear pressed against it because he opened immediately at Fräulein Alice's knock. From the expression on his face it was clear that he had expected it to be me, alone.

"Rudi, I have told Kurt, and now I am telling you. Kurt is strictly forbidden to go skijoring again. Is that perfectly clear?"

"Yes, Fräulein Alice." He had the good sense to look chastened.

"And before you or Kurt", here I got another direct look, "even consider going somewhere without my knowledge, you had better first give thought to what the results of your actions will be. Is that perfectly clear?" This implied threat of informing his mother was the one effective weapon against Rudi.

"Yes, Fräulein Alice", we said together.

"Very well. Now both of you change for dinner."

After we had once again said, "Yes, Fräulein Alice", she disappeared into her room. Rudi and I grimaced at one another. He sighed silently and mimed the act of wiping perspiration from his brow with the back of his hand. I gave him a shove and mouthed the word *coward*. His only response was an exaggerated shrug of his shoulders.

Really, we both had gotten off the hook lightly. We ducked into our rooms, and in no time reappeared: changed, spotless, and on our best behavior. Fräulein Alice really was a genius at managing us boys.

# *Separation*

It was a wonderful Christmas, the likes of which we would not see again for a long time. I bade Father good-bye and, in youthful ignorance, returned to my world that was still as I expected it to be.

Father attended his last meeting of the members of the Rome Protocol. Regardless of Italy's decisions, he could not allow Austria to join the Anti-Comintern Pact or leave the League of Nations.

An "entirely reliable source" reported to Ludwig Jordan, Austria's consul general in Munich, that "a party functionary belonging to Hitler's entourage said that there would be 'a move against Austria' in the spring. Unless the Federal Chancellor 'came to his senses' he would share the fate of the late Chancellor Dollfuss."[1] The rumblings from the neighboring Reich turned into a deafening roar, and the chancellor moved from one crisis to another trying to maintain a balance.

There was the Tavs affair. One of the Committee of Seven, Tavs had outlined plans for fomenting armed insurrections throughout the country. These would necessitate the German occupation of Austria to reestablish order. When the plans came to light, both Tavs and Leopold, the head of the Committee of Seven, were expelled from the country.

That there was an alternative to the Tavs plan was not yet known, but it was soon put into effect. An invitation arrived through Ambassador Papen for the chancellor to meet Hitler in Berchtesgaden. Since before the summer of 1937, Nazi terrorism and extremist propaganda had picked up again and was now in full swing. The Austrians hoped that this meeting would be used to reduce tensions. Papen explained that he had been specifically instructed to say that Hitler's interest lay in the renewal, reinforcement, and perpetuation of the July 11 agreement and that no new demands would be made. He assured Father that "whatever the course of the

---

[1] Schuschnigg, *Im Kampf gegen Hitler*, 256.

negotiations in no case would they alter Austro-German relations to the disadvantage of Austria nor lead to any aggravation of the Austrian situation."[2] The invitation was accepted.

The Austrian delegation consisted of the chancellor, his aide-de-camp, the Austrian foreign minister, and a secret service agent. When the Austrian delegation arrived at the railway station near Berchtesgaden, they were greeted by high-ranking German military officers who, through a remarkable coincidence, just happened to be present: Gen. Wilhelm Keitel, Gen. Walter von Reichenau, and Gen. Hugo Sperrle. Also present were Joachim von Ribbentrop, the foreign minister since February 4, 1938; Franz von Papen; and Otto Dietrich, the Reich's press chief.

The chancellor left behind a description of the proceedings:

> The Berghof was exactly as one imagined it from numerous pictures: it was tastefully, not ostentatiously arranged; there were many flowers; on the walls were heads by Lenbach and a particularly beautiful Madonna by Dürer—pictures one had already seen elsewhere ... For the first part of the discussion Hitler and I were alone: for the second, in the afternoon, others were present. The struggle, for such it was, lasted some ten hours in all. Hitler frequently spoke very loudly. I spoke quietly.[3]

When the Austrian chancellor opened his cigarette case, the German dictator said, "I do not like smoke!"

To this the Austrian politely replied, as he lit his cigarette, "That is unfortunate for I must smoke." The morning session continued in that vein.

The chancellor's commentary continues: "Hitler on the offensive all the time ... opened with a general attack on the 'un-German history' of old Austria.... [A]fter two hours in the morning neither side had yielded an inch."

Lunch was bizarre. Hitler's personality changed completely. He played the host, speaking of the great things to come in the Reich: building projects, from the largest bridge in the world to mushrooming skyscrapers. After lunch the pressure and the threats resumed.

---

[2] Hopfgartner, *Ein Mann gegen Hitler*, 199.
[3] Kurt von Schuschnigg, *The Brutal Takeover* (New York: Atheneum, 1971), 191–92.

Among Hitler's many demands was the appointment of Nazi Seyss-Inquart as minister of Austrian security. Hitler made an extraordinary statement: "I am well aware that your friend, the Jesuit Muckermann, one of the bitterest enemies of the German people, is in Vienna plotting to assassinate me—and with your knowledge and your government's assistance." [4]

To this irrational accusation, the chancellor replied evenly, "Austria does not use assassination as an instrument of policy."

Father Friedrich Muckermann, SJ, (1883–1946) was a scholar and writer who divided his time between Rome and Luxembourg. Apart from a brief visit in 1937, the chancellor had not seen him since 1933. A story had been passed to Papen that the anti-Nazi priest was in Vienna to exterminate Austrian National Socialists and that he knew of a plot to assassinate Hitler.

The Austrians were led to another salon and left alone. When Hitler was told that Schuschnigg refused to appoint Seyss-Inquart, he replied, "Tell Schuschnigg if he does not accept this demand, I shall march this very moment." [5]

The chancellor countered this threat by maintaining that three days would be required to examine the Austrian Constitution and that the appointment must be approved by the Austrian president. Three days were reluctantly granted.

"What does he want three days for?" Hitler said to his entourage. "I really don't want to give them to him. All right then. I don't like it; I would much rather have marched. Gentlemen, I will have one last try; let him have his three days." [6]

Shortly before the departure of the Austrians, Hitler remarked, "It would be completely irresponsible and unjustifiable before history if an instrument like the German Wehrmacht were not used." [7]

The advantage of diplomacy by intimidation was that it left no room for misinterpretation. There no longer remained any question of playing for time. Time was up.

---

[4] Schuschnigg, *Im Kampf gegen Hitler*, 237.
[5] Ibid.
[6] Ibid., 238.
[7] Ibid., 243.

Ribbentrop presented the German demands to the Austrian delegation. They were on two typewritten pages and bore no resemblance to the assurances previously given by Papen that the July 11 agreement would be affirmed. Instead they amounted to an invasion from within: Arthur Seyss-Inquart, head of the banned Austrian Nazis, was to be appointed minister of security; Glaise-Horstenau, now a self-proclaimed Nazi, was to be put in charge of the armed forces; all the National Socialists in prison were to be freed, with a general amnesty and full restitution for all discrimination suffered by them; and, a merging of the two economic systems was to be effected. Germany was to be consulted in everything. These were the high points, as it were. The Austrian government managed to have some of these demands modified, but with the threat of imminent invasion looming in the background.

The US ambassador to France, William Bullitt, sent a "strictly confidential" report to Secretary Hull, which was received at three forty-seven P.M. on February 16, 1938:

> The Austrian Minister just read to me a telegram which he received this morning from Schuschnigg. It indicated that Schuschnigg had by no means given up hope of maintaining Austrian independence ... he would continue to struggle for Austrian independence; that he believed this independence could be maintained in the long run only if there should be reconciliation between England, France and Italy ... Schuschnigg felt that the actions, which he was about to take, would produce a temporary breathing period but in the end would prove to be just as unsatisfactory to Hitler as his actions, which followed the accord of July 1936. At some future date Germany would mobilize on the Austrian frontier. He would make no further concessions. He could not attempt to fight Germany alone and, if faced by German mobilization, would have to resign.[8]

On the following day, Gabriel Puaux, the French ambassador in Vienna, reported to Paris: "It is the duty of the French and British governments to speak frankly to Mussolini before it is too late. No defense of Austrian independence can be arranged without Italy. Whatever démarche the French and British governments may make

---

[8] Ibid., 266.

in Berlin, they would neither impress Hitler nor help the Austrian patriots, unless Italy was openly and genuinely associated with them." [9]

With inflexible resolve, the chancellor set himself and his cabinet to the task of creating any obstacle that might impede the Nazification of Austria, while at the same time trying to avoid the spread of panic among the people.

Papen had phoned Berlin to report:

> There was considerable agitation in Vienna because of the political and economic consequences of the German-Austrian Agreements. Vienna at the moment resembled an anthill. Quite a few Jews were preparing to emigrate. The stock exchange was agitated and the banks were under heavy pressure. Besides, Prague was doing its bit to add to the confusion, spreading rumors that Austria had decided on large-scale rearmament with German aid. [10]

Hitler delivered a speech at the Reichstag on February 20. Winston Churchill commented on the passages referring to Austria: "One can hardly find a more perfect specimen of humbug and hypocrisy for British and American benefit. . . . What is astounding is that it should have been regarded with anything but scorn by men and women of intelligence in any free country." [11]

Four days later, in an address to the Austrian Parliament, the chancellor said that no further concessions were forthcoming since they would be incompatible with maintenance of an independent Austria and in open contravention of the recently concluded Berchtesgaden agreement. "We knew", he said, "that we could go and did go, up to that boundary line beyond which appear clearly and unequivocally the words, 'Thus far and no further'." His speech ended with a ringing, patriotic call: "Red, white, red until death!" [12]

The demands for the official recognition of the Nazi Party never abated. The Nazis desired the resignation of the chancellor's cabinet

---

[9] Ibid., 268.

[10] Ibid., 269.

[11] Ibid., 262.

[12] Gottfried-Karl Kinderman, *Österreich gegen Hitler: Europas erste Abwehrfront 1933–1938* (Munich: Langen Müller Verlag, 2003), 391.

and the collapse of the government, but Schuschnigg refused to bend. Seyss-Inquart, beginning to realize that he had been marginalized by Berlin, made a public declaration of his inability to control the situation, and an uneasy peace still held.

That changed on March 4, 1938, when Wilhelm Keppler arrived from Berlin. The Reich commissioner for economic affairs presented himself at the chancellor's residence the next day with a fresh list of demands. He declared himself interested only in the economics of the situation, which he said made the Anschluss a necessity. The chancellor repeated what he had said to Parliament on February 24: it was impossible to go beyond the Berchtesgaden agreement. "Keppler", he wrote later, "took note of my rejection with polite sorrow and neither hectored nor threatened." [13] The question of a plebiscite on the Anschluss had been raised before. Now there was nowhere else for the chancellor to go.

On March 11, Keppler delivered to Father Hitler's final demands: cancel the public vote on Anschluss and disband the government, or German troops will march into Austria. The next day, the Wehrmacht invaded the country. The number of planes, tanks, and infantry was so large and well orchestrated that there was little doubt Hitler had long intended to take Austria by force.

On March 12, I was summoned by Father Montjoie. I had been to his office in the past as from time to time he had called me in to check on my school progress. This time was for a different reason. He came to the point swiftly, "I have some bad news for you, Kurt. Your father has been arrested." I was sure that I had misheard him and sat staring—waiting for him to say something I would understand. Putting his hand on my shoulder, he repeated his words. I had understood him. Father Montjoie went on to say that this was only the beginning. He feared for the whole of Europe and said that terrible times lay ahead. National Socialism would put an end to the life we knew. That night the soon-to-graduate seniors armed themselves with hunting rifles and camped outside my sleeping hall. A cold, all-night vigil passed without incident, and we tried to maintain our daily routine.

[13] Schuschnigg, *Im Kampf gegen Hitler*, 293.

Several days later, I was once again in Father Montjoie's office. He told me that my father would be allowed one phone call; we waited. When it came through, Father Montjoie spoke to him first. My eyes were riveted on his face, but it remained impassive. Then gently smiling, he handed me the phone. Father sounded the same as he always did. He said we wouldn't be seeing each other for some time and told me to do my best in school and be a good boy. At the end of the school year, I would stay with Fräulein Alice. He loved me, he said, and then the line went dead.

"He's gone." I looked up at Father Montjoie. Taking the receiver, the kind-hearted priest said that I was the only thing about which Father was worried and that the best way to help him was to be strong.

Kalksburg was permitted to operate until the end of the spring term. The Third Reich then closed the eighty-two-year-old school. Its students, previously entrusted to the Jesuits, would now come under government control.

The Nazi ship of state, with a full wind at its back and captained by the little Austrian-born corporal, sailed on. In its wake bobbed the flotsam of its victims. For those who survived, the horror they experienced by day was followed by the hopelessness of night with its terrifying dreams. But the mind numbs, and the will to survive is stubborn. One day followed the next—time passed. One grew older.

In May Father was moved to the Vienna headquarters of the Nazi secret police, the Gestapo. There was one cause for celebration, however: Aunt Vera had become my stepmother. Free to marry Father with the blessing of the Catholic Church, she did so by proxy on June 1. The ceremony took place in the Dominican church in Vienna with Uncle Artur standing in for Father. Grandfather, Aunt Marianne, and the church sacristan served as witnesses. In honor of the occasion, a papal representative called on Vera to deliver an apostolic blessing from Pope Pius XI. There was an accompanying message for Father, Vera, and me. It stated that if at the hour of our death we were unable to pronounce the name of Jesus, we would still be absolved from our sins (assuming that we were disposed to receive this grace). Throughout the war years, I carried this assurance of God's mercy in the back of my mind; it gave me courage and a degree of solace.

During his time in government, Father had called on the pope each time he visited Rome, as was customary because the Vatican is a sovereign state. Those visits went beyond protocol, however, as Father was serious about his obligations as a Catholic. Thus he and Pius XI developed a close bond.

Pius XI died in February 1939, and his successor, Pius XII, Father had long known as Eugenio Cardinal Pacelli, the former apostolic nuncio to Germany who had become Vatican secretary of state in 1930. It was he who signed the concordats of the thirties. After he became pope, Pius XII sent Father his prayers and blessing.

When the school term ended, I was claimed by my golden Fräulein Alice, who then lived with her parents in Vienna. The Ottenreiters' apartment on Neubaugasse had three bedrooms. There were six of us. In addition to her parents, Fräulein Alice's sister and her husband, Grete and Fritz Sammer, also lived there.

Everything that summer was new to me. When I arrived Fräulein Alice's mother cautioned me about the building's janitor, a woman from Bohemia. The new authorities had impressed on all janitors the importance of keeping a watchful eye on the comings and goings of tenants on behalf of the fatherland. Having a Schuschnigg in the building, even a young one, was cause in itself for scrutiny.

Reality forced its way into my consciousness. The privileges, benefits, and even the sympathy given me because I was the son of the chancellor were now things of the past; however, the challenge for me was not deprivation, but the challenge of adapting to the sudden and complete disappearance of all that had been normal in my life and in the world around me.

To be the son of Schuschnigg now meant to be the son of the man who had tried to thwart the führer and prevent Anschluss with the glorious and prosperous Reich that now embraced Austria. Fräulein Alice did her best for me but often made unpleasant discoveries. When she contacted the mother of a friend of mine who had often played with me at the Belevedere house, the woman told her not ever to call again, adding, "His type is not welcome."

The conversation had left Fräulein Alice stunned. Worse than the rejection had been the woman's attitude. "No one ever talked to me like that in my entire life!" said Fräulein Alice, indignantly. "It was in the same way that one would say, 'I just stepped in something awful!'" From that point on she was more selective and much more cautious.

Fear had begun to grip even the staunchest of Father's friends and allies as their old way of life and the people they had known began to disappear. The rot of National Socialism was spreading faster than the plague.

Life with the Ottenreiters had become my world. We dined together, went to Mass together, and lit many, many candles together. The idyllic summers in Saint Gilgen were only a memory. Mostly, I read or wandered about Vienna, though always keeping to myself.

When the Gestapo took Father from Belvedere, they forced Grandfather, Colonel Bartl, and Liesl to leave. Liesl returned to Innsbruck and married the policeman who had been patiently waiting for her these many years. Colonel Bartl was immediately arrested, and Grandfather found an apartment on the Beatrixgasse in Vienna's Third District. He spent the last months of his life looking for a solution to his son's Kafkaesque predicament. But there was no one left to listen to a retired field marshal of the old empire. Slowly Grandfather realized that acquiring something as basic as humane living conditions for his son was not possible and spent his remaining days with the few relatives and friends he had left or in the Café Prückel on the Karl Lueger Platz.

Vera also sought to help Father and plunged into a letter-writing campaign. She sent eloquent pleas to innumerable officials of the Reich but to no avail. Not easily denied, she changed her tactics; she simply arrived unannounced at an official's office and waited. Vera was a lovely woman with a commanding presence, and she had two additional advantages: she was relentless and—like many beautiful ladies from well-known families—she was accustomed to getting what she wanted. Moreover, her marriage to Father legitimized her cause. Within the month, Vera met with her first victory.

Austrian Ernst Kaltenbrunner was the commander of the Danube Region Schutzstaffel (SS). The SS was the dreaded Nazi paramilitary organization that was later held responsible for many of the crimes against humanity committed during World War II. Kaltenbrunner had been implicated in the assassination of Dollfuss and had assisted Hitler in his takeover of Austria, yet Vera amazingly convinced him to let her see Father. At Father's cell, Kaltenbrunner curtly informed her that as the wife of the traitor Schuschnigg, she could visit for exactly three minutes on Fridays.

Recalling the conversation, she exclaimed, "Three minutes! What can anyone even say in three minutes?"

I immediately asked if I would be allowed to come with her.

"Certainly not. Are you mad?"

I blinked at her and then realized that yes, I was mad. I was furious that all of this should ever have happened. Father—honest, brave, and honorable—whose sin had been working too hard and caring too much for his country, now sat in prison, called a traitor by a traitor! Mother, my real mother, had been a loving parent and a good person, and she was dead. And I? I was a long way from perfect, but I wasn't a malicious boy; yet, I was also sitting in the soup. How could so many horrible things have happened to us? Mad as I was, in reply to Vera's question I simply said, "No, Mami."

With the end of summer, the question of my education was resolved. It had nothing to do with Fräulein Alice's efforts at finding a school for me. The state had decided. Early one September morning, Herr Krause arrived at the front door. This dedicated, heel-clicking Nazi said he was authorized to be my tutor. My lessons were to be conducted in the Ottenreiters' apartment. I was almost as sorry for Frau Ottenreiter and the others as I was for myself. Now they had to sacrifice their dining room during the day. I was already sleeping in there on the couch at night. Worst of all, Frau Ottenreiter would also have to put up with this horrible man.

The Nazi's manner toward me was artificially correct. Smugly self-righteous, Krause had a personality that would have made a rock seem exciting by comparison. I sensed that his frosty civility disguised fury at being slighted by what he viewed as an offensive and degrading assignment.

When Fräulein Alice inquired how long I would be educated in this manner, his reply left no illusions about my status and not much reason for optimism. I was an "undesirable person" and would not be allowed back in the Austrian educational system.

Thus began my school year in the autumn of 1938 with joyless and seemingly endless hours of Krause. Frau Ottenreiter, upon his departure, did her best to air out the lingering "odor of Nazi" from the apartment. I would clear the table, and we would have tea of some description.

During the first weeks with Krause, my mind wandered back to the previous year. The difference was as if I had been put in a dark room after living in sunshine. I no longer knew what to believe. How could Father be all right as I had been told? He was in prison! How could people believe that National Socialism was good when it did terrible things to people? How could people say that there was now order in the streets when almost anytime you walked through Vienna, you saw the Swastikas beating Jews? How could life be normal when people were being encouraged to spy on one another? Would anything ever again be as it was? I was back on the endless merry-go-round of unanswerable questions and silent petitions. I prayed that God would help Father come back to us and that Purzel was all right.

For the hundredth time I worried about what had happened to Purzel. Had the Nazis given him to someone nice? I wondered about his new owner; dogs were such constant, trusting, and loyal companions. They needed only food and affection; in return they were loyal until death. And, unlike humans, dogs were without malice. Fräulein Alice said she was sure he was happy wherever his new home was. This was a comfort. Fräulein Alice was always right.

Most children who grow up without brothers or sisters learn to adjust to solitude. My great diversions—the legions of tin soldiers and other toys—were gone along with the rest of our belongings, which had been crated up and shipped somewhere. Fräulein Alice had somehow managed to save my stamp collection. She buried it in the basement's dirt floor beneath the Ottenreiter country house outside Vienna. I began replacing my missing treasures with a growing passion for reading—Schiller, Goethe, and countless others. But thrilling were the adventures of Karl May in America's Old West.

I struggled through September, and near the end of the month I went to visit Grandfather. He took me to lunch and, as an exceptional treat, a Shirley Temple movie. I wanted to see it a second time, but Grandfather said no: one could have "too much of a good thing". That was the last bit of wisdom that he shared with me. His son and his Austria had been taken from him; the combination was more than his heart could stand. One morning as he was dressing, his heart simply stopped: one more huge hole in my life.

That November brought Kristallnacht, the night Jewish homes, shops, and synagogues in Germany and Austria were destroyed by the Nazis. One of their targets was the candy shop on the ground floor of the Ottenreiter apartment house. A part of my weekly allowance contributed to the flourishing trade of its owners, a kindly Jewish couple. It was past the shop's closing time when I rounded the corner onto Neubaugasse. I was surprised to see that a small crowd had gathered outside the shop. As I drew nearer the shop front, my feet crunched over broken glass. Thinking that there had been an accident, I stepped closer. The crowd shifted, and I had a view into the shop. It looked as if lightning had struck the interior. Not a pane of glass—neither countertop nor display case—was intact. But that was not all. Nothing of any description was left whole. The cash register had been smashed. The wooden stools were split. Loose candy lay everywhere. I stood there gaping while youths wearing the swastika were looting the store they had destroyed.

The bolt of lightning had a name—anti-Semitism—an age-old plague in Europe. An image of the shopkeeper and his wife flashed through my mind; I felt sick. I wanted only to get back to the Ottenreiters' apartment.

Suddenly one of the Swastikas noticing me called out, "You there, catch!" and threw a box of candy toward me. I froze and let the box fall. It landed at my feet. Smiling maliciously, the thug barked, "Take it! It only belonged to a pig Jew."

Not moving a muscle, I just stared at him.

"What's the matter? Are *you* one of them?"

There were many blonde, blue-eyed Jews. My mind finally connected with my adrenaline. I ran around the corner and up the building staircase. I did not stop until I had slammed the apartment door behind me and locked it. I stood there panting and shocked.

What was happening? Vienna had gone mad! Hate and evil filled the streets as Nazi songs echoed throughout the night. The torch-carrying Swastikas marched, destroyed, and looted. It was a night to hide—it was a night of shame.

The next day we learned that more than one hundred synagogues in Vienna had been desecrated and burned. Hundreds of Jewish businesses had been destroyed, thousands of Jews arrested, and many killed outright. In Germany the numbers were more shocking. Not known, however, was the fact that the Third Reich had ordered all insurance money for damages to the Jews to be paid to the Reich as reparation.

The incident did not deter Vera, whose letters had reached all the top officials in Berlin, including Hitler. She learned in early December that she was to be granted an appointment to see SS Reichsführer Heinrich Himmler, who was in charge of all the Gestapo throughout the Third Reich.

Himmler met Vera at Gestapo headquarters in Vienna, where Father was still being held. Punctual to the minute, Vera entered the lobby of the former Hotel Metropol and was ushered to a waiting room. After a few minutes a door opened and the reichsführer entered.

"Ach, Frau von Schuschnigg. I am sorry you have been waiting. Please do come in."

Himmler's slimy politeness continued as Vera seated herself on the chair he offered. She got straight to the point: the unjust and inhuman conditions of Father's imprisonment. She did not use the word *inhuman* to me nor had she told me of the actual circumstances of his confinement. None of this was news to Himmler, however. He had seen Father and knew the way things were.

Her request for better conditions drew a murmured, noncommittal response. Considering their respective positions that in itself was a surprise. Vera would later say that she had never realized how difficult it was to talk to someone while avoiding eye contact. But the last thing she wanted to do was irritate Himmler by staring at his glass eye. After ten minutes of Nazi rhetoric, Himmler escorted her back to the corridor. Little had actually been accomplished. There was nothing else left to do but bombard Hitler again with letters.

My life continued without incident until one morning several days after Vera's audience with Himmler. I was in the middle of my daily session with the tutor when I heard the telephone ring. A moment later, Fräulein Alice stepped into the dining room.

"I dislike interrupting Kurt's lesson, but I must have a word with him."

"Yes", answered the tutor in his usual flat tone. His raised eyebrows communicated that he expected the message to be delivered in his presence. Nothing was further from Fräulein Alice's mind.

"Come with me, Kurti", Fräulein Alice said. I was already on my feet and moving toward the kitchen. Quietly closing the door, she pulled me to the far side of the room.

"Kurti," she said quietly, putting her hands on my shoulders, "that phone call was from the office of Reichsführer Himmler."

I waited.

"This afternoon at four P.M. you are to be at the Hotel Metropol. You are to ask for Reichsführer Himmler himself."

"All right, Fräulein Alice," I said, shrugging my shoulders, "I will go."

"I will go with you and wait in the lobby."

I paused and gave Fräulein Alice a lingering look, knowing she would do anything she could for me.

"No, Fräulein Alice, I will go alone. It is Gestapo headquarters, and you probably won't be allowed to wait in the lobby. You stay here, and I will go and see what he wants. I haven't forgotten where the hotel is." The Hotel Metropol wasn't far from the Augarten Palace. How long ago it seemed since Mother, Father, and I had lived there.

"I know you haven't, Kurti. I would just like to go with you."

"Fräulein Alice, please don't worry. I will be fine."

I gave her a reassuring smile and a pat on the arm. Opening the kitchen door, I heard the contrived cough of Krause clearing his throat. Well, I couldn't bother about Krause now. There was an even bigger swine I would have to deal with that day.

As soon as Krause left, Fräulein Alice came in.

"Kurti, I have ironed your sailor top. Your brown shoes are polished."

"Thank you, Fräulein Alice, but I am going like this. I would not think of changing."

She regarded me thoughtfully.

"Wash your hands and face and brush your hair before you go."

"Yes, Fräulein Alice."

We all had tea and the special treat of a fresh kuchen and pretended that it was just a day like any other. I then scrubbed and brushed myself as instructed. When I reentered the dining room, Frau Ottenreiter and Grete were speaking earnestly to Fräulein Alice.

"Well, I'm off now."

"Kurti," Fräulein Alice's voice stopped me, "you have been brought up to behave correctly and to be polite. Remember what Uncle Willy Elmayer told your class: that a lady or a gentleman is unfailingly polite, even to the devil himself. Don't forget that when you see Himmler", she said, hugging me. "You deal from strength when you keep your own counsel and are polite. Do you have your money for the streetcar?"

I nodded.

"Well, then, aren't you a little early?"

"Maybe, but I might have to wait for the streetcar."

This drawn-out conversation was unlike Fräulein Alice. I realized then she was nervous. That didn't happen often.

"We are having wiener schnitzel for dinner", said Grete. That was my favorite dish.

"Wonderful!" I said with genuine enthusiasm. "I'll be back soon."

Fräulein Alice helped me into my coat, wrapped the scarf around my neck, and handed me my gloves. Then all three of them hugged me. I gave them a smile and a wave. Despite their cheerfulness, they all looked like parents whose child was about to have an operation. I felt as I did when I had to go to the dentist; it was nothing more than an unpleasant inconvenience.

It had stopped drizzling, but gray dampness persisted. I walked the short distance to the streetcar stop without even the delay of a stoplight. I arrived just as the streetcar pulled up. I stepped in, paid, and found a seat. My thoughts immediately went to Vera and her description of her recent meeting with Himmler. Vera had said Himmler was far from distinguished. Were it not for his glass eye, there would be nothing about him worthy of comment. It was said that his glass eye was the one that made him look human.

The streetcar reached my stop, and the connecting streetcar arrived immediately after. If I took it I would be half an hour early, and I did not want that. I started walking instead. There was a wonderful stamp collector's shop on the way. I thought I would take a look in its windows.

Soon I was staring at a beautiful stamp from an island halfway round the world. I was sure the stamp's cost was far beyond my means, but I decided to ask its price in any case. The proprietor was absorbed in a discussion with an elderly man who apparently wanted to buy a present for his grandson. Another customer was waiting ahead of me. I occupied myself by studying the stamps in the display cases. The waiting customer grew impatient and left. A glance at my watch told me that I had been there for nearly fifteen minutes and was running out of time. Just as I turned toward the door, the elderly customer slammed his hand down on the glass countertop with such force that it rattled the display stands, causing the proprietor and me to jump.

"You Jews are all alike!" he said with contempt. "You want to wring the last mark from every Aryan. Well, you won't get any of my money!" With that he stormed out, slamming the door so hard that the glass shook. I was stunned by the man's violence and embarrassed to have witnessed the shopkeeper's humiliation. With sad eyes he then turned to me.

"And what can I do for the young gentleman today?"

Coming directly to the point I said, "I haven't any money just now, but I would like to know how much the Hawaiian stamp is."

His worn, lined face lit up. "It is a beautiful stamp, isn't it?" Before I could reply he continued, "But aren't you the son of our chancellor?"

For the second time in as many minutes I was stunned, so stunned that I didn't answer.

"Of course you are! I have seen your picture a number of times. Your father is a wonderful man. He did everything he could to help us Jews. Two years ago my sister and her whole family were allowed to move here from Germany. The hatred and brutality that Hitler fostered there made life impossible. Now the sickness has spread here as well."

He walked to the window, took the Hawaiian stamp, and returned to the counter. Placing the stamp under a magnifying glass, he remarked, "This stamp is neither old, nor is it particularly expensive. Instead of your having to save up for it, please take it as a present."

Unable to believe my ears, I quickly looked up from the stamp to him. Smiling, he picked out another stamp and placed it in the space left by the Hawaiian stamp. I watched as he put my new treasure in an envelope engraved with the name of his shop.

"When you see your father, please remember to thank him for me." With that he handed me the envelope.

I bade him good-bye. Now I really needed to hurry and began walking briskly toward the Hotel Metropol, but my mind was racing, going over the episode in the philatelic shop.

Since the Anschluss and Father's arrest, the National Socialists had constantly vilified him as a traitor. Father! Vera had said the Nazis had wanted to put him on trial but gave up the idea because they knew the Austrians wouldn't have tolerated it. Hearing a stranger praise my father made a deep impression on me and raised my spirits more than if I had kicked Herr Krause in the shin. Admiring a "traitor" was a dangerous thing for the shopkeeper to have done. If an Aryan had been overheard voicing such an opinion, he would have found himself in serious trouble. But a Jew! I could not imagine the consequences.

The clock struck four as I hurried along the Danube Canal toward the hotel. I had miscalculated my timing, and I would be late for my appointment with Reichsführer Himmler. And so what? I asked myself. I slowed my pace.

At the front desk, I heard a bell strike the quarter hour. A uniformed clerk scanned a clipboard for my name.

"You are late!" he said with a frigid voice and an even icier stare.

"Yes," I said, without adding, "and so what?"

"You will follow the sergeant."

I had to hurry to keep pace. Halting abruptly he rapped sharply twice on an unmarked door, turned the handle, and entered. I followed. The sound of typing ceased. Over thick-rimmed glasses, a pair of hostile eyes fastened on me. The uniformed secretary looked over at me then down at a desk calendar.

"Be seated!"

The sergeant left. I looked around. The walls were lined with pictures of Hitler in various poses: here triumphant, there with an expression of benevolence, and in another it seemed to me he was fighting constipation. The last photo looked as if he'd just sat on a bee. These thoughts cheered me, and I began to smile.

Still wearing my coat and scarf, I had grown very warm. The room was overheated. As I removed my gloves and scarf, the clamor of the typewriter stopped. I had earned myself a disapproving look. Just then the door opened to admit a distinguished looking officer who held the door at rigid attention for an unremarkable man of average height. I knew this was Himmler, who looked at his watch and then at me. I prepared myself for a rebuke but none came. His watch must have stopped.

"Come in, come in", he said, his arm outstretched in an awkward gesture, not that ridiculous salute. As if he were just resuming a conversation he said, "Now, I don't want you to worry about your father." We were both still standing. He put a hand on my shoulder and continued earnestly, "The führer and I want you to become a good Hitler Youth. That is the best thing you can do for your father!"

Nonsense, I thought, but I answered him with suitable gravity: "I understand, Herr Reichsführer."

"Good. Now I have many pressing matters to attend to, and you must go home to study."

The conversation was over, and I had not even taken off my coat. Himmler steered me toward the door, and I stepped back into the waiting room. He Heil Hitler-ed me and, without waiting for a response, closed the door. In return, I said the traditional Austrian greeting: "*Grüss Gott.*"

Himmler had not heard me, but the secretary had. "You had better learn to say Heil Hitler if you know what is good for you", he spat.

I gave no indication of having heard him. I was beginning to establish what sort of person existed for me and what sort did not. That idiot fell into the second category. I wondered how long that list would grow before sanity returned to my country. Then it came to me suddenly that I had forgotten about the glass eye.

Once outside I looked up at the hotel, wondering if Father's room had a window and whether he could look out of it. Perhaps he could see me? Just in case, I stood for a moment and waved. On the way back home, I took both buses. It was dark, and I was growing hungry.

I had not even closed the door behind me when all three Ottenreiter women rushed toward me from the dining room. Frau Ottenreiter: "Kurti, you did see Himmler himself? What was he like—as dreadful as his reputation?"

Fräulein Alice: "Mother, let me get his coat off first. Kurti, was it all right? Did you manage what we discussed?"

I was assuring her that I had not stamped on Himmler's foot when Grete broke in, "Did you notice his glass eye?"

Usually quiet and unflappable, their reactions surprised me.

"Himmler was boring. I didn't get a chance to say anything more than, 'I understand, Herr Reichsführer', and I'm embarrassed to tell you that I forgot to look at his eye. I wasn't even there long enough to take off my coat."

"But it is after five o'clock. You left almost two hours ago!" Fräulein Alice's tone was almost reproachful, a sure sign that she had been worried.

They led me into the living room and wanted a detailed account of everything that had happened to me from the moment that I had left the apartment. I told them about the scene in the stamp shop and showed them my present. When I repeated the shop-keeper's message to Father, Frau Ottenreiter, close to tears, could only shake her head slowly and say, "Life in this beautiful city has become wretched! It is hard to believe the times in which we are living. How did this happen? We're not a belligerent people. But this violence is everywhere and grows worse daily!"

"Tell us exactly what Himmler said to you", insisted Fräulein Alice.

I repeated Himmler's words.

Her brow furrowed. "He told you not to worry about your father; that he is fine?"

"Fräulein Alice, I am sure Himmler could convince the devil that it is cool in hell."

She got to her feet abruptly. "All right. As I recall you were in the middle of a very interesting scientific experiment, Kurti. Tell me again what it is."

"I am working on a thermometer. It is not exactly a scientific experiment. It's more of a test to see if I can actually make one."

"It sounds fascinating. Show me what you have done so far."

I was happy to have an audience and just as happy to have something else to think about. I put the day behind me.

Saint Nicholas Day came and went, as did Christmas and New Year's. I do not remember any of them. Grandfather was dead and Father was locked away. There was little to celebrate. Mentally, I distanced myself from everything that was not immediate. It kept bad thoughts away. I fervently wished that Father could do the same, but his reality was far different from mine.

Father was confined in a small chamber under the Hotel Metropol's roof. A guard was posted outside his door, and another within. A straw mattress lay on the floor leaving space for the guard, a table, and a chair. He was often awakened at two or three in the morning: drunken guards would foul the toilet and order Father to clean it. His utensils were his toothbrush and towel. Next he was made to brush his teeth, and then he was manhandled back to his room. On other nights, metal objects were struck against the pipes under Father's window. The racket continued until morning's light. He was not permitted a shower for nearly four months. His bank account was frozen, but the cost of three meals a day was deducted from it. The meals came from the café next door—when it was open. When it was closed, Father had nothing to eat. On holidays and on those days when the café was closed, Father had to make do with what he had saved of the previous day's meals, or go without food. I am still grateful that these horrors were hidden from me at the time. What twelve-year-old son could bear such knowledge?

Like a horse with blinders I went though my days. I resolved not to let the tutor affect me. It was my daily challenge to irritate him in some oblique way while wearing a mask of innocence and politeness. Whether or not I succeeded was unimportant. It was the effort that mattered.

Peter Mayer and his family had fled the previous summer. Rudi was sent to boarding school in Bavaria, while I was left with the Ottenreiters. While I had been accustomed to the solitude of an only child, I experienced a deeper kind of loneliness, knowing that I had been erased from the minds of most of those who had known me. I had become anonymous, but in a peculiar way this new status was something of a relief—a resolution. Above all, the Ottenreiters' routine, the regularity of their lives, and their deep faith in God provided a modest sense of well-being—a sense of security.

The Nazi drumbeat grew ever louder. The Sudetenland had already been reclaimed by Germany, and on March 15, 1939, the people of Czechoslovakia woke to find that the Nazis were now the masters of their country and their lives. Why should the National Socialists be satisfied with a small piece of the pie when they could easily have the whole thing? What was to stop them? Who could stop them?

# Munich

Vera was notified that Father would soon be sent out of Austria, and mentally, at least, she began to pack her bags. His destination was Munich, but it was unclear when this transfer would take place. Meanwhile, Vera turned her attention to my situation. I could not be left indefinitely with the Ottenreiters.

After a year with Herr Krause, the time had come for my examination to enter *Hauptschule* (high school). An oral exam consisted of correctly singing all the Nazi songs, and I was given a passing grade.

Vera searched for a high school in Munich that would accept the son of Schuschnigg and was inexpensive—very inexpensive. Father's uncle Professor Hermann Wopfner helped with our expenses, but money was scarce.

First Vera arranged for me to live with Frau Paula Niedermayr, the widow of a distant cousin of Father who lived in Unterhaching with her mother and son. Eight miles from Munich, the town was within reach of the city and its schools. I had never met the Niedermayrs, who were brave and generous to take me under their roof, especially since Vera had, as it were, plucked them from our family tree.

The excellent Catholic boarding school at Ettal in Bavaria had recently been closed by the Reich, so Vera turned to the Munich academy run by the Salesians. Her idea was that a Catholic school would hardly turn away the son of Schuschnigg.

During our tour of the school, Vera was optimistic and encouraging; however after we completed our inspection, I was convinced that the only thing I would learn at the academy was how to treat bedbug bites. The school was more than just run down; it looked like something one might come across in a rural area of the Balkans. Vera was adamant that this was a respectable Catholic school and a solution to my academic needs.

We sat in the office of the school principal, where Vera attempted to win me over. As she continued to extol the merits of the school, a huge water bug crawled down the wall toward the floor. Without speaking I rose, advanced toward the bug, and smashed it. Satisfied, I returned to my seat. Turning to Vera, I matched her determination and said, "Absolutely not!" We bade the Salesians good-bye and left.

Aunt Paula's twenty-one-year-old son, Karlheinz, was my third cousin. The problem of my education was dumped into his lap. He first approached the Luitpold Gymnasium and made the mistake of mentioning my name, which sealed my fate. He subsequently sought the advice of one of his former teachers, a non-Nazi. The professor told him to approach the German Board of Education, requesting admittance for an unnamed Austrian student. Having accomplished this, Karlheinz's next challenge was to find an appropriate school.

The Alte Realgymnasium, a school with a strong academic reputation, had space for another student. Fortunately, the school's principal was in ill health and was being temporarily replaced by the non-Nazi assistant principal, Herr Zettner. Karlheinz was bravely honest with Herr Zettner, who replied, "We do have room for a new student, and I don't see that the admission board needs to know his name."

With a school in Munich and a place to stay in nearby Unterhaching, I could now enjoy the summer. Fräulein Alice, whose previous association with Father had made her unemployable, was accompanying me to the Alt Aussee.

Only thirty miles or so from Saint Gilgen, the Alt Aussee was in the Steiermark, which had a capital city known for its university and a large population of retired government employees. The road to Alt Aussee went over the 3,300-foot-high Potschen Pass that afforded a magnificent view of snow-laden glaciers.

We had been invited to stay with a family whom neither of us knew: Herr Kurt Walter; his wife, Luise; and their two sons, Otto and Waldemar. Vera's far-reaching hand was once again felt.

The Walters had a spacious country house. Built of dark wood, it had a two-tiered bay window with an enormous window box from which flowers spilled down the wall. Best of all, it was within easy walking distance of the lake.

Fräulein Alice and I blended seamlessly into the Walters' household. They graciously made room for the two refugees from Vienna. Herr Walter and his wife were delighted to have Fräulein Alice.

She was an enormous help. Otto and Waldemar were crazy about her. She never scolded. Her long, deliberative looks quietly exercised discipline among us three boys.

The summer ended but not the Third Reich's appetite for lebensraum. When Germany and Russia overran Poland, there was, finally, a reaction: Great Britan and France declared war on Germany. Life on the European continent lost all semblance of normality, and people's lives were no longer their own.

In spite of my family's circumstances, being delivered from Krause and entering the Alte Realgymnasium was like reentering the land of the living. I had forgotten how much I had loved school. My new life had another plus. Having seldom traveled alone, the daily trip from Unterhaching to Munich was a pleasure for me. I realized that I could actually take care of myself. On the other hand, there was my ambiguous situation with the Niedermayrs. I was a dependent relative, and how could one turn down such a person? The Niedermayrs were unfailingly kind to me, and in gratitude I made myself as unobtrusive as possible.

There was just one incident that possibly marred the period during which I was with the Niedermayrs, but Karlheinz was the only one affected by it. As a special treat for me, Aunt Paula had booked tickets for a bus tour of Munich. I knew that Karlheinz could make more entertaining use of his time than overseeing a thirteen-year-old; but being a dutiful son, he consented to go with me.

The tour culminated at the statue of Bavaria. Lady Bavaria, protectress of the arts, is a sixty-two-foot-high statue, and one could climb to the top and look out of her eyes. As it was a school holiday there was a throng of visitors. Karlheinz and I brought up the rear of our group as it entered the statue's base. Scores of legs pumped their way up Bavaria's interior staircase. Halfway to the top, I paused. With a barely audible sigh I leaned against the wall. Karlheinz eyed me suspiciously.

"I am a little tired. You go on. I'll catch up in a few seconds." Karlheinz shot me a disbelieving look but continued on.

Once alone I whipped out my most recent acquisition: a small glass sphere containing "essence of rotten egg". My stink bomb guaranteed an unforgettable experience, but it had to be handled carefully. The sphere was made of glass so thin that the slightest pressure would break it. Stretching my arm straight out, I dropped the small globe. The concrete did the rest. The stench began to rise instantly, and I shot down the stairs; I must have reached the sidewalk in record time. Not wanting to miss the reactions of tourists enjoying the Third Reich, I took up a position at a slight distance from the entrance. Thirty seconds later, masses of groaning and squealing sightseers erupted from the bottom of Bavaria. Among them was Cousin Karlheinz, who had put two and two together and was not amused.

"Karlheinz, it's not healthy to be that color", I said trying to keep a straight face. "You're going to make yourself sick."

"You should be arrested, you maniac!" he hissed at me. "This is perfect. This is really perfect; and with your name! Get away from me. I have no intention of sharing a jail cell with you!"

A little later when his face returned to a more normal color, I attempted to talk to him, but he refused to listen. When we returned to Unterhaching, I felt uneasy because I had no idea whether Karlheinz would tell his mother. I believe he held his tongue; for when I thanked Aunt Paula, truthfully saying that I had not enjoyed myself so much in a long time, she seemed pleased.

After a year and a half in the Gestapo's Hotel Metropol, Father was finally sent to Munich in December 1939. His transfer was due in part to Vera's unceasing petitions and the annoyance they and she had become. Another factor, however, was the state of Father's health. His imprisonment had taken its toll: six feet tall, he weighed about ninety pounds. The Nazis did not want the past chancellor of Austria to die, a martyr, in prison. The move to Munich offered itself as the solution.

My life was vastly improved with a new school and the expectation of being closer to Father. Then something terrible happened: the ailing principal of the Alte Realgymnasium died. The student body gathered two days later to meet his permanent replacement—the very embodiment of the glory and strength of the fatherland, a ramrod-stiff, steely-eyed Nazi wearing one of the party's most prestigious decorations—the Blood Order medal. My name on the school roll would have the same effect on him as a red flag on a bull. I knew that my days at the Alte Realgymnasium were numbered and that I was beyond Herr Zettner's help.

The summons came the next day. I entered the new principal's office, and before I could even close the door, he began: "You, Schuschnigg," he sneered, "are a total disgrace to the Alte Realgymnasium, in fact, to the entire fatherland. You will not be tolerated here one minute longer. Gather your books and get out!"

"Very well, Herr Director. Thank you, Herr Director", I said politely, keeping the tone of my voice level. With a crisp turn and a measured pace, I left his office, gathered my books, returned to Unterhaching and to a very distressed Aunt Paula.

Vera was notified and the school search resumed. Soon, Vera learned about a boys' residence for boarding school students who didn't care to, or couldn't, live at their school. This establishment also had its own tutors. Suitcase in hand, I set out for the Schülerheim Schmitt, which was situated in the well-tended Bogenhausen section on Possartstrasse. Here I would stay for the duration of my secondary education. My visits to the Niedermayrs would be limited to occasional weekends and holidays.

The Schülerheim Schmitt housed twenty-five or thirty out-of-town boys. "Considering the new director of the Alte Realgymnasium, I am not in the least surprised by your situation", said Herr Schmitt as I stood before him. "Since we are more than well into the school year, all of the tutors have long since been assigned; therefore, it falls to me to tutor you myself."

A kind man and an excellent teacher, Herr Schmitt, together with the occasional substitute, produced remarkable results. At the Schülerheim Schmitt, instruction was untainted by propaganda, and this was, for the times, a rarity. During my stay there, I developed an indifference to events—Christmas, Easter, birthdays, deaths— perhaps as part of my survival. I also came to know Munich well, exploring it by streetcar and by a very old bicycle with rusting handlebars and bald tires that conveyed me through parts of the city unreachable by public transport.

Vera had moved into a boarding house just behind the Gestapo prison in a converted section of the Wittelsbacher Palace. Bogenhausen was some distance. I went each Tuesday by streetcar to see her. Vera had obtained permission to see Father once a week for about two hours. Vera kept his mind and hopes alive as she presented the possibility of a future, of a life beyond prison. In Vienna

Father had been held in isolation. He was permitted neither news-papers nor radio—no contact with the outside world. Munich was an enormous change. He was allowed reading material, and Vera took him my letters.

On most Sundays I would pick up Vera at her boarding house for Mass. The church in the Odeonsplatz was a five-minute walk. Preferable would have been the Frauenkirche on the Domplatz to attend Mass by Cardinal Michael von Faulhaber. An opponent of the Nazis, he was called the world's greatest pulpit orator. An army chaplain during World War I, Faulhaber was the first cleric to be awarded the Iron Cross. He became archbishop of Munich in 1917 and preached against the Communists and the 1919 uprising. A cardinal since 1921, he was already denouncing the Nazis for their persecution of the Jews in 1933. The esteem in which he was held by the Catholic Church and the public certainly kept him out of a concentration camp. As much as Vera admired him, her desire to hear his sermons was tempered by the certainty that the Gestapo had knowledge of her whereabouts at all times. I knew from Herr Walter that the same was true for me. I had been warned about which conversations were safe to have in public.

One day, I set out on my ancient bicycle for the apartment of my new friend Peter Schlessinger, who lived with his mother on the Prinzregentenstrasse. The weather was brisk, but I was enjoy-ing the day. I became aware of a column of vehicles overtaking me, and I saw that it was a motorcade. I turned my head and found myself locking eyes with none other than Adolf Hitler himself. I was completely dumbfounded and momentarily forgot that I was on a bicycle. I swerved and this brought me very close to the open Mercedes. I steadied myself and looked again, observing his fanati-cally gleaming, piercing blue eyes and his fleshy nose that swelled over a preposterous mustache. Then an absurd thing happened: he raised his forearm—a gesture that reminded me of the American Indian greeting—and then was gone.

I approached Peter's apartment, knowing what I would find across the street: Hitler's empty Mercedes. My friend Peter and his mother had the misfortune of living directly opposite Hitler's Munich apart-ment. Whenever he was in residence, all the neighbors had to lock their attics and basements and hand the keys over to the police.

Those with a view of his apartment building were required to close their windows and pull down the shades. Frau Schlessinger declared that the arrangement suited her perfectly: "The less I see of that grotesque little man, the better!"

Frau Schlessinger was a Catholic from Alsace-Lorraine, but her husband was Jewish. For her sake and his son's, Herr Schlessinger had made his wife divorce him. When I first met Peter, his father was waiting for his official exit papers, the acquisition of which was being arranged by one of Vera's acquaintances. Having lived in Munich before, as the wife of Maj. Gen. Count Leopold Fugger, Vera had a wide range of friends and acquaintances. She knew an official who was considered a decent Nazi: the man apparently had a conscience, and Vera pressed Herr Schlessinger's case with him. There was money, she assured him, for whatever had to be done. Had Herr Schlessinger been a simple man without means, eventually he would have been marked for transportation to a concentration camp; but Herr Schlessinger not only came from a well-to-do family, he also was a highly successful timber trader and wealthy in his own right. He could afford the cost of freedom, but the process was taking considerable time. Meanwhile, people around him were disappearing. He watched as friends and acquaintances were removed for "relocation".

By the time the papers finally arrived, Herr Schlessinger was an absolute wreck. After a final farewell to his wife and son, and a brief telephone call to Vera, he raced to catch his train for Switzerland. From Munich he traveled to Innsbruck, where he needed to change trains. From there, Switzerland and safety were just two and a half hours away. Exiting the train at the Innsbruck station, he saw a double column of SS soldiers coming down the platform toward him and panicked. The anxieties of life as a Jew in Munich, the wait for the travel documents, and the workings of his own imagination must have overwhelmed him at that moment, for Herr Schlessinger took out his pistol and shot himself in the temple. The suicide took the SS unit completely by surprise—they too had only been changing trains. Tragedies such as that of Herr Schlessinger were becoming commonplace. One braced oneself for bad news, for bad news was as inevitable as was the Nazi greeting, "Heil Hitler!"

In addition to Peter, Walter Treuleben and sometimes his exceptionally good-looking sister, Gertie, took part in my exploration of Munich. The Treulebens lived in an apartment just around the corner from the Schülerheim. On weekends we would travel about either on foot or by streetcar, and I was often invited to dine with them.

One Saturday we returned late, having lost track of the time. Walter and Gertie jumped off the streetcar and raced home to accompany their parents to a birthday party. Rather than return to the empty Schülerheim Schmitt, I decided to tour the area. The only object of any interest was the small chapel behind Saint Georg Church. It was dark, and moonlight filtered through the trees. I came to the deserted chapel and noticed a pale light flickering through the window. Cupping my hands around my eyes, I pressed my face against it. I made out a large indistinct mass. After a few moments of intense concentration, I jumped back from the window in shock. I looked through the window again, and it was still there: a large cart piled high with the corpses of German soldiers. Body was heaped upon body. Arms and legs stuck out at odd angles, and all their feet were bare. What had happened to their boots? In the sputtering candlelight inside, those lifeless faces looked terrifying. Why had they been left there like that, sloppily stacked like peddlers' wares? Did the parents of these soldiers, "the future of the fatherland", know that their sons were lying here like this? From somewhere an owl hooted. I sprinted all the way back to the Schülerheim Schmitt. I never again ventured in the direction of that chapel.

The remainder of the school year passed quickly until the spring of 1940, when Vera told me, during one of my regular Tuesday afternoon visits, that the next day I was going to be allowed to see Father. Vera had worn down the commandant of the Wittelsbacher prison. I would have half an hour. Who knew, when Father and I had bidden each other good-bye after Christmas in 1937, that we would not see each other for more than two years? Vera gave me a copy of Ferdinand Raimund's play "Der Alpen König und der Menchenfeind" to take to Father; and clutching it as if it were a priceless object, I returned to the Schülerheim in a state of elation.

I hardly slept that night and was useless with Herr Schmitt the next day. Apologizing, I told him about my visit to Father in a few hours. I was immediately dismissed for the rest of the day and went directly to the streetcar stop. Predictably, I had forgotten the book for Father, and I didn't even notice. I was just in time to catch the streetcar, and I arrived in the city before the lunch hour.

Afraid that I might be turned away if I were too early, I strolled around the Wittelsbacher area. I rejected the idea of an unannounced visit to Vera. She was not fond of surprises. Finally, casting caution to the wind, I walked through the entrance of the Wittelsbacher prison, gave my name, and stated the purpose of my visit. The guards were more than civil; they were actually polite. Following their instructions, I presented myself to a guard who unlocked Father's door.

When I saw Father I tried not to show my astonishment at his shocking appearance. Vera had tried to prepare me, and I was almost fourteen—old enough to know that mental and physical suffering change people—nevertheless, I was simply not expecting him to look so altered.

The thirty minutes flew by in a blur. Walking toward the streetcar stop, I felt a bolt of electricity go through me: I realized I had forgotten the book from Vera and was overwhelmed by my stupidity. I spent the rest of the day in a torment of indecision. In the end, I decided to return and throw myself, my stupidity, and the book on the mercy of the guard. It was wiser and much safer than facing Vera.

The next day after finishing my lessons, I rode the streetcar back to Wittelsbacher. I took a deep breath before approaching the guard, the same man who had admitted me yesterday, and he recognized me. I thanked him for letting me see Father yesterday and thrust the book toward him. "Would you please give this to my father? I stupidly forgot to bring it with me yesterday."

To my total amazement, he replied, "A boy should be able to see his father. You can give it to him yourself."

I knew I heard him speak but didn't think I understood what he said. I looked at him blankly for a moment.

"Come. Follow me", he said and began walking down the corridor. I hesitated. He glanced back and with a smile said, "Well, come on! Let's not keep your father waiting."

I raced down the hall after him. He unlocked and opened the cell door. Father was speechless with surprise. Turning to the guard, I could only say, "Thank you very, very much."

"You come back whenever you want." Then he added with a wink, "Just don't overdo it."

It had taken Vera years to get permission for me to see Father, and we had assumed that yesterday's meeting would be the only one. Now, this good-hearted man had given me back my father. Who knew there could be so much kindness in a German prison guard? Thus began my weekly visits to Father.

# Sachsenhausen

There was no question of my remaining in Munich the summer of 1940.

The Schülerheim Schmitt was a substantial expense that could be eliminated until the fall. After a brief return to Vienna, I would join the Walters again on the Alt Aussee. Unlike last year, I would travel alone, for in April Fräulein Alice had married Walter Lillie, a pharmacist from Steiermark. He too now lived with the Ottenreiters.

Before I left Munich, Vera had given me a parting present: the news that the Wittelsbacher School had accepted me for the autumn term. It was one of the best schools in Munich and one of the very few with neither political nor military affiliations. With Herr Schmitt's help at the Schülerheim, I had achieved the highest marks in the entrance examination at the Wittelsbacher School. Vera and Father were very pleased, and I was deliriously happy—another chance to be just a boy at a normal school. I left for the Alt Aussee knowing that when I returned to Munich, it would be to a new life, one that included both Papa and school.

At the end of the summer just before the school term began, I went to Vienna. I wanted to visit not only the Ottenreiters but also Herr Rittmeister, Uncle Willy, who wanted to be kept abreast of things. Like many others, Uncle Willy missed life as it had been in Vienna, and his conversation was full of comparisons to the past. The city had not yet suffered deprivations. Compared with what they would encounter, the Viennese were living in good times.

Uncle Willy always felt compelled to feed me, and we went invariably to Demel's. He enjoyed seeing me and also being seen with me. Appearing with me in public was a wordless condemnation of our fellow citizens who had made me, as my father's son, an outcast. I thought Uncle Willy a brave man for standing up for us. He was also a generous man, for there was the little something that he always slipped into my pocket. Although I was now given more than fifty groschen a week, my allowance seldom lasted me very long. Uncle Willy's "loose change" made a big difference in my life.

With the luxury of regular visits to Father and of again being a normal schoolboy, the days back in Munich went quickly. I was thriving at the Wittelsbacher School. I was happy, and I was careful not to look back.

A number of other lodgers at the Schülerheim attended the Wittelsbacher School. On most days, shortly after seven, we took the streetcar together. It was a half-hour trip from the Schülerheim to the school. When I was late, I rode my bicycle. It was a quicker trip by bicycle but also something of a luxury. Replacement parts for my dilapidated bicycle were not available.

I was bicycling home one day when the skies opened. This was no ordinary Munich rain. Sheets of water literally blew sideways; the boundary between sidewalk and street was simply obliterated. I had reached the Lenbachplatz when I decided to pull over. I didn't care about being soaked to the skin. It was the risk of being run over by a car or the trolley that mattered.

As I stood under the covered entrance of a bank, I could almost hear new rust growing on my poor bicycle. I waited twenty minutes for the rain to let up. When it showed no sign of doing so, I realized that I had to find somewhere to store the bicycle and return for it the next day. I saw a shed around the building, the sort of structure in which garbage cans were usually kept. Behind its two metal containers there was just enough space for my bicycle. I parked it against the wall and carefully replaced the containers. After closing and latching the wooden door, I shook myself off and set out for the trolley.

The next day dawned sunless but dry. After school I made my way to the shed and unlatched the door. The bicycle was gone. I walked up and down the street, circled the entire block, and returned to the shed but no bicycle. I had one option left: go into the bank and inquire. I went inside.

Near the doors sat a man who did not look particularly busy despite the stacks of papers on his oversize desk. I kept my eyes on him as I approached. He was rolling his fountain pen around on the desk blotter. "Excuse me", I began. He slapped his hand down over the pen. "My bicycle seems to have been removed from the side of your building. It was raining so hard yesterday that I had to leave it inside the wastebin shelter. I wonder if you might have seen it."

For a moment the fellow seemed not to have heard me, then a scowl spread across his face. I wondered which disturbed him more: the trivial question or that his daydreaming had been interrupted. "Young man, I am particularly busy, and I have no time for your bicycle. I suggest you find it yourself. And what do you mean leaving a bicycle on bank premises in the first place? This is not a parking lot. What is your name?"

"Sorry to bother you", I said as I hurried toward the door. Now I had only streetcars and my feet to travel the city.

A few days later, I told Vera about the bicycle. She listened quietly. Then she said, "Well, the bike is gone. I can't replace it, but I do have a present for you. Before the end of winter, you are going to have either a baby brother or a baby sister."

I could only gape at her.

"Well, aren't you happy?"

"Happy? I'm over the moon with happiness!" I shouted, giving her a big hug. It was true. This was one of the greatest gifts of my life. I had long ago given up wishing for a brother or sister. Not having had much exposure to expectant mothers, I was unsure of what I should be doing.

"May I get you a glass of water? Here! I can put this pillow under your feet. How would that be?"

She laughed, really laughed at me. It was wonderful to see her happy. Things were going to be a lot better now—I was sure of it. I did every chore I could think of for Vera. She seemed unchanged, composed, and as ever, in command. And Father? Father was quietly happy.

Father and I talked mainly about my studies and friends at the Schülerheim Schmitt. I could see how satisfying this was for him, so I told him everything that came to mind, even about the goldfish I swallowed on a dare. I was not used to having Father's full attention. I had never before been able to spend so much time with him.

Life had regained some of its flavor. No, much more than that had happened: I had regained my father, and now I was going to have a new baby brother or sister. The Nazis no longer oversaw my education. Instead, I had the Wittelsbacher School and the Schülerheim Schmitt, both full of decent fellows. God was listening! Life, in fact, was wonderful.

It was settled that I would go back to Fräulein Alice and the Ottenreiters for the Christmas holidays. The Schülerheim emptied out, the Niedermayrs had other relatives coming to stay with them, and Vera had her children who wanted to be with her for Christmas. It was strange to think that they were my brother and sisters. All four were scattered in schools throughout Bavaria, and I had seen none of them since 1938.

On March 23, 1941, Vera gave birth to a baby girl, Maria Dolores, who would be known as Sissi, and I was ecstatic. Vera brought her home to the boarding house. Owned by longtime family friend Countess Kuka Harrach, the boarding house was occupied by good, decent, reliable people. Vera was safe and certainly not alone. They were people on whom she could count.

I went to see Vera and Sissi at every opportunity. I had never before been exposed to anyone as small as Sissi, but after mastering the art of diapering I turned into a competent babysitter. The prison commandant allowed Vera to bring Sissi when she visited Father. She was a golden child—blonde, blue-eyed, and from the very beginning full of smiles.

If the officials whom Vera had harassed into submission thought that the move to Munich had silenced her, they were mistaken. After Sissi's birth, Vera launched a new offensive. If Father could be moved from Vienna to Munich, he could be moved once more. Again she wore someone down. The authorities agreed to move Father to a location where Vera could join him. She began talking about the move. Friends had told her that there were many confiscated houses and estates that had already been converted into holding areas.

The end of the school year was soon upon me. I was consistently at the head of my class—my marks reflecting the satisfaction that I felt with my life. I don't think Father expected anything less; both Father and Uncle Artur had excelled at their studies. Still, Father was pleased, and my teachers were practically patting me on the back in delight. It was a good way to end the first year at my new school.

After stopping briefly in Vienna, I went on to the Alt Aussee. Over the years, Otto, Waldemar, and I had become used to one another's company and were good friends. The summer of 1941 was unlike all other recent summers: at the end of it I could look forward to my family and a school that I loved.

On my last evening, Herr Walter said he wanted to have a talk with me. When I entered the room that he used as his library, I was told to close the door. Herr Walter reached far back into a drawer. When he faced me again, I could feel the blood draining from my face. He held a pistol in his hand and took a step toward me.

"This is to be a secret between us, Kurt", he said in a quiet, confident voice. "You are not to tell anyone that I have given you this— neither of my sons and certainly not my wife. They wouldn't understand. Someday it may be of use to your father."

"Yes, Herr Walter."

I knew none of the Walters would understand; I did not understand. I didn't like guns but knew that Herr Walter was right— maybe my father would need it.

"In here", he said, holding up a cotton sack tied at the neck, "is an ammunition clip."

As I watched, he wrapped the small Browning handgun with another piece of cotton cloth. Ammo clip and gun were then wrapped up in heavy paper and tied with twine, making it look like an ordinary parcel.

"Take this up to your room and pack it with your clothes."

As I was wondering where I was going to store the thing, eerily Herr Walter put the same question to me. It made me jump.

"I can put it in my closet at school—it's my best place."

"That will have to do. Under no circumstances are you ever to show it to any of your friends at school. Do you understand?"

"Yes, sir. I understand." I would bury it in the closet and try to forget why I had it. That was the last time I saw Herr Walter.

In November Vera was informed that Father would be moved in December. She and Sissi would be allowed to accompany him; however, they were not going to a confiscated property but to something called a concentration camp. It was situated between the towns of Sachsenhausen and Oranienburg, outside the city of Berlin.

Berlin! That was a world away. So Father would be out of reach once again, but this time Vera and Sissi would be leaving too. I felt as if I had been kicked in the stomach. When Father had been taken away from me the last time, I had at least been in Vienna with the Ottenreiters. I forced myself to remember that I was older now and more responsible. I had to pull myself together.

As the moving day approached, my studies began to suffer. I could not concentrate. Unless I was directly under a teacher's supervision, my thoughts were never in the classroom. I couldn't even say where my mind went: just out, far away. My brain seemed to have a will of its own; it simply refused to address practical necessities. One of my teachers had a phrase for this predicament: mental wanderlust. This failed to appease Vera, who had made and was making many sacrifices for Father; she was right to expect more of me. I was more disappointed in myself than she was.

I increased my visits to Father as often as I dared. Afterward I would go to see Vera and Sissi. I didn't have confidence that the Nazis would keep their word, but my belief in Vera's determination was absolute. As I knew it would, the call came. The three of them would be leaving just before Christmas, but there was one consolation. I would be allowed to visit them for holidays and in the summer.

Addressing my disappointment at their move, Vera tried to reason with me. "Kurti, contrary to your obvious reaction, you should be happy that your father will be out of that terrible Gestapo prison. His daily life will become so much better."

Of course, she was right. I was being selfish.

I made my last visit on the day before their departure and pretended a happiness that I certainly didn't feel. On the streetcar back to the Schülerheim Schmitt, I fought back my feelings of loss. Trying to ignore the stinging behind my eyelids, I stared out of the window at a group of boys on their bicycles and wished for my old bicycle. I began to calculate how long it would take me to save the money to buy a secondhand bicycle. My allowance was now one mark a week. Assuming the lowest possible price for a bicycle and some money spent on necessities, I figured that I would be about thirty-five years old before I could buy a bicycle.

A week later, I packed and went to the railroad station to catch a train for Berlin. I was to spend three days with Uncle Artur, Aunt Marianne, and their children in their new apartment. Against all odds, Uncle Artur had been appointed curator of the Berlin Museum. With doctorates in art history, philosophy, and music; no political interests; and a German-born wife, he was not unqualified for the post. That he was Father's brother made his appointment something of a miracle, however. Then his life changed shape with bewildering suddenness. After moving to Berlin, Uncle Artur was informed that he could better serve the Third Reich in the Luftwaffe. Too old to be a pilot, he was given the task of editing films produced for Luftwaffe pilot training.

Certain that my reputation as a babysitter had preceded me, I was prepared to help Aunt Marianne with her children. Young Artur, the oldest, was nine years my junior. Next came four-year-old Anna—called Dicki—and then the baby, Verena, who was a year older than Sissi. Watching Munich disappear from the train window, I thought how good it would be to live in a normal home again and also have a new city to explore.

When Vera arrived to take me to Sachsenhausen, I was nervously waiting with my suitcase packed and ready to go. No sooner had she stepped into the apartment than I began tugging at her arm. When Aunt Marianne offered her coffee, I answered for both of us, "No, thank you. We have to catch the train."

"Kurti! There are plenty of trains. In fact, there are trains all day long!" said Vera, surprised.

"But they will be full of people!"

It was Christmas Eve 1941, and Vera gave in to my impatience. We left for the railway station where she had arrived just an hour earlier. The Sachsenhausen-Oranienburg Camp was about twenty miles from Berlin. As we boarded the train, Vera explained that the main entrance to the camp was closer to Oranienburg but "our" entrance was closer to the Sachsenhausen stop. The camp consisted of about ten thousand people confined within its walls, she said.

The locomotive and its string of passenger and freight cars snaked through the bleak winter landscape. In wartime Germany there was no heat in the cars, and I could see my breath. In didn't bother me, because nothing else mattered besides the fact that this would be my first Christmas with Father in four years. In my excitement I nearly bounced off the seat.

"Sit still, Kurti," warned Vera, "or you will wind up on the floor!" I paid little attention to the passing countryside; instead I concentrated on the stops between the main railroad station and our destination, marking every detail in my memory for a return trip.

The German railway system had a reputation for punctuality, but it had begun to experience delays as a consequence of Allied activity. Our journey, however, proceeded without interruption, and our train arrived on time. I stepped down from the train first and turned to help Vera when it struck me how tired she looked.

"I am going to help you take care of Sissi", I said, smiling up at her. "I helped Aunt Marianne with the cousins. She told me I did a good job too!"

"That will make me very happy! I would love to take a nap this afternoon before I make Christmas dinner."

It had never occurred to me that Vera might be able to cook. In fact, I could not imagine her in a kitchen. I had always thought her too beautiful, too glamorous for such chores. Her lovely hands with lacquered nails seemed to belong to a world quite remote from kitchens.

The wind had picked up. I could feel it at our backs, pushing us along. After a relatively short walk, we approached the corner of a high stone wall and made our way toward the entrance about halfway down. The guard tower and guards were clearly visible. A blustery wind was blowing, and stray snowflakes had begun to float down. I thought it a good sign; snow in the country is clean. I had no idea of the human misery waiting on the other side of that wall.

The guards incuriously watched us. I thought this odd; surely, visitors here were an uncommon sight. A door swung open, and a guard ushered us into a room with a stark interior: a table and four chairs, a coal stove, and a single metal cabinet. The one window afforded a view of the camp.

After a brief search, we followed the guard through a door to a gravel corridor between two concrete walls. On one side was the high common wall with the inner camp. Both walls were topped with electrified barbed wire. The guard led us to the door of "Doctor Auster". Since his arrest Father's real name had not been used—a useless endeavor for his face was easily recognizable. The guard unlocked the wooden door and stepped aside allowing us to enter. The door slammed shut behind us. The noise of the key turning in the lock had a sound of finality to it.

I found myself standing on bare earth, looking at a small cottage surrounded by the concrete wall. There were two small dormer windows under an A-shaped roof and, below them, two slightly larger windows. All were without shutters. The windows on the second floor barely cleared the wall in front of the building. Something told me that there was nothing one would ever want to see through them.

The front door opened, and Father stood before us with little Sissi in his arms and a huge smile on his face. In no time at all, he had covered the distance between us, handed Sissi to Vera, and hugged me. I could feel all his bones in that embrace, but the arms around me were as strong as ever. It was wonderful to be home.

# Summer Vacation

Christmas 1941 had seen the world change again. Hitler had reacted to the United States declaring war on Japan by declaring war on the United States. Many believed that with the Americans finally joining the Allies, Germany could not win the war.

That Christmas also marked my first conversation with Vera in which I was treated as a responsible adult. While Sissi slept and Father read, Vera called me into the kitchen. "Sit down, Kurti," she said, "I want to talk to you about our situation. I need every bit of leverage I can muster on your father's behalf. I am writing a letter to Hitler, offering him your electric trains, toy soldiers, and whatever other toys are in storage for the poor children of the Reich."

"He can have every last one of them, but do you think that these things are really interesting enough?" She made no reply, and so I went on. "What would tempt him is the Vermeer."

I had learned about this piece of her family's history from Rudi. His grandfather had inherited the jewel of the Czernin art collection—Vermeer's celebrated work *The Art of Painting*, also referred to as *The Painter in His Studio*. It depicted an artist, said to be Vermeer himself, painting a blue-robed young woman holding a book in one hand and a trombone in the other. The masterpiece seemed to me to be a far greater enticement than my collection of toys, even if it wasn't for the poor children of the Third Reich. I was completely unprepared for what Vera said next.

"Kurti, you know I am considered a non-person. She paused and focused on a point somewhere beyond my awareness. Taking a deep breath, she said, "The painting is gone. The Nazis already have it." Her younger brother had been advised that if the painting were not for sale it would be confiscated.

The loss was devastating. I had heard Vera refer to the painting as their "future". As I considered the implications of this revelation, I wondered if Rudi knew. He had told me that in 1935 Andrew W. Mellon, one of America's richest men, had offered a million dollars for the painting, but Austrian law did not allow any "national treasure" to leave the country.

I watched the tears well up in Vera's eyes and searched desperately for something reassuring to say. She got up, went to the sink, and began to busy herself with her chores. I went to her, patted her arm, and said, "Please don't cry. Somehow, it will be all right. We know the Allies will defeat Hitler. They will return the painting."

Vera gave me a hug and smoothed my hair. "You are right. I too think that—I'm just being silly. But I am still writing to Hitler and offering him your trains and soldiers. With any luck you'll also get them back after the war."

We looked at each other and both laughed. The führer was offered my electric trains, my hundreds of tin soldiers, and whatever else there was for the poor children of the Reich. In the end, Vera's effort was in vain, for the premise was flawed: there were no poor children in Hitler's Third Reich.

At the Wittelsbacher School my grades began to plummet, and my report cards were becoming painful to read. My teachers began having chats with me. They were kind, but baffled. I was not sick, had not suffered a terrible accident, and no new catastrophe had interrupted my life—yet something was wrong. I felt Father's disappointment in my grades keenly. He said little about it in his letters, but it became increasingly clear that Vera was more than a little unhappy about my lackluster performance. A school such as the Wittelsbacher imposed considerable demands on our resources. There were also the expenses attached to the Schülerheim Schmitt.

These expenses Vera herself had helped us to bear. She had been born into an aristocratic life of privilege, and her father's family had been rich for centuries. Her mother was by birth a von Hohenlohe. Vera had a small income that she used to improve our circumstances. She believed that anyone who looked and acted downtrodden would be treated as such and held her head up. Her spirit and courage were contagious and had an effect even in the camp. I hated to disappoint her.

The prison at Sachsenhausen brought us close to Berlin, where Vera continued to press for Father's release with an immense amount of planning, energy, and imagination. She was not discouraged by Nazi bullying or affected by Nazi charm, such as it was. Nor did she did linger on the lower slopes of the hierarchy; she directed all her efforts at the highest authorities.

One of her contacts came by way of her new obstetrician. Doctor Rust was the son-in-law of the famous stage actress Olga Tschechowa and was considered both a very good doctor and a gentleman. Better still, one of Doctor Rust's patients was Emmy Sonnemann, the vivacious and blonde stage star who had married Hermann Göring. Rust's proximity to Hitler's second in command made him more than irresistible; and in no time at all, Vera began to campaign on a new front.

Doctor Rust was not unmoved by Vera's plight, which had become famous. The English magazine *Sketch* had published an article about Vera that included a full-page picture of her. The story declared that she had married Father in the presence of 150 German storm troopers and made other equally extravagant claims. In the United States, *Time* magazine put Father on its cover and ran a long article inside. As was to be expected, many of the facts in *Time* were also incorrect because no one outside the Nazi hierarchy had access to the truth. These errors were nothing compared with the monstrous falsehoods circulating in the Reich: Father was said to have several villas and bulging bank accounts in other parts of the world and to be living in seclusion somewhere in the heart of Europe, protected by the Nazis. In these fabrications one could detect the hand of Joseph Goebbels, the Nazi's brilliant propaganda minister.

Doctor Rust offered to raise the subject of the Schuschniggs during Frau Göring's next visit. Subsequently, he said that Frau Göring had been intrigued by Vera's voluntary presence in Sachsenhausen and had expressed surprise that Sissi was also at the camp. It is difficult to know whether this conversation had any material consequences for our lives. Doctor Rust's effort on our behalf was, nevertheless, another instance of selfless kindness freely given, and at a time when it was unsafe to help those who had fallen on the wrong side of the Third Reich.

As the summer vacation approached, my spirits soared. Father had taken to correcting my letters with red ink and returning them. Since we would be together during the summer, I would gain at least a temporary relief from the red marks. One obstacle remained: my annual progress report. I wistfully recalled the old days with

Purzel; I might have been able to claim that he had accidentally chewed up the report. I even contemplated losing it. In the end, I accepted the inevitable.

A summer without the Walters and the Ottenreiters would be a curious experience; I had become so accustomed to being among them. For the first time since before Mother's death, I would pass an entire summer without so much as a glimpse of Fräulein Alice. I would miss her.

I was not to join my family as soon as the summer holidays began. My services and those of all sixteen-year-old boys were required by the fatherland. There was a shortage of farm workers, and Wittelsbacher students were assigned to two weeks of picking hops. In the company of the other sixteen-year-olds from Wittelsbacher, I took the short train ride to the nearby hops region of Hallertau. In groups of five, we waited at the railway station. Our names were called, and we stepped forward in turn. Our host farmer looked at each of us as one might look at cows at a cattle auction. My 110-pound frame did not impress him favorably. He turned to the supervisor, a woman.

"That last one", he said, jerking his thumb back in my direction, "is so skinny that one good puff of wind would carry him away. Give me another one."

Four pairs of eyes regarded me enviously, and for one fleeting moment I could smell freedom.

"The assignments have been made", the woman said. "You take all of them, or they go elsewhere."

Our farmer stood there, irresolute. Not ten seconds later, another unhappy farmer complained loudly about a prospective picker's size. This picker was so fat that just bending over was going to be a challenge for him; there was also the cost of feeding the stout youth. The woman supervisor stared icily at this farmer and turned to leave. Both men now quickly accepted their bad luck. With a tone of finality, our host farmer told us to climb into the back of his wagon. He flicked the reins against the horse's neck, and we were off.

I consoled myself with the thought that this too would pass. If one considered the matter more objectively, there really were several positive aspects to this two-week sojourn on a farm. The food should be good and plentiful, and we were to be paid for our work—fifty pfennigs a basket. No one would grow rich, but after two weeks it would add up. A book for Father would be a nice surprise, and I hoped to find something that would please Vera. It was easy to make Sissi happy; she liked anything. I would get her an inflatable ball. As we drove along in the bright sunshine, I began to feel quite cheerful.

We arrived at a large farmhouse, and out came the farmer's wife. She was sturdy and graying, and her face seemed more deeply lined than her husband's. There was kindness in her eyes, and her attitude was more welcoming than anything we had encountered so far. We were shown to the extra room on the ground floor where we were all to stay. We shoved our small suitcases or sacks under our cots and set off for a tour of the hops plots.

None of us had ever seen hops. Their vines grew up along a series of sturdy wooden poles six feet high and angled into the ground. The hops snaked upward and then laced themselves through the grid of webbing that stretched over the earth below. Picking them was easy; one simply stripped off the fruit. The farmer pulled down an overhead vine and with his calloused hands plucked several of the fuzzy, green clusters. They seemed to me a long way from beer.

We rose before the sun and were dropped off at our assigned plots. Before he left, the farmer gave me a long look. I carried one of the four huge, empty baskets to the corner of my plot and set to work.

After stripping a portion of the climbing hops, I pulled the corresponding vine from the grid. When the furry green hops covered the bottom of the basket, I began to calculate how much time I would need to fill it. The morning sun was now beating down on my bare head, and I wished I had brought a hat. My hands had begun to itch. I went on with my work, but the itch persisted. I tried to work more quickly and began to drop the hops on the ground instead of putting them in the basket. Soon, every inch of my exposed skin itched.

We had been advised to take long pants and long-sleeved shirts as well as sturdy shoes and socks. I was not going to slave away under the summer sun in long pants and long-sleeved shirts, so I packed shorts and short-sleeved shirts. These, I realized, were a terrible mistake. They were also probably the reason for the farm-er's long look. I considered my situation: could I endure this dis-comfort for two weeks? Scratching only exacerbated the itch. I racked my brains, but no solution presented itself. I was certain of one thing: the farmer must not be justified in his initial impression of my prospects as a hops picker.

I gritted my teeth and continued to work. When the farmer's wife arrived with my lunch, I had gotten through a respectable amount of picking. But my arms and no doubt my face had turned a bright red. I did not allow myself the temporary relief of scratch-ing them in her presence. Her glance took in my reddened skin and my basket of hops. She said I was doing a good job and moved on to the next plot. By the end of the day, I had filled one and a half baskets.

We took stock of the day at dinner. The three dark-haired boys had suffered not at all. But fair-haired George's face and hands bore evidence of torments similar to mine.

"How are you?" I asked him.

He rested his forearms on the table and leaned toward me. He whispered hoarsely, "Honestly, I might have to run away. I don't know how long I can stand this."

This made me feel much better.

"But you look worse", he added. I had to admit the justice of this observation.

"My mother told me to take a hat. I said I'd rather get sunstroke than be the only boy here with a hat on."

We both sat there thinking what a wonderful invention the hat was. In our room after dinner, I pulled out a deck of cards I had brought and asked if anyone wanted to play skat. The game required only three players, so the other boys took turns. I played every game. After all, they were my cards.

After soaking my face and arms in a sink of cold water, I stum-bled to my cot. A long-sleeved shirt and a pair of full-length pants had been laid out for me. I would have leapt for joy if I had had the strength. Instead, I dropped onto the bed and fell asleep.

I went out the next day armored in my new clothes. There was no question that they helped, but by the end of the day I was once again frantically scratching. There appeared to be no protection against the hops. They seemed to find their way to my skin no matter how careful I was. When we knocked off work on the third day, I had begun to think of fleeing with George. At dinner George was in a subdued state of excitement. He claimed to have had an enlightening conversation with a neighboring farmer's twelve-year-old son.

"You were enlightened by a twelve-year-old? George, the sun has gotten to you."

"Wait until you hear!" He leaned conspiratorially toward me, looked both ways and said, "This boy came over and watched me pick hops for a while. Then he said, 'Looks like you got a pretty bad case of hops itch. You shouldn't be touching them.' I told him I didn't particularly have a choice in the matter. Then he said, 'What if you did have a choice?' When I asked him what he meant, he said, 'How would you like to buy baskets of picked hops?' Well, I took another look at this kid and wondered if he were just trying to be a smart aleck. 'Already picked by whom?' I asked him. The boy said that he and some of the other farmers' sons had been picking their own hops a little at a time and were willing to sell them for seventy-five pfennigs a basket. If those run out, they can come and pick our plots for us. What do you think of that?"

I thought it the best news I had had since arriving. We were paid fifty pfennigs a basket. These substitute pickers wanted seventy-five. How to find eleven times twenty-five pfennigs? Having long since spent my allowance, I had only my daily wages, and these amounted to a paltry one and a half reichsmarks. How was I going to raise the rest of the money? I turned to George.

"Would you buy my cards from me, please?"

His father was a wealthy industrialist, and George always had plenty of money.

"How much do you need?"

"I have exactly a mark fifty. I'm short two marks seventy-five for the balance of the two weeks."

"So, two marks seventy-five pfennig and I own the cards? Done!"

Other than an early release from hops picking, nothing could have made me happier. George was more than a good fellow. I knew he did not really need those cards, and at two marks seventy-five he was being robbed. So, our baskets—George's and mine—were filled daily.

I passed the time by picking whatever hops were within reach of the stool upon which I sat. And when my stint in the fatherland's hops fields finally drew to a close, I headed north.

That second journey to Sachsenhausen-Oranienburg was not as gloomy as the previous one. Despite the war, German farmers went about their work; the plowed checkers of rich, brown earth were a soothing sight. I arrived at Sachsenhausen to the sight of fresh, green grass and leafy lindens. At the gate, the same guard as before admitted me.

"Here you are again! Must be happy to be out of school for the summer, eh?"

Coming from Fräulein Alice or Liesl such a greeting would not have been out of place, but here it was positively startling.

"Yes, I certainly am", I replied, trying to conceal my surprise.

I put my suitcase on the guardroom table and slowly reached to undo the clasps when the guard, placing his hand on the top of the suitcase, said, "That's all right. You can go on through."

I was careful not to show my relief. The second guard locked the door behind me, and I stepped once again into this other world. There was Father, digging. And from what I had once thought barren soil there now sprouted green shoots.

"Kurti."

I dropped my suitcase and hugged Papa. He looked twice his age, but the listlessness produced by the years of confinement in Vienna and Munich seemed to have dissipated.

"Papa, I am so happy to see you! Tell me, how are Sissi and Mami?"

"Fine. They are just fine. Come inside and unpack. Then I have something to show you."

It cheered me enormously to see Father in such good spirits. I hurried upstairs to unpack. Though I slept on a cot downstairs in the ersatz dining room, I shared Sissi's small chest of drawers in her sleeping alcove next to our parents' bedroom. After putting my clothes away, I went to the stairs. Father, having climbed half of them, reached up and took my arm. He fairly bounded back down the stairs with me in tow.

"You must see my new gift", he called over his shoulder.

"A gift? From whom, Papa?" I felt a twinge of guilt about nothing to show for the hops picking.

"Come, come, come!" he said. "Do you recognize this?"

It was a *Volksempfänger* (people's receiver). This small rectangular box on the kitchen table was a radio specially designed with a limited range. Father could not do without music. In days gone by, he thought nothing of rushing to the opera house just to hear a certain aria and then returning to the chancellery to work far into the night. More surprising than the radio was the identity of the person who gave it to Father—the new camp commandant.

Soon after his arrival at Sachsenhausen, SS Col. Anton Kaindl paid my parents a visit. He had been exceptionally pleasant and had asked if there was anything in particular that my parents needed. Father doubted that the man was serious but told him that he greatly missed his books and most of all music. Kaindl agreed that life without culture was indeed something of a wasteland and then left. A short time later, Father received several crates of books from his former library. That was an enormous comfort. Then when Kaindl brought him the radio, Father was almost speechless. The short, bespectacled SS man had provided a tonic for Father's spirit and a greater measure of stimulus than he had ever thought possible in those surroundings.

That evening we all eagerly listened to a concert on the radio. Afterward, out of curiosity, I began to fiddle with the dials. Then I removed the back to have a look inside.

Vera said, "Kurti, if you break that radio, I personally will kill you. That is your father's most important possession."

"I'm being very careful, Mami. Just let me look."

Father said nothing, but his eyes remained fixed on the radio.

"Peter Mayer and I used to experiment with radios. I won't break it. I promise."

During those years before he fled with his family to England, Peter and I had wireless radio sets. Those were only basic radios, but the principle—using a wire to pick up radio waves, isolating the frequency, and amplifying the signal—was the same. I was tinkering with the radio when something miraculous took place. The familiar knocking sound signaling the beginning of the BBC broadcast from London came from the little radio's speaker. London! Father froze and turned pale. Vera just stared at me waiting for words to come to her. Sissi gurgled happily and went on playing with her toys.

"It is strictly forbidden to listen to the BBC. Turn it off!"

I looked at Father. "But, Papa," I said gently, "what can they do? You are already in a concentration camp."

After a moment color trickled back to his face. He smiled. "Kurti, you are absolutely right. What was I thinking? Go upstairs quickly and bring the blanket from the bed. It would be stupid not to muffle the sound."

Thus, a nightly routine became established with us. The hourly BBC transmissions began on the stroke of the hour. We listened, each in turn, huddled under the blanket. Here, at last, was some reliable information. More than anything, it strengthened our spirit.

After the war we learned about the terrible punishment inflicted on those caught listening to "enemy" radio transmissions. Father's cousin Olga Hekajllo had lived in Salzburg, where she secretly listened to the BBC at night. One morning she shared news of Allied bombings with her grocer. After Aunt Olga left, a fellow shopper who had overheard her remarked to the shopkeeper that perhaps Aunt Olga was a friend of a friend. Would he help with her name? Before Aunt Olga had put away her groceries, Gestapo were at her front door. Arrested as a subversive, she was shipped directly to Ravensbrück and summarily gassed. Before her death, Aunt Olga had been allowed to write one letter. Sent to her brother, it contained the circumstances of her arrest. The letter was dated July 24, 1944. Arriving in the same post as Aunt Olga's letter was also a small packet from the camp's commander. Her brother first read Aunt Olga's letter then opened the packet. The latter contained Aunt Olga's ashes. An attached note stated that her death was the result of "acute pneumonia". Along with the note was the official death certificate, signed and dated July 22, two days prior to her letter.

The urge to share our good news was irresistible. The guardhouse was on our left, but to our right, separated by a twelve-foot wall was another cottage like ours. Father wrote his name on a small piece of paper. Vera wrapped the paper round a rock and tied it with sewing thread. Father went out at dusk, seemingly to work in his garden. Gathering up the spoons he used for digging and a few cans of dirt, he walked around to the far side of the cottage. When he was sure that he was not being watched, he lobbed his message over the wall.

A note was lobbed back from the other side. Our neighbors were Rudolf Breitscheid, a liberal German Socialist, and his wife. He had been the Prussian minister of the interior from 1918 to 1919 and then a member of Parliament from 1920. He left Parliament in 1933. Like many other German Social Democrats, he had been strongly opposed to Hitler. When Hitler came to power, he emigrated to France with his wife. They lived there until 1941, when the Gestapo found them. They were subsequently arrested, taken back to Germany, and confined to the cottage on the other side of the wall.

There were four of these cottages. The practice of lobbing notes back and forth soon took root and became our means of communicating with one another. Caution was necessary, but it was a worthwhile risk.

Vera and I regularly walked to the nearby village of Sachsenhausen to use our ration cards. Sachsenhausen was a collection of simple, colorless buildings. The butcher's shop was on the main street. Farther down the street was a grocery store. Our ration cards allowed us to buy two ounces of meat per person each week. Meat was in short supply throughout the Reich, and the butcher's shop bore testimony to that fact. Vera saved our weekly rations and bought meat once a month. As meager as it was, what reached the table was actually recognizable as meat.

Though interned in the camp, Vera and I were not confined to it. As soon as Sissi was able to walk, Vera took her to Berlin as often as possible. It was important that Sissi have some sense of normal life. These visits were like stepping from night into day. One's ration cards didn't go any further in Berlin, but being able to shop there did more for Vera's spirit than buying in Sachsenhausen.

That first summer, as the guard escorted me to the door of the cottage, he asked me what my favorite pastime was.

"Fishing", I said.

"Well then, you're in luck!"

He now had my total attention.

"There's a lake only half a mile or so away."

"With fish?"

"With fish!"

From that day on, whenever I had time, I took my fishing rod to the lake and sometimes returned with dinner. It was hard not to recall those very different days on the Wolfgangsee and Liesl's exasperation at being presented with one trout-filled bucket after another.

Weeding Father's vegetable garden was another of my projects, but Sissi, who was becoming increasingly more mobile, made this no easy task. She wanted to help, but she couldn't recognize a weed from a tomato vine. It cheered us to see our little patch of garden come to life that summer. Tomatoes, lettuce, and potatoes grew even in that God-forsaken place. Vera had found tobacco seeds somewhere in Berlin. These had been planted, and they too began to sprout. We focused on these small, bright occurrences in our lives and put away our memories of other family summers.

I had brought with me into the camp my most cherished possession: an Argus 35-millimeter camera. It was carefully hidden among the clothes in my suitcase. I knew I was taking a colossal risk, and I had some idea of the trouble it would cause if the camera were discovered. I had several fretful moments until that trusting guard waved me through.

The Argus was a present from a young American reporter whom I had met at the house of one of my friends from the Schülerheim. He asked if he could question me about my family. I briefly considered the matter. I was in Nazi Germany. I knew the rules included no discussion about Father. So, I kept my answers simple. Later that evening, the journalist took our pictures with the most extraordinary camera that I had ever seen. After removing the film he held out the camera to me.

"For you, and thanks", he said, smiling.

I imagine my eyes nearly popped out of my head.

"I couldn't take your camera!" I said, my hands at my sides.

"I go back to America tomorrow and my editor will give me a new one. Please, I'd be happy for you to have it. My editor would be happy for you to have it."

I continued to shake my head until I remembered that current circumstances were far from what they had once been. Father would want me to have the camera. I reached for it.

"This is a dream of a camera! I don't know how to thank you."

"You already have. Enjoy it." He clapped me on the back. "I hope you take some worthwhile pictures."

Soon after my arrival at Sachsenhausen, I took off for the lake early one morning, carrying my fishing pole, a digging fork, and a sack containing a can in which I stored worms. I looked the part of the dedicated angler. But hidden in the can was my new camera. I smiled at the guards and said that I hoped to return with dinner.

I walked some distance from the guard tower to a spot from which the silhouettes of the guards were still visible. I then stepped behind a tree, leaned back against the trunk, and slid down to a sitting position. The camera had to be unwrapped carefully; then the distance to the tower estimated, and the lens focused. I lay down on my stomach and wriggled out far enough to frame the picture and click the shutter. Then I rolled back behind the tree and held my breath. All was quiet. The guards did not blow their whistles; their dogs did not bark. I had not been detected. I had to be content with this one photograph, however. It was too risky to attempt any more, and I had very little film left.

Wrapping up the camera I considered my options. Taking a photograph of the outside of our cottage was out of the question, and the light inside was too weak for me to photograph the interior. A thought did occur to me: the upstairs window with its clear view of the camp. I looked at my watch. Five minutes had elapsed. I got to my feet and headed for the lake. At the lake I stuck my fork in the soft earth and immediately uncovered a nest of worms. I baited my hook, cast my line, and settled down to think about my list of subjects.

I normally tried to avoid the upstairs window, so I wasn't sure what the angle of the afternoon sun would be. It didn't really matter. I could take photographs from that window only in the afternoon. Although the family always stayed downstairs during the day, Sissi never left my side until she took her nap. The columns of prisoners returned to the camp in the late afternoon.

I had four exposures left: a view of the guard tower, another of the rows of prison barracks; the two remaining exposures would be spent on the columns of prisoners. I would take the film to Fritz Sammer in Vienna. He and Greta had moved from the Ottenreiters into their own apartment. Though an architect by profession, Fritz was a passionate amateur photographer and developed his own negatives. I could, of course, give them to Uncle Artur in Berlin. Editing tapes and developing films were perhaps daily tasks for him, but I knew better. His nerves would not be able to withstand the tension, and inevitably my parents would find out from him. No, I would have to wait until my next trip to Vienna. Fritz Sammer's nerves were in a much better state than Uncle Artur's. After all, Fritz was not burdened with such notorious relatives.

There was a tug on my fishing line: dinner.

The warm weather forced us to leave our windows and doors open. Although a wall separated us from the camp, it did little to hinder the smells and sounds from reaching us. There was a persistent, pervasive stench of unwashed, sick, malnourished, and mistreated human beings. The sounds were the worst: groans, cries, and gruesome screams that curdled one's blood and filled one's dreams.

During the course of the war, Sachsenhausen-Oranienburg held over eighty thousand prisoners. By war's end, over two hundred thousand persons had passed through its gates. The Nazis had flung their nets far and wide. In addition to common criminals, the camp's population consisted of Gypsies, political prisoners, homosexuals, Communists, members of targeted religious groups—the Jehovah's Witnesses were particularly persecuted—and, of course, Jews.

The prisoners wore uniforms of blue and white stripes; on each prisoner's head there was a brimless cap that was either striped or solid blue. Each uniform had a colored triangle and the prisoner's camp identification number. The colored triangles identified the category to which the prisoner belonged: Jews had yellow triangles, homosexuals pink, Gypsies purple, and so on.

I will never forget what they wore on their feet: heavy felt nailed with metal studs to thick wooden soles. No one who has heard the sound produced by those thousands of marching feet will forget it. Regardless of the weather, every morning at seven A.M. the prisoners trudged out through the electrified gates to work in a nearby brickworks, the sound of marching feet echoing long after they had disappeared. The prisoners returned late in the afternoon, and they could be heard long before they became visible. The noise made by their clogs increased to a crescendo as they neared—the musical mayhem of a demonic composer.

That gate, through which the prisoners marched, also saw Vera, Sissi, and me depart for something like normalcy. We could come and go every day while Father immersed himself in his books and writing. These were more than a distraction for him. Along with the radio they preserved his sanity.

Our greatest concern, however, was for Sissi. That tiny blonde bullet, ricocheting from one room to another in the cottage, was the center of our world. I was the horse she saddled for wild, bumpy rides, and I was "it" during games of hide-and-seek. My hands steadied her as she learned to walk, and my arms carried her when she was tired. To be needed was a new experience for me, but to be needed by her was the greatest joy of my life.

Time at Sachsenhausen was strongly marked by Sissi's milestones as she grew healthy, strong, and mobile. The more she could walk, the more important it was to keep watch over her. Our fears for Sissi were concentrated on the upstairs window: not that she might fall out of it, but that she might look out of it. The authorities strictly forbade us to cover any window, day or night, so it became one of my duties to guard Sissi from the one that looked down into the camp. I hated and loathed that window. From it I had witnessed enough brutality for a lifetime of nightmares—looking through it was like peering into hell.

Ironically and tragically the *Kapos*—those prisoners appointed to oversee their fellow inmates—were responsible for more heinous brutality than were the guards. The Germans picked the most brutal, violent, and often mentally unstable members of the camp's population to serve as kapos. Those who unflinchingly made examples of other prisoners inched a bit further from death.

One afternoon as the sound of the wooden clogs signaled the return of prisoners, I ran upstairs to get a sweater for Sissi. I heard a shrill whistle outside, then all went quiet. I approached the window with a sense of trepidation. A prisoner lay flat on the ground. I watched as he feebly struggled to get up but his arms had turned to rubber. After each attempt he fell back on the ground and finally made no further attempt—no one moved to help him. The barracks were almost within reach, only yards away. The kapo approached the prone man. A metal whistle, dangling from the string around his neck, glinted in the failing light. He surveyed the rows of prisoners on his right, then those on his left. Knowing he was the focus of their attention, he raised his foot and held it motionless for a full ten seconds over the man's back. I silently prayed for the man to will himself to get up, or crawl. He didn't.

"Get up . . . roll over!" The sound of my own voice surprised me. "Roll on your side!" I called out more loudly.

The kapo brought his foot and full weight down on the man's torso. I could hear bones shatter—like the sound made by boots trampling on dried branches. The kapo stomped again and once more. The prisoner—his upper body flattened—barely reacted: a few jerks and twitches. Movement ceased. The kapo circled the body and again languidly ran his eyes over the rows of prisoners.

"Kurti!" Vera called from downstairs. "What did you say?"

Next, like a football player going for a field goal, the kapo savagely kicked the dead man in the head. Then he sauntered toward the barracks. Almost as an afterthought, he raised his whistle to his mouth. The piercing sound cut through the camp air like a knife.

"Nothing, Mami, nothing."

From my vantage point at the window I looked at the faces of the remaining prisoners. They were without expression. Could they have been otherwise? Death at Sachsenhausen had no meaning. The prisoners resumed their march to the barracks. Several pairs of arms picked up the corpse, passed it back, and tossed it into the cart that trailed behind. That very same cart passed through the gates every morning and returned every evening, often with a cargo of dead prisoners. I turned away from the window and leaned weakly against the wall.

"Kurti! Where is that sweater?"

I grabbed the tiny garment. "I've got it." I headed back downstairs, vowing never again to let a noise from the camp yard lure me to the window.

An early inhabitant of Sachsenhausen was the French general Henri Giraud, who became the subject of many conversations. It was not his arrival but his adventurous escape that occupied our attention. Commander of the French Seventh Army and, for several days before his capture, the French Ninth Army, General Giraud had been taken prisoner in May 1940, just before France's capitulation to Germany. Sachsenhausen was intended to serve as only a way station for him. After a brief stay, General Giraud was transferred to the high-security prison for Allied officers at Königstein Fortress near Dresden. The general made his daring escape by lowering himself down the wall of the castle and the mountain on which it was built and jumping onto a train.

The wily general had also escaped from the Germans during World War I—some twenty-eight years before. After fleeing Königstein, he surfaced in North Africa and joined the Free French Forces. He remained one of our favorite subjects for conversation for a very long time. News of him came to us via the BBC through the little radio, our ears to the world.

There was another occasional source of information—the guards of the special section who were assigned permanent duty. Their constant presence resulted in a relationship between prisoner and jailer different from the one in the main camp. In 1943 Yakov Dzhugashvili, better known as Joseph Stalin's son, died in Sachsenhausen. An artillery officer in the Red Army, he was captured during the German invasion of Russia and brought to Sachsenhausen. Our guards told us that he was shot trying to escape.

Father's neighbors seemed to change often. Princess Mafalda, daughter of King Victor Emmanuel III, came and went. So did Crown Prince Rupprecht von Bayern's family and the head of the enormous Thyssen steel works, Fritz Thyssen, and his wife, Annelie. Over the years numerous prisoners from many different political and social backgrounds passed through Sachsenhausen. It made me wonder why Father was never moved and whether that was good or bad. I never raised the question. It did little good to speculate on such matters, and it made no difference. Sachsenhausen-Oranienburg was Father's reality.

# House of German Armaments

Werner Feurich was one of the few friends I retained from the Alte Realgymnasium. Werner exerted himself as I did—just enough not to be considered unathletic. He had a sense of humor, and we seemed to like many of the same things. He lived in the Bogenhausen section of Munich, only a few blocks from the Schülerheim Schmitt. His father, a wealthy industrialist, was the "Cookie King of Germany", and I was a loyal consumer of Feurich cookies.

From time to time, Werner invited me to stay over for the weekend. The Schülerheim could be a somewhat desolate place on weekends because those who could go home did. One weekend I was in a position to accept Werner's offer of hospitality. I eagerly looked forward to Friday; not only would I have a wonderful weekend, but I would be able to feast on Feurich cookies to my heart's content.

That Friday I threw a shirt, pants, pajamas, and toothbrush into a bag and walked over to Werner's. The Feurich house was large and handsome. The yard and gardens, however, were testimony to the gardener's occupying himself with the defense of the fatherland.

Werner himself answered the door, and we went to meet his parents. They were friendly and seemed to be genuinely nice people. They asked about life at the Schülerheim Schmitt and about my new school, the Wittelsbacher, but made no mention of the Alte Realgymnasuim, the school from which I had been summarily dismissed for being the son of Kurt von Schuschnigg.

The next day Werner's mother suggested we go to the library and say hello to Herr Feurich. I was particularly eager to see the library, where Werner said their fantastic telescope was set up.

"Wait till you see how powerful it is", he said, reaching for the doorknob.

"Wait, Werner. He's got somebody in there; maybe we should come back."

"It doesn't matter. Come on."

We opened the door and caught Herr Feurich midsentence. Standing up he said, "Werner, my son. Come in, come in!" Addressing the several men there, Werner's father continued, "Gentlemen, this is my son, Werner, whom some of you know, and his friend, the young Kurt von Schuschnigg." At the mention of my name, one man looked surprised. Another said, "Well, well", while shaking his head.

Werner's father struck me as a jovial, good-natured Bavarian. Sensing that we wanted only to use the telescope, he said, "You boys can look to your hearts' content, but quietly—we're in a meeting."

"Thanks, Papa. We'll be quiet."

"Yes, sir", I added

Herr Feurich took his seat, and their conversation resumed.

"Look at this", Werner whispered.

Having focused the telescope, he stepped aside. Pressing my eye to the lens, I could see ants crawling on a fence several hundred yards away. They were so clear, as if I could reach out and touch them. I would have loved to have a powerful telescope. I could think of a thousand uses for it. Our silence had the effect of amplifying the men's conversation.

"Of course, the führer will see to it! What do you think?"

Surprised, I glanced at Werner, who just shrugged his shoulders and focused the telescope on another target. I glanced around the room: slightly worn dark leather chairs; finely polished old wood; heavy silk curtains; and huge vases of flowers—these struck me with a bout of nostalgia. I missed having a home. A distant thought, a shadow, danced on the edge of my mind and nagged at me.

Werner backed away from the telescope and nodded toward the door. We thanked his father, and he waved us out, saying that if we needed anything—just ask. Werner had a very nice life. I was happy to be there, if only for the weekend.

The next day we all had Sunday lunch together. Presiding at the head of the table, Herr Feurich was both patriarch and host. "Kurt," he began in an earnest tone, "your father is in Vienna, isn't he?"

I was puzzled. "No, sir. Father was moved to Munich Gestapo headquarters in October 1939 and then to the concentration camp near Sachsenhausen in December 1941."

The Reich did not allow discussions about concentration camps and had issued an edict specifically forbidding all those linked with the concentration camps to speak about them or to acknowledge their existence. I did think, however, that Father's fate was somewhat common knowledge among important party members and leading industrialists.

"Well, yes, of course, that is perfectly understandable", Herr Feurich said, unsurprised. "That would certainly be for your father's own safety and no doubt a temporary solution until balance in Europe is restored. The führer would not want harm coming to your father at the hands of Austrians—best that he is now living in Germany."

Herr Feurich was either following the Nazi party line or was woefully ignorant of Father's circumstances. Those of us at the Wittelsbacher School who were friends of Werner had assumed that his father had contributed to Hitler's war chest out of expediency, rather than because he embraced the beliefs of the National Socialists. Practically all industrialists had aligned themselves with the Nazi Party to be able to participate in the German economy, which was booming.

I liked Werner, and I wanted to like his parents. All that was required, I thought, was to tell them of the true state of affairs as regarded Father. Putting my fork and knife down, I looked up from my plate. "Herr Feurich," I began carefully, "my father, stepmother, and baby sister are actually in a concentration camp. Officially their status in the Third Reich is that of non-persons." I had once again ignored the edict ordering silence on the subject; but since no bolts of lightning had struck, I pressed on.

"They've been put in one of four cottages in the camp. Directly on the other side of their wall is the main camp with tens of thousands of prisoners who are used as slave labor. The conditions under which they exist are unbelievable. They're barely even fed! I have seen them from the cottage's upstairs window. They're nothing but skin and bones. They can only dream of being treated as well as farm animals!" I paused, as Werner's mother had put down her fork and was looking decidedly uncomfortable, but there was no turning back for me now. "I don't think you will find too many Jews left here in Munich."

I was completely unprepared for what came next. Staring straight at me, Herr Feurich launched into an impassioned defense of Hitler. "The führer would never do anything that was unjust. You really should be careful of making such sweeping statements, Kurti. Those prisoners are a hard-core criminal element that the National Socialist Party refused to put up with any longer.

"Yes, I know that Jews have been removed. So what if the führer put them in Sachsenhausen? Eventually they will be resettled in countries that have offered them asylum, but that's not going to happen overnight. The Jews knew resentment had built up against them. They should have left before it came to this. It was all so unnecessary.

"The Jews have made money in every imaginable way, becoming rich, some very rich, and they have pushed themselves into any avenue of society they could. The führer has been patient, but he finally had to say enough is enough. I personally have no problems with the Jews, but one must consider the whole of society. I am sorry to have to say it, but the Jews have brought this upon themselves."

It was deeply unsettling that Herr Feurich would give credence to this Nazi lie about the Jews—resettlement in other countries. How then could he explain the other groups in the camps?

"But Herr Feurich, you don't have to be Jewish. That concentration camp has clergy from every faith along with military personnel and political prisoners the Nazis have collected. Anyone can land in a camp these days, whether a Jehovah's Witness or a member of European aristocracy. You won't find any more Gypsies either. The Nazis have rounded them all up. That camp has many people whose only crime was being born with a physical defect; others just for disagreeing with Hitler over something."

I was about to mention the empty mental wards in the hospitals, but I could see from his steely expression that Herr Feurich was past listening. There was no point in continuing. Prosperity had returned to Germany, and the German people were proud of it. They refused to believe these stories and were intolerant of criticism of their führer or their Reich.

"Nonsense!" he threw his napkin on the table. "Kurti, you are just a boy. You know nothing of the world, and you have no idea what you're talking about. I do", he said looking straight at me. "I am a businessman and a patriot."

Now I realized what had escaped me in the library the day before—the tone of his voice that expressed such a ringing confidence in Hitler. Herr Feurich seemed to be a considerate man and a good father. How could he be so successful and also so naive? I recalled Uncle Willy telling me that propaganda can't be contradicted by facts if people really don't want to know the truth.

Frau Feurich, now clearly unhappy, made a determined attempt to change the subject. "Yes, you are, my dear—and everyone knows it. Would you like dessert?"

I decided to enjoy mine. It was unlikely that I would partake of the Feurichs' hospitality again. After dessert, Werner and I were excused from the table. "I'm sorry, Werner," I began, "but everything I said was true."

He looked as unhappy as his mother had. "I saw a bunch of Nazis beating up an old Jewish man a couple of weeks ago", he said. "It was awful. And you're right. There are fewer and fewer people wearing yellow stars. But all of the others you said were in the camp—well, it's hard to believe. And if all of this is true, how could my father not know? He wasn't pretending—I know him. There's no way in the world he believed you!"

I had said as much as I could. When I returned to Vienna, I would send Werner one of the photographs that I had taken at the camp.

As the war ground on, the fatherland expected ever greater contributions from its children. I was now no longer a mere hops picker; I was inducted as a flak helper. Flak helpers assisted soldiers with the antiaircraft guns. As the Allied bombing of Munich increased, more boys were assigned to flak units defending the city.

Several times a week we left our classrooms and reported to the antiaircraft towers. There we performed the tasks assigned to us, spent the balance of the night sleeping on cots, and returned the next morning to our schools. My main responsibility was to set the antiaircraft gunner's searchlight with the coordinates of incoming Allied aircraft. Some of us were required to carry live ammunition to feed the 88-millimeter antiaircraft guns. Others had to clean those guns. Extraordinarily, there were no accidents with either the guns or the ammunition. Though Munich was being bombed relentlessly, none of our positions ever took a direct hit.

Some mornings, as we made our way back to school, the sky above us would be completely obscured by clouds of billowing smoke, a remnant of the previous night's bombing. With wet handkerchiefs clamped over our noses and mouths, we ran through streets illuminated only by the fires that consumed one building after another. The silence that followed the massive Allied raids was chilling, eerie. Entire city blocks were flattened. On others, only outlines in brick and mortar lent testimony to the buildings that had once been there.

Since December 1941 the world outside of the Axis powers looked to the United States of America to turn the tide of war. Patience was all that was needed and the ability, or luck, to stay alive.

At the end of November 1943, I was called up for Reichsarbeitsdienst (RAD), which was one more form of compulsory volunteerism. I was being requisitioned by the fatherland for six months, and my particular assignment involved rerouting and regulating certain streams in Westerwald, a region deep in the Rhineland. On the train I was assailed by thoughts that were far from pleasant. I had turned seventeen in May, and I would very likely be drafted for military duty after my six months in RAD were completed.

A *Feldmeister* (field master), the RAD's equivalent of a sergeant, stood on the platform of the railway station waiting for the small army of seventeen-year-olds on the train. He held a large placard directing us to assemble for transport to the RAD camp. We got out of the train and milled about until the feldmeister ordered us to line up and count off.

"Number twenty-seven, Schuschnigg!"

We were transported in an old bus that bumped, coughed, and sputtered but got us to the camp. After being told how important our work was to the fatherland, we were assigned to barracks. The next morning we donned our brown uniforms and swastika armbands. After marching in step, we presented arms—our shovels—then set off to the task of digging ditches and canals.

It was backbreaking, mind-numbing work, and winter in the Westerwald was brutally cold and damp. Our job was not only to dig a new canal for the stream but to do it fast "for führer and fatherland": this irritating phrase echoed constantly in my mind during those early days of ditch digging.

Though the work was exhausting, my difficulties were mental. I could not reconcile myself to being in that place. Feeling that I would lose my sanity before overwork consumed me, I had a thought. My medical history listed asthma, allergies, grippe, pneumonia, and scarlet fever, and I had both experience and knowledge of the symptoms of these ailments. Being chronically thin I could, with very little effort, look sick. A bit of acting skill was all that was needed.

We were at our work site at dawn, well before the sun would have a chance to take some of the chill out of the air. Working about thirty feet from the next youth, I waited until he paused for a rest. Then, slowly, I doubled over and began to hyperventilate. Rudi, Peter Mayer, and I used to have fainting contests—I always won. Lying on my back I tried to focus, as my vision had become blurred. An acne-spotted face loomed over me.

"Can you hear me?" the section leader shouted down.

Stifling the impulse to say, "I'm not deaf; I just fainted", I answered instead, "I'm all right" and struggled to stand.

Slamming a beefy hand on my chest to keep me flat, he almost knocked the breath out of me again.

"Hold still. Don't move!"

"You two," he said to two of the other faces now looking down at me, "get him over to the infirmary, quickly. Then report back to me." So far, this was going well.

My 110 pounds were no problem at all for the strong pair. They carried me with very little exertion to the infirmary and put me on a stretcher. The nurse examined me and left the room—just long enough for me to swallow a mouthful of hot water from the sink. When she returned, I wiped my brow and said, "Do you think you could open the window? It's really warm in here."

She took out her thermometer, put it under my tongue, and looked at the second hand of her watch. A minute later my temperature reading had put me on the verge of death. I was immediately assigned a bed in the infirmary. My ongoing performance kept me there for the next two weeks. Had a specialist been called, I would have been in trouble. In the end the part-time doctor, a general practitioner, could do no more than recommend I be returned to Munich.

Munich and the Schülerheim Schmitt had never looked so good. I would be able to spend Christmas with my family. From Munich I went to Berlin on crowded trains as Christmas travelers and soldiers strained the war-stressed railway system. Trains carried more and more soldiers. I watched them make their way through the cars—most of them were about my age. It was a sobering thought. I wondered if it was also like this in the Allied countries. I thought of Father, who had volunteered to fight in the First World War when he had been only slightly older than I. He had fought and, like his father, had been taken prisoner. In deference to Grandfather's high rank, the Italians interned them together. In the prisoner of war camp, they had orderlies who polished their boots and laundered their uniforms. That world had long since disappeared.

Upon arriving in Berlin, I wanted to visit Aunt Marianne, Uncle Artur, and the cousins to wish them a merry Christmas. But first I wanted to photograph the Brandenburg Gate and other picturesque parts of Berlin while they were still standing. Allied bombings were irreversibly altering the city's features.

As I walked down the Unter den Linden, it began to rain, and I wished I had changed the roll of film in my Argus while I was still on the train. I ducked into a doorway, took out the used roll of film, and dropped it in my coat pocket. After putting in a new roll of film, I put the camera back in my coat pocket and resumed walking. I had gone no more than ten paces when I felt a firm tap on my shoulder and heard those unforgettable words: "You are under arrest."

I found myself confronted by an ordinary-looking man dressed in civilian clothes. His face was forgettable except for the eyes— cold, small. We stared at one another for a second before he said, "Give me your camera and that film you just removed from it." Then he flashed a sliver badge with "Geheime Staatspolizei" (Gestapo) in unmistakably clear letters.

I did as ordered.

"You will come with me."

We walked toward the building in whose doorway I had changed the film. A sign above the first floor read, "House of German Armaments". I went through the doorway as directed. No one even looked at us. We crossed the lobby, then went up a flight of stairs. The firm grasp of the Gestapo agent never left my shoulder. We headed down a long, gray hallway. The agent opened a door. The room was already occupied. Another Gestapo agent gestured angrily as he questioned a man. The latter sat hunch-shouldered, with elbows on the bare table before him and his face buried in his hands. It was a picture of complete despair. We went on.

The Gestapo man opened another unmarked door, this time to an unoccupied room bare of furniture except for a table and metal chair. He told me to sit. I did. Without further ado, he began shooting questions at me. I provided my name, address, and occupation as requested; then he came to the real point: "What did you photograph?"

"Nothing, I was just changing the film in my camera."

He repeated the question several times, and I gave him the same answer. The agent changed direction, "You have an American camera!"

"Yes, I do", I replied firmly. "Is there a law against that?"

Raising an eyebrow, he said, "Wait here."

After he left, I glanced about the room. The only window was so dirty that even bright sunlight would never penetrate its panes. It took a lot of imagination to guess when the room had been painted last—determining its original color was out of the question. How I wished I had waited for a sunny day to take pictures.

After about forty-five minutes, a uniformed police sergeant opened the door, looked at me, and said, "You will please come with me." We walked back down the corridor. "Any attempt to escape will result in my having to use my gun." It was not a warning that I needed to hear twice. I walked with measured steps before him.

We left the armaments building and after a few blocks entered a police station on the Unter den Linden. I was turned over to another policeman, this one a captain, who had just finished dictating a list of names to another officer. "Bring them all in immediately for questioning", he concluded and then turned to my escort. "Is this the one your captain called me about?"

After he was assured of my identity, he led me to an empty courtroom. The front third of the room consisted of judge's bench and opposite it two tables with chairs—for the prosecutor and defendant, I thought. A wooden rail and a number of wooden benches completed the room. Portraits of the führer and Himmler oversaw the proceedings from opposite walls.

"Empty the contents of your pockets", he instructed, motioning toward one of the tables. I took out a heavy gold cigarette case given to me by a family friend, matches came next, then my wallet, some money, and a comb. My wallet held my Sachsenhausen-Oranienburg identification document. This had my picture and date of birth and identified me as Kurt Auster. Then I took out my RAD discharge papers, which identified me as Kurt von Schuschnigg.

"Sit down", the policeman said when I had finished. He then took up each item and meticulously examined it. He seemed fascinated by the cigarette case, studying its six surfaces and pressing each in turn. Only the lid sprang open. I turned sideways in the chair to shift my focus and avoid being intimidated.

He looked at my papers and then slammed his fist down on the table. I was startled, and he noticed it. He had gotten my attention, and I was furious with myself. He placed his hands flat on the table and leaned toward me, his face stopping a few inches from mine. "Why do you have documents with two different names? You're a spy, aren't you?"

"That is absurd. I am no more a spy than you are!" I said, trying to sound as dismissive as I could.

"Germany has been at war with America since December 7, 1941. That Argus was only produced in the United States in 1941. What are you doing with an American camera, and how did you get it?" he shouted.

The situation was going from bad to worse. Again I repeated the same story that I had told for the past couple of hours. He gave me one last hard look and then left.

Next came a bull-necked youth whose only comment during his two hours of guarding me—"No smoking is permitted while on duty"—was spoken when I offered him a cigarette. His replacement was an older man. His manner was completely different, even friendly, and he seemed to want to talk. He began as soon as he closed the door. "I am an old Communist. I cannot wait to get rid of these Nazis."

I said nothing—not wanting to be taken in by what could be trickery.

"They are nothing but trouble," he went on, "and half of them are thugs and hooligans—upsetting everyone when they could get the same job done in a much calmer manner."

I stared at the portrait of Hitler and said nothing.

He bent down toward me and asked, "Don't you agree?"

I turned and looked squarely at him: "I do not have an opinion on such matters. I am not political." He was quiet for the remainder of his shift.

The last man was unlike the two that preceded him. He began questioning me as if I had not yet already been questioned. Suddenly I had a thought. "Please, if you have more questions call the commanding officer of the Sachsenhausen-Oranienburg camp. My case is complicated, and I am not allowed to talk about it."

He called in another guard and left the room. This one sat in complete silence. Two more hours passed, and the captain returned. "The situation is cleared up. You may go now. The camera is still being examined in the lab. You may come back tomorrow to claim it."

I gathered my belongings and left. It was now dark, and the rain had stopped. I had been in the police station for more than eight hours. There was no point in visiting Uncle Artur now. On the way to the railroad station, I went back over the entire episode in my mind.

I was not happy about having to tell Father about it, but it was unavoidable. Vera, however, was the one who was alarmed. "What an idiotic thing to do, Kurti. You must pay attention to everyone and everything around you. These days even the trees have eyes and ears! Don't you realize that?"

After a moment Father drew a breath and spoke: "Son, your mother is right. There is no longer anything normal about the times in which we live. People disappear for no reason. It might be for something as innocent as what you were doing today. The irony of the entire incident is that your prison camp papers probably saved your life—please, be careful." After a brief pause, he continued, "Given a bad situation you kept your wits; you kept thinking— I'm proud of you."

Later, I mentioned that I hated not visiting Uncle Artur and his family. Father and Vera looked at each other, and then Father spoke.

"Uncle Artur no longer lives on the Burggrafenstrasse. The buildings were all flattened by Allied bombing the other week. They weren't there, so they're all right." Silence settled over the room.

The next day I went back to Berlin for my camera. When I returned, Father was reading. I sat down and placed a box on the table. "I returned to the police station in Berlin. I gave my name at the desk and asked for the camera. A policeman returned with this box." I took out the magical Argus—both halves—and placed them on the table. We sat looking at the camera in silence. Father sighed and patted me on the shoulder.

Waking one morning to bright sunshine, I told my parents that I would try my luck at fishing again. The week before, I brought back an eel for dinner. Vera said, "Kurti, fishing will have to wait. I have a very important errand for you. You are to take the train to Berlin, then go to the residence of Bishop Preysing.[1] Saint Hedwig Cathedral was bombed, and he is now living just outside of the city. He will give you an envelope. It will contain Holy Communion for your father."

Vera certainly had her network in Berlin. I was proud that she trusted me and excited over the prospect of wandering around the environs of Berlin on my own. But most of all, I was happy for Father. His faith had sustained him these many years; but for the devout Catholic, to be denied the sacraments was a great deprivation.

Following Vera's precise directions, I took the train to the city and found my way to Bishop Preysing's residence. When I entered, he was sitting behind a desk that was heavily laden with correspondence and books. He rose and circled the desk. "And you must be Kurti", he said, smiling.

"Yes, Your Excellency."

The bishop put his hand on my shoulder and guided me to a chair. He had a quiet manner and asked thoughtful questions about our lives. I was happy to be in his presence although somewhat

---

[1] Count Konrad von Preysing (1880–1950). Born in Munich, Germany, he entered the Bavarian Ministry for Foreign Affairs in 1906. Instead of pursuing a career in diplomacy, he studied for the priesthood and was ordained in 1912. Pius XI consecrated him a bishop in 1932, and he became Bishop of Berlin in 1935. He preached from the pulpit against the Nazis, and in 1946 Pius XII named him cardinal.

intimidated. I didn't always get myself to Mass on Sundays, and a bishop *certainly* could divine this.

"Kurti," he said, "I know that I am not supposed to ask you where your parents are, because I am not supposed to know. But I send them my blessing, and I pray for you all. Now, you realize what a responsibility it is to transport the Host. Don't you?"

I did. I was nervous, but I was also an altar boy. I could do this. I placed the envelope in the inside breast pocket of my coat and traveled all the way back with my hand over it. Though successful, my mission had worried Father. After that Vera decided she would go herself. After two or three trips, she too grew afraid of detection.

A couple of days later, after putting a sleeping Sissi on the sofa, I tiptoed into the kitchen. Vera stood over the sink with her back to me—it took me a moment to realize she was crying. I thought I was familiar with all of Vera's facets: her charm, her beauty, her wit, and even her anger. But this was new. I was not prepared to see her like this. Sensing someone standing behind her, she turned around.

"Mami, what's the matter? Are you sick?" I asked.

She fumbled in her pocket. "No, of course I'm not!" she said, pulling out a handkerchief.

"Then why are you crying?"

"Oh, you wouldn't understand—it doesn't matter", she answered, dabbing at her eyes.

"Please, I would understand if you would just tell me."

"As unbelievable as our lives are now, I can't help wondering what will become of us when this all ends."

"When this all ends everything will be fine!"

"It's not that simple, Kurti. What are we going to live on? We have nothing!" Vera was the most practical person in our family. She handled what money we had. Father was hopeless in such matters.

"But Father will have money again." As soon as the words escaped my lips I regretted them—it sounded like such a feeble thing to have said. "And we have our furniture, our pictures, and lots of silver. We can sell them!"

"Kurti, we were told that many of the warehouses were bombed. There may not be any furniture, silver, or paintings."

Father had not told me—this was a shock. It made me sad too— not for the possessions themselves but because they were the last material links to the past. I took a different tack. "After the war I'll finish school and find work, but Father can start making money right away—after all, he isn't so old."

Although he might look like a contemporary of Grandfather, Father had just turned forty-six. Ten years ago, he had been one of the youngest—if not the youngest—heads of government in Europe. In those early days, Mother always said that Father's demeanor and bearing had the advantage of making him look older.

"Who isn't so old?" asked Father, as he entered the kitchen.

"Oh, no one", Vera offered as she turned back to the sink.

Father walked over to her and turned her around. "What's this?" He stroked her cheek tenderly, wiping away the last trace of a tear.

"Father, Mami is worried about how we will live after the war."

He led her to the table and looked at me. "Now, both of you sit down, and we will discuss this."

I continued, "I told Mami that even if our things did get blown up ..."

"What?" He gave me a very sharp look.

"I told him, Kurt", Vera said. "He's old enough to understand, and he should know."

I went on, "You can go back into government when this is all over—to earn money, I mean. Can't you?"

"My son, money isn't a legitimate reason to work in government. One should mix in government only with the right aims: strengthening the positives that exist and correcting the negatives. Up to the last day, that is what I concentrated all of my strength on. Now, considering my advanced age"—he smiled at me—"I am sure there are others who will take my place after the war. As far as our future is concerned, I am certain that I will find the right path. Now, no more of this sort of talk."

Everything was going to be all right.

# The German Navy

After Christmas 1943, I returned to Munich and started classes again at the Wittlesbacher School. The war was going horribly for Germany, and by May a wartime diploma program would be in place. That meant students who were seventeen or older would be graduated from school without the necessity of passing exams and dispersed among the various branches of the armed forces.

Vice Adm. Kurt Slevogt, the father of my friend and fellow boarder Kurt-Erich Slevogt, had prepared me for the inevitability of my military duty in early 1943. Admiral Slevogt was in command of the German Navy's Baltic Fleet, and he took Kurt and me out to dinner and discussed the war and our future. "It is too late to discuss the fact that Germany is in a war that should never have been started by a man who should never be a leader", he said. "There is no doubt that your age group will be called up for active duty within this next year. Kurt-Erich will volunteer for the navy. Kurti, I strongly recommend that you do the same.

"In fact, as I see it," the admiral paused and looked me straight in the eye, "volunteering for the navy is the only chance you have of surviving active duty. If you do not volunteer, you'll be drafted. Draftees in your category—you know that you come under the heading of politically unreliable—will be assigned to *Himmelfahrt* (travel to heaven) units. These do especially dangerous duties like mine sweeping or are sent to the Russian front."

When I was twelve I thought my being politically unreliable was a joke. It was no longer funny. The admiral continued, "By volunteering for the navy you will automatically be sent to the Naval Academy. From that point on, I will at least have access to knowledge of your whereabouts. To some degree, I'll be able to keep an eye on you."

Admiral Slevogt spoke with the bearing of one who had seen death and known death. Kurt-Erich had told me his father was vehemently opposed to Hitler but had his duty to perform for his country.

At Christmas, I had told Father about Admiral Slevogt. He had agreed with the admiral's plan, saying, "These are extraordinary times when I find I am indebted to a German admiral I don't know and will probably never meet. Don't ever confuse Hitler with the true German people. The Nazis have nothing to do with the real spirit of the German people."

In January 1944 I reported to the recruiting office and volunteered for the German Navy. A few months later, Kurt-Erich and I received our call to duty. As Admiral Slevogt had accurately predicted, I had been admitted to the Naval Academy. I was to report immediately. I bade farewell to my friends at the Schülerheim Schmitt, said my good-byes to teachers at the Wittelsbacher School, then boarded a train headed north to Heiligenhafen.

I sat in my third-class compartment and watched the landscape fly by; the sun streamed through my window. It was a relief to see grass growing and trees blooming—a sign of normalcy even in these times. I unpacked my lunch, grateful for the Schülerheim Schmitt's thoughtfulness. These days, if you didn't bring your own food, you did without, as dining cars were now a memory of the past.

It took almost ten hours to travel from Munich to Hamburg. But that was only the first leg of my journey. At Hamburg I waited for hours before boarding the connecting train to Kiel. Then I was told to look for either a local train or bus into Heiligenhafen. I arrived at the Naval Academy in the early evening, whereupon the duty clerk informed me that I had missed mess. I just stared at him.

"I know, I know! You've had a long trip and you're hungry, right?" He looked again at his watch. "Hold on, I'll see if I can dig up something from the kitchen."

The next morning the petty officer in charge assembled the newly arrived volunteers and marched us to a building for uniforms and supplies. "Wait over there until your name is called."

I was still dressed like a student at the Wittelsbacher School, but I leaned against a wall and tried not to look like the newcomer I was. A few minutes later my name was called. I stepped forward and was struck in the head by something heavy and solid. I looked down dazed, my head ringing, and saw a boot lying at my feet.

The petty officer snarled, "That's for being the son of that Austrian criminal! The other boot is with your gear."

I returned with the other new cadets to the barracks hoping that this man was an anomaly, not just one of many. To my enormous relief, the five cadets with whom I was billeted all seemed to be decent sorts. The next morning we were assigned to another petty officer; his name was Engel (angel in English).

The first week of basic training in any branch of the military, probably in any country, is the same: brutal. For maneuvers we wore our field grays—the wool jacket and pants of the regular army—boots, helmet, pack, and Karabiner 98 Kurz rifle. After some days of training, we were ordered to run through an obstacle course in this gear wearing a gas mask. It was midday and hot. We had been at it for half an hour when, stifled and queasy, I sought to loosen the gas mask that covered my face.

Petty Officer Engel had been waiting for someone to do just such a thing. He pulled me out of the detail, and the exercise continued without me. Some of the cadets collapsed out of sheer exhaustion. They were made to get up and repeat the obstacle course—from the beginning.

Petty Officer Engel returned to consider my case. I had been standing at attention for well over an hour under the blazing sun. "It is obvious that a skinny weakling like you needs special attention, Cadet. I am fully prepared to give you my absolute attention. It seems that your mask is something of a problem for you. Is that right?"

"No, sir. No problem at all!"

"Oh, but I think it is, Cadet. Remove your mask. Now, you will do double-time up that hill and do ten knee bends with rifle at full, horizontal extension. Then double-time it down the hill and do ten knee bends with rifle at full, horizontal extension. Then double-time back up the hill—you get the idea? I'll tell you when you're finished. Have I made myself clear, Cadet?"

"Yes, sir!"

I double-timed up the hill, did my knee bends, and double-timed down the hill thinking that a baby elephant would be a lighter burden than my uniform, helmet, and rifle. After three round trips, I was still on my feet. I was then given another order. "Cadet von Schuschnigg, I can see that this is child's play for you. You will now do push-ups with music." This meant I had to clap my hands together between each push-up. Soon after he began shouting out the count, I started smiling at him.

"You think this is funny, Cadet?"

"As long as you can count them out, I can smile."

"Resume double-time up the hill, Cadet!" he bellowed. I could see the veins sticking out on his neck. I felt better. It was a cloudless day and mercilessly hot—sweat blurred my vision, and my muscles began to cramp. My last memory was that of trying to make my rubbery legs work. I slid, rolled to the bottom of the hill, and came to rest, unconscious, at Engel's feet. A bucket of water was poured on my face as Engel enumerated my physical shortcomings in very colorful language. After being dismissed, I was helped back to the barracks by some of the other cadets.

After engine-room training the next day, I was called to the barracks. Engel was waiting for me; his arms were crossed before his chest, and he was leaning against a wall. "This place is a pigsty, Cadet von Schuschnigg! The Naval Academy does not tolerate filth and mess. You have three minutes to put everything in perfect order, Cadet!"

My bunk looked like the sight of a platoon exercise; all of my belongings from my locker and trunk were everywhere. It would take an act of God to put this right in three minutes. "Come on, boys, let's give our mate a hand!" said the sturdy, fearless Dietrich, who had come upon Engel in the middle of his rampage. My barrack mates and I threw ourselves into the task. Three minutes later, our mission accomplished, we stood at attention. Engel was not amused. He stalked out of the barrack, slamming the door behind him. It was clear to all of us that Engel had only begun.

Later that day, I was ordered to report to the admiral's office. This was a startling development. I searched my mind but could find no possible reason. I had given my best effort from the moment I had entered the Naval Academy. I arrived at the building, took a deep breath, and marched in. There, seated near the duty clerk's desk was Engel. When he saw me, he gave me a surly smile. I ignored him and gave my name to the duty clerk.

"The admiral is expecting you. Go straight in."

I marched in, stopped in front of the admiral's desk, and stood at attention. I was facing a sharp-eyed man in his sixties who, except for a precise fringe of gunmetal gray hair, was completely bald.

The set of his chin projected determination. I had the clear impression that this was a man who would stand for no nonsense.

"Cadet Kurt von Schuschnigg?"

"Yes, sir!"

"You are a hair's breadth away from going on report. Do you understand?"

"Yes, sir. Very good, sir!" I said crisply.

"Cadet von Schuschnigg, are you aware that it is a violation of duty not to report ill treatment by an instructor?"

"Yes, sir!" I said, though I had no idea that was the reason I was there. Engel's attitude in the outer room indicated that he had no idea either.

"You've been warned, Cadet. Abuse of power is not to be tolerated in the German Navy. Is that clear?"

"Absolutely clear, sir!" I could have jumped for joy.

"Dismissed."

"Yes, sir! Thank you very much, sir!"

Later, I learned that Engel's fellow instructors had finally been pushed beyond their endurance of his abuse of cadets. Engel's treatment of me had been the final straw. It was they who had reported him to the admiral.

There was one last memorable incident before I left the Naval Academy. On July 20, 1944, another attempt was made on Hitler's life. The plot led by Count Claus von Stauffenberg had failed, but because there was concern that it could be part of a larger action, a coastal alert was put into effect. I was put in charge of a detail assigned to guard the Heiligenhafen grain silo—a far better assignment than protecting the ammo depot. The detail consisted of five other men, side arms, and a machine gun.

Reporting to the armory, we collected a light machine gun and, after loading it into the jeep, drove to the silo. First the driver circled the silo's base, then I chose a site for the gun and ordered that it be loaded. Without a trace of sarcasm, one of the other cadets suggested that it first be mounted on its tripod. There were no sidelong looks or witty remarks made at my expense. We were all happy to be off the base. After mounting the gun and loading a belt of ammunition, four of the cadets dispersed around the silo. I sat down with the fifth cadet, whose job it was to man the gun. Then we waited.

An eternity seemed to pass before the all clear finally sounded. The cadets took the ammunition belt from the gun's chamber, dismantled the machine gun, and returned to the armory.

The petty officer in charge there was at least six feet five. He had bulging biceps and the broad, flat nose of a boxer. After snapping open the firing chamber of the machine gun, the petty officer stared and hesitated for a moment. Next he picked up the gun and peered down the barrel—then he regarded me in silence.

"You didn't fire this", he stated flatly.

"No. We had no cause to."

"Well, young Cadet Engineer, that was a stroke of luck for you!"

I was beginning to feel slightly uneasy.

"This is a training gun, Cadet Engineer." He turned the barrel toward me, holding it at an angle to catch the overhead light.

"The barrel is blocked. Can you see that? If you'd fired this, it would have exploded—ripping the barrel apart and taking the gunner's face with it."

"And what idiot gave my detail this weapon?" I shouted.

Leaning toward me he answered quietly, "I did." He picked up the gun and carried it into the weapons room. I returned to the barracks.

The rest of my training passed without incident. I acquired a highly localized knowledge of a ship's engine room. Our three-month course was designed to give each cadet enough training to be useful in as little time as possible. As the end of August approached, my fellow cadets and I began to speculate on our coming assignments. They all were German, but none had sympathy for or belief in the cause that was propelling us toward our future. Still, naive as we were, we thought war was an adventure and the prospect of being on a battleship exciting.

Our classes came to an end. We were told that the fatherland's need for us was urgent. I was assigned to the *Prinz Eugen*, an Admiral Hipper-class heavy cruiser and one of the fastest, most modern ships in the German Navy. It had been built in Kiel at the Krupp Germania shipyard and was said to have cost the German nation 104 millon reichsmarks.

After the First World War, the Allies had decreed that Germany would not be permitted to build any vessel whose displacement exceeded ten thousand tons—which, officially, was the tonnage of the *Prinz Eugen*. Its declared maximum speed was 32.8 knots. Unofficially, the ship weighed over nineteen thousand tons and was capable of a speed of almost 40 knots. Its keel was laid in April 1936, and the *Prinz Eugen* was launched on August 22, 1938. After sea trials it was commissioned in August 1940.

On the train to Danzig (Gdansk, Poland), I found a window seat. I was going to miss the beauty of the countryside in full bloom, the smell of the earth, and all that grew from it. But I would get used to life at sea soon enough because I was nothing if not adaptable.

After arriving in Danzig, I was still ten miles or so southeast of the German naval base at Gotenhafen (Gdynia, Poland), which had one of the largest harbors on the Baltic. Traveling the last leg to Gotenhafen, I could not help but consider how ironic it was for me to be assigned to a ship named after Prince Eugene of Savoy, one of the greatest field marshals ever to have fought for Austria. The irony bordered on the absurd when I recalled that Hitler, during the famous Berchtesgaden meeting, had invited Father to christen the *Prinz Eugen*. Uncle Willy's comment about that brought tears of laughter to my eyes: "Ah, yes. There was that small scheduling conflict in 1940—your father was in a Gestapo prison."

A navy bus took me to the dock. I joined the throng of sailors waiting to board. Among them, I saw one of my fellow cadets from the Naval Academy. "Manfred, I can't believe you're on the *Prinz Eugen*."

"Oh, yes. We're going to be shipmates, Kurt."

After exchanging more small talk, we discovered that we were also quartered together. It was a bit of luck not to be totally among strangers. We were assembled, and an ensign took us on a tour of the heavy cruiser. Listing the highlights of the ship, he spoke with pride. "The *Prinz Eugen* has eight 20.3-centimeter guns, four fore and four aft. In addition, there are twelve 10.5-centimeter guns, seventeen 4-centimeter guns, and twenty-eight 2-centimeter guns. Finally, there are twelve torpedo tubes and three seaplanes."

"Really!" said Manfred, now clearly impressed.

"Where are they?" I wanted to know.

"Well, you can see one amidships on its catapult. The other two are below deck. After a plane lands, it is taken from the water by crane. It is quite an operation. One miscalculation and the plane hits the side of the ship."

Now I too was impressed.

After thanking him, Manfred and I walked off on our own. "Well," I said, "if we have to be in this war and on a ship, then it's good to be on the best thing that floats."

We completed our tour of the 212-meter-long ship then went below to find our quarters. The ensign assigned to our crew wasted little time on formalities. He stated his name, and motioning to the lockers along the wall he said, "Pick out one and stow your gear. Take the key. It's numbered."

Except for the lockers the cabin was empty. Manfred and I chose ours. By the time we had stowed our gear, the cabin had filled up. There were now ten of us. Neither I nor Manfred, for he also remained silent, was going to be the one to ask, "Where do we sleep?"

We leaned against the wall and waited. The last cadet to arrive slammed his locker door, looked around the cabin, and arrived at the same question as Manfred and I had. He bluntly asked, "Where the devil is my bunk?"

After giving the cadet a long look the ensign answered, "No bunks on ship, you idiot! Where did you go through basic training?"

Just then the intercom crackled to life.

"Cadet von Schuschnigg. Report to the captain."

That sent a bolt of electricity through my stomach.

The ensign pointed to me and said, "That would be you, Cadet. Get moving!"

The ship's current complement consisted of about eight hundred men. Not an hour after setting foot on the *Prinz Eugen*, I was being summoned by the captain. I didn't think it was a good omen. From the expression on Manfred's face, neither did he.

Upon arriving at the captain's door, I took a deep breath, knocked, and—obedient to the voice inside—entered. "Cadet Engineer Schuschnigg reporting as ordered, sir!"

The captain was a man of medium height, with fair hair and regular features but much younger than I had expected. He rose from behind his desk and said, "Good afternoon, Cadet von Schuschnigg." Then he stuck out his hand. Dumbfounded, I shook it.

"Please take a seat", he said, motioning to one of the chairs in front of his desk.

"Would you care for a brandy?"

I selected the chair and sat down out of total reflex as my brain was in a state of shock. "That is very kind of you, sir. Thank you."

"Cadet," he handed me a half-full glass, "I want to make something perfectly clear. I do not allow politics on board my ship. We are at war. If someone on the *Prinz Eugen* gives you any trouble because of your name and who you are, I want it reported to me at once. By the same token, I expect you to do your duty just like everyone else."

"Captain Reinicke, I fully intend to do what is expected of me", I said, meaning it.

"Good. That is what I presumed." He concluded the subject with a slight smile and a nod.

Out of politeness he then talked about the ship and our part in the war at sea. I felt sorry for Capt. Hans-Jürgen Reinicke. He had taken command of the *Prinz Eugen* only in January 1944. He was another decent German who was certain to come out of this war badly. The prevailing attitude, which percolated down to the lowest reaches, was that the war was lost for the Axis powers—it was just a matter of time. The thought never failed to cheer me.

I finished my brandy, stood up, and thanked the captain. When I returned to my quarters, incredibly relieved, Manfred answered the bunk question. "You see those holes in the ceiling? Look straight down at the floor—matching holes. Cables are attached and form three-by-six-foot rectangles. A piece of canvas is hooked to the cables, a straw mattress goes on top, and you've got a berth!

"Well, that's all right. It's better than sleeping on the floor", I said to Manfred.

"Wait, Kurt, that's not the whole story. That is our sleeping arrangement right now, today, in port."

"Yes, and?"

"When we're under way, the mattresses and hammocks are stored in a fireproof room."

"Are you saying that we have to stow them every day in the fireproof room—or something else?"

"Something else", Manfred answered slowly.

"Like what?"

"Like we sleep wherever there is a comfortable corner."

"What! You mean on the floor?"

"Yep!" I knew my mouth was hanging open.

Manfred almost smiled.

"Do you mean to tell me that everybody does this?"

Manfred sighed deeply and said, "I have no idea, Kurt. All I know is that *we* do."

My ship duty was straightforward. I had been trained for the engine room. My job was to monitor the gauges, set various dials, and do other routine tasks. It was not overly demanding work; simple, in fact—but one thing was made clear to me as critical. The turbines had to be maintained within a certain temperature range. Above all, they must never be allowed to overheat. Should any gauge show fluctuations beyond the limits set for it, I was immediately to alert the bridge. There was one additional duty, an unwritten one: do nothing to irritate the regular crew. They did the real work aboard the *Prinz Eugen*. Cadets were viewed as a temporary burden—no substitute for real sailors. We were tolerated.

I was assigned to engine room three. My day began with a four-hour watch during which I monitored various gauges that reported data such as turbine temperatures and speeds as well as fuel consumption rates. Then came four hours of manning the phone, in readiness for any emergency that might arise. This shift also required that I act as a backup to the next operator. During the last four-hour period, I was off duty. Then the rotation began again. There were between ten and twelve cadets in each cabin, and they went off duty at the same time. This schedule had nothing to do with fostering camaraderie; it was meant to coordinate our mess schedule.

Our group of ten cadets ate together in our quarters. Our mess gear was kept in our lockers. After each meal, we washed our utensils and stowed them again. Our food was brought to the cabin by the two cadets assigned to meal duty that day. When a cabin's number was announced over the loudspeaker, they dashed to the galley while the others returned to quarters. Latecomers got whatever was left.

Eating and sleeping during off-duty hours was a challenge. A man was doing well if he managed three and a half hours of sleep per off-duty shift. There was also the matter of trying to fall asleep on the floor.

Our stored mattresses were stacked in the small area adjacent to our cabin. After two days at sea, I was worn-out from insufficient sleep and decided to try a new sleeping arrangement. I climbed onto the pile of mattresses and slid into the narrow space between them and the ceiling. I slept like a baby.

On the second or third day of this new routine, an ensign discovered me. I had left the connecting door to our quarters slightly ajar. From a sound sleep on my pile of mattresses, I was jolted awake by the shouted, "Cadet Engineer!"

Groggy but awake I finally answered, "Yes, sir?"

"How long have you been up there?"

"Uh, what time is it?"

"Nineteen hundred hours."

"What? Good God!" I started up and struck my head against the ceiling. "I've been here since 1400 hours."

"Didn't you tell anyone to wake you before your next shift started?"

I climbed down and stood there looking blankly at him. Why hadn't I thought of that? I could feel the blood draining from my head. I had been on duty for the last hour. Every sailor knew that falling asleep on duty was deemed "cowardice in the face of the enemy" and that the punishment for this was death by firing squad. It was one of the first things we were taught at the Naval Academy.

The ensign informed me that I had managed to sleep through an engagement with a Russian ship in which the *Prinz Eugen* took up pursuit of the vessel and had a lengthy exchange of gunfire with it. The action, having taken place in rough seas, had caused considerable pitching and rolling of the ship. "Unbelievable", the ensign concluded, shaking his head.

I didn't know if he meant the battle or my ability to sleep through it. I apologized profusely for my stupidity and thanked him for waking me.

With dread mounting within me, I hurried to my station praying for protection to whichever saint was in charge of the seas.

There were three of us in this section of the engine room; to my relief, neither of the other two seamen was visible, and all of my gauges registered "normal". No one had seen me arrive at my station. That didn't mean I hadn't been missed, but they wouldn't know how late I was.

I had been there only a few minutes when the seaman whose job it was to observe and maintain the oil and coolant levels appeared, saying, "That was some action, wasn't it?"

"Unbelievable!" replied another sailor who followed him into the engine room.

That word made me wince, but I chimed in, "It certainly was! Thank God nothing blew!"

It didn't seem as if there were any accusations that would be coming from the engine room crew, but there was another potential danger: the ensign. I waited tensely for my name to be called over the intercom or for the appearance of a security officer. Every time the intercom came alive, I held my breath. I finished that shift with raw nerves.

When I entered the cabin for mess call, one of the cadets good-naturedly slapped me on the back; I jumped. "You need some sleep, my friend!" he said earnestly.

No thanks! Sleep was responsible for my predicament.

For the rest of the day, I watched the faces around me, but no one seemed to know about my oversleeping. I was on my guard the next day, and again nothing happened. On the third day, I began to think that the ensign had shown me a great mercy; otherwise I would have been in the brig by then.

What had I been thinking to let myself make such a terrible mistake? I recruited Manfred to be my alarm clock. That way when I went off duty, it was safe to sleep. Gradually, I put the incident out of my mind but not my dreams.

Raymond Vohman was one of the ten cadets with whom I was quartered. He was four years older than I and had previously been a sub-lieutenant in the French navy. It was Raymond's good fortune to be Alsatian. The Third Reich had declared that Alsace was again German, making Raymond now a German citizen. Had this not happened, Raymond after June 1940 would have found himself an Allied prisoner of war. Instead, he had been sent to the German

169

Naval Academy, made a cadet engineer, and assigned to the *Prinz Eugen*. Raymond was a true navy man: he loved the sea and serving on a ship. He was easygoing and excellent company. There was another thing about Raymond: he hated the Nazis. I had an ally, a good friend, and also another reliable alarm clock.

On October 15, the *Prinz Eugen* was steaming for Gotenhafen. The ship had just passed the Hela Peninsula at about eight P.M. I was on duty in engine room three when suddenly I was thrown forward as the ship lurched violently. We had hit something solid. The lights immediately went out—it was now pitch-dark. I sat at my post as instructed. Seconds later, the emergency lights came on. I could hear the *Eugen's* siren wailing.

A heavy fog blanketed the entire area from the nearby port of Gotenhafen outward past the peninsula. The fog was so dense that the *Eugen* had turned on its running lights, a practice rare in wartime, and was sounding its foghorn. Our ship was not the only ship in the area: the light cruiser *Leipzig* was departing Gotenhafen, its home port. Like the *Prinz Eugen*, the *Leipzig* was also assigned to help protect the German retreat from the eastern front by shelling enemy installations and troop movements. The *Leipzig*, without the benefit of running lights, was slowly departing when it was hit broadside by the *Prinz Eugen*.

Even though the light cruiser was traveling at only fourteen knots, the 177.1-meter-long *Leipzig* was nearly severed amidships. The collision left the *Prinz Eugen* at just enough of an angle that its propellers were partially out of the water and ineffective. The ship could not reverse itself. Separating the two ships took fourteen hours, but repairing the ships would be more involved.

In addition to the damage done to the *Leipzig*, twenty-seven of her crewmembers died and numerous others were injured. One of the *Leipzig's* officers, white scarf wrapped around his neck and attaché case in hand, was observed preparing to leap to safety onto the bow of the *Prinz Eugen*. In making his way to the side of his ship, he had literally stepped over the body of a seaman injured in the collision. A crew member seeing this reacted swiftly—punching the officer squarely in the mouth, knocking him to the deck, and yelling, "Take care of the wounded before you save your own skin!" Interestingly enough this seaman was only reprimanded—not court-martialed.

It was publicly acknowledged that neither Captain Reinicke of the *Prinz Eugen* nor Captain Spörel of the *Leipzig* was to blame for the deadly collision. The rules of transit and passage in extreme weather had been followed. Hitler must have been furious, however. He had just ridiculed the British for an at-sea naval collision. There was one positive outcome for the crew of the *Prinz Eugen*—we would have an unexpected shore leave. The crew of the *Leipzig* probably sat out the rest of the war waiting for it to be repaired.

In November 1944, after the *Prinz Eugen* returned to home port following the *Leipzig* collision, Cadet Franz Burkert and I were fetching and carrying during mess call. As we neared our quarters with the food, we heard a loud and animated discussion in progress.

"What do you think that's all about?" I asked Franz.

"Could be anything", he said. "I just hope it isn't about waiting for mess." Raymond came over to help us unload the food.

"What's going on?" I asked.

"Something pretty awful happened earlier today. One of the enlisted men assigned to gun duty stepped inside for a moment; he thought his hands were frozen."

Conversation in the cabin subsided.

"You know how brutally cold it is out there, easily minus forty degrees."

There was a chorus of nods and murmuring.

"Well, you can hardly blame the fellow for that", I said. "Earlier I was on deck; there had to be a forty-mile-an-hour wind blowing."

"Yes," Raymond said, "but stepping inside wasn't the problem."

"What then?" Franz asked.

"The problem was that he fell asleep."

Now there was dead silence. I felt a numbness starting at the bottom of my heart. Raymond went on, "The duty officer looking for him found him huddled in a corner, eyes closed, mouth open, and sound asleep."

"Well, what happened?" My voice was too loud and I knew it.

"He was arrested on the spot and taken to the brig."

Franz asked, "What's going to happen to him?"

"What do you think? Cowardice in the face of the enemy: death by firing squad. All cadets are required to be on deck tomorrow at noon."

This seemed incredible to me—it could not be cowardice to fall asleep. I was so intent on this thought that I wasn't sure that I hadn't said it out loud. I ate without knowing what I was eating, then tried to sleep—impossible. My mind clung to one thought—that might have been me. Somewhere on this ship was an ensign to whom I owed my life, and I couldn't even remember what he looked like.

My entire off-duty shift had been a waste, and I reported early for the next watch. My mind was elsewhere, and I couldn't focus. I considered faking an illness like the one that had gotten me released from RAD, but my heart just wasn't in the effort.

The following morning our ensign reminded us that every cadet had to be present on deck for the execution. My fellow cadets and I were on deck five minutes before noon under a gray sky teeming with thunderclouds. How cruel it was: a man about to die for falling asleep was on his last day denied a glimpse of the sun. Behind us in the stiff wind, flags whipped against the metal flagpole—its sounds an ominous foretaste of those to come.

Would the corpse be wrapped in sacking and disposed of immediately? Or would there be a ceremony afterward conducted by the ship's chaplain? Was there a chaplain? I had neither seen nor heard of one aboard. I busied my mind, trying to distance myself from what was to be.

The firing squad of six sailors marched in a file, halted on command, then turned toward starboard facing an angry sea. Raymond, who had witnessed an execution by firing squad, told me that one of the rifles would contain a blank cartridge. Each sailor in the detail could think, pray, or hope that his rifle had the blank.

The condemned was brought on deck by two sailors. Neither shackled nor blindfolded, he was walked to a point about ten paces in front of the firing squad. I didn't look at his face. I didn't want to remember it. The charge was read out: "Cowardice in the face of the enemy. May God have mercy on your soul."

The deck, crowded with hundreds of men, was absolutely still. Not a sound was heard; no one coughed, whispered, or sneezed. The guards stepped away from the man. I closed my eyes. Then I heard, "Detail, ready." After "Aim!", I opened my eyes and looked down at my shoes. Despite my intentions, at the command "Fire!",

I looked at the sailor. He hung there for a moment, as if suspended from an invisible rope. His face registered disbelief. His body fell heavily on the deck. I looked at the ocean.

The *Prinz Eugen* returned to Gotenhafen, for replacement of its main gun tubes. Twelve-hour shore leaves had been granted; but before the first party could disembark, an announcement came over the intercom: the park adjacent to the naval base was off limits to all navy personnel. Polish partisans were active in that park, and there had been a number of fatal incidents there.

One of the seamen listening to the announcement with me could have been a model for Aryan manhood—blue eyes, dazzling white teeth, a strong jawline, blonde hair, and an olympic build. He had what women called movie star looks and a girlfriend waiting for him on shore. I worked with him in engine room three and knew that he was his own favorite topic. He liked to brag about his fearlessness; no one and nothing could intimidate him.

Before the announcement had ended he burst out indignantly, "Not walk in the park? Ridiculous! That is my favorite park. I always walk in that park."

Those were the last words I heard him say. Sometime before midnight his naked body was found hanging from a tree in the park. For consorting with the enemy, his Polish girlfriend lay nearby with her throat slashed.

Armed resistance in Gotenhafen had grown since it became home port to German ships late in the war. When the *Prinz Eugen* first docked there, one guard had been posted at its bow and another at the stern. No sooner had this routine been established than it had to be changed. The relief guard detail found the first two guards decapitated—their heads bucketed in their helmets. A two-man watch, fore and aft, was instituted.

As I was leaving the ship with the other cadets for our shore leave, we passed some of the enlisted men from the neighboring ship. In the navy, ranking cadets are listed below officers but above enlisted men. The other crew stopped to salute us. One of them was my old nemesis, Petty Officer Engel. Recognition dawned. His face froze. I smiled—slowly—flipped a return salute, and moved on with my group.

The sleeping arrangements on the *Prinz Eugen* aside, life aboard ship was infinitely better than civilian life. Not only was there plenty of food, but there was a pack of cigarettes a day and a quart of alcohol per month included in our rations. Occasionally even this generous allowance proved to be insufficient. It wasn't that we were hardened drinkers. None of us had even been regular drinkers before the navy. But a shot of alcohol and a cigarette seemed to go well with our card games. There was little else to pass the time off duty.

One day my fellow cadets and I found ourselves off duty and without so much as a drop of liquor among us. Good fortune had smiled upon us the previous month. A rat had been spotted in our quarters, and I had caught it. Every rodent aboard had a bounty on its head: one bottle of confiscated French cognac. My prize cognac was now a memory, and for about the tenth time Goswin, one of my cabinmates, complained that our card game wasn't the same without it. Then he raised a question: "Kurt, what was the exact sequence of events with your rat?"

"I caught the rat, took it to the executive officer, and got my bottle of cognac."

"No! Go through the details. How did you carry the rat to the EO's quarters—by its tail, in your teeth, or what?" He seemed genuinely curious.

"Are you joking? Rats are filthy things. I picked it up with newspaper and wrapped it up."

"Then what?"

"I knocked at the EO's door, went in, and said I was there to give him the rat I'd caught."

"Go on—what did he say to you?"

"I don't know—something like 'good job.' "

"And then?"

"And then I held out the rat!"

"Yes, but did you take it out of the newspaper to show him?"

"No, I didn't. I held out the bundle and started to unwrap it. He immediately said, 'Just throw the thing out the porthole', which I did. That was it!"

"So, you never showed him the actual rat. He just took your word for it. He never saw the rat, did he?"

"Well, no, come to think of it, he didn't." I looked at the faces around me and knew I had been had. I was an idiot! I was now to wrap a piece of wood in newspaper, take it to the executive officer, and receive a bottle of cognac. "Great," I exclaimed, "do any of you know how to spell gangplank or even brig?"

"This is a sure thing! You threw it out the porthole—remember? We know he doesn't save it for the galley. People are creatures of habit; he won't change. Believe me!"

"Goswin's right", my friend Manfred offered. "The EO would never ask to see a dead rat. If word got out that he had, why, the captain would trade him to the Russians!"

The vote was solidly against me. I marched off, shaking my head, and holding a rat-like piece of wood wrapped in newspaper. I stopped in front of the officer's quarters, took a deep breath, and raised my hand to knock.

"Do I really want to do this?" I asked myself.

An officer appeared in the gangway. Seeing the piece of camouflaged wood he said affably, "Looks like a bottle of cognac to me!"

"Yes, sir!" Resigned to my fate, I knocked sharply on the door. "Enter."

I stepped inside. "Cadet von Schuschnigg reporting with a rat—a dead one, sir", I said trying to sound cheerful.

"Ah, Cadet von Schuschnigg. You are becoming a regular Pied Piper. Well done!"

"Yes, sir! If we don't stomp on these disease-carrying rodents, they'll find their way into the food supply." I stepped forward and, holding my breath, extended the bundle toward him. In what felt like slow motion, I reached out with my other hand as if to open the paper and expose a squashed rat. The officer, God bless his trusting soul, waved it away as before.

"Throw the thing out the porthole!"

In November 1944, while covering the massive German land retreat from Russia, the lookouts on the *Prinz Eugen* spotted a disabled Russian submarine flying a white flag. As the *Prinz Eugen* drew nearer, the submarine flashed the international SOS distress signal with its ship-to-ship light. The captain ordered stop engines about five hundred yards from the submarine, which was bobbing drunkenly in the rough, dark sea. Our 20.3- and 10.5-centimeter guns were trained on it.

An armed boarding party was dispatched, and the launch wove across the choppy waves. It soon returned with its first load of surrendering Russian sailors. A lot of the crew of the *Prinz Eugen* gathered along the railings. Many of us discussed how we were going to tow the submarine back to home port. Spoils of war or not, the thought of having to engage the enemy while towing a disabled vessel was distressing.

After the last of the Russians had been rescued, a German engineer was sent to the submarine. When he returned, and in less time than any of our hastily shouted wagers could be recorded, the submarine began to sink. Amid a plume of whitewater, the submarine disappeared beneath the waves. The Russians had intended to scuttle the vessel but couldn't figure out how to do so. This provided fuel for innumerable Russian jokes. The sailors didn't mind bearing the brunt of German humor; they were just grateful that we had respected their white flag of surrender in a war going badly for Germany.

The *Prinz Eugen* arrived at Gotenhafen the week before Christmas to take on fuel and supplies. All the cadets were issued a seven-day shore leave. I had been prepared to spend the holiday in the middle of the Baltic Sea but now found myself making my way south to Sachsenhausen. The journey was not as difficult as I had expected. Trains were working and adhered to something resembling a schedule; however, things would get worse as the Russian sweep continued westward. The defeat of the Axis powers was approaching. I was worried about what conditions could develop in Sachsenhausen during the last days of the war.

I had an important delivery for Father: the Browning and ammunition that Herr Walter had insisted I take with me so long ago. At the time, I hadn't appreciated Herr Walter's foresight; now I considered it genius. One gun with a clip of ammunition would not repel an army, but it meant that Father would not have to face danger unarmed if danger arose.

The guards at Sachsenhausen had searched me only once—when I visited my family for the first time in December 1941. Wearing a navy uniform now, I felt confident that the Browning and I would go through without a problem. The guards' greetings were full of Christmas good wishes. Then they wanted to know about the war at sea. Searching me was the furthest thing from their minds.

Father, Sissi, and Vera greeted me with surprise and joy. At this moment, at this place, and in this war, we were together and alive. The future would have to wait. We talked about everything and about nothing. Being together was Christmas and the best Christmas could be.

When Sissi had gone upstairs for her nap, I gave Father the Browning along with Herr Walter's message. Father looked at the gun, glanced at me, and shaking his head said that he was glad to have it. Now we had to hide it—not from the guards but from Sissi. She was everywhere, and her curiosity knew no bounds. Dangerously bright, she could climb anywhere by stacking things on top of each other. The kitchen provided a solution. Vera emptied a canister and hid the gun in it. The canister was then pushed to the back of the top shelf in the cupboard.

In January 1945 the *Prinz Eugen* was still covering the German retreat. Cruising its regular route along the Baltic coastline, the ship shelled Russian installations, troop movements, and targets of opportunity that were worth the price of a projectile.

One day, during an off-duty shift, I watched the main gun turrets swing around and lock onto a target that had been radioed in previously by a besieged German Army unit. The guns discharged two salvos within seconds of one another. The hits were confirmed, bringing a general cheer around the deck. Later we learned that the German ground troops had mistakenly advanced to the coordinates they had radioed to the ship. The *Prinz Eugen* had annihilated Germany's own confused and freezing countrymen.

Russian tanks and artillery constantly lobbed shells at the *Prinz Eugen* despite a distinct disadvantage in gun range and accuracy. The contest was German skill and precision versus Russian brute force and stubbornness. The Germans had the edge. To help alleviate boredom—weather permitting—we spent part of our off-duty hours on deck wagering on the inaccuracy of Russian shelling. Sometimes this was the high point of a morning or an afternoon.

One day a Russian T-34 on the shore favored us with its attentions. The tank's cannon spat round after futile round despite the fact that the *Prinz Eugen* was a mile or two beyond its range. With binoculars we could spot a puff of smoke from the shore and, some seconds later, a geyser of water a mile distant but vectored toward us. German high command had issued orders to conserve ammunition. Gunners were to fire only at military installations and troop movements when in pursuit or when Germans were in danger. After fifteen or twenty minutes of watching the tank's best efforts, however, the artillery officer ran out of patience. Our gun turret swung slowly. After sighting the target with great deliberation, it loosed a single salvo and blew the Russian tank to smithereens. A cheer went up on deck, and much backslapping and congratulations followed: we were easily amused.

Our humor could not disguise the fact that Germany's position grew grimmer every day despite German technological superiority. By mid-January 1945, the Russians' advance had not wavered. Swift and ruthless, they left in their wake death and destruction.

I had barely begun my shift one day when I noticed a definite fluctuation in the readings on my gauges. It seemed minor, but I had no intention of taking any chances. Using the catwalk I went to check the number three turbine, found everything in order, and returned to my post.

High above, a Heinkel He 111 advanced toward the ship. The *Prinz Eugen* had not been notified of a German bomber in the vicinity, but Axis intelligence had become steadily less reliable. Once the plane was directly overhead, it opened its bomb bay. That He 111 was an abandoned aircraft—now piloted by a Russian.

A fifty-kilogram bomb hurtled down through the ship's main funnel. The *Prinz Eugen* was massively armored with heavy steel plating, and the bomb's impact was easily absorbed; but the normal expulsion of steam was affected. The funnels that projected from engine rooms one and two were clear and functioning normally. But fragments from the exploded bomb had completely blocked engine room three's funnel, forcing the rising steam back down into the engine room.

Unaware of the unfolding events, I continued to watch the gauges. Other than the minor fluctuation I had just checked on, my entire tour of duty aboard the *Prinz Eugen* had been without incident. So when the turbine's primary dials suddenly leapt to within a hair's breadth of "explosion status", I prayed that it was a gauge malfunction but sprang for the phone. I tried to remain calm as I described the readings to the engineer. There was a hasty thanks on the line, which then went dead.

I just had time to wonder what had caused the aberration in the gauge before steam exploded into the engine room and blew up the boiler. Searing heat followed the deafening explosion—super-heated steam filled the room.

Some time later, I opened my eyes. My lungs felt as if they were on fire. I tried to roll onto my back—the pain was intense. I decided not to make that mistake again. Vaguely aware of the screaming and groaning around me, I lay where I had fallen, drifting in and out of consciousness. I could see about a foot above me; the scene resembled a winter whiteout in the mountains. I thought of blizzards and of the texture of very cold snow. I recalled making my first snowman and wondered if there were any snow yet in Sachsenhausen for Sissi to play in.

Then I was looking up at a ceiling light. I turned my head and saw a wall. Turning the other way, I saw a doctor putting his stethoscope on the chest of an immobile man. Behind him were glass cases containing instruments and bandages—sickbay. On one side of the doctor, two more white jackets were leaning over a body. I couldn't think what I was doing there. I tried to sit up; a wave of pain swept over me. I managed to raise my head. My leather jumpsuit and the slacks and shirt underneath had been peeled away on my right side. I was covered from my shoulder to my ankle with salve and bandages. Suddenly a white jacket was next to me; a voice floated down, "We've just given you morphine. You have burns covering your right side. Your face and entire side have already been treated. Do not move. Just try to sleep."

When I awoke, I was able to understand what had happened. The ship's doctor declared that I was, despite the burns and a torn lung, a very lucky cadet. Four more from the engine room were also in the ship's infirmary. The others were in body bags, awaiting burial at sea.

On the following day, the *Prinz Eugen* stopped engines just outside Königsberg, where I was to be hospitalized. The ship's tender transferred five of us to a boat headed for shore. As the vessel pulled into the port, deserted except for a single submarine, I got my final view of the *Prinz Eugen*. My sea duty had come to an end.

# Recuperation

The first few days in the Königsberg hospital passed in a morphine-induced blur. I was aware only of nurses and doctors in white uniforms, my bandages being changed, and conversations that I could not understand. About the fourth day, full consciousness returned, and with it knowledge that the Russians had surrounded Königsberg.

The evacuation of the port began. The Russian Army controlled all lands east of the city, and inhabitants traveling west had to pass through a Russian-controlled exit. Only civilians were given safe passage through the Russian checkpoint. That left an entire hospital full of wounded military personnel whose only escape route was by sea.

A nurse named Hilda woke me with the news that she had come to prepare me for the evacuation. As she explained the plans, she checked my bandages and applied salve to the burns on my skin. When she had finished, I mentioned that I had been brought to Königsberg by a small ship and that the only vessel in port at the time was a small submarine.

"Yes! That's the one. The whole hospital is being put aboard."

Nurse Hilda located my duffel bag and began stuffing what I had into it.

"I see. Well, Nurse Hilda, thank you for all you have done for me. I am here in this hospital because of an explosion on board a ship. There is no way in the world I'm getting on another sea-going vessel—least of all a submarine. I'd sooner take my chances burrowing my way out of here underneath the Russian lines using a spoon." I had not overlooked the fact that I couldn't even stand up on my own. I just knew that I would not travel by water.

"Of course, I understand how you feel", she said sympathetically. "I would probably feel the same way if I'd been in an explosion on a ship. Let me just see what I can do. Perhaps there is something else that can be worked out."

Before I could reply she had left. There would be few evacuation alternatives for wounded military. My thoughts all morning were of how to escape the Russian soldiers outside the city. Given my condition, the outlook seemed bleak.

Near the end of the afternoon, I spotted Nurse Hilda making her way through the ward in my direction. Not wanting to hear the inevitable and determined to avoid the submarine, I closed my eyes and feigned sleep. After calling my name several times she gently shook my shoulder—there was no avoiding Nurse Hilda. As soon as she saw my eyes open she began: "Cadet von Schuschnigg, I have good news for you."

"Yes?"

"Well, I am leaving with a very kind couple that I know, friends of my parents. They have a farm on the outskirts of Königsberg."

"Yes?"

"They leave early tomorrow morning in a covered wagon just like hundreds now rolling out of Königsberg. I am to ride in the back of the wagon. If we are questioned, they will say that I am their daughter."

I realized that I was holding my breath when I began to feel light-headed. Nurse Hilda reached for a damp cloth. "No, no, I am fine. Please continue."

"I went out to the farm today. I told them about you and asked if they would let you come with us. Farmer Becker said it was up to his wife, but instead of answering yes or no, she asked me how old you looked—not how old you are but how old you looked. I thought about it, and I told her you looked fourteen or fifteen years old but are really eighteen."

I could feel my face redden. My very young appearance always had been an embarrassment, but there wasn't much I could do about it. Perhaps reading my thoughts, Nurse Hilda said, "I am more than a year older than you. I'm sure you didn't know that, did you?"

"No, I didn't", I said genuinely surprised. With full, rosy cheeks and smiling blue eyes, she didn't look more than fifteen herself. "*Please* tell me what Frau Becker said."

"Oh, I thought I had! Frau Becker said she had always wanted a son." She clapped her hands in delight. It made her seem even younger.

For the first time in my life, I was thankful for not looking my age. It was bad enough being a new cadet fresh from naval school with a ranking above the enlisted men, but looking fourteen or fifteen years old had made my situation even more difficult.

What these people were doing for me was much more than an act of kindness. It was an act of bravery. If they were discovered aiding a German sailor, even a raw cadet engineer, the Russians would shoot all of us on the spot.

"You'd better get a good night's sleep. We leave before daybreak. I also brought you some clothes to wear from Farmer Becker", she said, placing them on the chair beside my bed. As she turned to straighten my bedcovers I reached for her hand. "I will never forget this. I don't have words to thank you for what you and the Beckers are doing for me."

It was her turn now to blush; on her it was becoming.

Early next morning one of the orderlies carried me out the side entrance of the hospital. I was put atop the loose hay in the Beckers' covered wagon. My duffel bag was buried under the hay.

Nurse Hilda sat on her own hay pile. She too was out of uniform but had added a touch of her own: she had braided her hair in pigtails. Now she looked twelve years old. In the front sat the Beckers, who were saving me from a very dark fate. They looked as if they could be in their fifties but despite their lined and weather-worn faces the Beckers were probably no more than forty.

As the horses began to pull the wagon, I tried to thank the Beckers but was interrupted by Nurse Hilda. "You can thank them after we stop for the night. This is to keep the dust from your torn lung", she said as she covered my face with a damp hospital mask. And with that we headed to join other covered wagons headed west toward Danzig.

The exodus from Königsberg stretched for miles. Horses and donkeys pulled wagons and carts overflowing with household goods, furniture, tools, and livestock. Choices had been made between necessities and things of real or sentimental value. The dust from so many people, wagons, and animals in the air made breathing difficult. Many tied bandanas, cloths, or kerchiefs over their mouths and noses. Moistened with water these helped against the invasive and choking dust.

The refugee line was passing between two Russian T-34 tanks when we were stopped by Russian soldiers looking for German military personnel, implements of war, and treasure. Frau Becker turned to us and hurriedly whispered, "Pray—Saint Christopher." Not an unreasonable suggestion; we did.

Nurse Hilda and I sat in the back of the wagon trying to look our part—sad but obedient youths—amid the Beckers' household items as the first Russian approached the wagon and said in broken German, "Soldiers get out or we kill you!"

Farmer Becker, unimpressed, replied calmly, "There are no soldiers here, which you can see for yourself. Here," he enunciated each word carefully, "is my wife. In the back are my children." He put his hand on Nurse Hilda's head. "Daughter", he said slowly. Then he put his hand on my head. "Son." To Hilda and me he said, "It is all right. Don't be scared."

Two Russians with rifles walked around to the rear of the wagon and leaned inside. Their broad faces and pronounced cheekbones were foreign in appearance to us. But it was their slightly slanted eyes—black and devoid of emotion—that made me feel cold. I had little doubt that either of them could shoot a man, woman, or child as easily as he could crush a gnat. Using the barrel of his rifle, one of the soldiers dug into the hay at our feet. A loud discussion broke out between him and the other soldier. It was settled when one soldier, knife between his teeth, crawled under the wagon and drove the knife up between the bottom slats of the wagon bed. When this exercise produced no dramatic results, they grudgingly waved us through. Farmer Becker flicked the reins, and the horses started forward.

Getting past this Russian advanced unit had been the simple part. There were many miles still remaining, and it was January 1945— winter. Despite the snow and the freezing wind, men, women, and children trudged on without complaining. It was a silent affair. There was no banter back and forth.

The journey to Danzig would take three full days. Farmer Becker said that he had enough hay for the animals. More important than our food, water, or comfort were the needs of the horses. Attending to the wagon was next on Farmer Becker's list of priorities. The axles were greased during rest stops for the horses and at night. He went over every inch of his wagon looking for any signs of a failing board or metal fitting as well as a missing nail.

This massive exodus had transformed the proud and prosperous Germans into hordes of cold, homeless refugees. Everything for which they had worked and saved all of their lives, except for the few possessions they carried with them, lay behind—spoils of war for the conquering Russians.

From the air the slow-moving wagons were an irresistible target for any overflying Russian aircraft. Luckily, Russian inaccuracy prevented any serious setbacks. Neither the occasional strafing nor our present circumstances caused me concern. I had been rescued from two stark choices: transport in an airless tin can—the Germans had lost over 240 submarines in 1944 alone—or becoming a Russian prisoner of war.

The caravan was on the move until dusk. After stretching out cramped limbs, the men would tend the horses and wagons while the women prepared food. Nurse Hilda saw to me first. After changing my bandages, she went about helping Frau Becker. Sleep came easily, and first light came early.

Before dusk on the third day we rolled into Danzig. Farmer Becker directed the team of horses to the hospital and reined them to a stop. This was the first time in my life I was happy to see a hospital. It represented a bath, bed, and hot food—luxuries in those days. Words were inadequate to thank the Beckers and Nurse Hilda for the risk they all took to keep me from being captured by the Russians in Königsberg. I would never forget them.

I was assigned to a ward and slept for the better part of three days, during which the progress of the advancing Russians was constant. Impervious to bad weather, rough terrain, and scarce supplies, the Red Army was nearing Danzig; capture of the city was imminent. An orderly brought the news that there would be an evacuation. He checked off my name on his list. "Cadet von Schuschnigg, your transfer is set for five A.M. tomorrow."

As he turned to leave I grabbed his sleeve. "Transfer—how?"

"You are one of the fifteen hundred patients who will be evacuated tomorrow on the *Wilhelm Gustloff*", he stated as if awarding a prize.

I knew about the ship. Before the war, the *Wilhelm Gustloff* had been built as the luxury ship for the working man. Named after the assassinated leader of the Swiss Nazis, it belonged to the Nazi party's *Kraft durch Freude* (Strength through Joy) organization. The *Wilhelm Gustloff* was the sea-going equivalent of the Volkswagen automobile—meant to give the average German a taste of the good life at a price that he could afford.

"That would be 1499 patients. This patient is not getting on that ship."

"What do you mean? The Russians will be here by tomorrow afternoon." He spoke as if to an uncomprehending child.

"My injuries came from being on a ship, and I will not get back on one. That is final—I'd sooner take my chance with the Russians."

"Now, I know you're sick. What on earth do you expect me to do?"

I thought for a moment. "There must be trains leaving Danzig. Please get me on one of them."

"What you are asking is not possible; there aren't any seats."

That was probably true. The population of Danzig was certainly in a state of panic. Everyone who could buy or bribe his way onto a train had already done so, not because a conquering army would occupy Danzig, but because Russians would be loosed upon the city. Their reputation had preceded them. The Red Army's reward for each victory was well known: officers granted their men three days of sanctioned rampaging, raping, and plundering. After three days, any soldier caught violating the inhabitants was shot dead on the spot.

"I am only asking—no, I am begging—you to inquire. I cannot, and will not, get on a ship again. If the Russians get me, then so be it."

"Look, I will do my best. I promise."

"Thank you. That is all I ask."

He stood looking at me for a moment then stuck out his neck like a turtle from its shell. "First you have to let go of my arm."

"Sorry."

After the orderly left, I swung my legs over the side of the bed, struggled to the washbasin, and slowly made my way back. I lay on the bed breathing hard; there was no way I could get any place on my own. Some other way had to be found.

The orderly returned later as nightfall came upon Danzig. It was clear that he did not bring good news. He came directly to my bed and spoke quietly, "I spent the better part of this afternoon at the

185

transport office—I did my best. It is not possible to get out of this city by land."

"You mean to say that there isn't one berth on any train out of Danzig?"

"Not one", he spoke carefully for emphasis. "All the hospital's patients are going to be on the *Wilhelm Gustloff*. You know it's practically a brand-new luxury ship. I wouldn't mind going on her myself."

"What do you mean? Aren't you going on the ship too?"

"No, there wasn't any more room. We orderlies are scheduled to go by train."

Another answer to my prayers had presented itself. A minute later, I had his place on the train, and he had my navy-rationed cigarettes—worth a fortune in wartime. This arrangement left us both very pleased. I was sure that being an orderly he might be able to finagle himself on the train. Otherwise he could take my place on the ship—the choice would be his.

The next morning the other orderlies took me to the station. I was wheeled into a three-berth compartment and placed on the middle bunk. Above and below me were wounded soldiers. The train would head due west to Stettin. In peacetime the trip had taken two and a half hours. Our trip would take almost a day and a half. Strafing by Russian aircraft caused innumerable delays. Each time, the train stopped and all aboard got off as quickly as possible— fortunately, Russian pilot accuracy didn't ever seem to improve.

The wounded soldiers in berths above and below me were non-stop talkers. I heard in great detail the views of the common man. They painted a grim picture of Germany's position. "We" were hanging from a ledge by "our" fingernails. The lack of fuel and ammunition was severe. Six years of war had consumed Germany's resources, and the once-famous German resilience had been ground down.

For a portion of the transit to Stettin, the railroad tracks parallel the highway. I was positioned in my berth with my feet pointing toward the window affording me a view of the passing countryside and roadway. Gazing out train windows was a habit that had given me years of pleasure; but as the train crept westward, the scenes that passed before my window grew more macabre by the mile. Still harnessed skeletal horses with icicles dripping from their manes

186

nosed for a blade of grass in the crusted snow. Spilling out of over-turned wagons were entire families—frozen together in death. Petrified animal carcasses lined the roads.

As far as the eye could see, for mile after frozen mile, the wintry, white wasteland stretched before us. I thought of the anxiety that must have filled the minds of those retreating German soldiers as they fled. How hopeless their mission had been once the Russian winter had them in its grip; how wretched their path now.

The medics making their rounds also dispensed information. The train, we learned, had about fifteen cars full of civilian passengers in addition to the string of hospital cars.

"I'll tell you how bad things are in the other cars", said the medic who was looking in on us. "You wounded are the lucky ones." He paused to check the pulse of the soldier in the berth above me and said, "Your pulse is good—much stronger. You'll be up in no time." Then he returned to his story. "You can't imagine how horrible it is for those civilians. Aisles, corridors, and berths are one solid mass of humanity. A couple of cars back a pregnant woman went into premature labor. A passenger near the door went for help, but it was too late. The poor woman had delivered a stillborn baby girl. She wrapped her shawl around it and threw it out the window. God help us."

Just outside Stettin a medic entered our compartment to check our destination cards. These hung from the necks of all patients stating where each was to be shipped. He checked the soldier in the berth over me, grunted, and made a note on his clipboard. Then he checked mine and said, "Naval Hospital, Malente—do you know where Malente is?"

I was sure it was still situated near the small town of Eutin in Holstein. This was up north near the Danish border—not where I wanted to go. I replied without hesitation, "Yes, of course. It's down south near Garmisch." Garmisch is in the state of Bavaria, close to the Austrian border. It was a believable answer, for Garmisch was well known for its military hospitals. Fortunately, my words drew no comment from the upper or lower berths.

The overworked medic proceeded to write "Garmisch-Partenkirchen" beside "Malente" already printed in black wax pencil on my destination card. "When I'm through with this car, I'll come back to help you put on a uniform." I rolled my eyes back, looked at nothing, and swallowed the urge to laugh out loud at my outrageous good fortune.

The train pulled slowly into Stettin with steam bellowing from the sides of the locomotive. My new crutches stood in the corner waiting for our first encounter. The medic returned and helped me dress, then asked if I was ready.

"I'm ready, but I don't know if these crutches are ready for me."

He laughed and said, "First time on crutches?"

I nodded, wondering how hard this could really be.

I tentatively made my way through the compartment door, down the car's hallway, and eased myself onto the platform. I thanked the medic as he handed me my duffel bag and wished him good luck. Balancing on my crutches, I looked for something southbound. Directly opposite my track stood the train to Berlin. Perfect!

The platform was crowded with soldiers and civilians. The combination of crutches and duffel bag challenged my balance. Suddenly there was a breach in the crush of people. I aimed and swung myself forward. Halfway across, my crutch hooked someone's leg. The leg kept moving and took my crutch with it. I struggled in vain to keep my balance, then braced for contact with the platform. Two pairs of hands grabbed me in the nick of time. I was thanking the two servicemen when I heard someone shout, "Kurt!" No sooner had I recognized my name than two arms went around my neck—Nurse Hilda!

"I can't believe my eyes! How did you get here?" I asked, as the surging crowd jostled us.

"Come on, let's move over there", she said, grabbing the duffel bag and clearing a path as authoritatively as a seasoned traffic cop. "Kurt, you won't believe what happened to me!" She took a deep breath and then began her story. "The nurses and doctors left Danzig on the *Wilhelm Gustloff*, along with fifteen hundred wounded that had been transferred from the hospitals."

"Fourteen hundred ninety-nine", I silently corrected her.

"We were supposed to sail from Gotenhafen to Kiel. You wouldn't believe the conditions on that ship. It was also carrying eight thousand refugees from eastern Germany. We wound up sailing with something like ten thousand people on board. Do you know what the capacity of that ship was in peacetime? Just shy of nineteen hundred with crew and passengers. We had over five times that on board!"

Her story was interrupted by a tarp-covered baggage cart bearing the bodies of dead German soldiers being pulled across our path. As I watched it being wheeled past, my mind went back to a field, looking through a chapel window at another cart of dead soldiers stacked one upon another. Or had that happened to someone else? Nurse Hilda's voice pulled me back to the Stettin Railroad Station.

"Kurt, there were people everywhere. They slept in the exercise rooms, on the dance floors—even in the emptied swimming pool! And more than half of them were women and children. By the end of the day, the other nurses and I were cross-eyed with exhaustion. But by the time we'd finished our shift, there was no room left below. Even the corridors were clogged with people trying to sleep. If there had been a free corner somewhere, there still wasn't a breath of air left—and the noise! All of those poor children were frightened and crying. Our only option was to take our cots to the top deck."

I silently congratulated myself on my stubborn refusal to take the ship.

"We wrapped ourselves in blankets and settled down as best we could. It was just after nine P.M., and I'd barely gone to sleep. Without warning the ship shook ferociously. I couldn't understand what was happening. Then it happened twice more, and we were scattered all over the deck. Someone yelled to get up and head for the side railing."

"What?" I couldn't believe what I was hearing.

"One of the doctors yelled out that we had either struck a mine or been torpedoed. Later they told us that we had been torpedoed by a Russian submarine."

I was stunned—this was inconceivable.

"Kurt, the *Wilhelm Gustloff* was painted with a huge red cross on both sides. Do you think that Russian commander didn't see that mountain-size red cross?" Her voice grew louder as she answered her own question, "I don't."

"Surely not even the Russians would fire on a Red Cross ship!"

"Well, they did and over nine thousand people died."

"Nurse Hilda! I was supposed to be on the *Wilhelm Gustloff.*"

"No!"

"Yes! But how could so many have died? Weren't there life jackets and lifeboats on board?"

"Kurt, the seawater poured into the ship so fast and climbed so quickly that no one below had a chance!" Her voice, now hard as stone, had lost all traces of youth. "The next thing I knew, I was in the water. I don't know if I jumped—I can't remember. After the shock of finding myself alive, I began to swim for my life. The sea was black and icy. At first I didn't feel the cold. I was completely focused on getting as far away as I could from the ship before it went down. Otherwise the tow would take me with it." She grabbed my arm.

"I swam like I didn't know I could! I swam and I swam until I had no strength left. My arms and legs had turned to jelly, and I'd swallowed about half of the ocean. As I looked back to gauge my distance from the ship, I heard a loud whooosh—the ship was gone."

After a moment she went on.

"I treaded water and stared into the darkness where the ship had been. There were now only distant cries of people in the water. Up to that point I had been running on sheer adrenaline, but now I was beyond exhaustion. I could feel the cold taking my last strength. I lay floating on my back when something bumped against me. I screamed—imagining it was a sea monster—I was going to die a horrible death! It was a plank of wood, but big enough to hold me up. I stretched across it and tried to catch my breath.

"There was complete silence, and I realized that I was there alone, bobbing up and down on an endless body of water in the blackness of night, and that I was going to die. All of those people, thousands and thousands of them, drowned like rats. I would just be one more. I'd never see my family or friends again. I'd never eat breakfast again. I'd never put on a pretty dress again. I'd never do any of the things that I'd always taken for granted—gone forever. I saw the faces of patients whose names I don't remember, scenes from my life when I was a baby. Events shot through my mind like lightning. I started praying. I prayed to God and to all the saints I could think of." Her hold on my arm tightened.

"And then a miracle happened. Out of nowhere a lifeboat appeared next to me. Kurt, I hadn't even called out. I was just lying there thinking the last thing I'd ever see would be the stars. Well, I got into that little boat and here I am!"

We stood in silence. I shook my head, Nurse Hilda still clutching my arm. The announcement of the immediate departure of my Berlin-bound train brought us back to the present. We hugged each other tightly; a final wave and she was gone.

I edged my way toward the waiting train. The bulk of the duffel bag and Hilda's tale of survival weighed heavily on me. A passing soldier seeing me try to enter the train told me to go ahead and he'd toss my duffel bag after me. I thanked him for his kindness.

Looking down the corridor of the passenger car, I saw three wounded soldiers being wheeled out on stretchers. I let them pass and then hurried as best I could to their compartment—it was empty. I dropped my gear at the foot of the lowest berth, propped the crutches against the wall, and five minutes later was asleep. An orderly distributing soup and bread woke me once. Fifteen hours later, the train pulled into Berlin. It was February 4, 1945.

God only knew when I would have another opportunity to see my family. My first order of business was getting a pass to Sachsenhausen. I checked my bag at the station and headed for Gestapo headquarters. Getting to the Prinz Albrechtstrasse wasn't difficult unless one was unused to crutches. I got as far as the pastry shop opposite Gestapo headquarters and decided to catch my breath. Inside I addressed the woman behind the counter, "Is that an apfelkuchen?" I was suddenly starving.

"Naturally. What else?" she replied, apparently irritated at the question.

"May I please have a piece?" After shifting the crutches from side to side I finally found the pocket containing my wallet. I pulled out some reichsmarks and held them out to her.

"First, I need your ration book."

My ration book was in my duffel bag at the railroad station. "Well, you see, I had to leave my duffel in the checkroom at the railroad station, and my ration book is in it." And in case she hadn't seen my crutches I held them up.

"No ration book, no apfelkuchen!"

"But I have the money."

"I cannot sell anyone anything without proper authorization."

She put the cake back and walked to the back of the shop. I was left standing there with money in my hand, no apfelkuchen, and a wave of frustration washing over me. This mentality drove me crazy. People who refused to think for themselves usually became their own victims. Well, I needed all my energy for the Gestapo. Uncharacteristically, I left the shop without saying another word.

Gestapo headquarters was humming with activity. I approached the main desk and asked to see Lieutenant Colonel Müller. After the several flights of stairs and time spent in his waiting room, I was admitted to Müller's office.

"Ah, Cadet von Schuschnigg. I am sorry to tell you this but these days the passes for your destination can be granted only by Reichsführer Himmler himself." (The term *concentration camp* never came out of their mouths.)

"Ah, I see. Well, thank you, Colonel." That was a blow. No matter how friendly the camp guards were, there was no possibility of my being admitted without a pass. With no idea what I should try next, I turned to go.

"Wait a minute!" Müller said, grabbing a stack of papers. "I thought I saw a memo with his itinerary and . . . yes! Here it is. He's supposed to be here one day this week, and it *is* today. I'll get you in to see him." Two phone calls later I was on my way to Himmler's office.

That 1938 visit to Himmler in the Hotel Metropol seemed like ages ago. Enough had been packed into these last six and a half years to last my family a lifetime. I had just registered at Himmler's office when my name was called and I was again in the infamous man's presence. The Nazi cyclops seemed to have shrunk. He looked smaller and older. "Ah, Cadet von Schuschnigg, I have been told of your request. I hope you are recovering from your wounds. Your sacrifices for the Third Reich are appreciated."

As at our previous meeting, his cordiality was unsettling, and I thought I detected the threat of a smile. The combination of my crutches and my pallid features was probably responsible. Himmler offered me a chair and immediately began asking questions. "Tell me, what is your impression of ship morale aboard the *Prinz Eugen*? How do the men feel about the course of the war?"

His willful ignorance was incredible—the man must be crazy: Rome was burning and he was fiddling. I knew immediately what to say—I would tell him what he wanted to hear. "Spirits are very high. Everyone is looking forward to a victorious end." This was, strictly speaking, true—an Allied victory.

A wave of rhetoric swept over me, the same empty speech, but I finally heard what I was waiting for: ". . . wounded for the fatherland . . . and of course any German soldier who has suffered for the fatherland has a right to see his family."

Himmler rang the commandant of Sachsenhausen. I listened as Himmler, using my real name, said I would be visiting the special block. So, we were no longer "Auster"; perhaps the name had run its course. Scribbling something on a sheet of paper, he then reached across the desk and handed it to me. It was an order that "Kurt von Schuschnigg" be permitted to enter the camp. I quickly folded it and put it in my pocket. By the time he'd hung up, I was out of my chair and gripping my crutches. I thanked him, and to his "Heil Hitler" I gave a nod of my head.

As I got to the bottom of the stairs, an air raid siren sounded. Doors flew open, and a horde of Nazi uniforms charged toward me. I was swept along in the surge for the basement. Finding a spot against a wall, I lowered myself to the floor and settled down for a long wait. This was Berlin, and there were far better places to be than Gestapo headquarters.

Bombs went off with the frequency of a machine gun. The noise was deafening, even in the bomb shelter, and it did not let up. When the explosions seemed close, women and men alike moaned or cried out. The emergency lights flickered throughout the first hour then went out altogether. Flashlights appeared from pockets and purses and were placed on the floor. Their beams threw giant shadows and turned ordinary faces into grotesque caricatures. Still, it was better than sitting in darkness.

I found myself holding my breath during the whistling of the bombs. It was impossible to say which caused more terror—the whistling or the actual explosion. The bombing was ferocious, and at times the whole basement shook—raining concrete dust on all below. What a way to die: cowering in a basement full of Nazis. I was certain they were fervently communing with God. I thought back to the *Prinz Eugen* and one of the many ship alerts. Sitting there, waiting for the incoming enemy fire, one of the regular sailors announced to no one in particular, "Now you all will remember how to pray."

Having done their best to level Berlin, the last of the thousand or so B-17s—the American Flying Fortresses—returned to their bases in England. After some three hours in the building's basement, we breathed a collective sigh of relief. Some laughed, some cried, some thanked God.

The basement's metal door opened to a mass of debris and dust. Collapsed beams had caused floor after floor to cave in. Digging began from above and below. Using our handkerchiefs against the dust, we covered our mouths and noses. Looking like grimy bandits, we finally burrowed our way through the rabble to the outside of the building.

It took me a moment to remember where I was, for Berlin was in ruins. The scene before me was like something from Dante's *Inferno*. Fires raged everywhere: the air filled with smoke and dust.

People were running in all directions. Here and there came a shouted command. Men and women were digging through debris with cans, broken bottles—anything at hand. Some wandered—dazed. For others, motion was to relieve the feeling of helplessness.

I stopped in front of the pastry shop—now a smoldering wreck. The woman from the shop, stunned but unhurt, stopped and stared at me, remembering. She turned her palms toward the sky and rocking back and forth wailed, "Look what I have left, dust and ashes! I wish I'd given you the whole kuchen. I was wrong, wrong."

I felt a tap on my shoulder. Ever since my encounter with the Gestapo agent on the Unter den Linden, I had lived in dread of a tap on my shoulder. I turned to find the young Austrian, Heidi von Boltenstern, who had sat beside me in the Gestapo waiting room. She had told me that her fiancé had been reported to the Gestapo by a neighbor for a fictitious crime. Unfortunately, this was not uncommon. The man had been sent to a concentration camp, and she had come to plead his case. I had wondered if she realized what she was up against. Even the most innocent statement could be dangerous when given to the Gestapo. It was possible to walk into their headquarters with a harmless question and wind up confessing to murder. I had nothing but admiration for the young woman's courage and loyalty, but I wouldn't have bet on her chances of success.

"I have to go back to my hotel—all of my belongings are there", she said. "Would you mind going with me? I'm not even sure in which direction I should be walking."

My answer didn't require thought: sympathetic company was both a relief and a pleasure. We started out in the general direction of the Hotel Adlon. Most of the streets lay under a maze of debris, and my crutches were becoming an impediment. I tried shifting my weight to my legs and using the crutches as canes.

I too had difficulty navigating. Every familiar landmark was gone, and some of the streets themselves had been erased. Odd portions of walls survived. Sometimes an entire front of a building was intact but with nothing left behind it. There were so many blazing buildings that the darkness, caused by a combination of the onset of nightfall and dense smoke, was relieved. Some still burned so intensely that we had to shield our faces from the heat.

A major portion of the population had long since been evacuated. Berliners knew they were near the top of the Allies' list of targets. Early in the war Göring had dared the Allies to bomb Berlin, bragging that not a single enemy bomb would fall on the city. It was only a matter of time before his bluff was called. Now, perhaps a quarter of the once majestic city still stood.

The Hotel Adlon had been heavily hit, along with most of the buildings in the area. After some searching we located a staircase, or at least a part of a staircase. I looked over at Heidi and motioned toward the stairs. "Are you game?"

"I have to be. Nearly all the clothes I have left in the world are up there. Thank heavens they gave me a room on the second floor."

One side of the staircase was gone, but the staircase's inner wall was still intact. Clinging to that wall we made it to the second floor. A lot of the walls had collapsed, but the floor seemed solid enough. Fortunately, Heidi's room was only a few doors down the hall.

Outside her door, Heidi rummaged through her handbag and pulled out the key and then a small flashlight. "I was hoping I might not need this for anything more than finding the bathroom at night."

I looked at the key in her hand and laughed, "I'm glad you remembered your room key—I believe the concierge is on break."

Heidi aimed the flashlight's beam ahead of us and said, "That's where I left my suitcase, in that corner over there, and the closet is next to it."

We picked our way through the parts of the ceiling that had fallen and dug out her suitcase. It was ruined, but her hanging clothes—though in need of cleaning—were undamaged and within reach. Heidi wrestled a sheet off the bed, dumped her clothes and other belongings onto it, and tied up the corners. "You will be the best looking hobo in Germany", I told her.

Heidi was delighted. We took a last look around, and she said, "Unbelievable that I have anything left in all of this."

Halfway down the stairs, we stepped on the same stair simultaneously. It groaned loudly. Heidi quickly shifted her weight to the step below and warned, "Careful, Kurt."

The step protested again under my weight but held. Then the staircase seemed to shift slightly, and I froze. Heidi had gone down two more steps and yelled over her shoulder, "We've got to get off this thing!"

"Go! Go! Go!" I yelled back.

She covered the last eight steps like a gazelle. I threw my crutch ahead and willed my sore leg to move fast—really fast. I arrived at the bottom of the stairs in a heap on the floor but otherwise undamaged. Heidi helped me up, and we looked back at the stairs: they had separated from the wall, and now there were gaps between them. Clearly, we would be the last people to use that stairway.

Outside the hotel we dusted ourselves off and took the subway (incredibly, still working) to the railroad station. Here too the Allied bombing had been deadly accurate. The station had taken a direct hit, but trains were still running. I couldn't believe it. The Teutonic spirit was indomitable. That any form of transportation still functioned in any part of Berlin after that round of bombing was amazing. The railway workers, though worried about their own families and homes, had stayed at their posts; they had done their duty.

The station was full of shattered glass; splintered wooden benches and heaps of gnarled metal were scattered throughout the terminal. Gaping holes in the ceiling looked down like hollow eyes on the destruction below. There was little left to bear witness to Berlin's once beautiful and vibrant transportation center. It had become a giant maze.

There was a placard announcing the departure of a southbound train. Heidi grabbed my arm, "That's my general direction." She kissed me hurriedly on the cheek then traced the sign of the cross on my forehead.

I said, "I'll expect a wedding invitation", but I had no confidence in her reunion with her fiancé.

I found the checkroom, somewhat the worse for the bombing. There hung my dusty duffel bag, still in one piece. Out of a desire for order or perhaps just a morbid sense of humor, I left my claim ticket behind.

"Is there anything going out to Sachsenhausen?" I called to a station agent.

"Third track over", he called back without looking up from his clipboard.

Finding a train today to Sachsenhausen was yet another piece of good fortune. The clacking of the train wheels as we pulled out of the station were strangely reassuring: order in the midst of chaos. As Berlin began to fall behind, the rhythmic beat of the wheels passing over the rails was oddly soothing.

Across the aisle, a mother was trying her to comfort her crying child. I thought about all the German children of these bombed cities and wondered how long it would be before houses, buildings, and churches would be rebuilt. Now, Germans could only plead temporary insanity for abandoning themselves to the visions of Adolf Hitler. The price paid in death, mental anguish, and suffering would never be determined.

My thoughts turned to my own country, to those Austrians who welcomed the troops of the Reich rolling across our borders in March 1938. When Austria awoke from this nightmare, how would Austrians view themselves? As participants, as victims, or as amnesiacs?

Appalling scenes of devastation passed before my window. Buildings still standing had assumed grotesque shapes and were altered beyond recognition; black smoke billowed into the sky from fires that still raged. How much longer could Germany endure the wrath of the Allies? I closed my eyes.

Soon the train pulled into the Sachsenhausen station. Winter's bleak progress couldn't alter the camp; it was still gray and forbidding. The naked trees lining the camp wall swayed slowly in the wind. Thank God they were mute. Who could bear to hear what they had witnessed?

The four SS guards greeted me like an old friend. Seeing my crutches and appearance, they reacted like Fräulein Alice would have in her time. Two of them escorted me to the cottage door. A moment passed before Father answered.

I hadn't considered the combined effect that my crutches and two-man escort would have on my father. I quickly sought to reassure him, "It's all right, Father. I'm fine."

He regained his composure quickly. In fact, Father's former resilience had returned in the last several years. He thanked the guards and closed the door behind me. "Son, what happened?"

Vera and Sissi emerged from the kitchen. Vera's reaction was a sharp intake of breath. Sissi grabbed my leg and, smiling, shrieked, "Kurti, Kurti!"

While Sissi played happily, I gave them a brief description of my experiences since I'd seen them last at Christmas. The bombing of the *Prinz Eugen* and my travels from Königsberg struck them deeply, but it was my description of the destruction of Berlin that was the most sobering. They listened silently until I had finished. Then Vera took Father's hand, "It can't last too much longer." He laid his other hand over hers and nodded.

Vera changed the subject, "You and Sissi have a new cousin—Heiner. Aunt Marianne and Uncle Artur had their fourth child in October." Amid so much death, Heiner's birth was reassurance of the continuity of life. It was the best news that I had heard in some time.

"Father, I need your advice on the rest of my journey."

"Come, Sissi. It is long past your bedtime", said Vera.

It was barely past eight the next morning when there was a knock on the door. Three pairs of eyes were fixed on Father as he squeezed

Vera's hand, smiled, and rose. It was the commandant of Sachsen-hausen, SS Colonel Kaindl. Apologizing for intruding, he hesitated a fraction of a second at seeing me. As Himmler's call had been before the bombing, perhaps the colonel hadn't been sure that I had made it out of Berlin alive. I gathered Sissi in my arms and left my parents alone with him. A few minutes later I heard the front door close.

"Kurt!"

"What did he say, Papa?"

"We will be picked up by a staff car—your mother, Sissi, and I. We may pack two suitcases. Kaindl knows only that we are to be taken to Berlin for transfer. He also said he was very happy for us. The end isn't too far away." It was a huge relief to know that they were leaving the camp. Life in Sachsenhausen could change in a number of ways with the approach of the Russians and the panic that would sweep over those in command.

Vera rose, looked at Father, and a tear trickled down her cheek. Father put his arm around her and rested his cheek against the top of her head. He reached to me and squeezed my shoulder. Left with only view of three pairs of legs, Sissi let out a shriek. I bent and picked her up. "You know we'd never forget you", I reassured her. To Father I said quietly, "The Allies destroyed a good part of the city. It's not likely that they'll be back soon. I think you are safer in Berlin than here."

Father replied, "You must get back to the station and try to get on a southbound train. After yesterday's heavy bombing, it will be full of Berliners also trying to leave."

I nodded and turned my attention again to what had become the center of all of our lives. "Sissi, I have to leave. You be a good girl. Take care of Mami and Father. Will you do that for me?"

Smiling, she gave a big nod of her head that sent her golden ringlets bouncing and said, "Yes!" She locked her arms around my neck and gave me a big, loud kiss on the cheek.

Releasing her was one of the most difficult things that I have ever done. I gathered my crutches and duffel bag and tried not to think of how I would ever find my family again. The four of us walked outside. I looked at Father's garden plot for the last time; there would be no harvest this year. I hoped to God that soon there would be no one left on these acres of misery and death. We reached the door to the guard's gate. After hugging and kissing all three of them, I rang for the guard. A second later, the door swung open and then closed behind me.

"You don't mean you have to leave already!" asked the guard.

"With Berlin in the state that it is ...", my words drifted downward.

"Well, the least we can do is get you back to Berlin", he stated in a matter-of-fact way.

I wondered that they could do anything of the kind and simply said, "Oh, no. It's all right. The train is still running."

"We have access to SS vehicles. You will be driven back in one and that is that", he said, patting me on the back. Life just seemed to get stranger and stranger.

Back in the guard house, he announced my departure to the others. That started an animated discussion on what was coming next. Before the war, these men had been ordinary German police-men. I doubted that they had the stomach for the jobs that the Reich had given them. Their behavior toward us over the years didn't match the terrifying death squad insignias on their uniforms—they had actually been kind to us. Their relief that our nightmare was coming to an end was genuine. Theirs, they said, was just beginning.

The main gate swung open. I looked around for the last time. Never again!

# Out of Germany

A black Mercedes staff car stood idling in front of the gate. I got in, wondering what the driver thought about a mere cadet engineer's uniform sitting in his backseat. He must not have cared, for we set off without delay for what was left of Berlin.

A gray haze still hung over the city from the bombing the day before. We drove through the ruined city, past portions of houses standing upright, seemingly out of sheer will power. It was impossible to view destruction on such a scale without compassion. The end was approaching—one could scent the odor of defeat in the air. The guards had been right. It would be their turn soon. Bouncing over some of the barely passable streets, I thought about what their plight would become once the Russians held this country in their grip.

The driver found an entrance to the station, parked the car, and helped me with the duffel bag. When I thanked him he replied, "Good-bye and much luck", instead of "Heil Hitler!"

I entered the station humming a few bars from Strauss' *Tales from the Vienna Woods*, but my mood soon changed when I saw the pandemonium inside. Civilians, desperate to board any train headed south or west, jostled with troops doing the same thing. An elaborate game of musical chairs was taking place on the trains—everyone was looking frantically for a seat. It was better to have a seat on a train leaving Berlin than money in one's pocket.

Only the station workers were orderly and focused. They were hard at work trying to create passageways through fallen sections of walls and ceilings. An enormous amount of debris from the previous day's bombing had already been loaded into a convoy of trucks that lined the outside platforms.

I went to the platform where I had disembarked the previous day. On the same track, a Munich-bound train was boarding passengers. Silently praising the German propensity for habit and order and shamelessly drawing attention to my crutches, I moved steadily toward the nearest hospital car.

The last stretcher patient was just being removed. I moved around patient and medics and entered the hospital car. I hurried along the corridor and several compartments down saw two figures asleep on the middle and top berths. The lower berth was vacant. A quick check of the metal lockers showed two full, one empty. I sank down on the bottom berth and managed to remove my boots and uniform before dropping into a dead sleep.

I woke up the next day feeling famished. One of the medics had left sandwiches and a container of soup on the floor beside my berth. Sleep had done wonders for me, and food—I expected—would restore me completely. The train had stopped for another air raid. As I reached for the soup, the patient in the middle berth must have heard me move and leaned over. "So you finally decided to join us", he said by way of greeting. "The two of us have barely slept between the air raid stops and the berth checks. It's hopeless. The medics seem to have nothing else to do but constantly wake us up. Isn't that right, Dieter?"

There was no reply from the top berth. He went on: "After about the tenth check, I asked the medic if they were having a problem with us wounded deserting during the air raid stops. Ha!" Overcome by mirth, he slapped the side of his berth and added, "The man had no sense of humor!"

"And what did he say the reason was?" I asked, out of politeness more than curiosity. The berth checks had not disturbed my sleep.

"It seems that a lot of the fellows are dying on the way. Not me! Never felt better. I'm finally getting to go home."

I didn't think he looked particularly well.

"You know, they couldn't wake you up—thought you'd died. The medic had to listen for a heartbeat. You are one sound sleeper."

"Yes, I know", I said, unwrapping the sandwich.

The train lurched forward. He must have been worn out by talk, as that ended his conversation. A few hours later, the medics came in and removed his body and that of the dead man in the top berth. A wounded soldier was moved into one of the two empty berths.

An hour or so outside Munich, two medics came in. I had carefully kept my destination card face down, but one of the medics flipped it over saying, "I know where the soldier above you is going; let's see what we're doing with you." He read my card, blinked, and looked again more closely. "What idiot wrote this?" he exploded. Obviously he had a firmer grasp of geography than the medic who had altered the card.

I shrugged my shoulders and tried to look too weak to care. He turned to the other medic. "Gunter, he is supposed to be heading for Eutin. That would be north, not south. No wonder we're losing this bloody war. Well? What are we going to do with him now? We can't possibly send him back up north. No telling how far the Russians have advanced."

"We could transfer him to the hospital in Munich", the other medic said.

"Good thinking, Gunter. That's perfect."

Thank you, Gunter, I wanted to shout with joy. To be able to recuperate in Munich—I could not have wished for a better solution. Listening to the rhythm of the train, I lay there thinking about how so many circumstances had combined to deliver me safely this far.

As we pulled into Munich, I looked through the window at the historic and once beautiful city. Much of what had not been destroyed was marred and damaged. There had been over seventy bombing raids on this early target in the war.

After the train came to a stop in the station, I heard the rattle of wheels in the corridor. Presently the door of our compartment opened, and two tired-looking medics rolled in a gurney. As they were transferring the wounded soldier above me, one of the medics knocked against the unsecured gurney. The next thing I heard was a thud followed by a stream of profanity from all three. Once the probably reinjured soldier was being rolled out, one of the medics said they'd be back for me. "My crutches are all I need," I said hastily, "but thanks, all the same."

Once the ambulance was full, we departed for the hospital. I still couldn't believe my luck. I had a place to recuperate, and my freedom was almost within reach. I desperately wanted to believe that liberation for Father, Vera, and Sissi was also at hand. Just knowing that they were in Berlin was a relief.

After a week of very good care, my burns were healing well, but lying in bed seemed to have done little to improve my lung capacity. A trip up the hallway and back left me wheezing like an old man. I wondered how I had managed the week before.

My physical therapy began the second week, and once under way I was given a day pass. This meant fresh air, more exercise, and best of all, lunch with my friends. Other than seeing my family, nothing could have made me happier.

One of the nurses had found phone numbers for two of my friends in Munich—all that was left of my Wittelsbacher Gymnasium and Schülerheim Schmitt group. Both were unfit for active duty—one was nearly blind, and the other had such severe asthma that walking too fast made him wheeze. We agreed to meet at the Schwarzwälder, one of the few restaurants in Munich that was still open.

I took a bus that stopped very near the restaurant and saw my friends, along with the three girls accompanying them, standing in a line that was as long as a city block. They were about a third of the way from its end, and I wondered how long we would have to wait for a table. They waved vigorously. After I had joined them, the Schwarzwälder maître d' came over. "How many are in your party, sir?" he asked me.

"There are six of us."

"Would you follow me?"

One of my friends slapped the other on the back. "You see! What did I tell you?" He let me in on the secret. "I just bet Bruno you'd get us in sooner rather than later. I won, didn't I?"

"You think I don't know that you lured me out of my sickbed just so you wouldn't have to stand in line?"

The boys caught my sarcasm, but the blonde beside me didn't. "Oh, we would never do a thing like that!"

Things just could not have been better. I had one of the best meals in years and a captive audience. They listened with open mouths to my accounts of the collision with the *Leipzig*, the engine room explosion on the *Prinz Eugen*, and the Russian advance. Then they wanted me to tell them all that I had seen in Berlin. I couldn't remember ever talking so much, and at the end of the long day I felt as fit as an aging pensioner. It was my fault. I had allowed myself to be an invalid. Tomorrow I would leave the crutches behind and walk like everyone else.

The following day, after the doctor's inspection, I left the hospital slowly, but without the crutches. The streetcar took me to the center of the city. I picked a café that Vera used to frequent and ordered a cup of coffee. I leafed through the only newspaper—the *National Socialist*. It predicted that victory was at hand—well, no surprise there!

I put down the paper and looked around the café again. Something seemed slightly odd, but I couldn't say what it was. I hadn't paid particular attention to anything on the previous day except the restaurant and my friends. Now I looked around more carefully. There were the usual lines at the butcher's, the baker's, and all the shops. Then it struck me. I saw only women around me. There were children and the occasional old man, but otherwise there were women. Even the middle-aged men had disappeared. It came to me that there had been a woman behind the butcher's counter.

The war had taken all the young men and even those in middle age. I remembered Grandfather saying that youths are the world's warriors. How many people from my childhood would be left when all this was finally over? I realized with a jolt that I was doing what I had noticed the old men doing—sitting alone, shaking my head, and probably talking out loud to myself. I paid my bill and went outside in search of fresh air.

The following morning, day pass in hand, I walked eagerly to the front desk. As I reached for the pen to sign myself out, the nurse turned and said, "Oh, the chief surgeon asked that you wait for him to finish his rounds. He would like to see you."

"No, I don't think so, Nurse. I just saw him and the other doctors in my ward less than an hour ago. You probably have me confused with someone else."

"No, Cadet von Schuschnigg, he specifically said for you to see him before you check out for the day."

The chief surgeon also happened to be the assistant medical director of the German Wehrmacht. I could do nothing else but put myself at his disposal. Several hallways after I began my search for the surgeon, I caught sight of him disappearing with some other doctors into a ward at the end of a corridor. I sat down in a chair in the hall and began waiting. About an hour later, the doctors came out of the ward, talking among themselves. As they approached where I was sitting, I stood up and smiled, expecting the chief surgeon to address me. Instead he walked right past me without any sign of recognition. Disappointed, I began walking after the group and followed them around a corner. I literally bumped into the chief surgeon as he turned to retrace his steps.

"Cadet, I'm glad you found me", he said, glancing left and right. "Would you step over here for a moment, please?" We stepped into a closet-size dispensary. Closing the door he pushed a stool toward me. "Sit down. I have been ordered by the Gestapo to turn you over to them as soon as I declare you healthy, meaning after a two-week hospitalization period, which, for you, is up tomorrow."

I was dumbstruck. I had persuaded myself that by now I might have been overlooked in all the chaos. The Nazis didn't often overlook anything. I gazed steadily at the man, wondering why he was talking to me in a supply room, not in his office with an MP (military policeman) present. Answering my unspoken question, the doctor said, "I do not see why you should have risked your life for that criminal Hitler, only to be killed ultimately by his henchmen." The man was more than decent—he was saving my life. "You already have your day pass. When you sign yourself out, just keep going. I cannot provide you with papers—you must try your luck at disappearing."

The alarm would be raised when I was found missing after curfew. My mind reeled at the prospect of traveling without documents, especially now that the Gestapo would be looking for me. Some aspects of the Third Reich were still intact. The *Feldgendarmerie*, Germany's military police, were especially efficient.

"Sir, I am deeply in your debt." I held out my hand. "I'll never forget your kindness."

Shaking my hand he said, "Cadet, a last medical word: your lung was torn and completely collapsed. You have damage to your other lung as well. I cannot stress this enough—you must not smoke another cigarette. If you do, I cannot guarantee your life for a minute more. Physical exertion is also out of the question. Do you understand?"

I nodded.

"I wish you the best of luck", he said softly and left.

I headed back to the front desk. The nurse was going over a roster, her back to me. Keeping my eye on her, I silently scribbled my name and went to get my duffel bag.

There was only one person in my ward, a sailor on the bed against the far wall. To my great relief I heard snoring; he was sound asleep. I shoved my belongings into the duffel bag and, avoiding the front desk, hurried to the hospital's employee entrance. The shift had already changed, and the area was empty. I quickly pushed the door open and headed for the streetcar stop. Taking no chances of being observed, I walked past the first streetcar stop to the next one—out of sight of the hospital.

I had to decide in which direction to travel. I had only my *Soldbuch* (navy pay booklet) as proof of my identity. I had plenty of money from my naval pay, but the fact remained that I needed travel orders to be able to buy a ticket. Captain Reinicke was an honorable man. If I made it back to the *Prinz Eugen* before the Gestapo picked me up, he would not turn me in. The odds weren't the best but they were all I had.

The Munich railroad station was not greatly improved since I had been there two weeks ago. I inquired about trains traveling north giving Gotenhafen as my destination. A harried railroad employee told me that the shortest route to Gotenhafen would be Munich to Berlin to Stettin, and then to Swinemünde. "From Swinemünde I don't know what to tell you. There is no surface transportation from there, and it's a good two hundred miles to Gotenhafen. I'd say you were on a fool's errand. If I were you, I'd rather risk deserting. The feldgendarmerie are apt to be a lot friendlier than the Russians!"

Well, I was already a deserter, and meeting a friendly MP seemed unlikely. In Swinemünde I would try to find an accommodating fisherman or boat to complete my journey to Gotenhafen. Meanwhile, as it was already midafternoon, I decided to wait three hours for an overnight train to Berlin. I would have all the next day to find some means of getting to Gotenhafen.

The station was teeming with soldiers and sailors. I could have tried to lose myself in the crowd, but there were also many MPs around. I decided to get something to eat at the military canteen in the station and look for a cinema afterward. It was as good a place as any for a nap.

A few hours later I went in search of my train. As I moved through the station, I told myself: Look and act natural—do not look nervous. I found the train to Berlin, but an MP stood between the passenger cars and me. I went back outside and found a side entrance.

One perfectly aimed bomb had ripped away the sidewalk—no MP stood guard. I entered, walked along the far side of the train, and half-way down, got on.

The distinctions of first, second, and third class had dissolved in the chaos of war. As a cadet engineer, I was entitled to travel second class with the officers; nevertheless, I headed for the enlisted men's third-class car. The farther back I was in the train, the longer it would take for the MPs who were inspecting travel documents to reach me.

I walked through five full third-class cars. About halfway through the sixth, I spotted a seat, or part of a seat, next to an exceptionally large woman. She had placed a wicker basket beside her and was staring out the window. I cleared my throat to get her attention. She turned to look at me, and I pointed to the partially available seat and said, "If you wouldn't mind . . ." With a grumpy expression on her face, she shifted the basket onto her ample lap and shrugged her well-padded shoulders. I thanked her but thought she should be thanking me. With a normal-size traveler next to her, she would be far less comfortable. I stowed my duffel bag and, fitting myself into the seat, folded my arms and crossed my legs; to be any smaller than that just wasn't possible.

I checked my watch and tried to calculate how long it would take before the MPs checking travel documents reached my car. Then I leaned back, determined to relax. The train lurched forward as the engineer released the clutch and spun the locomotive's steel drive wheels against the tracks. This procedure was repeated, and we got under way and began to build speed.

The blackout shades of wartime had already blotted out an overcast twilight. On this journey, the blackout shades had a disadvantage for me. Since the train wasn't visible from the air, there were no air raid stops—no train evacuations. Those evacuations would have allowed me to see where the MPs were and to reboard the train behind them.

Soon, a steady rain began to beat against the windows. The combination of rain and the clacking of the train's wheels had a lulling effect on the passengers. As if on cue, most of them fell silent and slept.

After an hour, I walked forward through the next car—still no sign of MPs. When I returned, I left the compartment door slightly ajar so I could hear their approach. Just then my neighbor woke up and started rummaging through her basket which was tilting at a dangerous angle. Wonderful smells came from it. "Can I help you?" I offered.

"Oh, yes. That would be easier."

I pulled part of the basket on my lap and tried to give her more room. She took out a hunk of cheese, a piece of salami, and half a loaf of bread. With a coquettish smile she said, "You look like you've missed a few meals—are you hungry?"

"Yes, I am. That looks delicious!" In that same moment I heard the sound of a compartment door opening.

"Papers, please!" a voice said from the forward compartment. I jumped up, hitting my head against the overhead rack and almost overturning the basket.

"Excuse me, I must just go and wash my hands first. I'll be right back."

"All right, little sailor. I'll save your food and your seat."

I stepped into the corridor. The MP had his back toward me. I stuck my hands in my pockets and forced myself to stroll down the corridor. When I reached the door, I looked back—empty. I made a lightning exit. Two cars back, there were available seats in the last compartment. I sat between two seamen, my eyes glued to the door, and thought sadly about the salami and cheese. Would my large new friend still be there when I got back?

The train slowed and came to a stop. I stood, carefully checked the corridor, got off, and ran forward as fast as I could. In what seemed no time, the train puffed a few times, and the wheels began to roll. I grabbed the metal handrail and hoisted myself onto my original car. Panting, I found the compartment—no salami, no cheese, not even an empty seat. I hadn't really been hungry before; now that the food had vanished into thin air, I was starving.

Out of pure frustration I kicked the men's room door. To my surprise it opened and an MP stepped out. Before I could find my voice he said, "Excuse me", stepped past me, and disappeared. Weak-kneed, I leaned against the wall. Would he remember that he hadn't checked my papers? But I was just one of hundreds of uniforms. I hoped the MP would remember which seats he had checked rather than the faces occupying them.

I spotted an empty seat and heard myself say, "Sorry, may I?" I didn't recognize my own voice. Nerves—that was a bad sign. Food would help, and sleep. Most of my fellow travelers were asleep. I wondered which was the greater privation—lack of food or lack of sleep? An older woman was the only other person still awake in the compartment. After wrestling with the bag she had brought with her, she pulled out a wurst and bread. I did not hesitate. "Would you be kind enough to let me buy some of your bread and wurst?"

"No, but I will give you half." Smiling, she passed over half of her food. I could have kissed her! Settling down into a companionable silence, we ate.

Knowing when to change cars in order to escape the MPs was an inexact science. One had to consider that there were the random conversations with soldiers or passengers, the cigarette breaks taken between cars, and so on. My guess was anywhere from two and a quarter to three hours. The last stop had been a small town north of Bayreuth, where my elderly friend who had shared her food got off. I calculated that I would have to change positions twice more before we reached Berlin. But at the moment I was tired when I needed to be alert. I had to have a nap.

I found a compartment with a window seat, wedged myself into the corner, and asked another passenger to wake me in an hour. That had to be enough. After that, if I felt myself dozing off I only had to call to mind that firing squad on the *Prinz Eugen*. After my nap, I periodically picked my way past the extended pairs of legs and checked the corridor.

Leipzig drew near, the beginning of the last stretch before Berlin. I got off and took a deep breath of icy air. The two MPs, who had also gotten off the train a number of cars back, were concentrating on hurriedly lighting cigarettes. How was it, I wondered, that they never slept and yet didn't look tired? Keeping my eyes on them, I climbed into the car directly in front of theirs.

I found a window seat next to a petty officer who looked even younger than I. "Good morning, Petty Officer. Are you going as far as Berlin?"

"Morning, sir. Yes, I'm afraid so."

"I wonder if you would be kind enough to make sure that I wake up at Wittenberg."

"Yes, sir. Happy to."

Wittenberg wasn't far from Berlin: first I would sleep, then I would get my duffel bag. I couldn't afford to make another mistake. Earlier, I'd had another close shave. I had just stepped out of my compartment. Instead of going to the back, I walked toward the MPs who were entering the forward compartment. I stopped and patted down my pockets, as if I had forgotten something. Then I turned and walked away.

The petty officer woke me up. I retrieved the duffel bag from my original compartment and went back toward the rear of the train. I chose a compartment in which everyone was asleep. There was no room left in the overhead rack, so I left the duffel bag in the corridor.

It was well past dawn, and I was considering raising the blackout curtain, when the compartment door opened. There was an MP speaking to someone. He stepped back out of our compartment and closed the door behind him. I leapt out of my seat and, forcing myself to breathe, stepped over several pairs of legs. I cautiously slid open the door and looked out—no one there. I grabbed the duffel bag and hurried to the next car. How had this happened? They were behind me at the last stop. Weren't they?

The train showed no sign of slowing down, and I was running out of time. I stood before the freight car. Surprisingly, it wasn't locked, only pitch-dark inside. By the light of a match I saw why: the car was full of dead soldiers. For once I was thankful for the cold weather. I found a spot where I could sit with my back to the macabre scene. Then I leaned against my lumpy duffel bag and closed my eyes.

I had fallen into a light sleep when I felt the train slowing. Lighting another match, I made my way to the door. The station was still some distance away. As the train crept toward its stop, I dropped the duffel bag onto the tracks and jumped after it.

Day was dawning pale and sodden in Berlin. As in Munich, large parts of track had been destroyed, and trains had to stop short of the platforms. The train to Stettin stood only three tracks away. According to the schedule, this train would leave Berlin at eight A.M. I quickly boarded the train, took a seat in a vacant compartment, and tried to catch my breath. I was gasping like a ninety-year-old who had just climbed the Matterhorn. Next I realized how hungry

I was, but the prospect of having to wander around the station looking for something to eat was too daunting. I lit one of my precious cigarettes. The compartment door jerked opened so unexpectedly that I almost swallowed it. With great relief I recognized the uniform of an army private. Nodding curtly, he sat down. After a moment he addressed the wall opposite. "Sort of a surprise not having an MP posted on the platform."

"Once we're under way they'll come through soon enough. That's why I sat back here. Figured I would be undisturbed longer. I've been traveling all night, and I need some sleep. The MPs are as bad as the medics on the trains. They come through every couple of hours to wake you up. But hunger is the worst thing about travel these days." Nervous chatter: a bad habit I had to break. I was sure that it made me look guilty—which, of course, I was.

"I'll give you a sandwich for one of your cigarettes", was his only comment. I could hardly get out the pack fast enough. Handing over the sandwich he said, "Gave my cigarette ration to my family. Our apartment was totally destroyed in the last raid. They can use the cigarettes for barter", he said, without any show of emotion.

"I'm sorry", I said, also offering him my partially smoked cigarette. "I'd much rather eat your sandwich. Thanks very much."

He accepted both with a smile. I practically inhaled the sandwich, neither recognizing nor caring what it was, and it revived me. The train pulled out of Berlin almost on schedule. It wasn't far to Stettin, maybe a hundred miles. How long it actually took was out of the train engineer's hands.

Two inspections by the MPs and three unscheduled stops later—nearly four hours since Berlin—we approached Stettin. A fine mist hung outside my window, and I watched the pastures and fields recede. As we approached the station, I stood on the train's steps and squinted into the haze. Stettin was a hub for northerly connections, and trains stood on nearly all the tracks—the Swinemünde train was the next one over.

A knot of civilians and soldiers were gathered at the front end of the train. I waited for them to disperse before I moved. A soft wind was causing small eddies of fog to swirl around the tracks—a piece of good fortune for me: there was a smaller risk of being seen. I entered the rear compartment of the first passenger car. The smell of stale cigarettes and cheap tobacco hung heavily in the air. I moved to the next car and sat down to wait. Just the knowledge that this was the last leg of my journey was an enormous relief.

Swinemünde lay roughly fifty miles to the north. A short trip—there was a chance that I might even miss the MPs altogether. That was my last thought before I dozed off. I was brought back to consciousness by a burly seaman who had tossed his seabag onto the overhead rack and thrown himself onto a seat. Letting out a deep breath he dropped his head back. I couldn't let him fall asleep before giving me some information.

"Heading back up to rejoin a ship, seaman?"

He opened his eyes reluctantly.

"Yes, sir, I'm hoping to, but I think it'll be rough going." He sounded exhausted.

"Is the train very full? I sat back here, hoping to sleep the whole way without being disturbed by the infernal MPs."

"No one is standing in the aisles yet, but every single seat is taken all the way back to here. We should make it through to Swinemünde without the MPs pestering us."

"Wonderful news, seaman. Thank you."

I again dozed off, waking only when the train pulled out of the station. The compartment had filled up with two middle-aged matrons and an elderly man dressed in a threadbare dark suit. The collar of his white shirt was clean but frayed, and his hands rested on the head of a curved silver-handled cane. Sharp-eyed and alert, he was the picture of a retired professor who had seen better times. I picked him. "Good day", I said.

Brown eyes looked inquiringly at me. "Good day."

"I was wondering if you are traveling all the way to Swinemünde?"

"Yes, I am."

"Ah! I wonder if you would be kind enough to wake me at the last stop before Swinemünde. I wanted to work my way back up to where a shipmate of mine is sitting before we pull into Swinemünde."

"I'd be glad to."

"Thanks. That is very kind of you."

No air raids disturbed me and I slept. Dutifully, the elderly gentleman woke me. I took my seabag down and said good-bye.

"Good luck", he replied.

Luck was just what I needed now. Again I took up my position at the rear door. I was soon on the platform in Swinemünde among all the other arriving passengers. Here at the end of the line there were no more documents checks. Confidently I approached the lone MP. "I am trying to rejoin the *Prinz Eugen* in Gotenhafen. How do I go about getting transport from here?"

It was obviously not the first time he had been asked this, for his answer came promptly. "You have to get to the docking area for small coastal vessels. Hold on a moment." He trotted the few steps to the road nearby and bellowed in the direction of an automobile that was just about to pull away. Everyone within half a mile of where we stood must have heard his shout. When the driver pulled up he said, "A cadet needs to go to the dock. Drop him off, will you?" Then to me, "My friend is going right by there. He'll give you a lift. It's not far, but it will save you some time."

"Thanks very much!" I said and waved as I hurried to the idling car. The driver was also an MP. My heart rate increased significantly. The trip was short enough to make small talk unnecessary—a relief since I had no wish to be remembered by him.

Four vessels were docked at the pier: three fishing boats and, at the dock's far end, a torpedo boat. What was it doing here? Eight men in navy uniforms stood next to one of the fishing boats. Like me, they were all trying to rejoin their ships. One of the seamen said, "The chief petty officer is talking to the fisherman now. Our cruiser's docked in Gotenhafen—yours too?"

"Unfortunately, yes—the *Prinz Eugen*."

Two minutes later, the chief petty officer rejoined us with the fisherman's price. After pooling our money, the ten of us filed into the fishing boat and seated ourselves wherever we could. The bearded old skipper gave us a perfunctory nod and brought the engine to life. Pulling away from the dock, the craft made for deeper water. As the boat picked up speed, the temperature dropped proportionally. Fifteen knots does not qualify as speed unless one is out in the cold, damp air. We used our seabags as shields from the wind. The sailors looked as tired as I felt.

The boat hadn't covered more than a mile when the wind dropped off and the engine slowed to a putter. Astonished, we looked around the area. Our skipper turned the rudder forty-five degrees to the right and then cut the engine. By now we were all sitting up straight—cold and exhaustion forgotten. The fisherman's gaze shifted from starboard to port. Ten other pairs of eyes followed. Everything looked normal. Then one of the sailors groaned. Another seaman said, "What is it? What do you see?"

"I'm turning around. We have to go back."

One of the younger seamen had risen. He bent down and grabbed the fisherman by his lapels. "No! We go on. I must reach my ship!"

This didn't ruffle the old man in the least. "Nobody is going to reach anything if we all get blown to bits! Use your eyes, boy. Look at that water. Don't you see that it has been peppered with mines?"

That was probably why the torpedo boat was lying in port. The seaman, dark smudges under his red-rimmed eyes, was still gripping the fisherman's jacket. "I must get back to Gotenhafen", he implored.

"Let go of it, boy. There is nothing more we can do", the fisherman said, not unkindly. The sailor slowly relinquished his hold on the old man and crumpled onto his seat. It was as if all his strength had deserted him.

The fishing boat turned around slowly, and we returned in silence. We chugged back to the dock and found the shore patrol waiting. They had watched us leave, probably placing bets on how soon we would return. One of the shore patrol said that since we were unable to rejoin our ships, we would be taken to the nearby navy-infantry barracks. Most of those in our group thought this was preferable to being left on one's own. I was not one of them; nor, I guessed, was the desperate seaman.

We climbed into the back of the shore patrol truck. As we approached the barracks, I saw machine guns positioned atop the gates and lots of barbed wire. The truck braked sharply in the courtyard.

A baby-faced sergeant led us up a flight of stairs in the multi-story brick building. "Pick out a bunk. Leave your bags and follow me." We were back on the first floor in an office. The sergeant informed the clerk that we were the group from the waterfront; then to us he said, "You will surrender your identity cards." I felt my stomach churning. I had handed over my navy pay booklet once before—in Munich. It had led the Gestapo to me.

The officer in charge, a lieutenant colonel, appeared. "Since you are all now hopelessly cut off from your respective ships," he said, "you will automatically become navy-infantry. Your uniforms will be exchanged for battle fatigues." Battle fatigues! That was the last thing I wanted to hear. But the news got worse. "And you will each be issued combat weapons." The officer droned on about our various weapons, but I stopped listening, remembering one of my achievements at the shooting range. I think I set a record. I not only missed my target; I hit the targets on either side of my own.

As the lieutenant colonel was winding up, he left out the call-to-arms bit: how much the fatherland needed us and counted on us. Instead, he abruptly dismissed us. Next came a welcome announcement—hot food in the mess hall.

Ten bodies hastened from the office. Nine went in search of food. I returned to our designated quarters for a pack of my dwindling supply of cigarettes and quickly returned to the first-floor office. With the clerk's attention fixed on me, I placed the cigarettes on the desk. Then looking directly at him, I politely asked for my pay booklet. He considered the cigarettes for a moment. Then he rose, picked up my pay booklet from the table behind him, and came around to my side of the desk. Handing it to me he said, "Do not let yourself get caught. We have heavy security both within the barracks and around its entire circumference. Thank you for the cigarettes and good luck."

By now I was ravenously hungry and suffering the effects of sleeplessness. At the canteen I grabbed a tray and joined the line. I saw my group; they didn't look happy. I heaped my plate with as much as it would hold—including extra salami and bread for breakfast—and, avoiding the others, found a spot near the door. I had to plan my escape.

In quarters I'd had the presence of mind to choose the bunk nearest the door. I sank down on it and fell asleep. Nothing short of an explosion would have roused me. I woke up almost ten hours later, got dressed, and quickly ate my sandwich. It was still dark but the camp had begun to stir. Opening the door to the courtyard, I could hear conversations going on in the distance. Lights were on in a building nearby. I stepped outside.

A number of trucks stood in a line. I shoved the duffel bag in the back of the first one, got in, and covered myself with the tarpaulin that was lying on the bed of the truck. Sooner or later that vehicle had to go somewhere. When it did, it would take me with it. Please, God, just let it be somewhere outside the compound.

I lay tense and alert, straining for the slightest sound. What if the truck has to be loaded first with something to be taken out of the compound? What if they didn't use this truck today? With every minute that passed, the chances of my being discovered grew. And, sooner or later, someone would notice that I was missing. I forced myself to think of something else. The tarpaulin gave cover but no warmth; my limbs were falling asleep. Moving as little as possible, I started flexing.

The camp was slowly waking. Distant voices drew steadily closer. I listened as two men stopped beside the truck's cab. "I'll be back within the hour", said one. Then the door opened, and the whole vehicle swayed under the driver's weight. The door slammed, then the engine turned over. After the sound of grinding gears, the truck jerked forward. After we hit two huge potholes, I peeped out from under the heavy canvas. The gates of the compound were disappearing in the distance.

Soon we were in Swinemünde. When the truck slowed down, I tossed the seabag out and jumped after it. The truck's taillights had disappeared even before I'd reached the curb. There was a store on the corner of the empty street. A young boy stood in front of it, gaping at me. I bent down to the freshly scrubbed face and asked, "Can you tell me where the train station is?"

He returned my smile and pointed to a street nearby. As I started walking away, the door to the shop opened and a woman came out. The boy called to her, "Mutti, that man just jumped out of the back of a police truck!"

Police! I got out of there as fast as I could. Fortunately, the train station was around the corner. I became just another uniform, for, though it was not yet seven A.M., the station was alive with activity.

My options had narrowed dramatically since the previous day. I had to go south again, but this time I would keep going: I had no wish to remain in Germany. The least complicated way out was over the Italian border into South Tirol. Mussolini or no Mussolini, the area had once been part of Austria, and the people there were still Austrian. My best bet, the quickest and safest solution, was to disappear quietly into the mountains. There, with some luck, I could conceal myself until the end of the war.

# *Tirol*

At the end of World War I, the Treaty of Saint-Germain gave Italy possession of South Tirol. When Mussolini came to power, the population of Bozen (Bolzano to the Italians) was still overwhelmingly Austrian. One still heard mostly German in the streets. This displeased Mussolini. He started trying to lure Italians to the area. Through a 1939 agreement with Hitler, Mussolini offered the former Austrians—now Italians—German citizenship if they would leave South Tirol and move to Germany. Even after seventy-five thousand South Tiroleans emigrated, South Tirol still remained predominantly German-speaking.

Bozen, with its temperate climate and rich soil, was an agricultural and wine-growing area. Mother's family owned vineyards and a fruit and resin export business. They had a house in town and one on the Ritten, the mountain above Bozen. Because of its architecture and culture, the village of Ritten was typically Austrian. Armed with provisions, I hoped to wait out the war on the mountain. But first I had to get there, and I was in the same old predicament—no travel documents.

The only train scheduled to leave at that early hour was a southbound freight train. It had two passenger cars; both were listed as full. Its departure was imminent. A disgusted-looking specialist first-class was also going over the schedules. He had a bad complexion and an even worse disposition. I ventured, "Don't you think it is strange for a freight train to have only two passenger cars? I mean especially now with the Russians almost here."

"It is completely unbelievable! I said exactly the same thing to one of the dispatchers. Do you know what he told me?" He didn't pause for breath but vehemently continued, "They are charters for the wives of the Nazi bosses. The wives! We, you and I, are the ones who've been protecting them. We should be on that train, not them!"

I couldn't have agreed more. I wished him good luck and melted into the crowd. Then a thought struck me: a chartered passenger car would have no MPs! I had to get on that freighter.

I worked my way over to the end of the train and began to check the doors. Every one of them was locked. I had reached a section of empty flatbed cars when the train's whistle sounded. The wheels groaned—the train began to roll. I started to run after the last flatbed car, heaved the duffel bag forward and threw myself at the side ladder. My knees and shin hit the iron steps, but my hands caught the metal sides. I climbed aboard and lay there, wheezing.

At the outskirts of Swinemünde, the train picked up speed. I didn't feel it until I stood and walked against the headwind. My coat flapping furiously around me, I staggered forward, seabag in tow, toward the end of the empty flatbed. Three more lay between me and the two passenger cars. I swung the bag onto the next flatbed and leapt across. I landed, then fell forward—two cars to go. I threw the bag onto the next flatbed. It landed as the train entered a turn, and began to roll sideways. I scrambled for it, snatching wildly as it reached the edge, caught the top half, and pulled it up one handful of canvas after the other.

Aching and sore, I made my way toward the last flatbed. My lungs were burning—hands, feet, and face numb from the cold. I would have swapped my pay book, in fact everything I had, for a pair of gloves!

The train entered another curve. This time I waited for it to straighten out before hurling the bag. Finally I reached the back end of the passenger car. It was an old model, with handgrips and a running board along the exterior. I shouldered the bag and, after first testing the runner for strength, crossed over. Hugging the car, I advanced to the first compartment one handgrip after the other. I grasped the door handle and turned. It didn't budge. I rattled it—nothing. I couldn't see inside because the window shade was pulled down. I had the same result with all the compartments in that car—doors locked, shades down. I tried not to think about my hands and ears, but I couldn't feel them anymore. I reached the end of the car, having tried and failed at every door, then leaned against the side of the train to catch my breath.

I moved to the next car. The first door was locked, and the shades were down. At that moment the train rolled over a ground-swell. Both my feet left the running board, finding it again after some heart-stopping moments, but the duffel bag jerked me off-balance. My left foot gave way, then my right knee. I hung on, flapping helplessly against the side of the train like a torn piece of awning in a storm. Instinctively, I had drawn my legs up. The bag swung and twisted against me; my left shoulder felt as if it were about to be ripped away from its socket. I managed to raise my body enough to hook my feet onto the running board. Every muscle in my arms shrieked in protest. The clatter of the wheels was deafening, and the tracks themselves seemed to reach up for me.

Pictures and faces from the past raced before my mind in dizzying succession. Impossible! With my last bit of strength I lifted myself up and got one knee on the running board, then the other. Badly shaken, I hugged the side of the train and forced air into my lungs. I don't know how long I knelt there, but my kneecaps couldn't take much more punishment. I ratcheted myself back up to a standing position and slowly inched toward the next door: lights and people!

Flooded with relief, I turned the doorknob. It was locked, but the shade was up. The people inside could see me, but no one moved. I beat on the window. Eight sour faces stared at me. Some made flicking movements with their hands, as one would do to shoo away a dog. I pounded fiercely on the window. "If you don't unlock the door," I screamed, "I will break the window."

That convinced them. The door swung out. I lay on the floor among eight pairs of feet while a torrent of insults rained down on me. "You stupid lout! What do you think you're doing on this train?"

"You brainless coward."

"Don't you even know which way the front is? You ought to be shot!"

I lay there, fighting for breath. When I was finally able, I struggled to a sitting position and pulled up my sleeve and my trouser leg to reveal the bandages. Then I placed my hospital papers in someone's lap. That silenced them. Grudgingly, they made room for me. There was a wood-burning stove in my corner. I resisted the temptation to embrace it, sank back, and reveled in the warmth. The remainder of the trip to Pasewalk, some thirty miles south of Swinemünde, passed in silence.

At Pasewalk the Nazi party bosses' wives got off. I stepped onto the platform, dusted myself off, and ran my hands through my hair. I had been correct about the MPs—none on the train. Here they were present only at the platform entrances. A Hamburg train stood opposite, but it was packed solid with people. I walked the length of the train outside. All of the corridors were clogged with standing passengers except for the very last car.

I thought it unlikely that the MPs would get through these crowded cars before we reached Hamburg, even though it was some distance away. If they did, it wasn't difficult to dodge them in the light of day. I wedged my seabag into a corner and sat down on it just as the train's whistle sounded. By the time the train reached the fringes of Hamburg, I had moved into a compartment.

Entering Hamburg, I was aghast at what lay before me. Berlin was terrible, Munich awful, but this city was a complete ruin. It may be that I was no longer able to make distinctions between grades of devastation. It was all calamitous. Even if Hamburg did represent an Allied victory, it was impossible not to have compassion for the Germans.

The train stopped thirty or forty feet short of where the platforms had stood. The ruin bore no resemblance to a railroad station. Cables crawled in every direction out of a mess of smashed concrete and brick. Just finding a path through it all was tricky. I hopped and jumped my way to the street. I had to go to another of Hamburg's stations, Dammtor, for the trains to Munich. I didn't see a single undamaged building between the two stations.

At Dammtor I found numerous unguarded entrances, but inside, despite the almost total destruction—or perhaps because of it—the place was crawling with MPs. Worse, there were several on each platform—all were checking documents. After finding out when and from which platform the Munich train was leaving, I remained in front of the schedule information board as if working out my route. Just before its scheduled departure, I approached the MP standing closest to the train, addressing him as I would one of my shipmates.

"You have a very cold duty today, my friend!" I rubbed my hands together and blew on them. It really was very cold.

"Yes, yes. But it is cold everywhere in this city now that nothing works!"

"Well, I've just arrived from Denmark on my way to Trieste. There it is really cold! Denmark, I mean. Trieste will only be a short relief because I must take the train again through here to

Denmark in only a few days. No fun traveling during these times, I can tell you! You are very lucky to have permanent duty here!"

"Ah, yes? You think so?"

I allowed him that one remark before launching into a nonstop monologue. I made up statistics, flinging odd bits of information at him. I described the *Prinz Eugen*'s maneuvers, the Russian advance, the state of the cities—anything, in fact, to hold his attention. "Can you believe it? I actually have a source in Trieste for silk stockings. Tell me, do you have a girlfriend?"

Only an idiot would pass up the chance of acquiring silk stockings. They were as valuable as cigarettes. "I certainly do. And she would kill for a pair."

"I'll tell you what. I can help you out. I'll bring you a pair—no, two pairs—on my return journey! That should make her very happy." I gave him a meaningful look.

I had timed things well. The wheels of the Munich train squealed sharply and started to roll. Pretending to be surprised, I let out a mild epithet and started running after the train. The MP was torn between duty and silk stockings. He ran after me for a few steps. "Your papers are in order, aren't they?"

I stood safely in the doorway of the car. "Yes, of course." I waved, then disappeared inside the train.

Before the war, the trip from Hamburg to Munich took between eight and nine hours, but this journey was an odyssey. With the constant strafing by Allied warplanes, it took thirty-three hours. Playing hide-and-seek with the MPs had become routine. On this train, I was barely challenged.

A red stoplight brought us to a premature halt some several hundred feet before Munich's main station. Two seconds later, I was crunching across the gravel toward the city's east railroad station. All southbound trains and all the local commuter trains left from there. As I approached, I saw that the main gate had been blown apart—there were huge gaps in the fence—so that the MPs were totally ineffective. Unnoticed, I found a train via Kiefersfelden and Kufstein to Innsbruck. It was through Innsbruck that one reached the Brenner Pass, the gateway to South Tirol.

I thought about the Radvanyi family in Kiefersfelden, old friends whom I had last seen in 1943. At the time, they were hiding a downed English pilot in a hut in the nearby mountains. It was the inspiration for my plan of the moment.

There was also a hotel in Kufstein that was owned by Grandfather's old friend Herr Rupprechter, a staunch Austrian patriot and a great admirer of Father. Both he and the Radvanyis would have taken me in. But I knew what would happen to anyone caught aiding the son of Schuschnigg, especially when he was also a deserter.

The Innsbruck train was preparing to pull out. I got on and walked to the end of the train and back—no sign of MPs. I sat down and kept my eyes on the door. These commuter trains carried very few military personnel. It was improbable there would be any MPs.

I couldn't remember when I had last eaten. Instead of thinking about food, I decided to sleep. That lasted until Rosenheim, when the door to the compartment suddenly banged open. "Travel documents!" a man in civilian clothes announced. I had prepared, during the long journey from Hamburg to Munich, a rough outline of a story. My brain was groping for the details that I had invented when I heard myself addressed. "Travel documents?"

"I will do nothing of the kind", I said indignantly. "Since when are civilians authorized to check the papers of military personnel?"

The man's eyes narrowed, and his lips grew very thin. He reached into his overcoat and took out a silver oval badge—Gestapo.

"Your papers?" he quietly repeated.

I gave him my navy pay booklet. He gave the pay booklet a cursory examination and snapped it shut.

"This is only your navy pay booklet. I asked for your travel orders!"

"My travel orders are with my transport leader, and I would really love to know where he is!"

Silence. Icy stare.

"I, four other volunteers, and a navy lieutenant—the latter being the transport leader with all our papers—are on our way from the naval base in Cuxhafen. We are to report to the Third S-boat Flotilla." I was warming to my subject. "During the air raid in Munich, we were dispersed. After the all clear sounded, I looked for them for hours. Nothing. I saw no alternative but to continue on my own. They would obviously resume their journey as well. Eventually we will reunite."

Thin Lips was not impressed. Without any further comment, he took the seat across from me until the next stop. Then he said, "Get up. You are coming with me."

I marched ahead with a straight back: my attitude—fed up and slightly irritated. When we were on the platform, I turned around inquiringly, but he only commanded, "Straight ahead!"

At the end of the platform was a row of offices. We stopped at a door marked "Railroad Station Commandant", far better than "Gestapo Headquarters". I breathed a little more easily.

The clerk at the desk and Thin Lips Heil Hitler-ed each other. My situation was briefly described; my pay booklet was handed over. Without a backward glance, Thin Lips then departed to search out his next victim. The clerk began typing up the account that he had just been given. When the racket ceased I spoke up. "Somewhat overly zealous, your Gestapo friend."

"He's no friend of mine, I can promise you that. He spends his time snatching people off trains, and then what does he do with them?"

"Exactly! He dumps them in your lap, and you have better things to do than someone else's work!"

His expression was that of one whose feelings were finally understood. Pulling the report from the typewriter, he knocked on the commandant's door, repeated my situation—but without prejudice—and withdrew.

The commandant—in the uniform of a colonel—called me into his office, greeted me civilly, and motioned me to a chair. He was well past middle age. His conduct left me optimistic. I recited my saga of the Third S-boat Flotilla. As he listened, he leafed through my pay booklet, giving no sign of recognizing my name. At last he said, "I see you were born in Innsbruck; so you probably just wanted to see your father."

"No, sir. Certainly not! It was simply a case of my losing my transport leader."

Was he calling my bluff? There was no way I could turn back now. Moreover, I was not about to fall for his air of reasonableness. It was a well-known Nazi tactic. I was preparing to express offense when he held up his hand.

"Well, anyhow," he said, sounding almost bored, "I am army and you are navy. You actually are none of my concern. You can

tell your story to the naval liaison officer in Brannenburg am Inn."
Brannenburg was a mere thirty-minute train ride. "To get there
you will, of course, need written orders. The clerk will issue them
for you."

I got to my feet. "Yes, sir. Thank you, sir. The naval liaison will
straighten this out for me." The colonel signed a form and gave it
to the clerk, instructing him to fill in the destination as Brannenburg. I gave a crisp salute, and the colonel returned to his office.

The possibilities stretched out before me. I had been worried
that an MP would be assigned to escort me, but that hadn't happened. I was free! I chose a seat in the first compartment of a
second-class car toward the front of the train, hoping that someone
would ask for my orders; no one did.

The lone attendant at Brannenburg am Inn station said that the
naval liaison officer had left for the day. He lived just across the
street. I entered the drab hotel typical of those found in the vicinity of railroad stations. The clerk didn't look up from his book.
When I asked for the naval liaison officer, the man sprang to life.
Herr Captain was in his room. On my way there, I passed the
hotel restaurant and hesitated. No, business first. I climbed to the
second floor and knocked on the door indicated.

"Herein!"

Sun had bleached the wallpaper in the room. The largest piece
of furniture in sight, a bed, was covered by a blood-red bedspread.
Next to it stood a scarred wood table; a lamp with a dingy parch-
ment shade rested on it. On the other side of the room, its sole
occupant was bent over the sheaf of papers that lay on his tidy
desk.

The captain was neatly set out. Every strand of the oiled white
fringe surrounding the top of his shiny scalp was in its place. Trim
in appearance, the man was probably in his late fifties. I thought he
looked reasonable enough. Then, without glancing up from his
papers, he screamed, "You miserable deserter! I'll put you up before
a military tribunal! I told you before to report back to your unit!"

"But, sir, I was never here before! I am with the Third S-boat
Flotilla and have lost my transport leader." I felt that my story grew
more convincing with every repetition. I would soon be persuaded
of it myself.

His head snapped up, and he said, "Sorry, Cadet. Forgive me! I thought you were someone else." As he grew calmer his face regained a normal color. "What is this about the Third S-boat Flotilla?"

I launched forth once again. I began with the air raid and concluded my fiction with "I am sure you have knowledge of the Third S-boat Flotilla."

"Yes, yes, of course! Cadet von Schuschnigg, I am from Berlin. Please tell me what you know of the state of the city. My whole family is there."

I told him all I knew. When I finished, he shook his head sadly. I paused a moment, then returned to the subject of my flotilla, which was "waiting for me in Trieste". I had just been visited by inspiration. Trieste was the German naval port closest to South Tirol. Emboldened, I proceeded to add, "The flotilla is under the command of Captain Reinicke." This was pure audacity; the man was, of course, currently the captain of the *Prinz Eugen*.

"Yes, certainly. He is a very good friend of mine."

"Ah! No wonder you are informed about the flotilla!" Our friendship was on firm ground now.

"When you see him in Trieste be sure to give him my best."

"Yes, of course, with great pleasure."

"Come! I have an office downstairs. I will give you your travel orders immediately."

"Yes, sir, thank you. I have been too long delayed as it is."

We went downstairs to his office, which was just off the lobby. He sat down behind the desk, typed out the orders, then signed and stuffed the document into an envelope. He got up and, with a bit of a flourish, presented it to me. I resisted the urge to snatch the envelope and run to the station.

"Cadet, late though you may be, you do still have to eat. Come, join me in the hotel restaurant! It is nothing special, but it serves my needs adequately enough."

"With what is ahead of me, it would be a pleasure to have one more good meal. Thank you for the invitation."

"I must confess I actually find the restaurant rather pleasant. They make such a fuss over me. I've almost become a little spoiled."

I'd had my last hot meal in Munich, and that seemed a long time ago. I sprang to open the restaurant door for him as the proprietor hurried over to greet us. With a ceremoniousness that wouldn't have disgraced the maître d' at the Schwarzwälder, he seated us at his best table.

The captain had not exaggerated the solicitousness of the staff. When they were not delivering one steaming course after another, they hovered nearby. The food was more than tolerable, and had I been able to forget that my host was totally on the wrong side, the occasion might even have been enjoyable. I was careful to direct one question after another to him, and for most of the meal he was the one who talked.

After coffee and a parting brandy, the captain insisted on seeing me off. I had mentioned that I intended to travel via Verona to Trieste. That was the excuse to travel through Innsbruck, which was the direct route to South Tirol using the Brenner Pass. Instead, the captain led me to the Rosenheim train, which connected in Klagenfurt—a shorter route. As a result, I first had to travel in the wrong direction. When I reached Rosenheim, I simply remained in my seat. I knew the train reversed directions and continued to Innsbruck.

It was amazing how salutary the effects of food and official travel documents were. I slept through the hissing of the train, its stopping and starting, the slamming of doors. Only the conductor's booming announcement that we were in Innsbruck finally roused me. I collected myself and hastened to the door.

The station had been hit hard. Wondering how much the rest of Innsbruck had suffered, I headed for the exit. It was too late to catch a streetcar even if they were still running after dark. I had to spend the night in the city. I would replenish my supplies and find a train that would take me farther south. I decided to present myself at the Mayrs' door.

Former neighbors and also friends, Clemens Mayr and his wife had been "Uncle" and "Aunt" to me since early childhood. I wanted very much to see them again, and I thought that if I slipped in at a late hour and left early the next morning, when it was still dark, my visit would not put them in any danger.

As I turned onto the Innrain and was again among all those familiar sights, I realized how much I had missed Innsbruck, how much I had missed Austria. I could make out, even in the darkness, the irregular silhouettes of damaged buildings. I had naively thought that Austria, as a victim of the Germans, would escape the wrath of the Allies. But after the Anschluss she too was their enemy. Targeted cities were just as dangerous here as in Germany.

After finding their name, with the help of my weak flashlight, I rang the Mayrs' buzzer at the darkened apartment house. The street was empty and silent, and the sound of the buzzer seemed as loud as an air raid siren. When there was no response I tried again, holding the button down for a long time.

The sound of footsteps and grumbling grew louder. Uncle Clemens sounded grumpy. He was the director of the Bank for Tirol and Vorarlberg and was always the first to arrive at the office in the morning; he would have been asleep for hours. Moreover, Uncle Clemens was a man of orderly habits, fond of routine; he did not like to be surprised. I shone the light in my face and braced myself.

When he opened the door, I quickly said, "It's me, Uncle Clemens, Kurti!"

He squinted into the darkness, and his grumpiness evaporated. "Kurti, mein Gott! Come in, come in!" After closing and carefully relocking the door, Uncle Clemens turned and gave me a big hug. "As soon as Elizabeth sees you, the first thing she'll want to do is feed you! Even for you, you are thin", he said, peering at me in the dim light.

"I am fine, Uncle Clemens. Forgive me for dragging you out of bed at this hour." He looked much older than the last time I had seen him.

"It doesn't matter. I am just so happy you're here! Come, Elizabeth will be dying of anxiety. We don't get many unannounced visitors at this hour. With her imagination she probably thinks the Gestapo has taken me away by now!"

"Uncle Clemens, would it be possible for me to sleep on the couch? I will be leaving very early in the morning."

We were almost at the top of the stairs. He stopped. "What do you mean, 'first thing in the morning'? If you can you must stay longer!" He noticed my uniform and the seabag. "You have to tell us everything that has happened since we last saw you."

Light spilled from their partially opened front door, where Aunt Elizabeth was waiting.

228

1. *Christmas 1931*    2. *Seven years old in 1933*

3. *With my mother at a Presentation of Colors*

4.
*My father, Kurt von
Schuschnigg, 1933*

5.
*My mother, Herma von
Schuschnigg, 1933*

6. *With my mother at a dedication*

7. *Children's party at Kriegsministerium, 1934*

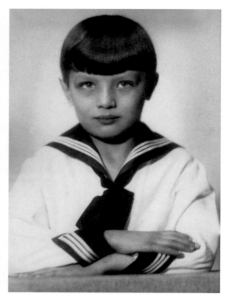

8. *In costume for an Elmayer theatrical performance*

9. *Eight-year-old student in 1934*

10.
*With Fraulein Alice, 1934*

11. *With my paternal grandparents and my mother in Kriegsministerium, 1934*

12. *The new chancellor of Austria, Kurt von Schuschnigg, in his office at home, 1934*

13. *Chancellor von Schuschnigg meeting Benito Mussolini in Florence, Italy, August 1934*

14. *Dignitaries at meeting with Mussolini in Florence, Italy, August 1934*

15. *Chancellor von Schuschnigg and Archduke Eugen at a troop inspection, 1934*

16. *Watching a parade*

17. *Greeting Cardinal Theodor Innitzer with Austrian Chancellor Engelbert Dollfuss, 1934*

18. *Austrian government ministers Fritz Stockinger, Karl Buresch, and von Schuschnigg with Vice Chancellor Ernst von Starhemberg and Chancellor Engelbert Dollfuss*

19. *Mother and I*

20. *Herma von Schuschnigg greeting supporters shortly before her death*

21. *Our car after the fatal accident on July 13, 1935*

22. *Doing homework, ca. 1935*

23. *With Grandfather von Schuschnigg, 1935*

24. *Arrival in a government plane, 1935*

25. *An Elmayer theatrical production*

26. *Riding at the military barracks in Vienna, 1935*

27. *Serving as an altar boy, 1935*

28. *With Rudi Fugger on vacation in Sistiana, Italy, 1935*

29. *Wearing the uniform of*
*Ostmärkische Sturmscharen*

30. *My stepmother, Vera von*
*Schuschnigg,* Sketch *magazine,*
*March 1938*

31.
*Breakfast with Father
on vacation in
Saint Gilgen, 1935*

32. *The von Schuschnigg vacation home in Saint Gilgen*

*33. Rowing with Father in Saint Gilgen, 1936*

*34. Fishing with Fraulein Alice in Saint Gilgen*

35. *Duchess of York, Chancellor von Schuschnigg, Princess Royal, Duke of York, and Prime Minister Ramsay MacDonald at the Austrian Embassy in London, 1935*

36. *Chancellor von Schuschnigg in Prague with Edvard Beneš, president of Czechoslovakia, 1936*

37. *Chancellor von Schuschnigg riding with General Wilhelm Zehner , state secretary for the army, ca. 1936*

38. *Funeral procession of Hungarian Prime Minister Gyula Gömbös, October 1936: Beginning second from left, German Air Force Commander Hermann Göring; Italian Foreign Minister Count Galeazzo Ciano; and Chancellor von Schuschnigg*

39.
*My grandfather
Field Marshall Artur von
Schuschnigg, ca. 1936*

40. *January 1938 meeting of the signatories of the Rome Protocols: Austria, Italy and Hungary*

41. *Chancellor von Schuschnigg refusing Hitler's demands before the Austrian Parliament on February 24, 1938*

42. *Playing with toy soldiers at Belvedere, 1937*

43. *Campaigning for a public vote against Anschluss, March 1938*

44. *Father and Grandfather during house arrest at Belvedere, March 1938*

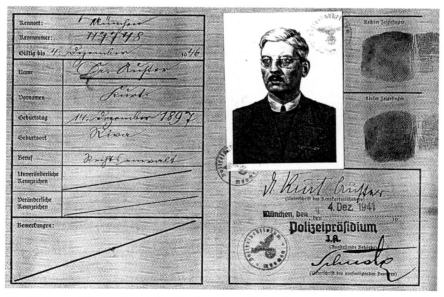

45. *Kurt von Schuschnigg's identification papers for Sachsenhausen concentration camp*

46.
*Drafted as a flak helper
in Munich, 1943*

47. *Photo of Sachsenhausen bungalow 1 (far right) taken from outside the camp,
summer 1942*

Am _24. XII._

zugezogen nach _Sachsenhausen, Friedlandstraße_
(Ort)
_Nr. a_

als — Mieter — Untermieter — Schlafstelle — Dienst — Besuch — bei ......
(Zutreffendes unterstreichen)

Letzte ) : _Wien I_ _Am Graben_
Wohnung (
(Ort und Kreis; falls Ausland auch Staat¹)

| 1 | 2 | 3 | 4 | 5 | 6 | | |
|---|---|---|---|---|---|---|---|
| Lfde. Nr. | Familienname (bei Frauen auch Geburtsname und gegebenenfalls Name aus der letzten früheren Ehe) | Vornamen (sämtliche; Rufname ist zu unterstreichen) | Familien= stand (ledig, verh., verw., gesch.) | Beruf (genaue Bezeichnung der Berufstätigkeit und Angabe, ob selbständig oder Angestellter, Arbeiter usw.) | Geburts= | | |
| | | | | | Tag | Mo= nat | Jahr |
| | v. Schuschnigg gen. Auster | Kurt | l. | Schüler | 22 | 5 | 26 |
| | | | | | | | |
| | | | | | | | |
| | | | | | | | |

**Für Kraftfahrzeugbesitzer**

Ich bin Besitzer des / der
Lastkraftwagens Nr. ...........................
Personenkraftwagens Nr. .....................
Kraftrades Nr. ...................................
Meiner gesetzlichen Verpflichtung zur Anmeldung der Wohnungsveränderung bei der Zulassungsstelle für Kraftfahrzeuge werde ich unverzüglich nachkommen.

**Für Ausländer und Staatenlose**

a) Art des vorhandenen Ausweises (Paß, Paßersatz): 
.................................................
b) Nummer des Ausweises: ..................
c) Ausstellende Behörde: ....................
d) Datum der Ausstellung: ...................

ASCHELM Vordruck a DIN A 4

**Für Angehörige de...**

Welche Verwendung haben ...
1. Sicherheits= und Hilfsdienst
2. Werkluftschutz: ............
3. Erweiterter Selbstschutz: ...
4. Selbstschutz: ................
5. Luftschutzwarndienst: ......
Im Luftschutz verwendete mit u...
falls in der für sie in Frage kommen...

¹) Es ist die politische Gemeinde... Amtsbezirk oder ein Ortsteil.
²) Bei mehrfacher Staatsangehö... losigkeit: staatenlos und früher...
³) Von außerhalb zuziehende Weh... Abgabe der Anmeldung ihre e... gegebenen Ausweise vorlegen.

48. _Sachsenhausen registration form for Kurt von Schuschnigg, alias Doctor Auster_

Meldebehörde

Tagesstempel der Meldebehörde

−7. JAN. 19 11

ift — find

Brandenburg

(Kreis)     (Wohnung)     Straße / Platz   Nr.

O  als  Mieter / Untermieter  bei  Fr. Kammer ; oder   vom Reichsarbeitsdienst _____
                                                      vom Wehrdienst _____

| 8 | 9 | 10 | 11 | 12 | | | 13 |
|---|---|---|---|---|---|---|---|
| Staatsangehörigkeit 2) | Bezeichnung des religiösen Bekenntniffes (ob Angehöriger einer Religions oder Weltanschauungsgemeinschaft, gottgläubig oder glaubenslos) | Wohnort und Wohnung (Ort, Kreis, Straße, Hausnummer) bei der letzten Personenstandsaufnahme bzw. am letzten vor der Anmeldung liegenden 10. Oktober | Wehrdienstverhältnis (z. B. Erfatref. I ufw.) Wehrnummer? Zuletzt zuständige Wehrerfatzdienststelle? 3) | Bei Zuzug von außerhalb: a Haben Sie schon früher in der hiefigen Gemeinde gewohnt? Bejahendenfalls, wann und wo? | b Für den Fall, daß die oben angegeb. letzte Wohnung daneben beibehalten wird, Zweck und vorausfichtl. Dauer des Aufenthalts in der hiefig. Gemeinde? | | Bei Zuzug aus dem Ausland, von Reisen, Wanderschaft, Schiffahrt oder Reichsarbeitsdienst und Wehrdienst, Angabe, wann und wo Sie zuletzt im Inland polizeilich gemeldet waren (Ort, Kreis, Straße, Hausnummer) |
| D.R. | kath. | Uhr Westgwald RAD Abt 5/251 | ER I. | Juli 4) dtr | | | |

Gemeinde Sachsenhausen Kreis Niederbarnim

Luftschutzes

_____

Kurt v. Schuschnigg
(Eigenhändige Unterschrift des Angemeldeten)

Dr. Aistes
(Eigenhändige Unterschrift des Wohnungsinhabers bei Untermietern)

a oder Kinder find ebenen.

nicht ein Wohnplatz, ein    (Eigenhändige Unterschrift des Hauseigentümers bzw. des Verwalters)

e angeben, bei Staaten=
rigkeit.
en der Meldebehörde bei    Sachsenhausen , den 2. I.        19 44
die an ihrer Stelle aus=    (Ort und Datum der Abgabe an die Meldebehörde)

49.
*Kurt von Schuschnigg, his wife Vera (left), his sister-in-law Marianne (center), and his daughter, Sissi, Como, Italy, 1946*

50. *Kurt, Vera and Sissi von Schuschnigg upon arrival in New York, 1947*

"Look whom I have brought you!" called Uncle Clemens.

She swung open the door and cried out, "I cannot believe it! Kurti! Why didn't you let us know? We would have waited up for you!" She threw her arms around me.

"Ssshhhh! Let's go inside, Elizabeth", Uncle Clemens said, shooing her inside and firmly turning the key in the door.

Our voices had brought out Hildtraud, the younger of the Mayrs' daughters. The conversation continued in the kitchen, where, as Uncle Clemens had predicted, preparations to feed me were already in full swing. I gave them a condensed version of the last couple of years, including all that had happened since my departure from the hospital.

"You must be careful, Kurti. Everyone believes that the war's end is just around the corner. You only have to remain invisible until then", said Uncle Clemens. I outlined my plans for the Ritten. I didn't know how much faith they had in my being able to camp out in a remote mountain hut, but they were good enough not to discourage me. Had they been able to think of something better, they would have said so.

I finished my second dinner of the evening. We bade one another farewell until a happier time. Their older daughter, Elsbeth, was away at school; I was given her room, and it couldn't have pleased me more. I sank into a heavy sleep. I woke up at five thirty, bathed, and got dressed. Then, after leaving a brief note for the family, I headed outside.

There was barely any traffic on the streets. My first stop was a café where I could wait until the government offices opened. The municipal office would give me ration books. I was entitled to them because of my legitimate travel documents. Uncle Clemens had given me, from his own stock, more than enough stamps for my breakfast.

I was the first one at the café. I asked for coffee and began to leaf through the reading material, which had been, of course, endorsed by the fatherland. The coffee was only a little more palatable than the Nazi newspaper. Resigned to the risk of wartime substitute ingredients, I bravely ordered breakfast.

After determining that I was both Austrian and a Tiroler, indeed one who had been born right there in Innsbruck, the middle-aged waitress seemed only too happy to deliver her opinion of the war. She began with the events of the middle of the last decade and carried on through the Allied bombings. These had evidently begun in December 1943; there had been so many raids, she said, that she had lost count. The Innsbruckers had certainly suffered. There was little point in telling her about cities like Munich, Berlin, and Hamburg. I listened to her with half an ear until she said, "Chancellor von Schuschnigg did his best to wake people up, but did anyone listen? No! People are fickle. Just look where all of this has gotten us. I'll bet you can't be too happy having to serve in the German Navy!"

I said nothing.

"You know that the chancellor and his family lived here, don't you?"

"Ah, yes, I did know that." So it went with the Austrians, I thought. She could very well have been among the madly waving crowds strewing rose petals and hailing the Germans as they marched across the border in 1938. Since that day long ago, as the tide slowly began to turn, so, it seemed, had people's memories. I thanked her for the surprisingly edible breakfast, paid, and left.

Having forgotten to ask for directions to the municipal office, I stopped at the streetcar shelter around the corner. Its only occupant was an old man. He was eager to help. "Ration book office! Of course I know where it is. Why, a blind man could tell you how to get there!"

The whole European world was living on ration booklets, and apparently everyone except me knew where this office was in the city. With the man's precise, lengthy directions I found the building easily, but it had not opened yet. I had a short wait before me, but I was in no hurry. Eventually, a long queue formed behind me. The doors of the office opened on time, and we all filed inside in an orderly fashion. I presented my documents to a crotchety old clerk who seemed unhappy to be there; he looked as if he had not had enough sleep the night before. Between yawns he considered first my pay booklet and then my Brannenburg document; then he reversed the order and reinspected them. I was becoming impatient, and I was not alone. From behind me a voice called out, "Is he still awake?"

The old geezer shot back, "I am! Any more distractions, and it will only take me longer!"

I asked, in the most civil way, for the maximum number of ration stamps, two weeks' worth. Normally, one could obtain only a week's worth at a time. "It isn't definite yet how long my travel is going to take me", I added. I might as well have addressed the blotter on the desk or so it seemed. He totally ignored me as he shuffled through a sheaf of booklets. He gave me, however, two weeks' worth and recorded the fact on my Brannenburg orders. I pocketed my new ration stamps and headed for the grocer's shop.

The last such shop that I had visited was the one in Oranienburg. I was sure that there would be, if not superior goods, at least more offered in Innsbruck. I was not the earliest customer at the shop. Taking my place in the line, I surveyed the shelves behind the clerk. I realized that, unfortunately, the shop in Oranienburg came off quite well in comparison. The narrow range of choices shortened the process of shopping. I picked up some passable salami and a piece of odorless cheese. After spurning the undrinkable coffee substitute and the tea on display, I asked for butter.

"Butter! Why don't you just ask for caviar?" the clerk said, pausing to lean with both hands on the counter separating us. He turned to his fellow clerk. "We haven't been able to get our hands on butter for ... how long, Peter?"

Peter ruminated. "At least a year, at least that. And that was a mistake ... supposed to have gone to the military commissary!"

"Fine. Do you have any margarine?"

"That, yes."

I also asked for the largest container of salt available (there being none in Italy, salt was another form of currency).

"What in the world are you going to do with all that salt?"

I stuttered something about its effectiveness as a disinfectant and remembered one more item: "Bread?"

That was one of the few things not deemed too extravagant. The bread was plopped down beside my margarine, salt, salami, and cheese. I looked glumly at the supplies that would have to sustain me for weeks. Mistaking my silence for satisfaction, the clerk went on. "Soon this will look like nothing! Once things get back to normal, that is."

I was being treated once again to the views of the common man on the present state of the war. The clerk looked as if he would make further comment, but perhaps realizing that he was talking to a person wearing the uniform of the German Navy, checked himself. I nodded and counted out my ration stamps and money. After stowing away my purchases, I started for the station.

Thoughts of the Gestapo returned. What was the likelihood of their tracking down a solitary runaway cadet engineer? Surely, as time passed, this would only become less likely? Nevertheless, I was resolved to make myself as inconspicuous as possible.

The damage to the station was far more apparent in the daylight. The authorities had made some effort at check points, but entering the station was, nevertheless, child's play. I should have avoided the sentry as a matter of principle, but I just couldn't help myself. I walked straight up and offered him my papers. Then I looked at the schedules: nothing but freight trains.

Spotting a southbound freight train, I went around to its far side and looked for an unlocked car. I was determined to avoid open flat-bed cars at all cost. In practically no time, I found an empty car and got on. It must have been used to transport either very dirty livestock or something far worse. It was only a brief journey, but when I got off at the station for the Brenner Pass, I became aware of a foul smell; it emanated from me. I flapped my overcoat up and down, then opened and closed it as fast as I could. That would have to do.

I strode into the commissary and presented my documents to the clerk behind the counter. "I am on my way to Trieste. As you can see, I was issued ration stamps in Innsbruck before I realized that they're no good in Italy. So I gave them to my friends in Innsbruck." That lie proceeded from the need to acquire all the provisions I could. What I had gotten in Innsbruck wouldn't go far. Who knew how long I would be on that mountain?

It was the government's responsibility to feed its servicemen, and I met with no resistance, not even so much as a raised eyebrow, when I asked for two weeks' worth of rations. There was more of everything here, and it was of better quality than the goods in the stores for civilians in Innsbruck. I chose a fragrant farmer's cheese, a pungent salami, and butter—real butter. I saw cigarettes—a blessing, for I had none left. I had just picked up more salt and bread, and was beginning to turn away, when I saw at the back of the counter, and so well concealed that I almost missed it, coffee. I stared in disbelief. The beverage served in every café, and everywhere else, was the wartime substitute. I claimed the real thing.

I hoisted my very heavy seabag onto my shoulder and went out to await the next southbound train, another freight train. An hour and a half later, I was in Bozen seeking my mother's brother.

Father had always said that Uncle Sepp was a very decent man with a good head on his shoulders. Coming from Father, that was high praise. If anyone could give me intelligent advice on the Ritten, it was my uncle. After a brief conversation with him, I would be on my way. Keeping my eyes open and my cap pulled down low, I set out for the family's house on Kapuzinergasse.

I dropped the seabag in front of the door and stepped back to look up at the four-story stucco facade. It was relatively unharmed by the air raids. The roof had suffered a little damage, and exposed bricks peeked out in several spots. Otherwise, except for streaks of soot here and there, the sturdy cream-colored house had fared well. Uncle Sepp had been fortunate.

I rang the doorbell. There was no answer. I rang again and looked up, hoping to see at least a window opening. Instead a middle-aged woman stepped out of the house next door. "There is no one home. What do you want?" she demanded loudly, as she eyed my uniform.

"I am Herr Masera's nephew. Can you tell me where everyone is?"

She looked me up and down before replying. "Well, Frau Masera and the children have been staying up on the Ritten ever since the bombings." She gave me a hard look to accompany the note of accusation in her voice. "You can see what we have had to go through here!" She lifted her hands from her broad hips to indicate her house, which had suffered even less damage than Uncle Sepp's. I made exclamations of sympathy, but she shrugged her thick shoulders and, sighing, went on, "Yes, poor Herr Masera. He was conscripted. And every day now he sits in City Hall."

I wasn't sure exactly how bad this news was. Uncle Sepp was about the same age as Father. If his duties entailed going only as far as the town hall, how terrible could his suffering be? That my Aunt Louise and my cousins, Grete and Norbert, were in their summer house was reassuring, for the area was heavily wooded. It was very unlikely that the Allies would be dropping their bombs there. I thanked the woman and shouldered my bag. Then I started walking toward City Hall. When I looked back, she was still there watching me. I had considered leaving my seabag with her. In the end, I decided that her curiosity would have had its way with her. I had no doubt that she would have thoroughly inspected the seabag and wondered what was I doing with a supply of food that would have fed an entire family for some time.

The bag was very heavy. I felt as Sinbad must have when he had to carry the old man on his shoulders. Every half a block or so, I had to stop and shift the bag from one shoulder to the other.

It was a relief to see that everything in the city looked fairly normal. There was plenty of activity; shops were open. Indeed, the people of Bozen were luckier than they knew.

At City Hall a clerk gave me directions to my uncle's office, and I gave thanks that I did not have to climb any stairs. When Uncle Sepp saw me, he jumped up and hurried around his desk—his arms flung out, a huge smile on his face. "Kurti!"

The smile on my face froze. My Uncle Sepp stood before me, kitted out in all the splendor of the Tenth SS Panzer Division Alpenvorland.

# South of the Border

I had assumed that Uncle Sepp had been conscripted by the Italians, not the Germans. Seeing my surprise, he reassuringly said, "What? Ah, yes, the uniform. Easier to put it on and play the game, Kurti. Come, my boy, sit down."

After we had recovered from the shock of seeing each other, Uncle Sepp described his predicament. When the Allies began pushing north through Italy in 1943, Germany had declared that all Austrians in South Tirol were now Germans and had pressed the men into service. This was part of a last-ditch effort to mobilize additional men. Uncle Sepp said he was lucky not to be serving on the front. He was an auxiliary SS policeman. Taking in my German Navy uniform, he said, "Now you. Tell me everything that has happened."

He balanced himself on the edge of his desk and folded his arms. I began slowly and only touched on the most significant events. When I came to the explosion in the engine room on the *Prinz Eugen*, I knew I had to mention that I was wanted by the Gestapo. I described my meeting with the chief surgeon at the hospital in Munich. My uncle's face went pale, and I saw a flash of fear in his eyes; but he quickly straightened his back and squared his shoulders.

"Kurti," he said, "you are my sister's son. I shall do for you what I would do for my own children. Right now that means hiding you immediately. No one must see you. No one must know that you are here. This is not out of concern for me but for your aunt and for Grete and Norbert. They are safe right now, but you know how long the arm of the Gestapo is!" He went behind his desk and sat down heavily on his chair.

"Uncle Sepp, I didn't come here to ask you to hide me. I have a lot of rations with me. What I had planned to do was go up into the woods on the Ritten and find an empty hut. I came to see you because I thought you might know of one. With luck I can wait out the end of the war there. Everyone says it will be any day now. That is my plan. What do you think of it?"

Because he said nothing I went on. "I actually have legal travel orders. This document allows me a forty-eight-hour interruption in my designated travel to Trieste. Even if I were to be picked up, as unlikely as that is, according to my official travel documents, I am not in flight. Bozen is merely a transit point."

"Kurti, I want you to wait here in my office. Wait here and do not leave, not for any reason!"

"Yes, Uncle Sepp."

"I shall be back very shortly."

As I sat in his office unoccupied, I was consumed by one thought: What were the responsibilities of an auxiliary SS policeman? What did Uncle Sepp have to do? The possibilities were dreadful. I waited, and I reflected uneasily. In the end I managed to collect myself.

I tried to consider things from Uncle Sepp's point of view. Here *I* was, in the uniform of the German Navy: Who was I to judge him? I had neither a wife nor children to worry about. And this was Italy, not Germany. Uncle Sepp had lived here all his life. He was a good man and highly respected in Bozen. He was also resourceful. If Uncle Sepp had to carry out an order that was morally difficult, he would do so only in a way that was acceptable to his conscience.

When he returned, some forty-five minutes later, he did not sit down. "Everything is arranged. We're going somewhere safe for the night. Come!" He picked up my bag and opened the door. I hurried after him.

We left City Hall by a back entrance and walked along a deserted alley. Uncle Sepp walked with a firm, purposeful step. He seemed disinclined to talk. The sight of my seabag hanging over the shoulder of his field-gray SS uniform struck me as bizarre, but then, at present, nearly everything in life was. We strode over bumpy cobblestones—past refuse containers, foraging cats, and chained bicycles.

At the end of the block, Uncle Sepp headed down another alley. We wove through a maze of backstreets for another ten minutes. Uncle Sepp never hesitated. By the time we finally stopped, behind a large, solid-looking multi-story house, I had lost my bearings completely.

Uncle Sepp's knock on the back door was answered at once by a woman. She took in my appearance and gave Uncle Sepp a brief greeting. We were led through a labyrinth of corridors, past several pantries, into a dimly lit hallway. We found ourselves in a living room that looked down on the main street. After gently closing the door the woman turned to us.

She was at least as old as my uncle and generously proportioned. She undoubtedly dyed her hair. Still visible despite the camouflage of powder were deep lines that creased her forehead and framed a mouth that bespoke an intransigent nature. She put her hand on Uncle Sepp's arm and said, "Wait here a moment and just let me check that there are no guests around."

She was apparently the owner of this boarding house. Father always said that my uncle was shrewd and resourceful. Uncle Sepp was also, it seems, a good judge of character, for this was certainly a serious and cautious woman.

We watched as she quietly climbed the steps to the floor above us. Almost immediately afterward, she was bending over the banister and beckoning us. My uncle grabbed my seabag and bounded up the double flight of stairs; I followed. The woman handed him a key and pointed toward the far end of the murky hallway where a door stood open. I followed Uncle Sepp inside the room and tripped over the threshold. I bounced off the door and only just managed to stay upright. His arm shot out to steady me, and he whispered, "Shush! We don't want to announce our arrival. Do we?"

"Sorry, Uncle Sepp", I said, noiselessly closing the door.

My uncle locked the door and stood the seabag in a corner; then he dropped into a brightly colored velvet armchair. I sat down on the end of the bed and looked around. A hanging lamp was the only incongruity among the otherwise mediocre furnishings. Its shade was draped with a cheap tasseled scarf that absorbed half the light that the lamp shed. I was reaching up to yank it off when Uncle Sepp stopped me. "No, no! You don't want to change the decor in here, Kurti", he said. Then, smiling somewhat sheepishly, he explained. "After all, this is the best bordello in Bozen." I looked at him, wondering if I would be able to tell this story afterward. When Father had said that Uncle Sepp was resourceful, he hadn't known the half of it.

Uncle Sepp explained that he needed to return to his office "before anyone becomes curious" but would be back at the end of the day.

"Uncle Sepp, you really don't have to bother. I'll be fine. I can take care of myself."

"Are you joking? Listen, Kurti. You are not to show your face to anyone. The only reason to leave this room is to go to the loo. And before you stick your head out, first listen through the door to make sure no one is in the hallway. You understand how important this is? No one must see either of us here."

"Yes, of course, Uncle. I will be extremely careful. Go back to City Hall and please don't worry."

Following his own advice, and probably as an example to me, Uncle Sepp went to the door and flattened his ear against it. He slowly opened it and peered out. Then, after a hurried wave of his hand, he went out.

I seated myself in the chair and looked more carefully at my surroundings. The only window in the room overlooked the back-street from which we had entered the building. Except for the scarf-covered lamp and the double bed, the room was like one in any other boarding house. I emptied my seabag and, after sorting through my stock, decided to try out the cheese and the salami. It was either incredibly good, or I had become much less discriminating. After eating too much of both I stretched out on the bed and instantly fell sleep.

On waking hours later, my first thought was that I would never again take a bed for granted. It was still light outside. Uncle Sepp wouldn't be back for some time. My seabag contained no books, and the room didn't have so much as a Nazi newspaper to divert me. Then I remembered the small bookcase in the living room downstairs. If I were careful, I could be down and back without anyone knowing about it. It was preferable to lying idly in the room.

I rolled off the bed and went to the door. The house was as still as a grave. I left the door slightly open and padded down the length of the hall. All seemed clear downstairs. I took the steps two at a time, crept into the living room, and gently closed the door behind me.

The heavy curtains left the room in semidarkness. A cluster of burning candles provided a little more light. I thought it very unlikely that I would find anything in my line of reading. I was groping in the dimness when my right leg made contact with the sharp edge of a low and very solid mahogany table. Its surface had been covered with bric-a-brac, which were now scattered all over the rug.

My leg throbbed with pain. I clenched my teeth and, gripping that leg, hopped up and down on the other. Having exerted myself for some time in this way, I sank to the floor, exhausted. I prayed that I hadn't torn the skin that was still healing.

I managed to recover all but one of the objects that had been knocked off the table. It had rolled under a sofa and lay just beyond my reach. I crawled behind the sofa and stretched out my arm for the scrimshaw Buddha. My fingers had just closed around it when the door to the hall opened. I recognized the madam's voice immediately. "We are more than honored by your visit, Colonel. We have the greatest respect for the Gestapo and the work it must perform to keep the Reich safe."

The Gestapo! Here?

"Let us not speak of professional matters for the moment", answered a deep male voice.

"Please be seated, Colonel. May I offer you some sherry?"

Sherry! What was the fellow doing here at this time of day? Wasn't he supposed to be in an office somewhere? A crystal stopper clinked back into a decanter. Someone else entered the room.

"Good afternoon!" announced the newcomer, a woman.

"Ah! Colonel, may I present our dear Theresa to you."

A giggle: very likely it was Theresa. The colonel said something that was unintelligible to me. Another giggle. It was fairly clear that the colonel hadn't come for conversation.

"Please make yourself comfortable", the madam said. "I have something I must attend to."

This was very bad. It was only a matter of time before I was discovered. Theresa giggled again, then she actually spoke. "My quarters are much more comfortable. Shall we?"

Evidently the colonel was a man of action, for the next sound that I heard was that of the door opening and closing. I exhaled and was just pulling myself up when the door opened once more. I dropped down on the carpet again. I heard the candles being blown out. Then I heard the sound of the curtains behind me being opened. Daylight flooded in. There was an audible intake of breath followed by "What the devil are you doing in here?!"

239

I scrambled to my feet. Replacing the truant Buddha, I started to explain but was immediately cut off. "Do you know what could have happened to you? Did you stop to think what could have happened to the rest of us if that pig had found you in here?" Her arms were crossed and her eyes blazed. I must have looked as remorseful as I felt, for her face softened somewhat. "You also nearly frightened me out of my mind! Hide behind the curtain until I return. I have to see if I can get you back up to your room." I was five years old again and standing in the corner. I had gotten off lightly then, and I was getting off lightly now.

A moment later she tapped on the door and softly called, "Get out here, now!" Holding a crimson-tipped finger to her lips, she motioned for me to follow. "Not a sound!" she whispered. We must have been a ridiculous sight—the madam with her unbelievable hair, heavily made-up face, and thickening body creeping up her own stairs with me in tow.

At the top of the stairs she moved swiftly down the hall to my door. It was still ajar. Practically shoving me through, she stepped in behind and gently closed the door. "What do you think you were doing, stealing around downstairs like that?"

"I cannot tell you how sorry I am", I blurted out. "I only went down to borrow one of your books."

"Books! What books?"

"The ones in the living room—that small bookcase on the table."

She regarded me in silence. It was the simple truth, and she saw that it was. Without a word she left, gently closing the door behind her. I went to lock the door but changed my mind. What was the point? I had just turned around when the door opened, striking my head and backside. I jumped and whirled around. There was the madam's head peering at me from the edge of the door. Her voice had lost its anger. "What in the world would we need with books in an establishment such as mine? Those weren't books. That is a liquor cabinet with a false front!" She laughed softly and went away.

A little later, Uncle Sepp bustled in, carrying two large burlap bags. He deposited them on the table and said, "Kurti, I have made all the arrangements, but first—dinner!" With a flourish, he brought

240

out a bottle of Terlaner, a local wine, and a pot of hot sausages with sauerkraut.

During dinner I showed my uncle the contents of the seabag that he had been carrying around for me. "I haven't seen so much food since the beginning of this idiotic war!" he declared. "But it doesn't look like you'll have the opportunity to eat it. Tomorrow morning, before dawn, I'm taking you to the Monastery Gries. From there you'll be transferred to a safe house."

"Uncle Sepp, I don't want you involved. Hiding out in the mountains is really the best solution."

"It is not a practical solution, Kurti. You haven't been up there since you were a small boy. It isn't as remote an area as it used to be. There are still farmers' huts, but those barely afford any protection from the weather; they have no electricity, no heat, and no plumbing. Where is your drinking water going to come from? You would have to use melted snow. That may only sound like a challenge, but it would quickly become tiresome."

He paused for a moment, and a twinkle came into his eye. "I would give you a week without a bath, two at most, and you'd be back in Bozen knocking on my door. It is still winter up in the mountains. Spring or summer perhaps, even autumn—but in the winter? You'd have to be crazy to do what you are proposing!"

"All right, Uncle Sepp. Thank you for your help."

We topped off our meal with some of the excellent cheese from the commissary on the Brenner Pass and then said good-night. He brought out one last item: an alarm clock. "This way we'll both have a good night's sleep." And so we did.

Uncle Sepp shook me awake at four A.M. A short time later, we stepped out into the ice-cold darkness before dawn. The monastery was on the outskirts of the city and about half an hour's walk away.

The abbot himself opened the door to us. He was no frail cleric but a solid, sturdy man who looked as if he could till the land and bring in the harvest all by himself. He greeted us heartily and let us in. The monastic life begins early, and the monastery was in full swing.

We were shown into a simple room, the abbot's office. Uncle Sepp and I sat down on straight-backed cane chairs while the abbot seated himself behind the rough wooden table that served as his desk.

"You know, Sepp, we are happy to be of service in any way that we can." And turning to me, he said, "You are welcome to stay here for as long as you like. But as I have already told Sepp, I do not recommend it.

"We have had extremely unpleasant experiences with the local Nazis. You see, the idea of the church as a sanctuary doesn't exist for them. Recently, we were denounced for allegedly harboring fugitives fleeing the Reich. None were found, but the mere allegation was enough to produce a vigorous search. Much of our furniture, modest though it was, was 'unavoidably' destroyed." He waved his hand around the room. "I don't doubt for a second that had anything unusual been found, however insignificant, we would all have been arrested and shot without the benefit of a trial.

"Since then we have been paid regular surprise visits by the Gestapo. We are on their active list. It is not for our safety I speak. I fear for yours because here I cannot guarantee it. I have taken the liberty of providing alternative lodgings."

Uncle Sepp and I both started to speak at the same time. I yielded. "We are most grateful for whatever arrangements you have made."

It occurred to me that it was probably some sort of mortal sin to put members of the clergy in harm's way. When Uncle Sepp had finished speaking, I said so to the abbot.

"Your father has been an example to his fellow man and to his fellow Catholic. To be able to help his son pleases us very much." Then the abbot addressed my uncle. "Sepp, I don't want you to worry. Go back to town. I will be in touch."

I walked with my uncle to the monastery's front gate. "Kurti, you're in good hands. Not only is the abbot a fearless man of God, he is also capable and shrewd. He knows what he's doing." He hugged me. "I am now going home to get some sleep!"

"Thank you, Uncle Sepp. Take care of yourself."

Uncle Sepp always seemed younger than his contemporaries; not only physically but mentally he was youthful, easy-going. Now, waving good-bye, he looked positively carefree.

The abbot was waiting inside. "I have things to take care of", he said. "I will see you later in the afternoon. In the meantime, Brother Michael will see to your needs."

A thin young monk took me to a cell-like room. Against one wall stood its only piece of furniture, a narrow cot. Below the curtain-free window hung a crucifix and on the opposite wall, two clothes pegs—high luxury compared with that lonely, unheated mountain hut. I put my bag in the corner and went to bed.

Some hours later I awoke, famished. I took out a salami and the farmer's cheese from the duffel bag. Perhaps ten minutes later there was a knock on the door. It was the young monk carrying a cup of coffee, real coffee. "I think this will go well with your meal", he said, handing me the cup.

"Is this coffee?" I asked redundantly.

"It is, yes."

"But how ...? Ah, you smelled the salami and cheese."

"They're very pungent."

It was a simple statement without any trace of envy or resentment. I was embarrassed to accept this luxury of coffee. I wrapped up the remainder of the salami and the wedge of cheese and handed it to him. "My compliments to the chef."

"How generous. We will all enjoy this."

It was almost four P.M. when someone knocked on the door again. It was an older, jolly-looking monk. "You may want a change of atmosphere. To a layman our rooms must seem rather stark."

"Well, after all, it's only a place to sleep. I was very comfortable. Thank you."

A few moments later, we were in the chapel. "If you take the doorway we just passed on the left, you will find a small, enclosed garden. Please use that if you prefer", he said. Holding out the two books that he had been carrying, he added, "And here is something to read, if you wish." They were biographies. One was the life of Sir Thomas More, the English martyr who had been canonized by Pope Pius XI in 1935. The other was about Saint Thomas Aquinas. I was grateful for the monk's thoughtfulness.

The winter day had turned dark and chilly. It had been some time since I had the opportunity to pray in a church, and there was a great deal to be thankful for. I then settled down to read.

I was collected punctually at five P.M. and returned to the abbot's office. "Your transfer to a local farm has been arranged. The farmer is both a parishioner and a valued friend of the monastery. First we will have a meal together."

He led me to the refectory. We all gave thanks for our meal before sitting down. Turning to me, the abbot said, "And we all thank you for the excellent cheese and salami."

"Since it doesn't smell you wouldn't know it, but I also have salt for you."

"Wonderful!" he exclaimed, clapping me heartily on the back.

The meal was like their lives, simple and good: a bowl of hot, frothy potato and leek soup, with a large piece of black bread, followed by some stewed fruit. Afterward, I trailed the abbot out to the monastery's backyard. A man had just finished loading a horse-drawn wagon with what smelled like compost. This was my conveyance.

I gave the abbot the salt. He handed me a brown cloak. "Put it over your uniform. This is Johannes. He is taking you to his farm, where you will be safe." Johannes was a man of medium height, but powerfully built. His honest, open face broke into a wide smile as we shook hands.

The abbot took my hand in his big, work-roughened hands. "We will keep you and your family in our prayers. You must be steadfast in your faith and believe that you will soon be reunited." His simple eloquence was moving. I turned quickly and climbed onto the wagon beside the farmer. The abbot blessed us, making the sign of the cross, then said to Johannes, "Thank you, my friend. I will see you soon."

I reached to take my bag from the abbot, but the farmer was quicker. He grasped it with one hand, as if it were feather-light, and stowed it under our seat. Responding to a flick of the reins, the horse began to trot homeward. The books still firmly in my grip, I waved and called out my thanks.

Dusk was approaching. The little traffic there was had dissipated. We bounced up the rutted path to the back of the house just as darkness fell. The three-story wooden farmhouse had the barn built onto the back, typical architecture for the area. Fruit trees surrounded the farmhouse. Johannes leapt down and unharnessed the mare. "I just have to attend to Lulu. I'll be back presently."

I settled on the back stairs to wait. The evening air was brisk and carried the odors of the rich soil. Johannes had told me that his property covered more than one hundred acres. During the growing and harvesting seasons, it kept his entire family, as well as a number of hired hands, busy. But at this time of the year, a farmer's only duties were mending fences, milking the cows, and making cheese.

With Lulu secured for the night, he led me into the kitchen and opened a side door revealing the staircase within: at the top of these stairs—my new living quarters. Against one wall were a chair, table, and lamp; a cot stood opposite. "The other door is to the toilet", said the farmer.

"Thank you, Johannes."

"I must ask something of you." He sat down. "I think I do not have to tell you that these are dangerous times."

I nodded.

"Only my wife knows that you are here. I do not want my children involved in any way with what I am doing. The less they know, the better. At present there are two temporary farmhands to help mend fences. I have known them all of my life. I can trust them. All the same, I also did not tell them of your presence. It is an unnecessary burden on them. Can you sleep during the day or read, anything that does not involve movement?"

"Sleeping anytime is never a problem for me," I held up the books, "and I have plenty to read. Don't worry. I will be as quiet as a mouse during the day."

"My wife will leave all of your meals outside your door."

I told him that I had brought provisions with me.

"Food, we have plenty", said Johannes, eyeing the seabag skeptically. "Save what you have. One never knows. The family has gone to bed, but my wife left us something to eat."

On the kitchen table was a heavy loaf of rye bread, butter, smoked ham, and sausage. From the cabinet Johannes brought out glasses and an open bottle of the local wine. For me it was a feast, as was every other meal provided by this generous family.

Each morning I found bread, cheese, and milk outside my door. Around noon after the soft footsteps on the stairs retreated, there would be a hearty, hot meal waiting for me. The suppers were cold, usually bread, cheese, and sausages. All the wholesome country food reminded me of my early childhood in Innsbruck.

When not sleeping during the day, I read my books from the monastery and played cards. I didn't really mind the confines of this solitary life. It was not very different from that of my childhood. Once the family had retired for the night, I did my calisthenics and paced around the room in my stocking feet for exercise.

Between the nourishing food and the long hours of rest, I had begun to feel like my old self. Just being off the German railroad system was a colossal relief, to say nothing of being out of Germany itself. The Gestapo and all its terrors seemed far away.

On the sixth day, having breakfasted at the usual time, I was preparing to do some light exercise before going to bed. I stood and, stretching my arms and legs, thought how easy it was to get used to such service. Then I happened to glance out of the window.

A big, black Mercedes staff car with an open roof was driving slowly up to the house. In it, besides the driver, were three uniformed men. I gasped and dizzily surveyed my surroundings—a medium-size, empty room with nowhere to hide. I went back to the window and looked down. It was a jump of eighteen to twenty feet. I would surely break an arm or a leg. I grabbed my seabag and, futile though the gesture was, shoved it under the cot. I ripped the covers off the bed and shoved them under as well. If it looked uninhabited, perhaps they could be deceived; but, what to do about me? Surely they would search downstairs before coming up. I could then slip down the stairs, out the back, and head for the woods. I would have to leave the seabag behind. I darted back to the window. Jumping was no longer an option: I would land *in* the car. It now was parked under my window, its driver behind the wheel.

The back door slammed. Boots tramped across the kitchen floor. Another door opened. I heard male voices growing nearer and louder; they were coming up the stairs. "Well, so. Finally, this is it", I said to myself.

I turned the chair around so that it faced the door. I sat down, crossed one knee over the other, and waited. An odd calm settled over me. The door swung open, and three men entered. The two younger men wore the uniforms of lieutenants. The older man was a colonel. Their Waffen-SS insignias and black boots and hats seemed to fill the room.

One of the lieutenants spoke. "Cadet Kurt von Schuschnigg?"

"Yes. I am Kurt von Schuschnigg", I said quietly.

"You will accompany us", he said.

Glancing briefly at the impassive face of the colonel, I wondered what he was doing spending his time on something like this. The officer who had spoken stepped back to the door. Slowly I rose and followed. The colonel let us out in silence. Only then did I realize that no one had drawn his weapon—reassuring, at least for the moment.

We marched through the kitchen to the waiting car.

Of Johannes, his family, or the farmhands, there was no sign. Where were they? There was no sign of life anywhere. I did not know whether this was good or bad.

As ordered, I got into the car. I was sandwiched between the colonel and one of the lieutenants in the backseat. The other lieutenant sat in front with the driver. Evidently our destination was known, for no one said a word.

As we bumped down the uneven track, I tried, with minimal movement, to scan the horizon for signs of the family or the farmhands. Nothing. It was as if the earth had swallowed them up.

# Resistance

The Mercedes maneuvered onto the open road and roared toward Bozen. No one spoke. The silence in the car was total. Traffic in Bozen was light. Near the Hotel Greif the driver braked for a red light. I considered jumping out and heading for the labyrinth of narrow, twisting alleys beyond. I wasn't worried about the colonel; he was on the wrong side of forty. But the other occupant of the backseat was a different proposition—not much older than I and well built. Either of the lieutenants could probably outrun and out-wrestle me. If I made it out of the car, one of them would probably shoot me. Even if they missed, they might hit some poor Bozener.

As if guessing what was passing through my mind, the lieutenant next to me slid forward to the edge of his seat, glanced around, and then looked directly at me—easing back only after the light had changed and the car had gathered speed. We traveled through Bozen in the direction of Meran. So, I wasn't being taken to the Bozen Gestapo headquarters. I was mystified.

The reprieve gave me time to consider what was going on. Who had led the SS to me? One of the farmhands? I had taken every precaution. Even had I been seen, no one but the farmer knew who I was. I prayed that Johannes, his family, and the farmhands were safe. What about the monks? Unthinkable. Please God, I begged, don't let the chain of guilt reach the monastery. Someone at the bordello? Surely not the madam. What reason could she have had? I left her establishment five days before. Why would she have waited until now? Uncle Sepp's neighbor was nosy and irritating, but thoroughly sympathetic toward Uncle Sepp and his family. She, like the madam, would not be easily intimidated.

That left my uncle, Mother's brother. He had a wife and two children. The possibility of Uncle Sepp having anything to do with my predicament did not bear thinking about. I felt the beginnings of nausea.

Soon I would be interrogated, and I needed a plausible story. I must not admit to having met Uncle Sepp. The Gestapo would think it likely that I did though. Why else was I in Bozen? I had to concentrate.

Why was I in the farmer's house? I was a deserter. South Tirol was out of the way, and I knew the area. Would I be stupid enough to tell anyone that I was a deserter? Especially my uncle, a member of the SS? Between his duty to the fatherland and the safety of his wife and children, he would never be willing to help me. I set out on my own for the mountains to look for an abandoned hut and came across the farmer's house. It was daytime and deserted. I found the unused room and took my chances. And so on.

The story sounded weak even to me. In any case, everything depended on what the farmer had told them. I made up a dozen other believable scenarios, but in my anxiety I was likely to jumble them all up. I had to remain calm. Meanwhile, it had grown cold. We weren't going fast, but we were in an open car, in early March.

As we also passed through Meran without stopping, I was more baffled than ever. Then a horrible thought struck me: What if they were just going to shoot me and bury me in the woods? I had heard stories about prisoners having first to dig their own graves, adding to their executioners' entertainment. Father would never know what had happened to me. Uncle Sepp, if he survived, might. I grew very still. The colonel's face was without expression, as was the lieutenant's beside me.

I closed my eyes, leaned back, and reflected. People were basically decent. All these people had been normal, ordinary citizens before the madness of the times. The fear of death—and worse—manifested itself differently in everyone. I could not blame whoever was responsible for betraying me. He wanted to survive, just as I did.

The driver made a sharp left turn, running over the curb in the process. The lieutenant next to me swore, reached forward, and gave the driver a shove. "Watch out! You made me bite my tongue."

I laughed. Surprisingly, he only frowned at me. Being docile was not in my nature. I thought of Petty Officer Engel and decided that the lieutenant deserved the same treatment. "Did that hurt you?" I said, sarcastically.

He pulled out his handkerchief and dabbed it on his tongue, but he ignored me completely. The colonel had relieved his feelings by giving the driver a mild reprimand. The lieutenant in front had retrieved his hat from the floor and said nothing at all. All this was most peculiar; it was decidedly un-Nazi behavior.

We drove through a neighborhood of solid-looking houses. I had not yet seen any woods. Then without warning, the car turned into a driveway and stopped. The gates before us yawned open, and we rolled through. The gates swung shut. As the engine was turned off, the colonel addressed me in German.

"Do you speak English?"

"Nein", I said, perplexed.

"Very well. We will continue in German. I am not really a German, nor are these men with me. I am a member of Allied intelligence. We have headquarters here behind enemy lines. My name is McCaffrey, and I really am a colonel—British, of course." He held his hand out to me. "You are safe with us."

I was dumbfounded. My first thought was that this was Gestapo humor. When I climbed out of the car, they would pull out their guns and shoot me in the back. Or maybe this was how they extracted information. First they gained my confidence. After I had named everyone who had helped me, then they would shoot me. I still hadn't moved when, out of the corner of my eye, I noticed the person who had closed the gate and was now standing beside the car—a little Catholic nun. She patted my arm reassuringly. "You really are safe now, you know."

I looked at her kind, worn face and then at Colonel McCaffrey's. Hesitantly, I shook his outstretched hand. He laughed. "You do speak German?"

"Yes, sir, and French."

"German will do perfectly well. Let's go inside. The good nuns run this boarding house. It also happens to be our headquarters for this sector. Come, Sister Maria has a room ready for you. I expect you'd probably like a bath and a change of clothes. I know we would all appreciate it as well."

I didn't know if he meant that they all wanted a bath and a change of clothes, or that they very much hoped that I wanted them. "Sir, I hid my seabag under the bed in the room. My uniforms along with a good bit of rations are in it."

"I am sure Johannes can find some use for the rations. As for the uniforms, they are no good to you anymore."

"Sir, I can't tell you how grateful I am to you, but why didn't you say something once we had driven away from the farmhouse?"

"My dear young man, if I had told you at any time prior to now, your relief would most certainly have been visible. We were traveling in an open car, for the whole world to see. Granted, if our conduct had been conspicuous, the chances are about a thousand to one that anyone would have noticed. But we haven't the luxury of even those odds. Countless people in an enormous network depend on each other for their safety. We would never jeopardize any part of our operation, even to spare your nerves."

"Of course not, sir. I hadn't realized."

"Think no more of it. You follow Sister Maria here. She has things prepared for you. We will see each other later."

Sister Maria led me to the two-story house. The neighborhood was a quiet area on the edge of the town. All the houses were some distance from one another. The boarding house was surrounded by a small park scattered with trees, giving the place an air of security and privacy.

Inside, another nun sifting through a stack of papers greeted us with a bright smile. Sister Maria took me past her to a room at the end of the hallway. Neat and simply furnished, it had a window that looked out on the side yard.

A shirt and a pair of trousers were laid out on the single bed. Sister picked up the shirt and glanced at me. "Close enough. The pants will just have to do. Originally they were meant for someone with a little more around the middle. I'll find you a belt." She left before I could thank her.

I was exhausted and lay down on the bed. I had been preparing to go to bed when I was arrested by Colonel McCaffrey and his men. Now, out of harm's way, I closed my eyes and fell asleep.

I awoke hours later, had a bath, and dressed. Then I found the kitchen, and in it a sturdily built cook who appeared to know who I was. She nodded toward the stool next to her counter. I watched her knead dough and fashion it into neat mounds. "Hungry?"

"Starving!"

She lined up some eggs on the counter—there was a chicken coop in the backyard—threw some freshly made tortellini in hot water, and cut newly baked bread while giving me a history of the boarding house.

After two helpings of the tortellini, the eggs, and almost a quarter of the loaf of bread, it was with some difficulty that I rose from my stool. The cook remarked, "I don't think I ever saw anyone your size eat so much food. You're not going to have any room left for dinner. We're having cheese spätzle and more of the tortellini you just sampled."

"I can hardly wait!"

I wanted to find the colonel, and the cook showed me the way. I found myself in a large, lamp-lit room. The curtains were drawn. Maps covered every wall. Charts were spread over several desks, and there were stacks of papers everywhere. A powerful-looking radio dominated one corner of the room. Here was the heart of the South Tirolean Resistance.

Colonel McCaffrey sat at one of the desks, poring over a pile of documents. The driver of the staff car was measuring distances on a map and dictating them to a partisan. The other five men in the room were inspecting passports and identity papers through magnifying glasses. The colonel made the introductions, then told me his extraordinary story.

"My father was a Scot and my mother a German", the colonel said. "My mother was adamant that I be given a German education. Father was not as enthusiastic about the idea, but he wanted to keep the peace. That meant appeasing Mother. So at a tender young age off I went.

"German schools provided me with an excellent education. As luck would have it, I had a natural ear. I spoke *Hochdeutsch* (high German) like a native, as well as regional dialects. I could imitate anything I heard. I'll skip over the in-between. It is enough to say that when the war began my linguistic expertise was needed. I was recruited by the British Secret Intelligence Service.

"SIS was watching as many German officers as they could. But they had their hands full. One day our agents intercepted a message from the German high command. A colonel posted in northern Germany was to take command of the Tenth SS Panzer Division

Alpenvorland. That made him a figure of great interest to the Allies. The Tenth SS Panzer Division Alpenvorland is based here, in the Meran–Bozen area. And the Brenner Pass, an important segment of the Axis supply line, comes under its jurisdiction.

"We learned the details of the colonel's travel orders, and partisans were dispatched to intercept him. The colonel's transport came across an accident: a farmer's wagon had overturned and was blocking the road. When the driver got out to help, our partisans—hidden in the nearby woods—surrounded the colonel's staff car, killed the driver and the colonel, and got rid of their bodies Their identification papers and orders were altered by our forgers. Here before you is the resurrected form of that officer, in command of the Tenth SS Panzer Division Alpenvorland!"

"Unbelievable!" I exclaimed.

Because of the colonel, the Allies were privy to all the information gathered by German intelligence in South Tirol. He oversaw rescues and escapes from Axis territory and was, as he put it, a sort of caulking material for the cracks that occurred. Highly successful, his intelligence unit was instrumental in carrying out many acts of sabotage against the Germans, saving innumerable lives. Colonel McCaffrey was justifiably proud of his people.

But that was only half his life. He was also the acting head of the Tenth SS Panzer Division Alpenvorland. He regularly made clandestine trips from his Alpenvorland office to the boarding house. His life was a massive, intricate operation.

Colonel McCaffrey turned to my situation. I had two choices: I could join the partisans and stay with them until the end of the war or escape—mostly on foot over the mountains—into Switzerland. "Even if one disregards the dangers presented by nature itself, there are German patrols throughout the Alpine region. Frankly, the crossing will be both strenuous and dangerous", the colonel said.

The partisans were also working on a project that lacked one element: someone who spoke German—ideally, a native Austrian—who would parachute into Kufstein, carrying four hundred thousand Swiss francs—an enormous sum in any currency. Allied intelligence had learned that orders soon would be issued to blow up all bridges spanning the Inn River. This was meant to hinder

Allied troops advancing from the south. The parachutist was to use the money to persuade local Austrian officials not to destroy the bridges. Colonel McCaffrey's narrative was interrupted. He was momentarily called away.

The very thought of giving or taking a bribe was repugnant to me. Even if I overcame my scruples and, for the sake of the cause, offered someone a bribe—what if he refused it? I could look forward to another encounter with the Gestapo. The last seven years had been oppressive. Mentally, I felt old beyond my years. I was tired. Physically, I would make an incompetent partisan. I couldn't hit the side of a barn even if I stood a yard away from it with a gun mounted on a tripod. Most of all, I couldn't stand the thought of injuring anyone. I had seen enough brutality to last me a lifetime. No, I could not take part in this operation.

The colonel returned and looked at me thoughtfully before speaking. "There is no need for you to agonize over this", he said. "I know your story and that of your family. This is not something for you."

He had relieved me of a heavy burden. I didn't want to appear ungrateful for my deliverance, and I expressed this as best I could. He assured me of the contrary. He judged the rigors of the training and the parachuting exercises to be beyond my physical capacities at present. His statement set off alarm bells in my mind.

"Colonel McCaffrey, I hope you don't have any doubts about my being able to cross into Switzerland on foot. If you can point me in the right direction, I can get there."

"My young friend, I have no doubts about your capability or your determination. Anyone who can crisscross Germany without documents, using only his wits, should be able to find his way over a little mountain. But first we must create a new identity for you. Once that is done, you must *become* that person. Most probably, your life will depend on it." He rose to leave. "I am on my way now, back to the other side. Probably won't see you again. Best of luck and, as they say, 'Keep your head down.'" He shook my hand and took leave of his group.

There were about twenty capable and dedicated partisans. My training was assigned to Luigi: twenty-five years old, bright, eager, and all business. I was told from the beginning that I was not to socialize with the other guests. Most guest bookings were for short stays, sometimes a week—two at most. There was one notable exception: the resident German, Lt. Gen. Axel von Petersdorff.

An elderly gentleman, perhaps seventy, and a widower, General Petersdorff had been a resident for a number of years. The German officer had distinguished himself during the First World War and was awarded Germany's highest military honor, the Pour le Mérite, informally known as the Blue Max. After the signing of the armistice, Petersdorff retired and began indulging his passion for travel—dividing his time among Germany, Austria, and Italy. Meran he found full of charm. It also had pleasant weather the year round and was close enough to visit often. Relatives in Germany, and his tailor and boot maker in Austria, made his circuit of travel complete.

Then Hitler came to power. Life under National Socialism was unpalatable, and he moved permanently to South Tirol. With the Anschluss in 1938, he also severed his ties to Austria. This was a stroke of good fortune for the Meran Resistance. With Prussian birth, appearance, and demeanor, he gave the boarding house a patina of collaboration.

The old gentleman was also the only distraction I was permitted by the inexorable Luigi. I studied and ate my meals in my room, so it was a welcome relief when Petersdorff arrived carrying his lunch or dinner tray.

He told me the story of one of his relatives, Col. Horst von Petersdorff, who like many other German military officers, had no love for Hitler but took up arms for his country. In 1940 he was decorated with the Knight's Cross of the Iron Cross, the highest honor for bravery or leadership in battle awarded by Germany during World War II. That was before he was suspected of participating in the failed Hitler assassination plot of July 20, 1944. The old gentleman believed that the colonel was a prisoner in the Buchenwald concentration camp, and he wanted to know about the camps. "Don't try to soften it for me", he said. "I've been through one war. I can imagine how things are."

I did not think so. It was like comparing apples and rotten oranges.

Meanwhile, I was being transformed into a lieutenant of the Tenth SS Panzer Division Alpenvorland. What would Uncle Sepp think? It was possible he knew already. I had heard from Luigi that Uncle Sepp was in contact with the head of the Resistance in Bozen.

Day and night, Luigi drummed dates and facts into my head. Three other partisans helped with the fabrication of my new identity. Aspects of my own background were woven into that of Lt. Karl Fischer of Munich. My schooling at the Alte Realgymnasium and the Wittelsbacher Gymnasium was retained. I was the only child of an ordinary set of parents. I memorized "our" various addresses, the names of the commanding officers of a number of units, including the one to which I belonged, and the names of my barrack mates.

Even the old general tested me during his visits. He would invent a scenario and then fire questions at me. If I hesitated, we started again from the beginning. It was excellent practice. My recent experiences—in fact, the last seven years—had forced me to learn how to invent on the spot. I could now create a plausible story out of thin air, improvising and embellishing as I went. A prepared, unassailable lie, committed to memory, felt almost like cheating.

When I jokingly said this to General von Petersdorff he replied, "You know, my boy, it is important to be able to use judgment regarding this sort of thing. There are times in life when the results of one's words are inconsequential. Then there are times when what one says can result in life or death. Given the latter, unnecessary improvisation would be reckless. You see the difference. Every lightbulb in one's brain must be burning at full wattage. When there is no alternative, improvisation is essential, but you have the advantage of all of these minds concocting an airtight story for you. One hardly needs to be a genius to decide down which path one should tread."

"When you put it that way, sir, I do see the difference. It would be stupid and, I suppose, a little egotistical?"

"Exactly, my boy. Good for you! Now, as you know, error is unacceptable. Let's do the thing again. Shall we?"

I had only to remember the feeling of being "arrested" at the farmer's. I began drilling again in earnest.

Three days later my papers were ready. They stated that I had been assigned to the frontier district for the purpose of tracking down German deserters. Meticulously prepared down to the smallest detail, the document was suitably worn in appearance—dog-eared and stained. Reflected in my new ID was the amount of rest I'd had as well as the amount of pasta I'd eaten; but I still looked like me.

256

On the fourth day I was outfitted in my new uniform. Sister Maria had taken great trouble over the alterations. I assessed the effect in the mirror, reminding myself that the figure looking back at me was not meant to be a dandy, just to pass muster.

After dinner with Petersdorff, I felt restless and claustrophobic. I wanted to test my performance. By ten P.M. all the lights in the boarding house were switched off. I waited and I listened. Then I put on my uniform and walked to the nearby café.

There was only one empty table. Facing the door, I sat and confidently ordered a beer. The room was full of locals: mine, the only uniform. The beer arrived, and at the door so did another uniform: an SS sergeant. Trying to avoid eye contact, I shifted my position. I felt rather than saw his gaze coming to rest on me.

"Do you mind if I join you?"

I turned and smiled at him. "Not at all!" I said enthusiastically.

A beer arrived. Since I hadn't heard him order it, I assumed he was a regular. Then again, beer was probably what 99 percent of the German soldiers would ask for, and it was unwise to keep members of the SS waiting.

"I haven't seen you in the district before."

I was ready: "I have only just been transferred. I arrived today, as a matter of fact."

"Under whom are you serving?"

"That information will be given to me tomorrow morning."

He raised his mug. "Wolf Dietrich Seidl."

I raised my own. "Karl Fischer." We clanked our mugs and gulped our beer.

"There isn't a lot by way of evening entertainment around here. In fact, you're looking at all there is!" said my new friend as he slapped the table. "I've gotten nowhere with that little signorina who brought my beer. And it is not for lack of effort, I assure you!" Wolf Dietrich's thwarted romance was not the most fascinating of topics, but he continued on.

"You have a girlfriend you left behind?"

This had not come up in my sessions with Luigi. It wasn't a difficult question. But I had to invent a person on the spur of the moment and then remember my fabrications afterward.

257

"Yes, of course. She's brokenhearted with loneliness." I swallowed my beer hastily, stretched, and yawned noisily. "I must get some sleep. I've been up for nearly twenty-four hours. No point in getting off on the wrong foot tomorrow."

I put down enough money to pay for both our beers and said as I stood up, "Auf Wiedersehen."

I was halfway to the door before he put down his beer. "Ja, danke!" he answered as I stepped out into the cold night air.

I hurried back to the boarding house, anxiously reviewing my performance on the way. I decided that it had gone well. I had not said Heil Hitler, but neither had he. No, that was all right. I was gone for only half an hour. As I quietly closed the door behind me, a strong hand grasped my shoulder. My knees turned to rubber. "Luigi! You nearly gave me a heart attack", I whispered loudly.

"You idiot!" he hissed. "What do you think you're doing? You nearly gave *me* a heart attack. What do you mean sneaking in here? More to the point, what do you mean sneaking out of here? Where the devil have you been?"

"Well, I didn't think it would do any harm to have a beer in the café. I also thought it would be a good idea to practice being Lt. Karl Fischer in public. It was just to test myself. That's all."

"That's *all*? You may have compromised all of us! Do you think this is a joke or a game—that none of us has anything better to do than sit around here all day long and entertain you? This was a juvenile stunt. You not only risked your cover; you endangered our whole organization. Go to your room and don't come out until someone gets you!"

As I found out the next day, Luigi was only the beginning. After lunch, I was summoned to a meeting. The senior partisans had gathered to consider the options. "What are we going to do with him now? He has been seen!"

I couldn't understand why anything had to be done and said so. Luigi ignored me and went on. "Moreover, he gave out his name to another SS man! Lt. Karl Fischer has been used."

The others agreed that this was insurmountable. I had to be moved to a different base; my cover and removal from Italy, modified. I was sent back to my room to wait.

I saw my position as unaltered. My performance had been convincing, and I was willing to bet that there was a 99.9 percent chance that the lovesick SS sergeant wouldn't remember what I had looked like, much less the name Karl Fischer. But then, what if the man did remember the name? What if he made inquiries? What if there had been no transfers? The stakes *were* too high.

I went in search of General von Petersdorff. I thanked him for his company and returned to my room to wait. I had one visitor. Sister Maria had come to say good-bye. Dipping her fingers into the holy water font attached to the door frame, she traced the sign of the cross on my forehead and recited a prayer for travelers.

Hours later, two men whom I had seen only from a distance came to collect me. I stopped at the operations room, made my apologies, and thanked the partisans for all they had done for me. It was late afternoon. Our destination was a farm somewhere up in the Vinschgau Valley. The Resistance had help from many of the local farmers there.

Darkness had fallen before we reached the farm. There was little moonlight, and we were driving without headlights. The partisan—confident of his destination—kept the jeep's pace constant, despite the inky darkness. The rutted road ended at the remote farmhouse. Slivers of light peeked through the blackout curtains covering the windows.

"Don't you find it peculiar", I ventured, "that a farmhouse has all of its lights on at this hour? Farmers usually go to bed with the setting of the sun."

"There isn't as much to do during the winter. Benno and his family repair fences, milk cows, make cheese—things like that. Benno's wife is the first one up. She gets to milk the cows and feed the chickens. Besides, Benno is expecting us."

The second partisan had barely finished speaking when the door opened, silhouetting a very large figure. He greeted the partisans, clapping them on their backs and tousling their hair. Then, wrapping a giant arm around each, he picked them up at the same time. This was Benno. Smiling broadly, he stuck out his hand. I shook it thinking how fortunate that Benno seemed so good-natured.

We sat around the big wooden table in the kitchen. Glasses and several bottles of potent, homemade brandy were brought out. More serious than the carefree teenagers they looked to be, the partisans permitted themselves only a small glass. After some good-natured shoving and vigorous handshaking they left.

Benno's family—two teenagers, a son and a daughter, and his wife were asleep. I asked him, "Do they know that I'm coming?"

"But certainly! Your room is next to my son's—come."

I followed him to a second-floor bedroom. I wasn't particularly tired; but since my days aboard the *Prinz Eugen*, I could fall into a dead sleep anytime, anywhere, whether I was tired or not—a sort of deposit to a savings account.

The morning dawned brisk and clear in the Vinschgau. It was past nine o'clock. I awoke to a silent house. The entire family was somewhere else. A glass of milk, several raw eggs, and a thick slice of bread had been left on the kitchen counter, and the iron plate on the wood-burning stove was still hot enough to scramble the eggs. I sat down to enjoy my breakfast.

After my circumscribed life at the boarding house, I was ready for some fresh air and exercise. I hiked around the woods before returning to the warmth of Benno's kitchen. There I found the family gathered for their midday meal.

They were a fair-haired, clean-cut family. Benno's wife was about my height, but he was at least six feet four; his children, not much shorter. I wondered if their mother felt dwarfed by them as I did. Introductions were made briefly, and then lunch was served. The talk at table was completely given over to the farm. Afterward, his family dispersed; Benno lingered over his pipe.

"Benno," I said, "I would be happy to have something to do around the farm. I can't just sit around all day long. Can't you use an extra pair of hands to mend fences or something?"

He looked at me thoughtfully.

"I am a fast learner and a lot stronger than you might think."

"You know," he said, "in winter we all fight for jobs. I wish I could take advantage of your offer, but my children would kill me if I gave away their tasks to a newcomer, an untrained new-comer at that. It would be as good as telling them that anyone could perform their tasks. No, my friend. I am afraid you will have to occupy yourself some other way." He moved on to another subject.

"I don't expect them again soon, but you should know about our local so-called resistance. Here in the Vinschgau, there is a small group that roams the area unhindered by the local authorities. At best they are ineffective—the authorities, that is. The men who call themselves partisans are no more than murderous thugs. They have nothing to do with McCaffrey or the South Tirolean Resistance. They show up, claiming to be the protective arm of our mountain region, and demand provisions and money if they can get it. My friend who owned the next farm a few miles away refused and called them thieves to their faces. Only after Karl pulled out his shotgun and aimed it at them did they leave, shouting threats over their shoulders. It did not end there. They came back in the dead of night and savagely murdered the whole family. Then they stole everything they could carry."

He seemed to have come to the end of his story, then added, "I found them myself. I hadn't seen Karl for a couple of days so I went over to check on him. It was horrible, finding them like that."

"You're sure it was this group?"

"I can't prove it, but there is no doubt in my mind. They were here only the week before, bragging about 'conquering' the enemy. It was disgusting. They had come across a couple of German guards who had stopped by the side of the road to relieve themselves. These 'heroes of the resistance' sneaked up on the Germans from behind, stabbed them in the back, and robbed the corpses. They took everything, even the boots on their feet. They told me the story as they sat laughing and joking about it outside my back door in their stolen German truck. I gave them provisions.

"As soon as they had left, I went to the three neighboring farms to warn them to do the same. Right now it is the easiest and safest thing to do. I went to Karl first, but Karl had a temper. He let his anger cloud his judgment and paid for it with his life and the lives of his family."

Benno's voice rumbled angrily. "That they call themselves partisans demeans every man, woman, and child who is trying to help stop the Axis war machine. We all have our hands full dealing with Germans. There is no way at present to control these murderers, let alone bring them to justice, but the time will come. I would like to kill them with my bare hands!" His fist came crashing down on the table, rattling the plates and making the salt and pepper shakers jump. I looked down at his enormous hands.

I had idled away a couple of days when the word came that arrangements for my trip were already complete. The next morning the same partisans who had delivered me to Benno's showed up. I was to leave the next day as "Karl Fischer", but I would have a new cover and company.

My companion was to be a recently downed Allied pilot. His was an unusual problem. He was a French-speaking Canadian whose second language was English. As both languages were equally useless in this part of the world, he had been kept hidden until the right circumstances arose. I spoke French. That was part of the solution.

The other part of the solution was provided by one of the partisans who had obtained an armband of the Twenty-eighth SS Volunteer Grenadier Division Wallonien.

There was a new star in the Nazi firmament: Leon Degrelle. A Belgian collaborator, Degrelle had formed a brigade of Belgian volunteers of Walloon background. The brigade was incorporated into the Waffen-SS and later elevated to the status of an SS division. Its insignia added to the uniform of an SS soldier produced a French-speaking Axis soldier.

The partisans returned with the pilot just after sunset. He filled nearly the whole door frame, and I wondered whether all Canadians came in this size. If he weren't a boxer—or at least a lumberjack—it was a serious waste of potential. I was introduced to "Jacques", and I addressed him in French, "Welcome to your last stop before freedom."

His face split into a huge grin, and his arm-wrenching handshake threatened to evolve into an embrace. Benno interrupted, "Come, we have work to do and not much time left."

The partisans had brought several knapsacks. These were now emptied one at a time. The only item in the first knapsack was a broken, British wireless radio transmitter. "This has to go to Switzerland to be repaired", said the partisan sitting beside me. "It is a very important piece of equipment, and we cannot fix it ourselves."

"How will you get it back?"

"As long as you get it there, we'll get it back somehow. Jacques has volunteered to carry it."

Out of the next knapsack came a revolver. Holding it by the barrel, the partisan handed it to me. "This is your weapon."

I took it and turned it over in my hands. "Is it loaded?"—a pertinent question, considering my competence in this field.

"No, not yet." He placed a clip of ammunition on the table.

"I don't know much about guns, but I've never seen one like this before."

"You certainly haven't. It was made in America."

"Are you serious? I am supposed to walk around with that thing?" The thought of carrying a gun with me was as appealing as walking around with a poisonous snake. Carrying an American-made gun seemed unusually dangerous. I thought about my Argus camera. "What if we get stopped and someone—a German—notices that I have an American gun? Wait a minute. Exactly why do I have an American gun instead of a German Luger?"

"Simple—we don't have a Luger right now."

"I see. Jacques is carrying around a broken radio transmitter—British—and I have an American gun."

"Well, those are two excellent reasons to avoid an Axis search!" said the partisan, grinning and slapping me on the back. "It will all go smoothly. Do not worry. If we had to wait to acquire another Luger, there is no telling how long the delay would be."

"My wife seems to have made enough food for the entire Degrelle division," interjected Benno, "and, my friends, she is a very good cook. Let's eat. Tomorrow will be a long day."

We occupied ourselves with timetables and the details of our journey while consuming a dinner fit for a condemned prisoner. Watching the food pile up on Jacques' plate for the third time, I couldn't resist remarking, "I think that you must have forgotten to feed Jacques for the past week or so."

"The man must have hollow legs. He ate at least that much at lunch!" offered one of the partisans.

The conversation returned to the trip. Our day would start at four A.M. Jacques and I would be driven to the Meran station. It was a short train ride to Mals. From there we would walk two or three miles, enter the forest, and, at some point, meet up with the South Tirolean guide. He was to lead us to the summit of Piz Chavalatsch. There Jacques and I would cross over into

263

Switzerland and find a hut with Swiss border guards—and food—waiting for us.

Being a mountain guide seemed like a dangerous occupation during wartime. I said so. "Well, he is not exactly a guide", the partisan admitted. "Let's just say the man has dedicated himself to the task of providing goods that are in short supply or nonexistent for his fellow Italians."

"The man is a smuggler?"

By the expression on his face, Jacques was getting the gist of the conversation. I wondered what he thought of the plan. How reliable *were* smugglers these days?

"All right", I said resignedly. "You certainly know what you are doing. The man is our ticket to the Swiss border."

Just then Jacques asked me, "And what if the smuggler doesn't show up?" I translated his question for the partisans.

"We have used him before, always with success. If we'd ever had a problem with him we wouldn't be using him now." The partisan who answered sounded defensive.

"He has your life in his hands. He knows that", the other partisan said.

"In the unlikely event that you are stopped before your rendezvous, your excuse for wandering the mountains is that you are looking for a deserter. This is certainly believable. They have plenty of them these days. "

The partisans had given us every scrap of pertinent information they had. There was no food left, and Jacques and I had no more questions. Silence fell. We were all bleary-eyed, so we retired for what was left of the night.

# The Ascent

"It is time!" Benno was saying loudly. "The partisans are waiting to talk to you before you and the Canadian leave!" I felt as if I had been asleep only a few minutes. "You are a very sound sleeper", Benno said. "I was just about to help you wake up with some cold water."

I sprang out of bed. "I am wide awake. I'll be downstairs in a few minutes."

I had hardly blinked, and Benno was gone. Despite his bulk, he was catlike in his movements. More than once, I had thought I was alone in a room only to look up from my book or turn my head and see Benno.

I got dressed quickly. My boots were too big: better than too small. I only wished I had asked for a second pair of socks.

All the lights at the back of the farmhouse were on. The family was up and probably already at their tasks. What I saw from the living room as I approached the kitchen made me stop. Two German soldiers stood with their backs to me. A hand gripped my shoulder. "Not a pretty sight first thing in the morning, eh?" said Benno. At the sound of Benno's voice, the two partisans—for it was they—turned.

"No, it is not", was all I could say.

"Help yourself to coffee", I was told. "Bread, cheese, and butter are on the table."

I shook my head; I was too excited to eat. I could think only of my first meal in Switzerland. "Thank you, Benno. Coffee will be fine."

One of the partisans spoke up. "Rule number two: eat anytime you can. You never know when you'll get another chance."

"And what would rule number one be?"

"Why, stay alive, naturally. You are one of the few who ever asked."

I took a thick slice of bread and a wedge of cheese. As Benno and the partisans talked, my thoughts went over the last seven years.

I couldn't remember how many narrow escapes I'd had: the most unbelievable of all—eluding the long arm of the Gestapo. I had one overworked guardian angel. Shaking my head in disbelief, I poured myself a cup of coffee.

Jacques appeared, the Degrelle insignia on his armband clearly visible. "Bonjour!" he said cheerfully. He sat and simultaneously grabbed a plate and a cup of coffee. In no time, a mountain of cheese, bread, and butter crowded his plate. "You never know when you'll get your hands on food again!" he said

"What did he say?" One of the partisans asked.

Reluctantly, I translated. Their only reply—raised eyebrows.

"Now that you are both fully conscious," said the senior partisan, "let us go over each of your backgrounds once more."

Having finished his breakfast, Benno rose. "My friends, I must go. The best of luck to you both. Come back anytime, just as long as it is after this bloody war!" I hoped that some of the good Benno had done for others would be returned to him. We shook hands. With a last wave, he stepped out into the darkness.

After both Jacques and I had recounted our stories at top speed, the partisans released us. Yawning and stretching, they rose and put on their heavy coats.

Jacques stood. Having consumed nearly half a loaf of bread and an enormous quantity of cheese, he still reached for more. Amazingly, Jacques was not fat, just solidly built. Vaguely I wondered who fed him at home. It would be a full-time job.

"We will warm up the engine", the senior partisan announced. He picked up the knapsack containing the radio transmitter. "I'll take this out with me now. Be ready to leave in about three minutes."

The door slammed behind him. In a loud voice the other partisan called to Jacques, raised three fingers, and—after pointing to his watch—gestured with his thumb toward the door.

"Oui", said Jacques. Then he asked me, "Do people do that to you?"

"Do what?"

"They know you don't speak their language, yet they still talk to you in that language but either shout or speak extremely slowly as if somehow that will make them understood."

I *had* noticed.

Jacques crammed in a last mouthful of food and slapped another wedge of cheese between two hastily sliced pieces of bread. Clutching his sandwich in one hand, he jammed his cap on his head and grabbed his coat.

"Stop!" I said.

Still chewing, he stopped. "What?"

"Do you see that? Newspapers." I jabbed my finger in the direction of the brown basket before the fireplace.

"Italian and German newspapers. I don't speak either language, remember? But you go ahead", he said, reaching past me for the doorknob.

"Not for reading, for insulation!" I said. I began stuffing newspapers under my shirt and tucked their edges into the waistband of my trousers. Jacques put his sandwich down and quickly padded himself with the newspapers too. Once we were satisfied that we were as packed as possible, we hurried outside.

The partisans were backing the *Kübelwagen* out of the barn. A race car wouldn't have caused greater excitement. This was a bucket-seat, open military vehicle comparable to the American jeep. A number of car manufacturers produced versions of these vehicles. The Volkswagen 82 is the most well known.

The kübelwagen had belonged to a German, dead now. The man had tried to romance one of the local Italian beauties. It had ended badly for him. Fortunately the vehicle already had a full tank of gas. We climbed in. It was a brisk morning. I silently congratulated myself on the padding under my uniform. This temperature would be mild compared with what awaited us on the mountain.

Jacques, still eating, seemed unaffected. The cold seemed to be having no effect on the partisans either. The senior partisan slouched in his seat and dozed. His partner drove, one hand draped over the back of the passenger seat, the other resting languidly on the steering wheel. Then we hit a deep pothole. The driver swore fervently and, after a brief struggle with the steering wheel, regained control of the jeep. We had nearly gone off the road. The sleeping partisan was now wide awake. "My God, be careful!" he said loudly.

I suddenly felt old and very, very tired—in mind rather than in body. We drove on in silence. I was assailed by memories. People crowded into my mind: school friends, family friends, enemies, acquaintances. All those scattered lives; so many people destroyed, and so many others missing. I longed for home, to be once again among family and friends. I had to keep telling myself that we would all find one another.

The kübelwagen was bucked again by the deeply rutted road. It was the Canadian's turn to swear: the remains of his breakfast had just bounced out of his hand and vanished into the semidarkness.

"Just concentrate on getting to Switzerland, Jacques."

"Ah, thank you so much for that, my friend."

We turned onto the smooth main road leading into Meran. An observer would have seen nothing out of the ordinary: just four German soldiers heading toward the railway station—a backup patrol. We had entered the town and circled around to approach the station from the rear. McCaffrey's men had replaced the lock to an unused back gate, hidden by trash cans and regularly checked by the Resistance. We stopped beside these trash cans. The partisans hopped out. I helped Jacques put on the knapsack, and quietly we followed the partisans to the gate and its big, rusty padlock. I braced myself for loud creaks of protest—none came. The key was noiselessly inserted and turned. Noticing my surprise, the partisan whispered, "We keep the lock well oiled."

There was no traffic. Should there have been, we were soldiers patrolling the entrances, a normal, daily occurrence. Jacques and I silently took leave of the partisans, closed the gate behind us, and approached the waiting trains. It seemed strangely effortless, and then I realized why—no duffel bag.

The doors to our train stood open. No MPs were in sight. As we had been told, in Meran the station's main entrance was the only place there was a document check. I fished out an issue of the *Völkischer Beobachter*, the Nazi *People's Observer*, from a wastebasket to read the latest propaganda. The newspaper was also a good prop.

In one of the compartments an elderly man sat alone. We stowed the radio in the overhead rack and sat down. The locomotive whistled, and we slowly rolled away from Meran. Jacques slid deeper into his seat and closed his eyes. I watched the town disappear.

Snowflakes began to float gently from a sunless sky. Soon it changed to a steady snowfall. I nudged Jacques. He looked out and raised his eyebrows and shoulders. He was right. So what? If necessary we would climb the mountain in a blinding blizzard. Short of being arrested or shot, nothing was going to spoil this day for me. Jacques dozed off again, but I was wide awake. I had to find someone in Switzerland to help me track down Father, Vera, and Sissi. I'd go first to the Red Cross and the embassies in Geneva. It was surely too late in this lost war for my actions to harm my family.

We left the train at Mals and headed toward the town of Latsch. Just behind it was the Swiss border town of Taufers. To avoid walking into that lions' den, we would enter the forest at Latsch, climb Piz Chavalatsch, and enter Switzerland.

"Well," said Jacques, "what should we do about the question of leadership? Toss a coin?"

"If you want to be the leader go right ahead."

"You know that pilots have a better sense of direction." He was clowning around.

"You realize that I'm Austrian, don't you? And that South Tirol, which includes Meran and the Vinschgau, formerly belonged to Austria? Do they know that in Canada?"

"Yes, yes. We were informed of its having changed hands."

"Well, I believe that qualifies me to be the leader. However, having said that, I have decided to defer to your obvious seniority."

"Very wise. What do you mean by 'obvious seniority'?"

"Why, those little gray flecks in your hair."

"Really?"

I smiled.

"Touché!" he said.

After we had made several turns and a couple of shortcuts through the small village, I stopped. "Jacques, this looks familiar", I said, frowning.

"Yes. That is because all of these streets look basically ..." He stopped and turned in a complete circle. "Sorry, Kurt." Then, after a lopsided grin, he cuffed me on the shoulder. "Why weren't *you* paying closer attention? We are back where we started."

"Well, with a pilot to lead me, why should I?"

We retraced our steps and headed out of the town. There was little traffic: a horse-drawn cart filled with milk containers and two women with large baskets over their arms. We found our marker for the path into the forest and headed for the cover of the trees.

"McCaffrey's men said our smuggler would be waiting for us less than a mile from our road marker", said Jacques. "Let's see how reliable these Italians are."

"Jacques, you know, of course, that while technically they may be Italians, in actuality they were South Tiroleans and my country-men until 1918. I'd appreciate it if you would show a little more sensitivity."

"Listen," he said, "technically, and in actuality, you weren't even born in 1918. Just to show you how sensitive I am, I will name my firstborn, boy or girl, Partisan as long as we make it out of here and over that border!"

Despite our banter, the thought came to me that this was the final leg of my journey. My seriousness affected Jacques, who also grew serious. I said, "Jacques, a lot of unbelievable things have happened to me. I have to call them miracles. I need to ask for one more."

"Kurt, I am not without my own miracles. Let us both ask." And so we prayed a *Stossgebet* (quick prayer) and set off for the summit.

The trees acted like a gigantic umbrella, keeping the snow off our wool uniforms—that was good. But we were already hiking through an inch or so of wet leaves. I knew nothing of the state of Jacques' boots. The insides of my boots were already damp—that was bad. It was a long way up to the top of the mountain. My feet would get neither dryer nor warmer.

It was long past sunrise. The snow had stopped falling, but the densely wooded forest resisted the light. I kept my eyes on the ground, careful where I stepped. My feet were cold, and getting damper. Jacques walked straight through whatever was in his path. At some point, I was going to have the challenge of relieving Jacques of the wireless.

Suddenly, in the near distance, we heard a man's voice. Our smuggler—finally! The feeling of relief quickly evaporated as we heard the second voice. Both spoke German.

"Do you see what I see?" asked Jacques.

"Look like you're glad to see them", I replied.

"Halt! Hands up!" barked one of the two approaching soldiers. Running toward us, their weapons drawn, were members of the SS Tenth Panzer Division Alpenvorland.

"Heil Hitler!" I called out.

They paused. "Ja, Heil Hitler", replied the sergeant, in a level tone. His comrade followed suit. They recognized our uniforms. No one moved. I pointedly looked up at my arms still held above my head, then back at him. "Yes, all right", said the sergeant.

Jacques and I lowered our hands, as I rattled off the details of my fictitious identity: name, rank, and serial number.

I added that we were searching for a deserter from our unit.

They holstered their lowered their guns. "Comrades, we are truly sorry if we seem overly zealous. We too are patrolling this general area, not for a specific deserter, but for any yellow coward trying to desert the fatherland."

"I am happy to see we are not alone. Naturally, we were aware of the forest patrols—sad that they are necessary. There is nothing worse than a deserter. I think I would rather shoot a deserter than a traitor."

"Ja, ja!" the other soldier joined our fraternal exchange. "You are absolutely right. Though shooting them is too easy. Better to hang them, slowly."

"Comrades," the sergeant said, "we would be happy to join forces and assist you."

"That's very kind but there is no need for you to extend your watch. We believe that our deserter is heading straight up." I poked northward with my thumb. "Our captain already dispatched two others from the unit directly to the top. We're sure he's between us and them; he's as good as caught. No sense in your being cold and wet for nothing. Thank you but nein, nein." I gave the soldier beside me a hearty slap on the back and added, "Danke vielmals und auf Wiedersehen!" We tramped off briskly but without unseemly haste. That took no small effort. Carefully, we looked over our shoulders. Their retreating figures were barely visible. We stopped and stood motionless for a minute. Then Jacques threw his arms around me, lifted me off the ground and let out a whoop of joy. We were like schoolboys again.

Our presence created little disturbances in the forest. A deer bounded away in fright, followed a few seconds later by a rabbit taking to its heels. We fell into a companionable silence. Jacques was the first to speak. "I am having an ugly thought about the new friend we are supposed to meet."

"What sort of ugly thought?"

"Do you think that he witnessed that last scene and decided the situation was too risky?"

"No, Jacques. I do not. We just haven't gone far enough into the woods yet. That's all."

We trudged on for several minutes more before the sound of a low whistle reached us. Some twenty feet ahead, there was a rustling in the bushes. A man stepped out and asked, "Are you men looking for cowardly German deserters?" That was the prearranged code.

I gave the reply, "Yes, but only those who speak Italian. You know," I continued, "if you had asked the two SS men we just ran into they might have shot you."

"You're joking! You were stopped by a German patrol?"

"I wouldn't joke about something like that. They wanted to join forces and help us search for 'our deserter'. I am Kurt. This is Jacques."

He just looked at us.

"Haven't you ever had to deal with German patrols before?" I asked.

"I was never careless enough to get caught by one."

I quickly translated for Jacques, who was struggling unsuccessfully to change the position of the knapsack. I turned to him. "What's the matter, Jacques?"

"Nothing really. Some of the newspapers must have worked their way up and bunched under the straps."

"Look. Just for the fun of it, let me give that thing a try", I said. I had no illusions about carrying it up a steep incline, but if I took a turn now, Jacques could carry it again later.

"Are you sure? It's a little heavy, almost like carrying a child on your back."

"I know all about that. I have a little sister. Give it to me."

"What is it?" The guide asked.

"Nothing. Jacques, he's impatient. Help me get it on."

"Let's move", the smuggler called out and briskly set off in a northwesterly direction. It occurred to me that we hadn't shaken hands with the man. He hadn't even told us his name. Fortyish and plump, along with his graying hair and thick mustache, the man looked more like an Italian waiter from the neighborhood trattoria than my idea of a smuggler. His pace, however, had nothing to do with middle age. Jacques was able to keep up with him. The knapsack *was* heavy; more moose than child. I fell back behind them.

We had begun to climb, and with the angle of our ascent, the knapsack became a challenge. The soles of my socks were sopping wet; my feet were numb. I tried distracting myself with the sights of the forest. Jacques silently pointed to a young deer springing away. Instead of admiring its grace, I played with visions of venison surrounded by chestnuts and red cabbage. I was famished.

The tramping of our feet and the snow cascading down from the tree branches were the only sounds to be heard. Then I tripped over a log in my path and fell heavily, face down. The weight of the transmitter knocked all the breath out of me. I could only lie there, gasping.

The noise of my impact with the forest floor brought Jacques back to my side. "Are you all right?" He stretched out his hand to pull me up.

"Give me a moment", I wheezed.

Jacques began untangling me from the knapsack.

"Did you sprain anything?"

"No. But my feet are both numb—cheap boots. They're soaking wet. So are my socks."

"Just catch your breath, Kurt."

The smuggler had joined us. Looking down at my boots he asked, "Are they Italian?"

I nodded in the affirmative. With a shake of his head the smuggler marched over to a fallen tree and waved to us to join him. Jacques gave me a hand up and silently slipped on the knapsack. My thanks brought only a brief flap of his hand.

"Tell your friend to hand me the knapsack," the smuggler said abruptly, "then take off your boots."

I looked down at his boots. He was technically an Italian living in Italy. "Are your boots Italian?" I couldn't help asking.

"Are you mad? They are German, of course."

With growing irritation, I realized that mine were the only pair of Italian boots—water-logged Italian boots.

Jacques wanted a translation.

"Wonderful!" said Jacques. "Your feet are already half-frozen. Now he wants you to take off your boots so that you can also catch pneumonia. Is he mad? I wouldn't be taking off my boots. I can tell you that!"

"What is he going on about?" the smuggler asked, none too pleasantly.

I was getting tired of interpreting. "Nothing, really", I said. "He is just irritated for not having brought something to warm up the insides." I didn't give Jacques a chance to ask for a translation and said to him, "Jacques, give him the knapsack."

"Tell him that the radio was already broken."

"There is only a broken radio transmitter in there", I told the smuggler.

"I already know exactly what is in there", he said. "A broken radio transmitter wrapped in thin rubber insulation."

While he unpacked the transmitter, I started struggling to remove my boots. The laces were dripping wet, and my numbed fingers got nowhere with the knots.

"Hold on! I'll get out my lighter", Jacques said.

"What are you planning to do, burn through the laces?"

"Did your fall knock out the little bit of brains God gave you? Pass your fingers back and forth over the flame. Remember it is better not to incinerate them."

Meanwhile our guide was cutting up the rubber insulation. "We haven't any daylight to waste", he said, putting the transmitter back in the knapsack. "Get your friend to help you take your boots off."

"Jacques, would you give me a hand with the laces? This fellow is in a hurry. We are losing daylight."

He worked one boot and sock off, then prepared to give my foot the same treatment that my fingers had received. But the smuggler reached over and, waving Jacques away, wrapped the thin piece of rubber around my foot.

"Now, while I hold the rubber in place, get your sock back over it." It took the combined efforts of all three of us to perform this action. Both my socks went on. The boots, two sizes too large, were not too tight.

We marched steadily upward for four hours. Undistracted by cold feet, I could appreciate the beauty of the forest. Not fifty feet ahead of us and completely without warning, a stag came crashing out of the undergrowth. Jacques and I dropped to a semicrouch. With a hunter's instinct the smuggler had been prepared. He stood his ground. As the stag disappeared from view, he called to it, "You are the lucky one this time, my friend. Under other circumstances I'd have your head on my wall!"

He motioned to a fallen tree, sat, and lit a cigarette without a glance in our direction. "Refreshments not included", Jacques said to me as we lit our own cigarettes. We sat smoking in silence and intermittently ate handfuls of snow. "Don't you think this fellow could have thought to include a swallow of wine for his guests?" Jacques asked.

I was fairly certain that our smuggler didn't speak French, but I knew it would be a big mistake to antagonize him. Jacques' tone had been aggressive, and the smuggler had given him a hard look. Best to let the subject drop, I thought, shrugging my shoulders at Jacques. Then, looking down at my cigarette, I remembered the warning of the surgeon in Munich. He wouldn't guarantee my life past my first cigarette, and I was to avoid physical exertion because the lung wouldn't stand the strain. If he could see me now.

"Come!" said the smuggler interrupting my thoughts. "We are on the last stretch now. I will take you as far as the tree line."

When I translated this, Jacques was on his feet so fast that the log rolled away, dumping me onto the snow.

"Sorry", he said with a laugh, pulling me up.

It was early afternoon, and the guide informed us that we had less than an hour to the tree line. From there we would climb about two thousand feet to the summit. I gave Jacques the information, and we continued on in silence.

With our jubilation after the encounter with the SS patrol worn off and our empty stomachs commanding all our attention, I was beginning to tire, and Jacques' step wasn't as jaunty as it had been.

Suddenly we stepped out of the forest into a pure-white expanse.

"Halt!" bellowed our guide.

"I think his missed lunch has made our friend cranky", Jacques said quietly.

"The Swiss border runs along the top of that summit", the smuggler said pointing up. He cut off a long branch, an inch in diameter, and marched into the snow. After three steps he sank to his thighs. Next he drove the branch down as far as it would go, notched the level, and handed it to me. "You are to follow a straight route from this spot to the mountain hut at the top, just a short distance over the border on the Swiss side", he continued. "Their patrol will be waiting to take you down into Santa Maria im Münstertal." He jabbed his index finger at the branch and said, "Use it!"

I had no intention of doing so. Measuring each step? It would take us forever to reach the top of the mountain.

The smuggler touched two fingers to his forehead, said, "Ciao, buona fortuna!" and was gone. We called out our thanks.

"I was worried about a long, emotional farewell from that fellow." Jacques' sarcasm matched my own feelings. I smiled at him and thought how much worse I could have done by way of traveling companions. He clapped me on the back, and we set off in high spirits.

Jacques veered to retrieve the smuggler's branch that I had tossed away. "You know," he called over his shoulder, "we just might need that stick." Seconds later, he sank, chest deep in snow. "What the devil?" Trying to turn toward me, he lost his balance and disappeared from sight.

"Welcome to winter in South Tirol!" I called, laughing so hard that I wound up sitting in the snow.

"When you can control yourself, perhaps you will be kind enough to give me a hand up. I am lying here flat on my back. That is, as flat as I can lie with this transmitter behind me." Jacques was no lightweight. It was a struggle for both of us. Finally he was upright.

"I guess we're going to need a measuring stick", I said.

"You tossed it away", he said, as he brushed himself off. "You can cut another one."

In doing so I acquired an appreciation for my knife, which I had regarded strictly as a prop. Jacques planted the new branch before each step and observed, "At this rate, it's going to take us until next year to make it to the summit."

We hadn't managed much of an advance when he paused. I followed his gaze, which took in the endless expanse of snow, all the

276

way up to the clouds. The browns and greens of the forest still lay close behind us. Jacques took up the pace again. After several hours I looked at my watch. There wasn't much daylight left, and Jacques, burdened by the transmitter, had begun to tire noticeably.

"You know, we'd better do this in shifts", I suggested. "At your age all this strain is likely to cause a heart attack. And I'm in no shape to drag dead weight up this mountain."

"I am in complete agreement with you," he said, "furthermore, I bow to what must be your superior knowledge of the local topography."

As I stepped around Jacques to take the lead, I had a flash of inspiration: I would travel through the snow like the prow of a ship through water. Handing the branch to Jacques, and hoping that I wouldn't vanish down some hole, I bent forward, laced my fingers and thumbs together and plowed—or tried to. It simply didn't work. I only succeeded in working snow up both of my sleeves. Then I tried to kick a path through the heavy snow using the idiotic Nazi goose step. The only result was a coughing fit.

Jacques watched the performance in silence. "Have you finished?" he asked. "Would you please explain your antics to me? From my viewpoint, you are not showing your best side."

"If you have a better idea, I would like to hear it."

We set off again. We had stopped mentioning food, but were now swallowing snow at regular intervals. The light was going fast. Jacques and I had managed perhaps a hundred yards in the past hour and were breathing hard, but we were finally drawing nearer the summit.

"You know, Kurt, we haven't veered off course. We have walked a line as straight as an Indian's arrow. You and I can both see the top from here. Do you see the hut?"

The thought had been occupying me for some time. "No. Nothing but snow and sky!"

Now that the subject had been raised, we could worry together openly.

"What do you think? That fellow wouldn't be in business if he couldn't at least keep his directions straight. Don't you think so?" When I said nothing, he continued. "Perhaps what he meant was that we'd see it when we reached the top. I mean, perhaps it's just set back from the top."

"Jacques, this conversation isn't cheering me up. It brings up the possibility that, despite everything, we may have misunderstood him." But "we" couldn't have misunderstood him. He had spoken to me in German. "Sorry, Jacques, I'd better amend that. Perhaps I misunderstood him."

"No. His gestures were clear enough. We were supposed to go straight up."

"Well, then I expect we didn't walk a straight line after all. What other explanation is there?"

We staggered on in silence. I tried my best to ignore it, but I was exhausted. I had not endured such exertions since I had been declared fit for service back in Munich. I felt a hundred years old. My feet seemed to weigh fifty pounds, and I couldn't stop yawning. I scooped up snow and rubbed it on my already-frozen face.

"Kurt, I've had it. Let's stop for a rest."

There was nowhere to rest. We could only sit in the snow—the wet, cold snow. Oddly, Jacques' admission of exhaustion actually revived me. "What? Canadians have the reputation of being either hearty lumberjacks or intrepid Mounties. Neither would need a rest. Come on!"

We slogged on. Soon afterward the same fatigue overtook me. If I didn't sit down, I would fall asleep walking. Just then Jacques stopped abruptly and I walked straight into him. "Look!" he shouted, pointing straight ahead.

I craned my neck forward and, squinting, could just make out a dark silhouette ahead. "Yes, it is something. But if that's the hut, then nobody is home."

As we approached it, the opaqueness slowly acquired definition. It was the burned-out ruin of what must have been a mountain cabin. There wasn't even a fraction of roof left on it.

"What do you suppose happened here?" All the disappointment we both felt was evident in Jacques' voice.

"Whatever it was certainly didn't happen recently—no smell."

We noticed a pale illumination beyond the hut. Jacques shrugged off his knapsack, and together we circled the cabin. Several hundred feet farther the earth began a downward slope. There, in the far distance below us, was an enormous, incandescent cross set in the middle of innumerable points of light. Switzerland!

Slapping each other on the back, we congratulated ourselves and stood in contented silence until the cold and our rumbling stomachs brought us back to reality. The way down to that bright cross lay in absolute darkness; continuing in the dark was out of the question. Unwillingly, we made our way back to the charred ruin.

Several partially burnt walls still stood. It had been a three-room cabin. The corner brick fireplace in the front room was intact. Closer inspection of the central wall proved it to be still solid. I began to clear an area at its base. When I had made room for two, I sat. Jacques joined me. We both fixed our gaze on the stars above.

"Do you think he did this to us on purpose? I mean, how could he not know this place was nothing but kindling?"

"You mean the smuggler?"

"No. My Aunt Martha. Of course the smuggler!"

"I can't think of any explanation for this, Jacques. The man is a smuggler. Smugglers have certain routes that they use all the time. This must be one of his. He had to know that this place had burned down. And what about the Swiss border guards? Were they really told to meet us? If they were, then where are *they*?"

"We know only that the partisans told us that they had arranged our meeting with the Swiss. The border guards' being here or not being here has nothing to do with the smuggler, Kurt. That's what makes this all so strange."

"I'm convinced that the border guards are expecting us", I said. "We have to assume that. Agreed?"

"Absolutely. In point of fact," Jacques said, "it is *they* who must be lost."

We were both beginning to realize that we could not allow ourselves to think otherwise.

"Okay. We need to do something to help the border guards find us. Right?"

"Yes, but what?" he asked impatiently.

"You know what I see here? What I see here is lots and lots of prechopped, prestacked firewood. I say we use this thing as a big torch. The Swiss border guards would have to be blind to miss it in this darkness."

"What? You want to set it on fire—again?"

"Well, why not?"

"Why not? Do you recall that rather unexpected encounter with a couple of German SS soldiers, the ones who were looking for deserters?"

"They are long gone", I said, waving my hand dismissively. "You think for one minute that they are wandering around up here after dark? Who would they be looking for? Certainly not us. They think that we are on their side. For all we know, they have already caught their quota of deserters for the day. But go ahead, tell me. If you have a better plan, I would love to hear it."

Jacques ruminated for about five seconds. Then he sat up straight. "All right." He jumped up. "Let's burn it to the ground!"

"I used up my last match. Where is your lighter?" Jacques fished out his lighter. "Good. Now what we need is something that will burn easily." We thought for a moment, and my eyes came to rest on Jacques' midriff.

"What? Oh, no," said Jacques, "I am not giving up my newspapers for a fire that might or might not attract those border guards. I won't be the one to freeze to death before dawn."

"All right, all right. Let's go through the hut and see what we can find. It can't all have gone up in flames."

We began digging through the two back rooms, and I unearthed what looked like a partially burned mattress. We dragged it to the front room, and Jacques slit it open with his knife.

"Looks like horsehair", he said.

"And it's dry."

We crammed the stuffing into the base of the wall. Then I looked for something to grate the charred top of the wall. Pieces of brick were the best I could find. I tossed one to Jacques.

"What is this for?'

"Try to scrape off some of the top layer of burnt wood."

The wood was practically petrified; the bricks, useless. But the exercise had brought some warmth to our bodies.

"This is harder than the entire climb, including carrying the transmitter," Jacques said loudly, "and I haven't accomplished a thing." He tossed the brick and sat down.

"It is not my idea of fun either", I said, dropping down next to him. "It must have been raining or snowing when the hut burned. There is no other way that so much of it could still be intact."

We tipped our heads back and contemplated the night sky. Except for a solitary cloud, it was a clear night; the stars sparkled down at us.

"Jacques, we aren't getting any warmer. Come on. Let's spread the rest of the horsehair." We began placing clumps along the top section. The interior walls had been built with wooden logs, which created gaps. We wedged the stuffing into these.

"That should do it", Jacques said, sitting down again. With his back against the wall, his knees raised, and his feet flat against the floor, he was the picture of a carefree man. He started calling out the constellations to me.

"As instructive as all this is, do you think you could get out your lighter? I am looking forward to some heat."

"Yes, absolutely."

He offered me a cigarette and, having helped himself to one, flipped open his lighter and spun the wheel. The flint sparked but—no flame. Again and again he tried, with the same results. He held the lighter under the horsehair and spun: this time, not even a spark. His hands dove into his coat, then he stuck out a pair of closed fists toward me. "Pick one", he demanded.

Thoughts of murder were coursing through my mind. "What the devil is in your hands?" I said. "You'd better say matches!"

"Matches", he sang out and tossed the box in my direction. Not prepared, I didn't react. The matches dropped into the snow. I gaped at him.

One of the mortifications of my life is my absolute lack of coordination. I have never been able to catch anything. It was a long-standing joke among my friends. Well, there was nothing to laugh about now. Jacques was aghast, and I could only stare back at him. "What is the matter with you? You didn't even move!"

"What is the matter with you? It's dark and I'm barely a yard away. You can stretch that far!"

"We can stand here arguing all night, but in the meantime, just how wet do you think those matches are getting?"

We dropped to the ground and crawled on hands and knees, pawing through the snow. Moments later my hand closed around the precious matchbox. It was slightly damp. Jacques selected one of the matches and ran it firmly and evenly along the rough, outer strip of the box. The match did not ignite. As he prepared to try again, I stayed his arm and asked, "How many matches do you have?"

"Eight or ten, I think."

"All right, if this one doesn't light we need to look for another surface. We don't have enough to waste one on a wet box, and we're going to need more than one to get a decent fire started."

I thought about the Saint Gilgen campfires. Although in the end they blazed, they wouldn't have started without Fräulein Alice's endless supply of paper and matches, the long wooden ones from the dining room. Jacques tried again—nothing. "Either the box or the matches are too damp. Try blotting the matchbox with part of your shirt, and I'll roll the match between my hands." Again Jacques tried to light the match, and this time it sizzled to life. "Get it over to the wall, Jacques!" Tiny red dots appeared as the horsehair began to singe, but it refused to catch fire.

"I thought you said that horsehair wasn't wet."

"Well, you felt it too. Did it feel wet to you?"

"No, not particularly."

"It is only logical that it should burn like paper." I said this more to myself than to Jacques. "Paper!"

Jacques held up his hand. "Please understand that under no circumstances am I alone giving up my insulation." He said this so earnestly that I had to laugh.

"That is only fair, Jacques. I wouldn't ask you to sacrifice yours alone." We unbuttoned our coats, then our uniform jackets. When I opened the extra civilian jacket and shirt that Benno had supplied, I realized how cold it really was.

"What do you think?" Jacques asked. "Should we remove the horsehair completely or stuff the paper in next to it?"

"The horsehair should have caught fire. I don't know anymore."

We decided to place each wadded piece of paper next to the horsehair, then we wedged it in between the base of the logs. Jacques touched the match flame to each wad of paper. Slowly the base of the wall started burning, producing a sharp odor. "That can't be the horsehair! Something must have died in there", said Jacques, stepping back.

The flames began licking at the wood, then consuming it in earnest until the entire wall was ablaze. We sat back on our heels

282

and watched in amazement. "Kurt, if we don't move back from here soon, we're going to have singed eyebrows." We retreated to just beyond the outer wall of the hut.

"Can you believe it?" Jacques said in wonder.

"That's what wood is supposed to do. It's the smell I can't believe. We have to get ahead of it."

"Upwind of it", volunteered the pilot.

We moved to the back of the burning cabin. After building a clothes rack out of logs, we hung out our damp coats and jackets, my shoes and socks, and were soon seated. Jacques leaned back, arms crossed, against the transmitter. Comfortable and relaxed, he eyed my bare feet, then looked down at his Canadian boots and smiled.

The warmth of the fire was an indescribable relief. The minutes ticked by; the silence lengthened. Wondering, I leaned toward Jacques—sound asleep. I grabbed a handful of snow and rubbed it in his face. He was only briefly annoyed.

We sat quietly for several minutes before he broke the silence. "This fire is bright enough to be seen by half of Europe. Where the devil are the Swiss?"

My feet were dry and warm, a marvelous sensation. I put on my socks and boots and said, "Patience, Jacques, patience."

"I have an idea. Let's send them a message that they can *hear*. What do you think?"

"With guns or hollering?" I asked seriously.

"With guns, you idiot! We will send them a signal in Morse code: three shots in rapid succession, followed by three shots with a pause between each shot, then three more fast."

"I know what Morse code is, but I have only one round of ammunition. What do you have?"

"The same, but it's better than sitting around here waiting for this fire to go out." His tone was curt, but we were tired and hungry.

"All right." I pulled out the American pistol. "I wonder how good the Americans are at making guns", I said, more to myself than to Jacques.

"You don't have to hit anything, Kurt; just fire straight up into the air."

I took a step closer to the fire, held the weapon toward the light, and awkwardly tried to open it.

"What are you doing?"

"Look, I had a close call with the last gun I handled. I'm checking to make sure nothing's blocked."

"Give it to me!"

He handled it expertly. After declaring it ready to fire, he handed it back to me. I pointed the pistol toward the sky and emptied the chamber. The echos hadn't yet died away when Jacques began firing his weapon. The reverberation was all-encompassing. For perhaps fifteen minutes, we stood in silence and waited. Nothing: no friendly greeting rang out, no gunshots returned—only quiet.

Rubbing his eyes, Jacques said, "I have a better idea. This one is more practical. Why don't we cover each other for fifteen-minute naps?"

I was sorely tempted but said, "Jacques, first of all, I wholeheartedly admit that sending the signal was a brilliant idea. But one thing is certain. If we both fall asleep, we will not wake up. Out here, in this cold, if we don't wake up, we die."

"Yes, yes. That is why we should take turns."

"Jacques, I cannot swear that I will be able to stay awake on my own. Can you be certain that you can without help?"

We were both hungry, utterly spent, and in desperate need of sleep. I saw it in his face. He saw it in mine. "If I even sit down, I'll fall asleep", he answered.

"So we've got to stay on our feet," I said, "and sing, dance, use each other as punching bags ... whatever it takes." We marched, hopped, and skipped; still the time dragged. After what seemed like hours of bruising exercise, I looked at my watch and said, "Jacques, it is two thirty-five A.M. We have only an hour and a half or so until we can begin to see something again."

"Good. We're still moving."

We sang songs, punched, pushed, and shoved each other until four A.M., when the inky darkness began to pale. That was enough. Jacques shouldered his burden and carefully we began the descent into the valley. With the fire out, we were threatened again with becoming lumps of ice, but at least our clothes were dry.

The angle of the ground got steeper. Below us lay an enormous outcropping of rock that partially obscured our view. As we circled it, the snow began to get deeper. We stopped, struck by the vision of the dawn as it began breaking over the valley. I laughed with joy and threw my arms wide. Jacques' shouts of delight echoed everywhere.

With heavy legs but soaring spirits, we descended as silver and pink tendrils crept across the paling sky. It was unlike anything I could remember. Jacques had fallen silent. I was sure his thoughts were far away, remembering relatives, friends, and the life that awaited him; mine were on all I had left behind. I had no basis for my optimism, but I was certain Father, Vera, and Sissi would reach safety.

Jacques gave me a hearty clap on the shoulder. "My friend, I am ready for breakfast. What do you say?"

With the energy of a full night's sleep, which we had not had, the two of us began to make our way down at full speed. The trek strained a completely different set of muscles. After several hours we encountered a particularly steep, snow-covered path. Half running, half rolling down it, we wound up wetter than we had been after the whole previous day's climb. It didn't matter. Santa Maria im Münstertal lay ahead: dry clothes, food, and warm beds.

When the border station did appear before us, it caught us by surprise.

"Do I really see it, or is it a hallucination?"

"If it is," I answered, "then I'm having the same one."

Breaking into a run, laughing, whooping, and waving like madmen, we arrived at the border station.

"Gruezi", said the guard. My opinion of Swiss German changed radically: a delightful language, and pleasing to the ear.

"Are you", the smiling guard asked in French, "the gentlemen that our gentlemen were expecting up in the hut last night?"

Jacques and I exchanged a look of astonishment. Then we cried out together, "Yes!"

"That hut was a burned-out ruin", Jacques said, with a great deal of feeling.

"What's more," I said, "when we finally got to it, it was pitch-dark. We couldn't continue with the descent."

"Didn't you see our signal?" Jacques asked. "We set what was left of the hut on fire."

"We saw the light, but then we heard gunshots and thought that the Germans had found you. That made it impossible for us to attempt anything. We are supposed to be neutral."

Jacques dropped his head on his chest and covered his face with his hands. "No!" he moaned. I clapped him on the back a few times.

"Who cares? If we hadn't stayed, we'd have missed the most beautiful sunrise ever."

"Do you have any cameras or", the guard looked pointedly at our holstered guns, "guns to declare? Do *not* say that you have any guns because then I will have to confiscate them."

"I have no weapons to declare and no camera."

"And I too have no camera, no guns. Nothing at all to declare except", Jacques grinned, "that I am hungry!"

"Would you please come with me, gentlemen? I am taking you to a more comfortable means of transport", said the guard, indicating his patrol truck. "We just have a two- or three-minute drive. Happy to see you are both in such fine shape." It was reassuring to learn that we had been expected after all. "How lucky you were to have crossed over this late in the winter season. We've had a number of earlier arrivals with frostbite and worse. I must say that you two look very fit indeed."

"Nothing to it really", said Jacques. "We just got caught by the dark."

We drew up to an Opel; a driver waited behind its wheel. The border guard introduced us as the passengers he was expecting, then took his leave. "Gentlemen, I wish you a very pleasant stay with us here in Switzerland."

We were driven to a solid-looking house nearby. The neighborhood had the look of quiet prosperity. The dark-suited man who received us introduced himself as Dr. Jörg Wais. We were introduced to an Englishman from British intelligence, to whom Jacques happily turned over the very broken transmitter. The head of police for the Canton of Saint Gallen was present as well as an Austrian from the Resistance.

"Gentlemen," Doctor Wais addressed the three men, "I must ask you to be patient for a little longer. I have to give each of our visitors a physical examination."

Jacques and I went through to a sitting room. Before us was a large table loaded with food. "First things first", said Doctor Wais. "You must be a little hungry."

"You have no idea!" said Jacques, who had already taken his seat.

"Thank you, Doctor. We do seem to have skipped a few meals."

There were pots of steaming tea and coffee, a mountain of toast, piles of bacon and sausages, and mounds of eggs: enough food to feed the Swiss border patrol.

"I too will leave so you can do justice to Berte's breakfast", the doctor said. "She has been hard at it in the kitchen."

"Please thank Berte for us", Jacques managed through a mouthful of food. "She is one of the treasures of Switzerland!"

"I will indeed", chuckled Doctor Wais.

After a thorough inspection and scores of questions, the doctor declared that I was miraculously fit, considering my recent medical history. Jacques' examination, little more than a formality, was brief. He exuded good health.

We rejoined our patiently waiting reception committee. The Austrian began in French. "We were waiting for you last night in the comfort of the Swiss border patrol hut with hot food and drink. What happened to you?"

"What border hut would that have been?" I asked. "We waited at what was left of the only structure that we found on the summit of the mountain."

"Yes!" said Jacques forcefully.

The Austrian looked at the Englishman and said, "You stopped at the old Italian hut that burned ages ago. The Swiss hut, which is in perfect shape, is only three hundred feet farther on. It is on the eastern side of that outcropping of rock."

"Our guide", Jacques said, "never mentioned anything about a second hut. We had no reason to look further. What's more, by the time we reached the summit, night had fallen."

"We didn't even see the Swiss hut this morning in the light of day", I said, shaking my head. But, really, it just didn't matter anymore.

# The Long Way Home

After a warm embrace, Jacques departed with the man from British intelligence. Capt. Konrad Lienert, the police chief, drove me to his office in Saint Gallen, where new identity documents would be drawn up for me. I would continue to be Karl Fischer. I was still German and had gone to work in Munich, but now my parents were Swiss. It was thought best, until my family reached safety, not to let the Germans know that one of us had slipped through their fingers. I waited with the captain in his office while my papers were prepared.

Captain Lienert began to question me about the *Prinz Eugen*. I found this to be curious. The *Prinz Eugen* had been afloat for approximately seven years, and during that time Allied intelligence must have learned what they needed to know about the ship. With the end of the war just around the corner, I could see no reason for his interest in the matter. I decided to put him off as politely as I could. "Captain Lienert, as far as I know, your country has no navy. Of what possible use could the details of a German ship be to you?"

"These are standard questions", he said offhandedly.

I pleaded weariness and managed to avoid further questions. Perhaps I had become warier than normal for my age; on the other hand, I had friends on that ship. I had heard that a number of officials were bartering information for money or using it to curry favor with the Allies. I had no grounds to suspect Captain Lienert, but the most prudent course would be to save my answers for the following day at the British legation in Bern. There, I hoped to learn something about my family.

Captain Lienert had recommended a hotel in Saint Gallen where I could spend the night, compliments of the Swiss. In addition, he handed me a hundred-franc note. I thanked him and set out on foot for the hotel. I had seen neither lighted streets nor well-stocked shop windows since the war began. The shops reeled me in like a fish.

The first window to immobilize me was a watchmaker's. I had never seen so many beautiful watches. There was one in particular; it had a black dial and silver hands. I would rather have had that watch than a bed for the night, but eighty francs was a fortune! Then I remembered that I had a hundred francs and didn't have to pay for the room at the hotel. A few minutes later, I was standing outside the shop and staring at my fantastic new wristwatch.

The combination of a real bed and a warm room was luxury enough; add to that Swiss hot chocolate and breakfast, and the effect was overwhelming. Switzerland was amazingly well organized and clean. On the train from Saint Gallen to Bern, I realized it was also a beautiful country.

I found my way from the railroad station to the British legation, where I was received by the head diplomat. In his late forties, well groomed, and perfectly tailored, he seemed to me the epitome of the English gentleman. His lack of information about Father was a great disappointment. He could only reaffirm the necessity of my continuing to pose as Karl Fischer. I wondered if he were going to raise the subject of the *Prinz Eugen*. He did not. Toward the end of our meeting, he reached into a drawer and took out an enormous bundle of hundred-franc notes, separated a wad, and handed it to me. I had never held so much money in my hand. In fact, I had never seen so much money before.

"You will want some new clothes," he said, "and while you're at it, buy yourself a piece of soap." It was only then I realized that I must reek like something from the farmer's stable.

"With the number of refugees entering this country every day," the legate continued, "lodgings are hard to come by. We've managed to secure a room for you at the Richemond in Geneva."

The Richemond! I knew it by reputation: the best hotel in Geneva and the most expensive. Still, one could hardly refuse British hospitality. Having done my best to thank the Englishman, I returned to the station and took the train to Geneva.

As the train ran along the shores of Lake Geneva, I thought wistfully of the Wolfgangsee. My reminiscences were shortened by the train's arrival. After Bern, the bustle and noise of Geneva's main railroad station was momentarily disorienting.

An ordinary-looking man stood directly in front of me. "Papiers, s'il vous plait."

I was more than familiar with the acute shortage of toilet paper and offered him some of my newspaper.

"Identification!"

Fishing out my new identity card from Captain Lienert, I began my recital of Karl Fischer's history but stumbled slightly over the altered details. The plainclothesman's eyes never left my face. He noticed. I gave him Captain Lienert's telephone number. After a brief conversation with Saint Gallen's police chief, the plainclothesman apologized and gave me directions into Geneva.

It was an easy walk. After the last two days in the mountains, everything was within easy walking distance. Silently repeating to myself that I was in Switzerland, safe, on my way to a fabulous hotel and soon to my family produced a feeling of euphoria long absent in my life. It wasn't easy to adapt to this new freedom. Being asked for my documents at the station had resurrected Himmler and the Gestapo. I had to remind myself that they lay in the past.

Geneva was cold and damp. A new overcoat was essential. In fact, I needed everything, from the inside, out. There was a magnificent display of men's clothing in the window of a shop. I stepped into its elegant interior and smiled at the shop assistant. This seemed to alarm her. She shook her head and tried to wave me out. I couldn't blame her; I had just caught a glimpse of myself in the shop window. To reassure her, I pulled out my bundle of francs, which only made matters worse. She frantically hailed the manager at the back of the shop.

When her employer shot out, I hastily explained that I had just fled across the mountains into Switzerland. I resorted once again to the name of Captain Lienert. "Here is his number. Please do call him. He will verify what I have told you."

The effect was immediate. I was fitted out for everything but shoes, which they did not sell. My old clothes were taken away immediately, certainly to the incinerator.

A favorite relative wouldn't have been treated with more kindness than I had been shown. I had even been given a parting gift of ration cards for chocolate. I stepped out onto the sidewalk a new man.

At the nearby shoe shop, I was greeted by a smiling clerk. His eyes traveled down my elegant exterior to my feet. One of my big toes was now visible. To his whispered exclamation, I hastily said that I'd simply worn them here to throw them away.

"But, naturally." The customer was always right.

Soon I was clad in shoes that blended with the rest of me. I was so busy looking at my reflection in every window I passed, and checking the time on my fabulous new watch, that the short walk to the hotel took me nearly half an hour. Oblivious to traffic, it was against all odds that I was not run over.

Walking into the Richemond, after all that had happened to me, was a source of deep pleasure and nothing short of miraculous. Seeing no luggage beside me, the concierge offered to have it fetched from the railway station. I thanked him and said that wouldn't be necessary.

"Ah, Monsieur has probably just arrived from another country?"

Monsieur had indeed.

I received a phone call the next day. The British legates wanted to ask me a few more questions; a car would pick me up at the hotel on the following morning at nine o'clock. This was puzzling. I considered the matter over a cigarette, and then I picked up the telephone and asked for the British legation in Bern.

"No, I did not call you, nor did I instruct anyone in my office to call you. Are you positive that the caller said he was from the British legation?"

"I wrote it down."

"Well, it could be a mix-up. Ignore the call. I do not need to see you; therefore, no car will be sent."

I then turned my attention to locating the Austrian community in Geneva. I had soon made three appointments, one for that afternoon and two for the next. I set out from the hotel, my spirits soaring. Geneva was like a tonic for my spirits. I liked the city very much: the kind and polite people, the quaint streets, and the charming houses. Spring was almost here, and the war would soon be over.

I returned from my appointment and found a message from the British legation. I tore up to my room and, after some fumbling with the telephone, was able finally to reach the head legate. He went directly to the point. "Just wanted to keep you informed regarding your call yesterday." Disappointed that he had no news about my family, I sank down on the chair. "I thought it best to be on the safe side—on the odd chance that perhaps the caller wasn't on the up and up—and I arranged for a reception committee at the front desk of the Richemond this morning. A driver did indeed show up at nine A.M. to fetch you, just as you were told yesterday. That driver was a Gestapo agent."

The Gestapo? Here in Switzerland? The news came as a blow.

"Hello? Kurt? Are you still there?"

"Yes, yes. I'm here, but what should I do?"

"Do? Why nothing at all, of course. We've got him, and the word that he's in custody is already out. They won't be trying anything again. The element of surprise is gone. They probably wanted to snatch you and hold you until they needed another pawn to exchange for one of their own. You just keep your guard up. This won't go on for much longer anyway. The war is all but finished."

Well, I had been in this position before; in fact, I had been in situations a thousand times worse than this. My present circumstances were immeasurably better. I was snugly among the Swiss and, essentially, safe. I just had to keep my eyes and ears open.

By the beginning of April 1945, I had made contact with the Austrians in Geneva who were active in the Resistance as well as Marcel Dupunnier, a Swiss who was deeply involved in supplying information to the Maquis, the rural guerilla groups of the French Resistance. Early one morning Marcel presented me with a copy of a Geneva newspaper. The headline proclaimed, "*Schuschnigg Assasine!*" ("Schuschnigg Assassinated!")

I had always suspected that Marcel knew who I was. Numb with shock, I groped my way to a chair. Saying nothing, Marcel also seated himself and waited. I began to read the article; the words "*identifie grace a son dentier*" ("identified by his dentures") leapt up at me. Father had no dentures! I slumped down in the chair, threw my head back, and said, "Thank God!"

Marcel was taken aback.

"No, no, Marcel. It is *not* Father. It says here that they identified him by his dentures. All his teeth are his own!"

Marcel was clearly relieved. "You must go to the US consulate here in Geneva. Their information is usually reliable. See what they have to say."

"An excellent idea." I rang at once, gave my name—my real name—and asked to see the consul general. I was given an appointment within the hour. Marcel drove me.

There were two men in the consul general's office. One of them introduced himself as the interpreter. The consul general was middle-aged, plump, balding. He rose from behind his desk and held out his hand. "But aren't you awfully young to have been chancellor of Austria?"

Glancing first at the consul general and then at the interpreter, I realized that the question had been asked in all seriousness. The interpreter looked embarrassed. I laughed, "I am indeed, but of course I am only his son."

"Of course you are!" And he too laughed.

I showed him the newspaper and explained about the dentures. The consul general frowned and retreated behind his desk. "Please be seated." He picked up his telephone and rang US headquarters in Strasbourg. The interpreter translated the results for me.

The report of Father's death was false. It was Admiral Canaris, the former head of the Abwehr, Germany's military counterintelligence service, who had been executed. Father had been ahead of the admiral on the execution list. That had caused the confusion. At the eleventh hour, word was received that Father was not to be executed. Instead, he and his family were to be sent to Dachau and held there. They were to be exchanged for several high-ranking Nazis now in Allied hands. I had struck gold! I knew now where they were. But, more importantly, I knew that they would be safe because they were of use to the Germans. I thanked the consul general for what was the most comforting news I'd had since leaving the concentration camp at Sachsenhausen.

Later that day Marcel informed me that a place was available for me with an Austrian family. The person who lodged with them had left. "You've been at the Richemond for what, two or three weeks now? Have you any idea what the bill must be?"

"None whatsoever. The British are providing for my lodgings. But they certainly have better uses for their money, and I would welcome living with an Austrian family."

It took very little time to pack my things, inform the British embassy, and check out that afternoon. I had a cardboard suitcase, a couple of shirts, socks, and another pair of trousers. These later purchases were modest, nothing like my initial extravagance.

Marcel's income came from the barbershop that he owned in Geneva's main railroad station, and his range of acquaintances was wide; it knew neither social nor economic boundaries. He took me with him to France, to the wedding of a friend's daughter in Annemasse. His friend was the French consul general in Geneva and the brother of Charles de Gaulle.

On May 6, a few weeks later, I learned from the newspapers that my family was free. There were no further details. On May 8, the Allies accepted the unconditional surrender of the German Wehrmacht, and the city of Geneva, along with the rest of the world, celebrated the end of the war. Confusion prevailed all over Europe, however. I heard nothing further about Father, Vera, and Sissi until mid-May. Once again the newspapers reported on my family. They were in Capri. The last stage of my journey began.

Before I could bury Karl Fischer, I had to revive my father's son. But in May 1945, Austria was divided into four zones of occupation, jointly administered by the Allied powers. It was treated as a political unit, but it wasn't yet a state. There was no Austrian body that could issue identity papers, legitimately, to Austrians. I turned once again to the ever-obliging British. When it arrived, my new identity document requested "both Allied military and civilian authorities" to "grant the bearer all assistance possible". I was soon to learn just how persuasive the signature of Her Majesty's representative was.

In one way I was sad to leave the transplanted Austrian community that had taken me in. Aware of my enormous debt, I said my farewells. Oddly enough, I left by the same route by which I had entered Switzerland. I took a train to Bern, and after a brief visit to Doctor Wais, I made my way to the border station in Santa Maria. The Italian officer checked my papers and asked my destination.

"A train to Bozen and on to Capri."

"You've missed the last train today, and there's no hotel in the area; but, you are welcome to sleep in the barracks. In the morning I will drive you to Bozen."

Either I had happened upon the nicest captain in the whole of the Italian Army, or the power of the magical signature on my papers was making itself felt. Either way, I couldn't have had a more handsome offer.

When we drove into Bozen, I noticed that the captain had taken a wrong turn.

"The station is the other way, isn't it?" I suggested politely.

"I know. We're not going to the station. I'm taking you to a hotel where a lot of the American officers are quartered. The Americans are the best solution for transportation."

The hotel's lobby was full of groups of uniformed men. Marching straight up to the central group, the Italian captain introduced himself, then me, and explained my predicament. An American officer stepped forward and addressed me in German: "I was with the group that liberated your family. I'm happy to meet you, son. We have courier planes flying between Bozen and our military base in Verona. From there you can hop a plane to Rome, and then down to Naples. It's hard to say when the first plane will head south, but I'll drop you off now. After I've had my breakfast, I'll run back out. If you're still there, I'll take you to Verona myself. How's that sound?"

Half an hour later, after I had said good-bye to the American officer, I perched myself on the fence along the tarmac and settled down to wait. "Just walk up to anyone coming out of or going into a plane", the American had said.

A short time later a twin-engine Caproni landed, stopping not far from my position. Originally designed in the late thirties, the Caproni had served as an Italian reconnaissance plane during the war and as a passenger aircraft. The door swung open, and its pilot nimbly descended the steps. I approached him, clutching my identity papers and praying that he spoke French or German.

"Yes, French", he said.

I offered him my identity papers and told him that I was trying to get to Verona. His eyes traveled from the document to me and back. Then he smiled and held out his hand. "Eight years ago I had the pleasure of flying His Excellency, your father, from Venice to Vienna. I would be very happy to take you to Verona. I am here only to deliver an official communiqué. Once I have done that, we can go."

Flying was pure pleasure for me. I had been in an airplane several times with Father. The aircraft we had used was the Austrian government's Junkers Ju 52. It was functional and efficient, but memorable only for the transportation it provided. The interior of this Italian-made Caproni had been lavishly remodeled. I noticed a man sitting toward the rear of the cabin in a large, beautifully upholstered armchair reading through a sheaf of documents. I returned his bow of greeting and began looking over the interior.

A Persian rug blanketed the entire floor. Chairs and couches were covered in heavy brocades, and highly polished occasional tables were scattered throughout. But it was the stately rococo desk to which the eye was drawn. I could have been in a salon in the Hofburg Palace in Vienna. The pilot pointed to a seat in the front and said, "Make yourself comfortable while I deliver this letter."

It was a very short flight from Bozen to Verona. I barely had time to savor the sensation of being airborne before we began to descend. We taxied to a halt, and the engines were shut down. After a somber nod to me, the document-reading passenger left the aircraft. I stopped to thank the pilot.

"Have you eaten yet?"

When I said that I hadn't, he asked me to follow him. "I have access to a wonderful breakfast."

The small building next to the landing strip bore a sign "*Solamente per Aleati*" ("Only for Allies"). But the pilot veered left of the building and struck out across the adjacent field. On its opposite side, a smiling farmer greeted him, and we entered a farmhouse kitchen.

The pilot asked, "How would you like a ride all the way to Rome?"

"Like it? I would love it!"

"On the way over from Bozen, I wired ahead for permission. I am here to pick up passengers who will be happy to share your company."

Breakfast consisted of four eggs—sunny-side up—two glasses of milk, and a quarter loaf of warm homemade bread. Afterward, we headed back to the Caproni.

My silent co-passenger from Bozen was waiting for us. He stood several steps behind four men of elegant appearance. The Caproni's captain made the introductions: the Count of Turin, cousin of King Victor Emmanuel III of Italy; Marquess Falcone Lucifero, chancellor of the royal household; and Lt. Lucca Dainelli, aide-de-camp to

Italian Crown Prince Umberto. I did not hear the name of the fourth member of the group. I bowed and shook his hand silently. The passenger from Bozen, who had reverently separated himself from this grand group, turned out to be a secret service man.

We were soon aloft. Lord Lucifero began to talk of Father. "Your father was the herald to Europe and the world", he said. "Because of its own preoccupations, this continent turned a deaf ear . . . until it was too late. That he was left standing alone is our collective shame." Each member of the group then spoke eloquently of Papa as a just man and a fearless patriot.

As we approached Ciampino airport, Lord Lucifero said, "I am sorry that I cannot send you on to Capri in the king's plane, but Lieutenant Dainelli will see to your hotel accommodations."

Keenly aware of my cardboard suitcase and its meager contents, I said, "Oh, it isn't necessary. I am certain I can find something." In fact, I had gone through nearly all the money the British had given me, and that needed to last until I reached Capri.

"You don't understand", the marquess said. "These days a hotel room in Rome is as rare as an ostrich egg. No, no. The lieutenant will apply himself to the problem."

The aircraft taxied toward what from above had looked like two huge black bugs on the tarmac. Now they were automobiles with royal flags posted on both sides of their windshields. We all got in and drove toward Rome.

On the outskirts of the city the traffic thickened. We made our way through a maze of streets, and before I could identify any notable sight, the car passed between two great stone columns. Lord Lucifero was deposited before the main entrance of a building. Further on Lieutenant Dainelli and I got out at a different entrance. I followed him through what looked like temporary barracks into an office.

"On your next visit," he said to me, "I will make sure you see the more impressive side of the Palazzo del Quirinale."

We entered an office where he sat down behind a desk and picked up a phone, motioning me to a chair. Dialing from memory, the lieutenant made one call after another without success until he reached the manager of the Grand Hotel. My heart sank. I had never been to Rome, but I had heard of the Grand Hotel. I had

350 lire left and calculated that I could probably afford to spend one night, possibly two. But then I would have nothing left for the onward journey to Naples. I thanked the lieutenant for his many kindnesses and made up my mind at least to enjoy the drive to the hotel before I started worrying about paying for my room. Wanting keenly to have the sights pointed out to me, I made desperate attempts at conversation in the car. But the kitchen Italian of my childhood was totally inadequate.

The manager of the hotel stood ready and welcomed me in perfect German. "I am happy to be able to give you the same suite that His Excellency, your father, had when he last stayed with us." That sealed my fate.

When the lift began its ascent, I asked the operator, "Just how much is the suite?"

"Three thousand lire, signore."

I was aghast and a little weak in the knees. "A month?"

"No, signore, a day."

After making a thorough examination of the suite, I decided that I couldn't afford to wash my hands. Three hundred fifty lire would probably not be enough for the soap.

Father's former personal secretary, Baron Victor Frölichsthal, lived somewhere in Vatican City. I had to find him and borrow some money to extricate myself from all this unaffordable opulence. I left my suitcase on the floor in the middle of the suite and went downstairs to the front desk. "I must go to the Vatican. Can you tell me how to get there?"

I was told that I could take either a taxi or a *camionetta*, a kind of jeep with lengthwise benches facing each other. I took the first one that was bound for the Vatican and seated myself beside a plump, pleasant-looking priest.

"Mon père", I said tentatively in French.

He held up a hand and said he spoke only Italian and German.

"Wonderful! I speak German. Do you by any chance know of a Baron Victor Frölichsthal living somewhere in the Vatican?"

"I do, my son. He lives with his family in the boarding house run by the Sisters of Charity. Why?"

"Father, my name is Schuschnigg . . ."

"No! Are you the son of Kurt von Schuschnigg?"

"I am, yes."

"God works in mysterious ways, does he not? I was a very young prefect at the Stella Matutina when your father was a student there. Moreover, I know Baron Frölichsthal very well. I will take you to him."

I could only slap my knee and smile at him. He mimicked my actions, and we both laughed. By fits and starts, our camionetta worked its way through the pandemonium that was Roman traffic.

"Have you been to Rome before?"

"No, Father."

"Well, keep your eyes open. Saint Peter's Basilica will be in view in a moment."

The little camionetta stuttered along beside the Tiber and started up the Via della Conciliazione. I half rose from my seat to get a better view. Almost before I could blink, the camionetta swung left and began to orbit the second half of Bernini's columns on the basilica's periphery. Barely using his brakes, the driver blasted his way through the traffic with his horn. Saint Peter's disappeared before I could get more than a glance or two.

We got out at the next stop, and from there the spry priest set off at a brisk pace. We went past a number of aging buildings and made but one turn. I was so absorbed by all that was around me that when the priest stopped I walked right into him. "That's quite all right", he laughed. "There is a lot to see in this city."

The door in front of us opened noiselessly. We stepped into semi-darkness lessened by a faint light from a curtained window. A nun whom I didn't notice when we entered closed the door behind us. She spoke so softly that I wasn't sure that she had spoken at all. The priest and I followed her to a door. She tapped several times. When it opened, there was Uncle Victor.

When he recognized me, Uncle Victor's expression was enough to make even the little nun smile. He nearly squeezed the breath out of me in his enthusiasm. The priest then bade us farewell, and I entered the altered world of Baron Victor Frölichsthal.

"Sit down, sit down, Kurti!" That was easier said than done. Uncle Victor's lodging, which he shared with his wife, was just a large bedroom with several extra chairs. "You will hardly believe the coincidence, but your father was just here."

"No!"

"He came in on a military plane to see the pope. He visited me for about an hour and then returned to Capri. But first tell me how you got here."

Briefly I told him of my journey from Switzerland that had ended in the terrifyingly expensive Grand Hotel. "It isn't an accident that that suite is the only thing available in Rome. No one can afford it." He rose and went to his desk. "I just had to give your father three thousand lire. You are going to need at least five thousand."

He pulled out a large, worn wallet and carefully counted out the bills. Handing me the money he said, "Go back to the hotel and ask for the manager. Tell him that you have already found transportation to Naples and you'll be checking out. Pay for one night and leave a good tip. Then come back here."

"Yes, Uncle Victor. Thank you very much."

"Go now. Can you find your way back all right?"

"I can find my way back, Uncle Victor."

Once outside, I realized I would see very little of the city, so I decided to begin walking in the general direction of the hotel. After a few blocks, my surroundings changed completely. The labyrinth of streets and alleys bore no resemblance to the place that I had just left. Washing hung on lines that streamed everywhere, and pungent, mouthwatering aromas wafted out of windows and doorways. I saw none of the damage that marred so many of the European capitals. A number of buildings gave the impression of disrepair, but that was from age not bombing raids.

Within the hour I had made my way back to the hotel, retrieved my suitcase, and presented myself at the front desk, where I related my fiction to the director. To my request for the bill he said, "Absolutely not! There is no question of a bill."

"That is terribly kind of you", I said, careful not to let my voice betray my relief. "Thank you."

"Not at all. Perfectly normal."

I peeled off several notes that seemed a fortune to me and left them for the staff. Then I asked for a taxi.

"Taxi? I won't hear of it. I will drive you myself. Do you want to go to the airport or the train station?"

I hadn't counted on so much kindness. It embarrassed me.

"I will be traveling from the Vatican."

The first thing Uncle Victor did was to call the local Allied headquarters and asked about transportation to Capri. He was told that an army jeep was leaving Rome for Caserta at first light the next morning and could take me along.

I stayed overnight with the Frölichsthals. Over a plate of pasta, we exchanged our stories of the past seven years. They had not been easy times, but still, there were some experiences that we could laugh over—and we were alive, weren't we?

When I climbed into the US Army jeep the next morning, I was greeted in German. I was amazed by Rome and peppered the sergeant with questions. We left the city behind us. The ride was long, hot, and very dusty. We arrived in Caserta in early afternoon, and I was taken directly to an American military officer, Brig. Gen. Charles Spofford. His greeting was gracious, but it took me a moment to realize that he was speaking to me in my own language. I listened attentively to the heavily accented German. "I have something here for your parents that I want you to take."

"Yes, sir. Thank you very much."

It was a wooden crate several feet long and half that in height and width. The general laid his hand on its lid. "I understand that your father is a heavy smoker."

"That he is, sir."

He lifted the lid and turned the crate around toward me. The crate was packed with cigarettes. A picture of the spindly tobacco plants over which Father had lavished so much attention in Sachsenhausen flashed through my mind.

"This will truly please him, sir. I thank you on his behalf."

"The jeep is waiting for you. I'll have the crate put in it later. Right now you're expected over at the private quarters. The king and queen want to give you something for your parents too."

"Yes, sir."

I climbed back into the jeep and, a few turns later, was deposited in front of an entrance to a building. I had had no sense of being anywhere near a palace. That changed immediately when I stepped inside. Marble, in shades of pink, gray, terra-cotta, and green, covered the floors and pillars. The sofas and chairs were draped in delicate fabrics, and oblong windows spilled sunlight over paintings by artists long dead. The high ceilings were ornamented: some painted, some gilded. My footsteps echoed as I followed the servant.

Passing ornate consoles that studded the walls, we walked through vestibules heavy with chandeliers and eventually entered a spacious, sun-drenched room. The scent of countless flowers permeated the air. Amid the furniture and the huge floral arrangements, I searched for the royal couple.

In appearance, Victor Emmanuel III and Queen Elena were an unusual couple. The king was diminutive; the queen well over six feet tall and stately. I bent over her hand, thinking how formidable she must be when she stood.

"We are very pleased that your own journey is almost over", she said in French.

"Your family has shown great courage during these terrible times", the king added.

It was generous of them, for they had their own pain to endure. Their daughter, Princess Mafalda of Hessen, had for a time occupied one of the four cottages at Sachsenhausen. She was moved to Buchenwald. There she was seriously wounded during a bombing raid on a nearby armaments factory. Already malnourished and exhausted, she died the next day.

"Please be seated and tell us about yourself", Queen Elena said.

The time flew by. A clock chimed, and I looked toward it. "You are naturally anxious to join your family", said the king. "A launch is waiting to take you to Capri."

Queen Elena rose from the sofa and walked over to one of the enormous floral arrangements. She took a large bouquet from a vase and held it out to me. "This is for your dear parents. Please give them our most sincere compliments."

"Thank you, Your Majesties." In my best Elmayer manner, I again bowed over her hand. To the king I said, "They will be deeply touched. Au revoir."

The male servant had returned unobtrusively to guide me back through this small section of the twelve-hundred-room wonder designed by Luigi Vanvitelli. I said good-bye to General Spofford and thanked him again for his help and especially for the cigarettes.

"Not at all. Please give my very best to your parents. Life can only be better from now on. The launch is waiting for you." As I got into the jeep, he added, "It's just a short ride. You'll be in Capri in no time."

"Thank you, sir. Oh, and please don't have anyone call my parents. I want to surprise them."

"Just get yourself going. The more you delay, the longer until you see them. Good luck!"

"And to you, sir. Good-bye."

When the jeep pulled up at the dock, the launch's engine was idling. The driver bounded out with the crate of cigarettes. I grabbed my suitcase and the enormous royal bouquet. Soon afterward, the launch was heading across the Bay of Naples toward the Isle of Capri. I looked for the Faraglioni rocks, but they were nowhere to be seen.

"What happened to the Faraglioni?" I called to the sailor at the helm.

"The what?"

"You know, those big rocks with the hole in the middle big enough to sail a boat through."

"Oh, those. They're on the other side. You don't see them from this approach."

Never mind. I had all the time in the world for the Faraglioni. I was not Ulysses. Nothing could delay my homecoming now. It was funny to call Capri "home", for I had never set eyes on it. But "home" wasn't marked geographically for me. Home was wherever my family was. This little island was the biggest part of my entire world right now, for there were the three most important people in my life. *Finally* I was going home.

In the distance one could just make out the tiny dock with figures the size of ants upon it. We neared, and the launch began to slow. I turned around and hoisted the crate and suitcase onto the seat. Then, as the launch's engine throttled down, I carefully picked up the royal bouquet. I looked toward the dock and realized those barely recognizable figures had become larger than life. Standing there waving wildly were Father, Vera, and Sissi.

# EPILOGUE

When one survives what this father and son survived, further accidents of fate are little more than irritants. In April 1945, fleeing German soldiers used the Ottenreiter country house to exchange their uniforms for civilian clothes. The advancing Russian troops, finding these uniforms, thought the Ottenreiters were helping the SS and burned their house to the ground. When Fräulein Alice came to the house later, she searched for Kurti's stamp collection, which was buried under several inches of dirt and by then also covered by a good half foot of rubble. She cleared away the rubble and earth. The colors of the album were as bright as when she had buried the book, but when Fräulein Alice placed her hand on the album's spine to lift the book, it disintegrated into ashes.

The negatives of the pictures taken by Kurti of Sachsenhausen and its prisoners were left in Fritz Sammer's apartment in Vienna. In March 1945, an Allied bombing destroyed the entire building. The only surviving picture is that of the Sachsenhausen bungalow of Kurti's parents.

When Vera moved to Sachsenhausen in 1941, she brought with her her Czernin family jewelry. For almost four years it remained with her. In transit between Dachau and Innsbruck, a Nazi guard detected the pouch concealed on her person. He took the jewelry saying, "Where you are going you won't need this anymore."

One of fate's ironies was what happened with the household goods of the Schuschnigg family. With German precision, what had not been "confiscated" in their residence was packed up and sent from concentration camp to concentration camp. Camp commander Kaindl signed an order that the seventy-two crates of "Doctor Auster" follow him to Dachau. When the US Army took over, the crates were never seen again. The Allies did return, however, the Czernin Vermeer with instructions to restore it to its rightful owner. Since then it has hung in the Kunsthistorische Museum in Vienna.

Astounding to father and son was the following story: after the war the former chancellor began immediately to write articles and give lectures in order to support his family. A couple of years later, he received a bill from the British government for expenses incurred by his son in Geneva. It was for the period of several weeks beginning March 14, 1945, of supposed British hospitality. Both father and son had to sit down when they saw the bill from the Richemond.

All four of the Schuschniggs emigrated to America and became American citizens. The former chancellor taught political science and European history at Saint Louis University and was a prolific writer and lecturer until his retirement in 1967. He returned to his native Austria, where he died in 1977. Vera died in Saint Louis in 1959. Sissi married, had one son, Marc de Kergariou, and died in Paris in 1989. All three died of lung cancer. "Kurti" is still alive and well at this publishing.

# ACKNOWLEDGMENTS

I had so much help with this long project. I will surely omit some of those who helped. Forgive me.

First and foremost, it is through Father Boniface Ramsey, pastor of Saint Joseph Church in New York City, that this publication was made possible.

I am grateful to Mr. William Eichenberger, who first reduced and clarified a very long manuscript.

Dr. Wilhelm Steidl and Prof. Fritz Molden, both witnesses to the Hitler era, afforded me incomparable insight. Doctor Steidl was also the source of innumerable answers to seemingly endless questions; and without Professor Molden's encouragement, I would have abandoned the project long ago.

My special thanks to my brother Joseph Kendall Cook, whose time and efforts were irreplaceable.

My great gratitude goes to my cousin Constance Whitney, whose intelligence and patience were invaluable.

Above all, I am most grateful to my husband, Kurt von Schuschnigg, for his long and sometimes very painful travels into the past.

# BIBLIOGRAPHY

Dollfuss, Engelbert. Protocol, May 27, 1932. Austrian Parliament Archives, Vienna.

Hopfgartner, Anton. *Kurt Schuschnigg: Ein Mann gegen Hitler.* Vienna: Verlag Styria, 1989.

Kindermann, Gottfried-Karl. *Österreich gegen Hitler: Europas erste Abwehrfront 1933–1938.* Munich: Langen Müller Verlag, 2003.

Schuschnigg, Kurt von. *The Brutal Takeover.* New York: Atheneum, 1971.

———. *Ein Requiem in Rot-Weiss-Rot.* Zurich: Amstutz, Herdeg and Co., 1946.

———. *Im Kampf gegen Hitler: Die Überwindung der Anschlussidee.* Vienna: Verlag Fritz Molden, 1988.

US Department of State. Records Relating to Internal Affairs of Austria, 1930–1944. National Archives and Records Administration, College Point, MD.

# INDEX

Abyssinia invasion by Italy, 57, 69–70
Adler, Victor, 14
Allied intelligence, 249–50, 253, 288
Alsace declared German, 169
Alt Aussee, 109–10, 118, 122
Alte Realgymnasium, 109–12, 144, 194, 256
Altwienerbund charity, 25, 39, 44
American B-17s, 194
the American officer in Bozen, 295
amnesties, 57, 71–72
Annemasse, France, 294
Anschluss
    crowd's welcome, 5–8, 197–98, 230
    date, 5–6, 92–93
    German invasion of Austria, 5–10, 91–93, 197–98, 230
    Hitler's demands, 5–7, 28, 89–93
Anti-Comintern Pact (November 1936), 76, 81
anti-Semitism, 15–16, 57, 98–100, 140, 146–47
    *See also* Jews
the apfelkuchen woman's sorrow, 191–92, 194
Aquinas, Saint Thomas, 243
*Arbeitsbuch* (Habicht), 17
*The Art of Painting* (Vermeer), 127, 305
assassinations
    attempts/plots, 7, 29–31, 33, 52, 90, 162, 255
    of Dollfuss, 7, 31, 33–35, 88
    propaganda, 292–93
    successful, 7, 31, 33–35, 47–48, 52, 69
    threats by Hitler, 88
Augarten Palace home, 24–27, 32–35
Aunt Elizabeth (Elizabeth Mayr), 227–30
Aunt Louise (Louise Masera), 233

Aunt Marianne. *See* Schuschnigg, Marianne von
Aunt Millicent (Millicent Rogers), 83–85
Aunt Olga (Olga Hekajllo), 136
Aunt Paula (Paula Niedermayr), 108, 110, 112, 121
Aunt Vera. *See* Schuschnigg, Vera von (Kurti's stepmother)
Aunt Zoë (Baroness Zoë von Schildenfeld), 57–58
Auster, Doctor (prison and concentration camp alias for the Chancellor), 125–26, 193, 305
Auster, Kurt (concentration camp alias for Kurti), 153–54, 193
Austria
    agreement with Hungary and Czechoslovakia (September 1937), 80–81
    appeasement policies, 28–30, 35, 57, 71–72, 77–80, 88, 91–93
    Army strength and size, 15n3, 29, 59, 70
    Berchtesgaden meeting (1938), 88–93, 164
    compulsory military service, 59, 70
    dependence on Italy, 29, 35, 37, 69–70, 72, 78, 81
    domestic loan plan, 79
    German invasion (Anschluss), 5–10, 91–93, 197–98, 230
    Hitler meetings, 29–30, 88–93, 164
    Hitler's Hossbach Memorandum (November 1937), 81
    independence, 5–6, 28–35, 57, 59, 69–70, 91–93
    international agreements, 29–30, 59, 77–78, 88–91, 164
    July 11, 1936 accord, 71–72, 80, 88, 91

Austria (continued)
League of Nations loan, 13–14, 45
Little Entente, 59, 77–78
Mussolini meetings, 35, 78
paramilitary groups, 28, 31–32, 57,
96, 105
Parliament dissolved itself March 4,
1933, 28
political parties in, 10–11, 14–15, 17,
28–30, 70
post WWI morale, 5–10, 15n3
pre-Anschluss government, 13–14, 24,
24n4, 28, 34–35, 76, 79–80
renamed Ostmark, 7, 31
Rome Protocols (March 1934,1936),
59, 77, 88
Social Workers' Union speech, 80
South Tirol German speakers, 218,
235
Ständestaat (corporate state), 24,
24n4, 35, 80
terrorism increasing, 7, 15, 17,
29–30, 47–48, 88
tourism tariff, 28–29
zones of occupation, 294
See also Austrian cities by name, e.g.,
Vienna
Austrian community in Geneva, 292–94
Austrian Legion (Austrian Nazis), 29, 70
Austrian Socialist Party, 10, 15, 28, 30
Austro-Hungarian Empire, 7, 9–10,
15n3, 36–37, 69, 78
See also Habsburg dynasty
autograph book, 65, 67

Bad Aibling, Germany, 5
Bad Ischl, Austria, 53–55
Balcom, Ronald, 82–85
Baldwin, Stanley, prime minister,
England, 9
Balkans, 77
Baltic Fleet, 158
barter economy
for already-picked hops, 133–34
cigarettes as currency, 186, 212, 216,
222
for confiscated French cognac,
174–75

for information, 288
rat bounty, 174–75
salt as currency, 231, 244
for a train ticket, 186
Bartl, Lt. Col. Georg, 6, 46, 49, 51, 57,
62, 82–83, 96
basic training, 160–62
Bauer, Otto, 10, 14, 28
Bayern, Crown Prince Rupprecht von,
143
Bayreuth, Germany, 210
BBC broadcasts, 135–36, 143
Beatrixgasse, Vienna, 96
Becker, Farmer, 181–84
Becker, Frau, 181–84
Belgium, 77, 79, 79n7
Belvedere home
Biedermeier salon, 16, 61, 65–67
five-shilling coin mystery, 67–68
Fräulein Alice's excitement about,
60–63
Grandfather at, 96
Prince of Wales's visit, 66–69
secret doors at, 60–61, 62
Beneš, Edvard (Czechoslovakian
president), 59
Benno, the farmer, 259–63, 265–66, 282
Berchtesgaden, Germany, 88–93, 164
Berghof (Hitler's home near
Berschtesgaden), 89
Berlin
devastation in, 193–97, 198, 200–201,
221, 226
Gestapo headquarters, 151–54,
191–93
Göring's dare, 195
museum in, 124
Mussolini's visit, 81
Bern, Switzerland, 288–89, 294
bicycles, 119–20, 123–24
Blood Order medal, 111
the Blue Max, 255
Bock, Fedor von (commander of
German Eighth Army), 6–7
bodies, piles of, 115, 189, 211, 232
bodyguards, 18–19, 26–27, 49, 52, 56
Bogenhausen area of Munich, 24, 112,
144

Boltenstern, Heidi von, 194–97
bombings, Allied
 Berlin, 151, 155, 193–97, 198,
  200–201
 Hamburg, 159, 221–23, 230
 Innsbruck, 230
 Munich, 148–49, 151, 203
 strafings, 184, 186, 222
 trains, 202
 Vienna, 305
Bozen (Bolzano), Italy
 best bordello in, 236–41
 Brenner Pass, 29, 222, 227, 232–33,
  241, 252–53
 history, 218
 Hotel Greif, 248
 relatives in, 25, 75, 218, 233, 235–37
 Resistance in, 236–48
Brandenburg Gate, Berlin, 151
Brannenburg am Inn station, 225–27
Bregenz, Austria, 5
Breitscheid, Rudolf, Prussian Minister
 of the Interior, 137
Brenner Pass, 29, 222, 227, 232, 241,
 252–53
bribery, 25–27, 216, 254
 See also barter economy
British Secret Intelligence Service (SIS),
 252
British wireless transmitter, 262–63,
 266, 268, 272–74, 276–77, 280, 283,
 286
Brother Michael (Monastery Gries),
 242–43
Brothers Grimm stories, 42
the Browning handgun, 122, 176–77
Brownshirts/Swastikas, 32–34, 52,
 98–99
The Brutal Takeover (Schuschnigg), 89n3
Buchenwald concentration camp, 255,
 302
Budapest, Hungary, 35, 78
Buddha, the scrimshaw, 239–40
Bullitt, William (U.S. ambassador to
 France), 91
the bunk question, 165–67
Buresch, Karl, Minister of Finance, 51
Burggrafenstrasse, Berlin, 155

Burkett, Cadet Franz, 171
burn wounds, 179–81, 184–92, 202–6,
 211–12, 219, 275
the burned-out hut, 278–84, 287
Busch, Wilhelm, 42
Byrd, Admiral Richard, 9

Café Prükel (Vienna), 96
Café Zauner, Bad Ischl, 53–56
camera, the American's, 138–39,
 151–55, 263
Canadian pilot, 262
 See also Jacques, downed Canadian
  pilot
Canaris, Admiral Wilhelm Franz (head
 of Abwehr), 293
the candy store, 99
Capri, Italy, 294, 299–300, 302–3
Caproni plane, 295–96
the car accident, fatal, 45–48, 52
Carinthia (Austrian state), 29
Cartel des Gauches (France), 9
Caserta, Italy, 10, 301
Catholic Church
 Chancellor's faith, 3, 11, 25, 95,
  155–56
 Kurti's faith, 32, 98, 142, 168, 178,
  182, 243, 270
 schools, 15, 24, 73–76, 93–94, 108–9
 Socialists against, 10
 Vera's faith, 20, 94, 155–56
Charlemagne's empire, 31
the cherrywood banquette episode,
 11–12
chief surgeon (Munich), 205–6, 235
Christian Socialist Party (Austria), 11,
 28
Churchill, Winston, 92
cigarettes, 174, 186, 212, 216, 222, 232,
 301–3, 305
code, the smuggler's, 272
coffee, real, 232–33, 243
Cols, Michael, 72
Cols, Suzy, 72
Cols, Vincent, 72
Committee of Seven, 88
Communism, 17, 25n, 28, 76, 113, 140,
 153

compulsory military service, 59, 70
compulsory volunteerism, 149–50, 172
concentration camps
  Buchenwald, 255, 302
  Dachau, 293, 305
  kapos in, 141
  Ravensbrück, 136
  speaking of, forbidden, 146, 192
  various demographics in, 140
  Vera joining Father in, 122–26, 129,
    137, 198–99
  See also Sachsenhausen concentration
    camp
Coolidge, Calvin, 9
corporate state (Ständestaat), 24, 24n4,
  35, 80
cousin of Victor Emmanuel III, 296
cowardice, 168–69, 171–73
  See also deserters
crimes against humanity, 96
Cuxhafen naval base, Germany, 223
Czechoslovakia, 15n3, 57, 59, 77–78,
  80–81, 92, 107
Czernin family jewelry, 305
Czernin family's Vermeer painting, 127,
  305
Czernin-Chudenitz, Countess Vera,
  19–20, 57–58, 94, 114
  See also Schuschnigg, Vera von
    (Kurti's stepmother)

Dachau concentration camp, 293, 305
Dagrelle, Leon, 262
Dainelli, Lt. Lucca, 296
Danzig/Gdansk, Poland, 164, 182–86,
  188–90
Daughters of Divine Love convent, 63
the Davids family (neighbors at
  Augarten), 32–33
de Gaulle, Charles, 294
Defregger (orderly), 36
Demel's cafe (Vienna), 118
Denmark, 221–22
"Der Alpenkönig und der
  Menschenfeind" (Raimund), 115–16
deserters, 207, 223, 225, 249, 256, 264,
  271–72
Dietrich, Cadet, 161

Dietrich, Otto, 89
disappearances, 96, 114, 154, 205–6, 217
  See also terrorism
ditch digging (RAD), 149
divorce, 20, 57, 69, 94, 114
Dollfuss, Engelbert (Austrian
  Chancellor)
  assassination of, 7, 31, 33–35, 88
  chancellor (1932–1934), 13–14, 24,
    28–30, 59, 70
  Rome Protocols (March 1934), 59
Dragelle insignia, 262–63, 266
Dresden, Germany, 143
Duke of Windsor, 66–69
Dupunnier, Marcel, 292–94
Dzhugashvili, Yakov (Stalin's son), 143

Economic Empowering Law of 1917, 28
Ecstacy (movie), 65
Edward VIII, King of England, 68
Egger-Lienz painting, 61
Ein Mann gegen Hitler (Hopfgartner),
  14n2, 89n2
Elena, Queen, wife of King Victor
  Immanuel III, 302
Elmayer, Wilhelm, 16–17, 102, 164
Elmayer's (finishing school), 15–17
emigration
  famous personalities, 65–66, 137
  Jews, 19, 65–66, 92, 107, 146
  the Schuschnigg family, 306
  South Tirol German speakers, 218,
    235
Engel, Petty Officer, 159–62, 173
England
  commitment to Austrian
    independence, 35, 69–70
  Edward VIII, king of, 68
  general strike in, 9
  war declared on Germany (1939), 110
Ethiopia, 57, 69
Ettal's boarding school, 108–9
evacuations
  Danzig, 184–86
  Königsberg, 180–84
  of trains, 186, 202, 208
  on the Wilhelm Gustloff, hospital ship,
    184, 186, 188–91

the Faraglioni, Naples, 303
farmhouse kitchen in Verona, 296
Fasching (carnival), 42, 42n2
Fascism, 9, 14, 65, 69–70, 81
Father. *See* Schuschnigg, Kurt von (Austrian Chancellor)
Fatherland Front militia, 31, 59, 70–71
Fatherland Front Party, 5, 59, 70–71, 76
Faulhaber, Cardinal Michael von, 113
Feurich, Herr and Frau, 144–48
Feurich, Werner, 144–48
Fey, Emil, minister of security, 30
firing squad, 168–73, 210
Fischer, Karl (alias), 254–59, 262, 271, 288–90, 294–95
the fisherman's refusal, 214–15
the five-shilling coin mystery, 67–68
flak units, 148
food shortages, 7, 137, 231, 288
"for führer and fatherland", 149
France
    Annemasse, 294
    on Austrian independence, 35, 69–70
    Bullitt, William (U.S. ambassador to France), 91
    Locarno Treaty, 79, 79n7
    the Maquis, 292
    Paris, 6, 91, 306
    on Starhemberg's telegram, 69–70
    Strasbourg, 293
    strength of, 5–7, 9, 142–43, 292
    surrender, 142
    war declared on Germany (1939), 110
Franco, General, 72
*Frankfurter Zeitung* (newspaper), 14
Franz Josef, Emperor, 54
Frau Something-or-Other, 22–23
    *See also* governesses (Kinderfräulein)
Fräulein Alice. *See* Ottenreiter, Alice
Free French Forces, 143
French Ninth Army, 142
French Seventh Army, 142
friendly fire, 177
Frölichsthal, Baron Victor, 298–301
Front militia, 59, 70–71
Fugger, Rudi, 19–22, 57–58, 74, 82–87, 107, 127

Fugger-Babenhausen, Count Leopold, 19, 114
Fugger-Babenhausen, Countess Vera, 19–20, 57–58, 94, 114
    *See also* Schuschnigg, Vera von (Kurti's stepmother)

Garmisch, Germany, 187
Gdansk, Poland, 182–84
Gdynia (Gotenhafen), Poland, 164, 170, 173, 188, 207, 214–17
Geheime Staatspolizei. *See Gestapo entries*
generosities amidst the war. *See* kindnesses, unexpected
Geneva, Switzerland, 35, 289, 291, 293–94, 306
George V, King of England, 9, 69
German Eighth Army, 5–6
German National Opposition, 71
Germans
    morale, 166, 178, 184, 186, 201, 203, 229–31
    character, 159, 170, 186, 192, 196, 201
    compassion for, 201, 221, 249
    as friendly guards, 116, 134, 143, 176, 198, 200
    Nazis different from ordinary, 154, 158–59, 163, 182, 201, 224
    opposition to Hitler but duty-bound, 158, 166, 200–201, 207, 255
    ordinary (*See* kindnesses, unexpected)
Germany
    absence of poor childlren in, 128
    Alsace declared to be German, 169
    compulsory volunteerism, 149–50, 172
    credits, redeemable only in Germany, 77
    France and England declare war on, 110
    Hossbach Memorandum (November 1937), 81
    invasion of Austria, 5–10, 70, 88, 91–93, 197–98, 230 (*See also* Anschluss)
    invasion of Czechoslovakia, 59, 107
    invasion of Poland, 110

Germans (*continued*)
  invasion of Russia, 143, 158
  July 11, 1936 accord, 71–72, 80, 88,
    91
  losses of, 115, 166, 178, 189, 211, 232
  reputation of soldiers, 177–78
  retreat from Russia, 175, 177, 180–84
  Rhineland re-occupation, 59, 79n7,
    80, 149
  Rome-Berlin Axis agreement
    (October 1936), 76
  South Tirol history and, 25, 217–18,
    235, 269–70
  unconditional surrender, 294
  war declared on U.S., 127
  See also *German cities by name, e.g.,*
    *Munich*
Gestapo (Geheime Staatspolizei)
  accidental encounters with, 151–54,
    194, 223–27, 291–92
  Himmler as head of, 100, 104–5,
    192–93
  prison in Munich, 112, 115–17
  seeking Kurti, 205–6, 235, 246–47,
    279, 290–92
  See also Nazis; paramilitary groups
Gestapo headquarters
  Berlin, 151–54, 191–94
  Bozen, 248
  Munich, 112, 115–17, 145
  Vienna, 100, 104–5, 107, 111, 192–93
Gilgen villa, 46–47, 49–51, 53–56, 59,
  62, 72, 80, 282
Giraud, General Henri, 142–43
Glaise-Horstenau, Edmund (minister
  without portfolio), 71, 91
Goebbels, Joseph, Minister of
  Propaganda, 17, 129
Gömbös, Gyula, prime minister of
  Hungary, 35
goose stepping snowplow antics, 277
Göring, Hermann, 129, 195
Gorizia, Italy, 10
Goswin, Cadet, 174–75
Gotenhafen (Gdynia), Poland, 164, 170,
  173, 188, 207, 214–17
governesses (Kinderfräulein), 18, 22–24
  See also Ottenreiter, Alice

Grand Hotel (Rome), 297–98, 300
Greater German Party, 28
greeting, official, 105, 114, 134, 201,
  224, 258, 271
Gsaller (orderly), 36, 39–41
guards, friendly, 116, 134, 143, 176,
  198, 200, 286
guide, South Tirolean, 263–64, 272–75,
  287
guns
  the Browning handgun, 122, 176–77
  friendly fire, 177
  Karabiner 98 Kurz rifle, 160
  Kurti's lack of skill with, 122,
    162–63, 176–77, 216, 254, 263,
    283–84
  the machine gun episode, 162–63
Gustloff, Wilhelm, 184
gypsies, 140

Habicht, Theo, 15, 17, 29, 32
Habsburg dynasty, 9–10, 78–79
  See also Austro-Hungarian Empire
Hallertau, Germany (hops region), 130
Hamburg, Germany, 159, 221–23, 230
Hammerstein-Equord, Baron Hans von,
  Minister of Justice, 65
Harrach, Countess Kuka, 121
Hauptschule examination, 108
the Hawaiian stamp, 102–4
Heil Hitler greeting, 105, 114, 134,
  201, 224, 258, 271
Heiligenhafen, Germany, 159, 162
Heimwehr (paramilitary), 15, 25,
  30–31, 70
Hekajllo, Olga, 136
Hela Peninsula, 170
Heldenplatz, Vienna, 88
Hess, Rudolf, 30
high school entrance examination, 108
Hilda, Nurse, 180–84, 188–91
Hildebrand, Dietrich von, 61
Himmelfahrt duty category, 158
Himmler, Heinrich
  Gestapo head, 100, 104–5, 192–93
  glass eye, 100, 102
  head of Schutzstaffel, 96
  and Hitler's snub to Chancellor, 30

Kurti's audiences with, 100–106,
192–93, 199
questions about morale aboard the
*Prinz Eugen*, 193
Vera's audience with, 100, 102
Hinkel He 111 (abandoned German
bomber), 178–79
Hitler, Adolf
assassination plots against, 162, 255
Berchtesgaden meeting (1938), 88–93,
164
Berghof home of, 89
Lebensraum, vii, 7–8, 110
*Mein Kampf*, vii
Munich apartment, 113–14
Papen and, 71–72, 88–90
personality, 72, 89–90
Reichstag speech (February 20, 1938),
92
snub of Austrian emissary in Munich,
29–30
war declared on U.S. (1941), 127
Hitler Youth (paramilitary), 31, 105
Hodza, Milan, prime minister of
Czechoslovakia, 80
Hohenlohe, family von, 128
Holy Communion in an envelope,
155–56
homosexuals, 140
Hopfgartner, Anton, 14n2, 89n2
hops-picking incident, 130–34
Hornbostel, Theodor, 70
Hossbach Memorandum (November
1937), 81
Hotel Adlon, Berlin, 195
Hotel Bristol, Vienna, 30
hotel, Grand (Rome), 297–98, 300
Hotel Greif, Bozen, 248
Hotel Metropol, Vienna, 100, 104–5,
107, 111, 192–93
Hotel Post, Saint Anton, 82, 85
hotel, Richemond in Geneva, 289, 291,
293, 306
House of German Armaments, 151–54
household goods, 98, 127–28, 135,
156–57, 305
Hull, Cordell, 76, 78, 80, 91
Hungary, 6, 15n3, 35, 59, 77, 80

Ibn Saud, King of Saudi Arabia, 64
"identified by his dentures", 292
*Im Kampf gegen Hitler* (Schuschnigg),
66n1, 70n1, 88n1, 90n4, 93n13
immigration to Germany, 218
incorporation of Austria into Germany.
*See* Anschluss
inflation, 7, 9, 45
the inhabitants rule, 185
Innitzer, Cardinal Theodor, 31
Innsbruck, Austria
devastation at, 227–30
home, 10, 30, 96, 227, 229–30, 245,
305
the Inn River, 225–27, 229, 253
Innrain, 229
Liesl from, 96
Nazis in, 5, 17, 30
shops at, 231–32
train station at, 222–24, 227
insurance payment theft, 100
Italy
African policy, 57, 69–70
Austrian dependence on, 29, 35, 37,
69–70, 72, 78, 81
Capri, 294, 299–300, 302–3
economic agreement with Yugoslavia,
78
Fascist Party, 9
Germany politically supported by,
70–72
League of Nations withdrawal, 81
Rome Protocols (March 1934,1936),
59, 77, 88
Rome-Berlin Axis agreement
(October 1936), 76
South Tirol German speakers, 218,
235
Umberto di Savoia, last king of, 65,
297
Victor Emmanuel III, king of, 143,
296, 302
*See also Italian cities by name, e.g.,*
*Rome;* Mussolini, Benito

Jacques, downed Canadian pilot
ascent of Piz Chavalatsch, 269–78
at border station, 285–87

Jacques, downed Canadian pilot
  (*continued*)
  broken wireless transmitter carried by,
    262–63, 266, 268, 272–74,
    276–77, 280, 283, 286
  the German SS patrol and, 270–71
  meeting Kurti, 262–67
  night on the mountain top, 278–84
  and the smuggler, 272–76
  walking in circle in forest, 269
Jacquingasse, Vienna, 63
Jansa, General Alfred, 70
Japan, 76, 81, 127
Jehovah's Witnesses, 140
Jews
  anti-Semitism and, 15, 57, 98–100,
    140, 146–47
  in concentration camps, 140
  deprived of German citizenship, 57
  emigration of, 19, 65–66, 92, 107,
    146
  gratitude of, 103–4
  insurance theft policy, 100
  Kristalnacht, 99–100
  laws against, 15, 57, 100
  lies about, 146–47
  speaking out for, 96, 113, 146–48
  suicide of, 114
Johannes, the farmer, 244–48, 251
Jordan, Ludwig, 88
Junkers Ju 52, 296

Kaindl, Commandant Anton, 135,
  199–200, 305
Kaliningrad, Germany, 179–84
Kalksburg boarding school, 73–76,
  93–94
Kaltenbrunner, Ernst, 96–97
kapos, 141–42
Kapuzinergasse, Bozen, 233
Karabiner 98 Kurz rifle, 160
Karl Lueger Platz, 96
Karl Marx Hof battle casualties, 30
Katholische Jugend (paramilitary), 31
Katholischer Schulverein, 15
Keitel, General Wilhelm, 89
Keppler, Wilhelm (commissioner for
  economic affairs), 5, 93

Kergariou, Marc de, 306
Kiefersfelden, Germany, 222
Kiel, Germany, 159, 163, 188
Kiesler, Hedwig, 64–65
Kinderfräulein (governesses), 18, 20–24
  *See also* Ottenreiter, Alice (Fräulein
    Alice)
Kinderman, Gottfried-Karl, 92n12
kindnesses, unexpected, 1–2, 4
  the Abbott, 241–44
  the Americans, 138, 295
  concentration camp and prison
    guards, 116–17, 134–35, 143, 176,
    198, 200
  concentration camp commandant, 135
  educators, 109, 111–12, 115
  evacuation with the Beckers, 180–84
  fellow train passengers, 209–10,
    212–13
  the Italians, 294–95, 298–301
  the madam, 236–40
  medical staff, 129, 205–6
  Niedermayr family, 108, 110, 112, 121
  of the Resistance in Bozen, 236–46
  stamp seller, 102–4, 106
  the Swiss, 286, 292–94
  Walter family, 109–10, 122, 176–77
  *See also* Ottenreiter family and home
Klosterneuburg, Austria, 31–32
Knight's Cross of the Iron Cross, 255
Königsberg, Germany, 179–84
Königstein Fortress, Dresden, 143
*Kraft durch Freude* (Nazi organization),
  184
Krampus, 11–12, 42–44, 56, 68
Krause, Herr (tutor), 97–98, 100–101,
  104, 107–8, 110
Kriegsministerium home, 35–36, 40–41,
  47, 56, 60, 66–67
Kristallnacht, 99
Krupp Germania shipyard, Kiel,
  Germany, 163
Kufstein, Austria, 222–23, 253
Kunsthistorische Museum (Vienna), 305

Lady Bavaria statue, 110–11
Lake Geneva, 289
Lamarr, Hedy, 65

318

Landeck, Austria, 76
Latsch, Italy, 269
laws
  after WWI, 15n3, 28, 57, 70, 163–64
  against discussing concentration
    camps, 146, 192
  Economic Empowering Law of 1917,
    28
  against Jews, 15, 57, 98–100, 140,
    146–47
  Nuremburg Laws (September 1935),
    57
  Thousand-Mark Tariff, 28–29, 45,
    71
  See also treaties and agreements
Le Richemond Hotel in Geneva, 289,
  291, 293, 306
League of Nations, 13–14, 35, 45, 59,
  72, 81, 88
Lebensraum, vii, 7–8, 110
Lehmann, Lotte, 65
Leipzig, Germany, 210
the Leipzig, 170–71, 204
Lenin, 9
Leo XIII (pope), 24, 24n4
Leopold III, King of Belgium, 77,
  79–80
Leopold, Joseph, 77, 88
letter bombs, 30
Lienert, Captain Konrad, 288
Liesl (head cook)
  in the car accident, 46
  and the fish, 52–53, 138
  gossip, 50, 57–58
  marriage of, 96
  our cook, 23, 42–43, 49, 67, 81–82
  and the pets, 38–40, 54
Lillie, Walter, 118
Lindbergh kidnapping case, 18
Linz, Austria, 30
Little Entente (alliance of
  Czechslovakia, Romania, Yugoslavia
  and Austria), 59, 77–78
Locarno Treaty, 59, 79, 79n7
London, 6, 80, 135–36
Lucifero, Marquess Falcone, 296–97
Luftwaffe, 124
Luigi (partisan), 254–58

Luitpold Gymnasium (Munich), 109
lumber, Austrian, 78
Luxembourg, 90

the machine gun episode, 162–63
Madonna (Dürer), 89
Mafalda, Princess, daughter of King
  Victor Emmanuel III, 143, 302
Malente, Germany, 187
Mals, Italy, 263, 269
Mama (Kurti's mother), 20, 23
  See also Schuschnigg, Herma von
Mami (Kurti's stepmother). See
  Schuschnigg, Vera von
Mandl, Fritz, 64
Manfred, Cadet, 164–65, 169, 175
the Maquis (French Resistance guerilla
  groups), 292
Märchentante, 42
Maria, Sister, of the Resistance, 250–52,
  257, 259
Mariahilferstrasse, 15, 25
Marianne, Aunt. See Schuschnigg,
  Marianne von
Marxists, 14, 48
Masera, Grete, 233, 235
Masera, Louise, 233
Masera, Norbert, 235
Masera, Sepp
  in a German uniform, 233–38
  prayers for protection of, 248–49
  resourceful, 237, 240–42
matches, argument about, 280–83
Matt, Rudi, 83
mattress, smell of burning, 280–83
Mayer, Louis B., 65
Mayer, Peter, 18–19, 74, 107, 135
Mayr, Clemens, 227–30
Mayr, Elizabeth, 227–30
Mayr, Elsbeth, 229
Mayr, Hildtraud, 229
McCaffrey, Colonel, 250–54, 261, 268,
  270
measuring stick, snow-depth, 276–77
Mein Kampf (Adolf Hitler), vii, 28
Mellon, Andrew W., 127
Meran, Italy, 248–49, 253, 255, 263,
  268–69

Meran Resistance, 255–57, 259, 263, 268–69
Messersmith, George, 30, 69, 76–80
Michael, Brother, Monastery Gries, 242–43
Miklas, Wilhelm (Austrian President), 6
Minoritenplatz, Vienna, 15
Mödling, Austria, 74
Monastery Gries, abbot, 241–44, 248
Monte Cavallaccio (Piz Chavalatsch), 263–64, 269–78
Montjoie, Father Hugo (Kalksburg), 74, 93–94
More, Sir Thomas, 243
mother, Kurti's. See Schuschnigg, Herma von
Muckermann, Father Friedrich, SJ, 90
Müller, Lt. Colonel, 192
Munich, Germany
    bus tour and stink bomb caper, 110–11
    devastation in, 203, 221–22
    Hitler's apartment, 113–14
    restaurants, 204–5, 227
music, 41, 135–36
Mussolini, Benito
    Berlin visit, 81
    Chancellor and, 35, 69–70, 78
    demographic changes to South Tirol, 218, 235
    international relations, 70–71
    regarding Austrian independence, 29, 35, 91
    See also Italy

Naples, Italy, 295, 303
Napoleon's army, 37
National Opposition Committee, 77–78
National Socialism. See Nazis
National Socialist (newspaper), 205
Nationalistic Party, 77
Naval Academy, 159–62
Nazis
    Austrian Legion (paramilitary), 29, 70
    Austrian Socialist Party, 10, 15, 28, 30
    character, 192, 224, 249–50
    compulsory volunteerism, 149–50, 172

Hitler's snub of emissary in Munich, 29–30
Kristallnacht, 99–100
laws against Jews, 15, 57, 98–100, 140, 146–47
National Socialism, 7, 37, 93, 96–98, 104, 107, 255
sabotage, 29–30, 47–48, 52, 253
Schutzbund putsch (February 12, 1934), 15, 29–30, 32–35, 57, 88
Schutzstaffel (SS), 96
Swastikas/Brownshirts, 32–34, 52, 98–99
unconditional surrender, 294
See also propaganda
NBC Symphony Orchestra, 65
Neubaugasse, Vienna, 24, 95, 99
Neumann, Dr. Heinrich, 63–64
neutrality, 6, 69, 79n7, 79–80
newspapers
    for insulation, 267, 272, 282
    as propaganda, 14, 205, 268, 292–93
Niedermayr home, 108–10, 112, 121
Niedermayr, Karlheinz (3rd cousin), 109–11
Niedermayr, Paula, 108, 110, 112, 121
non-persons
    educational system rejections, 97, 108–9, 111–12, 144
    Himmelfahrt duty for, 158
    officers from the First World War, 8, 96
    son of imprisoned Chancellor, 95–97, 103, 107–8, 118, 144, 158–62, 223, 298–99
North Africa, 143
NSDAP (Austrian Nazi Party), 15, 17, 28
Nuremburg Laws (September 1935), 57
Nurse Hilda, 180–84, 188–91

Oranienburg, Germany, 122, 124, 134, 140, 143, 153–54, 231
Österreich gegen Hitler (Kinderman), 92n12
Ostmark, 7, 31
    See also Austria
Ostmärkische Sturmscharen (paramilitary), 31

Ottenreiter, Alice (Fräulein Alice)
  admonishments by, 51, 75
  background of, 24
  camping skills shared with Kurti, 52,
    282
  cheerful and encouraging, 60–63, 74,
    82
  conversations with Liesl, 50, 57–59
  discipline by, 55–56, 64–65, 67–68,
    86–87, 110
  doubts about the kitten, 38
  at the fatal car accident, 45–49, 52
  with Kurti at Alt Aussee with the
    Walters, 109–10, 118, 130
  with Kurti at Gilgen Villa for
    summers, 49–52, 72, 80
  with Kurti for Christmas holidays,
    81–82, 85–87, 121
  Kurti's education arrangements, 97–98
  managing the moves to new homes,
    33, 60–64
  manners and grooming taught by,
    53–54, 64–67, 101–2
  marriage to Walter Lillie, 118
  with a mother's love, 46, 52, 59, 74,
    98, 198, 305
  nursing Kurti's illnesses and accidents,
    45–49, 63–64
  nurturing responsibiity in, 100–102
  skijoring incident and, 82–87
  unemployable after Anschluss, 109
Ottenreiter family and home
  Alice and Walter Lillie, 118
  cautioned about the janitor, 95
  on holidays, 109–10, 118, 121–22, 130
  house torched, 305
  Kurti to join, 94–96, 100–102,
    105–6, 130
outcasts. See non-persons

Pacelli, Cardinal Eugenio, 24, 95
The Painter in His Studio (Vermeer),
  127, 305
Palazzo del Quirinale, Rome, 267
Papen, Franz von, 71–72, 80, 88–92
papers
  "Auster" identification from
    Sachsenhausen, 153–54
  Brannenburg document, 225, 230–31
  destination card, 202
  Fischer identification, 254–59, 262,
    271, 288–90, 294–95
  hospital, 206, 220
  Navy pay booklet, 207, 215–16,
    223–24, 230–31
  ration booklets, 137, 191–92, 229–32
  travel, 114, 206–7, 209, 218, 222–23,
    227, 232
  von Schuschnigg identification, 294
paramilitary groups, 15, 25, 28–35, 57,
  59, 70–71, 88, 96, 105
  See also Gestapo (Geheime
    Staatspolizei)
Paris, 6, 91, 306
Partenkirchen, Germany, 187
partisans
  French, 292
  Italian, 252, 253–54, 256, 258–64,
    265–68, 270, 279
  Polish, 173
  Swiss, 292–94
  thugs rather than, 261
  See also Resistance
Pasewalk, Germany, 220
Pernter, Dr. Hans, Minister of
  Education, 51
Petersdorff, Axel von, 255–57, 259
Petersdorff, Colonel Horst von, 255
philatelic shop, 102–4, 106
photographs, 49, 61, 138–40, 148,
  151–52, 156, 305
Pinpin (kitten), 37–41
Pius XI (pope), 24, 24n4, 94–95,
  155n1, 243
Pius XII (pope), 95, 155nl
Piz Chavalatsch, 263–64, 269, 270–78
pneumonia, 63–64
Poincaré, Raymond, 9
Poland, 15n3, 80, 110, 164, 182–86, 188
political parties, 9–11, 14–15, 17, 28–30,
  57, 70–71, 76–77, 137
political prisoners, 140
  See also concentration camps
the pony and carriage episode, 26–27
Possartstrasse in Bogenhausen, Munich,
  112

Potschen Pass, Austria, 109
the Pour le Mérite award (Blue Max),
    255
Prague, Czechoslovakia, 78, 81, 92
Prater (amusement park) in Vienna, 67
Preysing, Konrad von, 155n1, 155–56
Prince Albrechtstrasse, Berlin, 191
Prince of Wales, 66–69
the *Prinz Eugen*
    in battle, 168, 177–79, 198
    built in Kiel by Krupp Germania,
        163–65
    cadet duties and rotation, 163–67,
        178–79
    captain, 165–66, 207, 226
    christening, 174
    collision with the *Leipzig*, 170–71,
        173
    cowardice, 168–69, 171–73
    disabled Russian submarine scuttled
        by, 175–76
    "explosion status", 178–79
    firing squad, 168–73, 210
    Hinkel He 111 bombing of, 178–79
    morale aboard, 193
    rat bounty, 174–75
    repairs, 170, 173
    Russian T-34 tank annoyance,
        177–78
    Swiss questions about, 288–89
Prinzregentenstrasse, Munich, 113
propaganda
    assassinations and, 292–93
    German, about return of Habsburg
        monarchy, 78–79
    Goebbels', 17, 129
    Habicht's leaflets and radio broadcasts,
        17
    newspapers as, 268, 292–93
    and a person's wish to believe it,
        147–48
    radio, 17, 31
    rumors and falsehoods creating
        confusion, 6, 13–14, 31, 78–79,
        88, 90, 92, 129, 146
Puaux, Gabriel, 91
Purzel (puppy), 36, 37–41, 49, 63,
    73–74, 98, 130

*Quadragesimo Anno* (papal encyclical),
    24

RAD (Reichsarbeitsdienst), 149–50,
    153, 172
radio
    Aunt Olga's, 136
    BBC broadcasts, 135–36, 143
    broken British transmitter, 262–63,
        266, 268, 272–74, 276–77, 280,
        283, 286
    German propaganda by, 17, 31
    receiver at Sachsenhausen, 113,
        135–37, 141, 143
Radvanyi family, 222–23
Raimund, Ferdinand, 115
Ramek, Rudolf, 28
the rat bounty caper, 174–75
ration cards, 137, 191–92, 229–32
Ravensbrück concentration camp for
    women, 136
The Red Army. *See* Russia and
    Russians
Red Cross ship, 184, 186, 188–91
Reichenau, General Walter von, 89
Reichsarbeitsdienst (RAD), 149–50, 172
Reichstag speech (February 20, 1938),
    92
Reinicke, Captain Hans-Jürgen, 166,
    171, 207, 226
religious education concordat
    (Austria/Vatican), 24
Renner, Karl, 28
Resistance
    Benno, the farmer, 259–63, 265–66,
        282
    in Bozen, 236–48, 255
    French Maquis, 292
    in Gotenhafen, 173
    Johannes, the farmer, 244–48, 251
    Luigi, the partisan, 254–58
    Meran Resistance, 252–57, 259–64,
        268–69
    South Tirol, 247–48, 252–53, 255–57,
        259, 261, 263, 268–69
    Swiss, 292–94
    unofficial, 121, 173, 201, 216, 249,
        259, 261

Rhineland, area of Germany, 59, 79n7, 80, 149
Ribbentrop, Joachim von (Foreign Minister), 89, 91
the Richemond Hotel in Geneva, 289, 291, 293, 306
Ringstrasse, Vienna, 31, 36n1
Rintelen, Anton (Austrian ambassador to Italy), 31–32
Ritten (mountain) above Bozen, 218, 229, 233, 235
Rogers, Millicent, 83–85
Romania, 15n3, 59
Rome, Italy, 267, 295, 297–301
Rome Protocols (March 1934,1936), 59, 77, 88
Rome-Berlin Axis (October 1936), 76
Roosevelt, Franklin D., 63
Rosenheim, Germany, 223, 227
Roth, Joseph, 66
rules one and two in war, 265
rumors. See propaganda
Rupprechter, Herr, 223
Russia and Russians
  advance of, 178, 180–86, 305
  disabled submarine scuttled, 175–76
  German invasion of, 143
  Heinkl He 111 pilot, 178
  the inhabitants rule, 185
  invasion of Poland, 110
  reputation of soldiers, 177–78, 184–86
  submarine and the *William Gustloff* Red Cross ship, 188–91
Rust, Doctor, 129

sabotage, 29–30, 47–48, 52, 253
  *See also* terrorism
Sachsenhausen concentration camp
  commandant, 193, 199
  communications into and within, 113, 135–37, 141, 143
  escape attempts, 143
  family life in, 121–26, 129, 137–39, 141–42, 146, 176–77, 198–200
  friendly guards, 134, 143, 176, 198, 200
  identification papers from, 153–54
  neighbors, 137, 142–43
  photos, 139–40, 148, 305
  purpose, 124, 135, 140–43
  smells and sounds of, 140–43
  tiny garden, 138, 199, 301
  the upstairs window, 126, 139, 141–42, 146
Sacre Coeur Gymnasium, 24
Saint Anton, Austria, 20, 81–82
Saint Christoph, Austria, 84–86
Saint Gallen shops, 288–89
Saint Georg Church, chapel, 115
Saint Gilgen villa, 46–47, 49–56, 59, 62, 72, 80, 282, 289
Saint Hedwig Cathedral, 155n1
Saint Nicholas, 11–12, 42–44, 106
salami sandwich signal, 59
Salm, Count Ludwig von (Millicent Rogers' former husband), 83–85
salt, 231, 244
Salzburg (Austrian state), 29
Salzburg (city), Austria, 5, 136
Salzkammergut (Austrian state), 49
Sammer, Fritz, 95, 139, 305
Sammer, Grete, 95, 101, 139
Santa Maria im Münstertal, Switzerland, 276, 285, 294
Savoy, Prince Eugene of, 164
scarlet fever, 63–64
Schafberg mountain, Austria, 49
Schärding, Austria, 5
Schildenfeld, Baroness Zoë von, 57–58
Schlessinger, Frau, 113–14
Schlessinger, Herr, suicide of, 113–14
Schlessinger, Peter, 113
Schmidt, Guido, Secretary of State for Foreign Affairs, 71, 80
Schmitt, Herr, 112, 115, 118
Schneider, Hannes, 83
Schönborn Cardinal Christoph, 1–2
schools
  Alte Realgymnasium, 109–12, 144, 194, 256
  Elmayer's, 15–17
  Ettal's boarding school, 108–9
  examinations, 108
  Kalksburg boarding, 73–76, 93–94

schools *(continued)*
  Katholischer Schulverein, 15
  lessons numbers one and two about,
    75
  Luitpold Gymnasium, 109
  Naval Academy, 159–62
  private tutoring, 97–98, 100–101,
    104, 107–8, 110, 112, 115, 118
  Sacre Coeur Gymnasium, 24
  the Salesian academy with bugs,
    108–9
  war-time diploma program, 158
  Wittelsbacher School, 118–22, 128,
    158–59, 256
Schülerheim Schmitt, 112, 118–21, 123,
  128, 144, 151, 159, 204
Schumann, Elisabeth, 65
Schuschnigg, Anna von (Kurti's
  grandmother), 48, 56
Schuschnigg, Anna von "Dickie",
  124
Schuschnigg, Artur von, 94, 121, 124,
  154–55, 170, 198
Schuschnigg, Artur von, 124
Schuschnigg family
  American citizenship, 306
  concentration camp life, 122–26, 129,
    137, 198–99
  liberation of, 294–95
  lung cancer, 306
Schuschnigg, Heiner von, 198
Schuschnigg, Herma von (Kurti's
  mother)
  appearance, 20
  character, 18, 40–42, 50
  charity, 25, 39–40, 44
  children's parties, 31–32, 42–44
  death by sabatoge, 45–52
  discipline, 11–12, 18, 33, 40–41
  humor, 44
  love of Chancellor, 10, 16, 157
  parents permit themselves to lie, 18
  relatives in Bozen, 25, 75, 218, 233,
    235–37, 248
  remembered with love, 61
  Vera's friendship with, 19–20, 57
  Wolfgangsee discovered by, 49
Schuschnigg, Janet von, 1–2

Schuschnigg, General Kurt von:
  Kurti's grandfather
  after Chancellor's arrest, 96, 98, 106,
    157, 205, 223
  character, 98, 151, 205
  death, 98
  joining the family, 49, 56–57, 59,
    74–76
  prisoner of war, 151
  at wedding (by proxy) of Vera to the
    Chancellor, 94
Schuschnigg, Kurt von (Austrian
  Chancellor): Kurti's father
  character, 3, 6, 25–27, 50–52, 76–77,
    80, 91–95, 151, 155–57, 177
  concentration camp life, 121–22, 124–
    26, 134–39, 143, 176, 198–200
  Dachau concentration camp, 293, 305
  death in Austria, 306
  death of first wife by sabatoge, 45–52
  faith, 3, 11, 25, 94–95, 155–56
  false report of execution, 292–93
  general respect for, 25, 91, 102–4,
    106, 223, 230, 242, 295, 297–99,
    301–2
  health, 111, 116, 134
  household goods, 98, 127–28, 135,
    156–57, 305
  marriage to Vera, 94, 129
  minister of justice, minister of
    education, 24
  in Munich prison, 111–13, 145
  prisoner of war during WWI, 151
  schooling and early life, 10–11, 74,
    121, 299
  skills of, 34–35, 59, 76–81, 88–92,
    162, 230
  in Vienna prison, 100, 107, 111
Schuschnigg, Kurt von: (Kurti)
  barter economy, 133–34, 174–75,
    186, 212, 216, 222, 231, 244, 288
  character, 94, 102–5, 110–11, 123,
    141, 164, 192, 249, 254, 256
  faith, 32, 98, 142, 168, 178, 182, 243,
    270
  Gestapo agents, 151–54, 194, 223–27,
    291–92
  gratitude (*See* kindnesses, unexpected)

gunsmanship lacking, 122, 162–63,
176–77, 216, 254, 263, 283–84
as non-person, 95–97, 108–9, 111–12,
118, 137, 159–62
Schuschnigg, Kurt von (Kurti):
childhood
afternoon tea and manners, 54, 63,
98
audience with Himmler, 101, 104–5
Augarten Palace battle, 32–35
bicycle, 119–20, 123–24
bodyguards, 18–19, 26–27, 56
the candy store incident, 99
the cherrywood banquette episode,
11–12
children's parties, 31–32, 42–44
death and funeral of mother, 45–52
fishing, 51–53, 72, 137–40, 155
five-shilling coin mystery, 67–68
governesses, 18, 20–24
pets, 36–41
responsibilities of, as child of
Chancellor, 31, 64–65
salami sandwich signal, 59
skiing, 76, 81–87
the snake in Café Zauner caper,
53–56
stamp collection, 37, 98, 101–3, 106,
305
summer holidays, 46–47, 49–51,
53–56, 59, 62, 72, 80, 282
toy soldiers, 11, 36–37, 39, 64, 66,
98, 127
train sets, 62, 64
See also schools
Schuschnigg, Kurt von (Kurti): youth
Alt Aussee summer holidays, 109–10,
118, 122
audience with Himmler, second,
192–93, 199
flak units, 148
health, 45–50, 63–64, 150, 172
hops-picking incident, 130–34
indifference to holidays as coping
strategy, 112
as Kurt Auster, 153–54, 193
lack of coordination, 281
photography, 138–40, 148, 305

on possessions as last link to the past,
98, 127–28, 135, 156–57, 305
on the post-war future, 156–57, 177
Sachsenhausen identification papers,
153–54
the upstairs window at
Sachsenhausen, 126, 139, 141–42,
146
visits to Father, 115–17, 119, 123,
125–26, 154–57
See also schools
Schuschnigg, Kurt von (Kurti): naval
career
bunks on the Prinz Eugen, 165–67
chief surgeon (Munich), 205–6, 235
destination card, 202
evacuations, 180–86
firing squad, 168–72, 210
the Gestapo agent on Unter den
Linden, 151–54, 194
gunsmanship, poor, 122, 162–63,
176–77, 216, 254, 263, 283–84
hospital trains, 186–87, 201–3
at the Naval Academy, 159–62
navy-infantry status, sudden, 216
rat bounty caper, 174–75
refusal to travel by water, 180, 185,
189, 214–16
wounds from the Prinz Eugen engine
room explosion, 179–81, 184–92,
202–6, 211–12, 219, 275
Schuschnigg, Kurt von (Kurti): deserter
arrest, 246–50, 256
ascent of Piz Chavalatsch, 269–78
attempts to return to the Prinz
Eugen in Gotenhafen, 206–13,
214–17
Benno's farmhouse and communications center, 259–66, 282
bomb shelter in Berlin, 193–95
bordello safe house, 235–41
broken wireless transmitter, 262–63,
266, 268, 272–74, 276–77, 280,
283, 286
chief surgeon's advice, 205–6, 235
deserter, 206–16, 223, 249
the German SS patrol on the
mountain, 270–71

Schuschnigg, Kurt von (Kurti): deserter
(*continued*)
  Gestapo agents, 223–27, 291–92
  Gestapo seeking, 205–6, 235, 246–47,
    279, 290–92
  health, 206, 211, 275
  Johannes' farmhouse, 244–47
  as Lt. Karl Fischer of Munich,
    254–59, 262, 271, 288–90, 294–95
  memories and grief, 267–70, 285
  in the Monastery Gries, 241–44
  night in the burned out hut, 278–84,
    287
  piles of bodies, 115, 189, 211, 232
  plans to escape to Switzerland, 217,
    244–47, 253, 270–78, 285–87
  plans to wait out the war on the
    Ritten, 217–23, 229, 233, 235–36
  and the smuggler, 272–76
  at Swiss border station, 285–87
Schuschnigg, Maria Dolores von (Sissi)
  birth, 120–22, 126
  concentration camp childhood,
    122–26, 129, 137, 198–99
  death, 306
  Kurti's love of, 141, 199, 303
  marriage and child, 306
Schuschnigg, Marianne von, 94,
  124–25, 151, 154–55, 198
Schuschnigg, Vera von (Kurti's
  stepmother)
  appearance, 20
  audience with Himmler, 100, 102
  character, 57, 86, 96–97, 112–13,
    137, 155–56
  concentration camp life, 97, 100,
    111–13, 115, 120–26, 129, 137,
    154–56, 198–99
  Czernin family treasures, 127, 305
  death, 306
  faith, 20, 57, 94
  family, 19–20, 57–58, 94, 114,
    120–28
  formerly Countess Vera
    Fugger-Babenhausen, 19–20,
    57–58, 94, 114
  household goods, 127–28, 135,
    156–57, 305

  as Kurti's "aunt", 19–20, 57–58, 94,
    114, 129
  as Kurti's stepmother, 97, 108–9,
    112–13, 115–16, 120, 123–28
  letter writing campaign, 96, 100, 115,
    121, 128–29
  marriage to Chancellor, 94, 129
  network of, 109, 114, 121, 155
  son, Rudi Fugger, 19–22, 57–58, 74,
    82–87, 107, 127
Schuschnigg, Verena von, 124
Schutzbund (paramilitary), 15, 25,
  28–30, 32–35, 57, 88
Schutzstaffel (SS) (paramilitary), 96
Schwartzwälder restaurant (Munich),
  204, 227
the secret doors, 60–61, 62
Seidl, Wolf Dietrich, 257–59
Seipel, Monsignor Ignaz (chancellor),
  11
Seyss-Inquart, Arthur, Minister of the
  Interior, 6, 89–91
"Shadow" (undercover bodyguard),
  18–19, 26–27, 56
Simpson, Wallace, 69
Sissi (Kurti's sister). *See* Schuschnigg,
  Maria Dolores von
Sister Maria (of the Resistance),
  250–52, 257, 259
*Sketch* magazine, 129
skiing, 20, 76, 81–87
skijoring, 83–86
Slevogt, Kurt-Erich, 158
Slevogt, Vice Admiral Kurt, 158–59
the smuggler, 263–64, 272–76, 287
snow antics, 277
Social Democrat Party, 14, 28, 30, 57,
  137
Social Workers' Union speech, 80
Socialist Party militia (paramilitary), 15,
  25, 28, 30, 32, 57
Soldbuch (navy pay booklet), 207,
  215–16, 223–24, 230–31
Sonnemann, Emmy (Frau Göring), 129
South Tirol
  Brenner Pass, 29, 222, 227, 232–33,
    241, 252–53
  history, 25, 218, 235, 269–70

Piz Chavalatsch, 263–64, 269–78
Resistance, 247–48, 252–53, 255–57,
    259, 261, 263, 268–69
Spanish Civil War, 72
Sperrle, General Hugo, 89
Spofford, Brig. Gen. Charles, 301–2
Spörel, Captain, 171
SS (Schutzstaffel) (paramilitary), 96
Stalin, Joseph, 9, 143
the stamp collector, 102–4, 106
Ständestaat (corporate state), 24, 24n4,
    35, 80
Starhemberg, Prince Ernst von (vice
    chancellor of Austria), 69–70
Stauffenberg, Count Claus von, 162
Steiermark (Austrian state), 109, 118
Stella Matutina (Jesuit college in
    Vorarlberg), 10, 74, 299
Stephan (the driver), 53, 74
stepmother, Kurti's. See Schuschnigg,
    Vera von
Stettin, Germany, 186–89, 207, 211–12
the stink bomb caper, 110–11
Stockinger, Fritz, Minister of
    Commerce, 37–38
Straffner, Sepp, 28
Strasbourg, France, 293
Stresa pact (April 1934), nullified, 57
Stubenring, Vienna, 36, 36n1, 41
Sturmscharen (paramilitary), 31
Styria (Austrian state), 31
submarines
    disabled Russian, 175–76
    German losses of, 184
    used for hospital evacuation, 179–81,
        184
Sudetenland, Czechoslovakia, 107
suicides, 113–14
summer holidays
    at Alt Aussee, 109–10, 118, 122
    at Gilgen, 46–47, 49–51, 53–56, 59,
        62, 72, 80, 282
Swastikas/Brownshirts, 32–34, 52,
    98–99
Swinemünde, Poland, 207, 212–20
Switzerland
    Bern, 288–89, 294
    border station welcome, 285–87

Geneva, 35, 289, 294
Herr Schlessinger's intent, 114
Kurti's plan to get to, 217, 244–47,
    253–54, 262, 264, 270–78, 285–87
marked by huge cross, 278–79

tadpole in the water pitcher episode,
    20–22
Tageblatt (Berlin newspaper), 14
Taufers, Switzerland, 269
Tavs affair, 88
telemark skiing, 83
Tenth SS Panzer Division Alpenvorland,
    234, 252–53, 255, 271
terrorism
    assassinations, 7, 29–31, 33–35, 52,
        88, 90, 162, 255, 292–93
    Austrian Legion, 29, 70
    Committee of Seven, 88
    disappearances, 96, 114, 154, 205–6,
        217
    increasing Nazi violence, 7, 15, 17,
        29–30, 47–48, 80, 88
    paramilitary groups, 15, 25, 28–35,
        57, 59, 70–71, 88, 96, 105
    sabotage, 29–30, 47–48, 52, 79, 253
    Schutzbund uprising (February 12,
        1934), 15, 29–30, 32–35, 57, 88
    suicides due to, 114
Theresa at the bordello, 239
Third S-boat Flotilla saga, 223–26
Thomas Aquinas, Saint, 243
Thousand-Mark Tariff, 28–29, 45, 71
Thyssen, Annelie, 143
Thyssen, Fritz, 143
Thyssen steel works, 143
Tichy (driver), 44, 47–48, 52–53
Time magazine, 129
Tirol (Austrian state), 29
Toscanini, Arturo, 65
trade blockade, 28–29, 45, 71
trains
    blackout shades, 208
    chartered passenger cars, 81, 218–20
    escape from concentration camp on,
        143
    evacuations of, 186, 202, 208
    flatbed, 218–20

trains (*continued*)
 freight, 211, 218–20, 232–33
 hospital, 186–87, 201–3
 kindnesses of fellow travelers, 209–10,
  212–13
 overnight cars, 81
 punctuality, 125, 176, 186, 191, 212,
  222
 stations, 60, 196, 207, 211, 221–22,
  225–27, 230
 strafing of, 184, 186, 222
 toys, 62, 64, 127–28
Traunstein, Germany, 5
travel tariff, 28–29, 45, 71
treaties and agreements
 accord ( July 11, 1936), 71–72, 80,
  88, 91
 Anti-Comintern Pact (November
  1936), 76, 81
 Austria and Germany economic
  (early 1937), 77
 Austria's international agreements,
  29–30, 59, 77–78, 88–91, 164
 commitment to Austrian
  independence (September 1934),
  35
 economic agreement with Yugoslavia,
  78
 Hossbach Memorandum (November
  1937), 81
 Italy's economic agreement with
  Yugoslavia, 78
 Little Entente, 59, 77–78
 Locarno, 59, 79, 79n7
 Rome Protocols (March 1934,1936),
  59, 77, 88
 Rome-Berlin Axis agreement
  (October 1936), 76
 Saint-Germain-en-Laye, 9, 15, 15n3,
  29, 70, 218
 Stresa pact (April 1934), nullified, 57
 Versailles treaty, 9
 *See also* laws
Treuleben, Gertie, 115
Treuleben, Walter, 115
Trieste, Italy, 221–22, 226–27, 232, 236
Trotsky, Leon, 9
Tschechowa, Olga, 129

Turin, Count of, 296
Twenty-eighth SS Volunteer Grenadier
 Division Wallonien, 262

Umberto di Savoia, last King of Italy,
 65, 297
Uncle Artur (Artur von Schuschnigg),
 94, 121, 124, 154–55, 170, 198
Uncle Clemens (Clemens Mayr), 227–30
Uncle Ronni (Ronald Balcom), 82–85
Uncle Sepp (Sepp Masera, brother of
 Kurti's mother), 233–38, 240–42,
 248–49
Uncle Victor (Baron Victor
 Fröhlichsthal), 298–300
Uncle Willy (Wilhelm Elmayer), 16–17,
 102, 118–19, 164
unconditional surrender, 294
undercover bodyguard, 18–19, 26–27,
 56
undesirables. *See* non-persons
unemployment, 7, 9, 79
Unknown Soldier memorial, 31
Unter den Linden, Berlin, 151–52, 194
Unterhaching, Germany, 108–12
the upstairs window, perspective, 126,
 139, 141–42, 146

Vanvitelli, Luigi, 302
Vatican, 95, 298, 301
Vera (Kurti's stepmother). *See*
 Schuschnigg, Vera von
Vermeer, Johannes, 127, 305
Verona, Italy, 227, 295–96
Via della Conciliazione, Rome, 299
Victor Emmanuel III, King of Italy,
 143, 296, 302
Vienna, Austria
 Gestapo headquarters, 100, 104–5,
  107, 111, 192–93
 Hotel Metropol, 100, 104–5, 107,
  111, 192–93
 hotels and restaurants, 30, 96, 118
 Prince of Wales' visit, 66–69
Vinschgau, Italy, 259–61, 269
Vohman, Cadet Raymond, 169–71
*Völkischer Beobachter* (newspaper), 268
Volkswagen 82, 184, 267

volunteerism, compulsory, 149–50, 172
von Hassell, Ulrich, 71
von Hildebrand, Dietrich, 66
von Reichenau, Walter, 89
Vorarlberg (Austrian state), 10, 29, 228

Waffen-SS, 246, 262
Wais, Dr. Jörg, 286–87, 294
Walloon volunteers, 262
Walter, Bruno, 65
Walter, Kurt, 109, 122, 176–77
Walter, Luise, 109
Walter, Otto, 109–10, 122
Walter, Waldemar, 109–10
war
    ability to lie well, 256
    celebrating the end of, 294
    costs, 197, 205, 267–70, 285
    crimes against humanity, 96
    demographic effects of, 205
    the inhabitants rule, 185
    kindnesses during (See kindnesses,
        unexpected)
    panic of, 199
    piles of bodies, 115, 189, 211, 232
    rule numbers one and two, 265
war-time diploma program, 158
Wehrmacht
    assistant medical director of, 205
    surrender, 294
    threat of invasion by, 6, 90, 93
Weydenhammer, Rudolf, 32
the Wilhelm Gustloff Red Cross ship,
    184, 186, 188–91

wireless radio transmitter, broken,
    262–63, 266, 268, 272–74, 276–77,
    280, 283, 286
Wittelsbacher Palace prison, 112,
    115–17
Wittelsbacher School, 118–22, 128,
    158–59, 256
Wittenberg, Germany, 210–11
Wolfgangsee, 46–47, 49–56, 59, 62, 72,
    80, 282, 289
Wopfner, Hermann, 108
World War I
    Austro-Hungarian Empire, 7, 9–10,
        15n3, 36–37, 69, 78
    awards and honors, 255
    Giraud, General Henri, 142–43
    laws after, 13–14, 15n3, 70, 163–64
    officers from, unwelcome in WWII,
        8, 96
    prisoners of war, 10, 151
wristwatch, 289

Young, James B., 78–79
Yugoslavia, 15n3, 59, 78

Zauner, Johann, 53–54
Zerlauth, Father (Kalksburg school
    principal), 75
Zettner, Herr (Alte Realgymnasium
    school principal), 109, 111
Zoë, Aunt (Baroness Zoë von
    Schildenfeld), 57–58
Zuckmayer, Carl, 66
Zwölferhorn mountain, Austria, 49